Chekhov in Performance

OTHER BOOKS BY J. L. STYAN

Drama, Stage and Audience
The Dark Comedy
The Dramatic Experience
The Elements of Drama
The Shakespeare Revolution
Shakespeare's Stagecraft

Anton Chekhov

Chekhov in Performance

A Commentary on the Major Plays

J. L. STYAN

Franklyn Bliss Snyder Professor of English Literature, Northwestern University

CAMBRIDGE UNIVERSITY PRESS

Cambridge

London   New York   Melbourne

Published by the Syndics of the Cambridge University Press
The Pitt Building, Trumpington Street, Cambridge CB2 1RP
Bentley House, 200 Euston Road, London NW1 2DB
32 East 57th Street, New York, NY 10022, USA
296 Beaconsfield Parade, Middle Park, Melbourne 3206, Australia

Library of Congress catalogue card number: 73-134614

ISBN: 0 521 07975 6 hard covers
ISBN: 0 521 29345 6 paperback

First published 1971
First paperback edition 1978

First printed in Great Britain by Alden & Mowbray Ltd
at the Alden Press, Oxford
Reprinted in Great Britain at the
University Press, Cambridge

Contents

Acknowledgments

Preparation of the book has been assisted by the Rackham Publication Fund of the University of Michigan, and to this Fund I wish to record a debt of gratitude. The approach in the commentaries is indebted to the kind of descriptive and stylistic analysis of Chekhov's plays begun by S. D. Balukhaty and M. N. Stroyeva, and to the implicit commentary found in K. S. Stanislavsky's and V. I. Nemirovich-Danchenko's notes on their productions. I am also indebted to the work of Ronald Hingley in the first three volumes of his *Oxford Chekhov*, and to M. H. Black, G. E. T. Mayfield, Susan Darvas, Susan Flower and other friends, students and critics for their extension of that everlasting dialogue which must surround the mature plays, and which is properly a debt to Chekhov himself.

J.L.S.

The University of Michigan
April 1969

vi

References

Short references to letters, notes and memoirs in the footnotes:

Balukhaty, *The Seagull Produced by Stanislavsky*, ed. S. D. Balukhaty, trans. D. Magarshack (London, 1952)

Friedland, *Letters on the Short Story, the Drama, and Other Literary Topics, by Anton Chekhov*, ed. L. S. Friedland (New York, 1924)

Garnett, *The Letters of Anton Pavlovitch Tchehov to Olga Leonardovna Knipper*, trans. C. Garnett (London, 1926)

Hellman, *The Selected Letters of Anton Chekhov*, ed. L. Hellman, trans. S. Lederer (New York, 1955)

Hingley, *The Oxford Chekhov*, vols. I–III, trans. and ed. R. Hingley (London, 1964–8)

Jackson, *Chekhov: A Collection of Critical Essays*, ed. R. L. Jackson (New Jersey, 1967)

Koteliansky, *The Life and Letters of Anton Tchekhov*, trans. and ed. S. S. Koteliansky and P. Tomlinson (London, 1925)

Magarshack, D. Magarshack, *Chekhov the Dramatist* (London, 1952)

Nemirovich-Danchenko, V. Nemirovich-Danchenko, *My Life in the Russian Theatre*, trans. J. Cournos (London, 1937)

Simmons, E. J. Simmons, *Chekhov: A Biography* (Boston, 1962)

Stanislavsky, K. S. Stanislavsky, *My Life in Art*, trans. J. J. Robbins (London, 1924)

Stroyeva, M. N. Stroyeva, 'The Three Sisters at the M.A.T.', trans. E. R. Hapgood, in *Stanislavski and America*, ed. E. Munk (New York, 1966)

Valency, M. Valency, *The Breaking String: The Plays of Anton Chekhov* (New York, 1966)

Plates

Introduction

Western tradition has accustomed us to thinking that great plays deal with larger-than-life people, important events, great experiences. Chekhov deals in the little things, the particulars that go to make up general experience; he leads us to the greater experience step by step by touching us with a thousand insights. It was the practising physician who wrote, 'Details are also the thing in the sphere of psychology. God preserve us from generalizations.'[1] And writing about the characters in *Ivanov* he claimed, 'I am telling you in all sincerity and in accordance with the dictates of my conscience that these people were born in my head and not out of ocean spray, or preconceived ideas, not out of "intellectuality", and not by sheer accident. They are the result of observation and the study of life.'[2] It is, moreover, his immense particularity which makes him so stageworthy and such a joy to act.

Tracing Chekhov through his details and seeing how all the elements of his craft work together is an attempt to plumb the depth of his subtext. This kind of exegesis can never, of course, be complete, but I am not alone in finding that the usual methods of dramatic criticism – describing plot and character and theme – are inadequate to realize the texture and density and the 'experience' of a Chekhov play. Robert Corrigan has said, 'To analyze these plays properly one would have to begin with the opening speech and then, making cross-relationships, work through the entire play until the final curtain in much the same manner one would give a critical reading of a poem.'[3] The analysis of theatre is more complicated than this, but I have tried to work roughly along such lines. The method of the book is, therefore, really designed to echo Chekhov's own practice, which prompts a host of controlled impressions from an audience as the play proceeds.

[1] Letter to his brother Alexander, 10 May 1886, in Simmons, p. 129.
[2] Letter to Suvorin, 30 December 1888, in Hellman, p. 77.
[3] Introduction to *Six Plays of Chekhov* (New York, 1962).

1

It goes without saying that this is also the method of the director in the theatre.

Yet there is an abiding belief that Chekhov did not bother his head with the rules of playwriting. Tolstoy, according to his friend A. B. Goldenweizer, was, like everybody, impressed by Chekhov's command of details, but without perceiving how these details were anything but casual in their ordering. Tolstoy found Chekhov a singular writer: 'He throws in words seemingly haphazardly, and nevertheless everything in him lives. And how clever! He never has superfluous details; on the contrary, each is either necessary or beautiful.' If this is true, it follows that it is unthinkable folly for a company to 'adapt' a major play by Chekhov for performance: cutting even one line would be working blind. But Tolstoy adds, 'Nevertheless, it is all only mosaic without a genuinely governing idea.'[1] We must watch to see how Tolstoy's 'impressionist painter with his brush strokes' works on the stage. We must examine how his details fuse in a complete, if dramatically ambivalent, harmony. The governing idea may be discovered in the governing experience.

The task of piecing together one of Chekhov's giant jigsaw puzzles in order to discover little by little what the whole picture is, must also be the only way the student of Chekhov can recognize the hidden beauties of his art. But it is not possible to anticipate what these beauties are. His poetry of the theatre is to be sensed in his balancing point with point, in his fine control of contradictory feeling, in the delighted objectivity an audience assumes when all its senses are in play. The literal meaning of the words of the dialogue offers little help when the minute behaviour of the character, or at the other extreme, when the centripetal mood of the whole stage, betrays another tone and rhythm in the real action of the scene. The submerged life of the text, in Chekhov's little silences and tensions, in the pacing and lyricism of the action, can finally be recreated, of course, only in the theatre. And only there can it be judged. 'What is so wonderful about Chekhov's plays,' declared Stanislavsky, 'is not what is transmitted by the words, but what is hidden under them, in the pauses, in the glances of the actors, in the emanation of their inmost feelings.'[2]

[1] Quoted by Dmitri Chizhevsky in *Anton Čechov: 1860–1960. Some Essays,* ed. T. Eekman (Leiden, 1960) and reprinted in Jackson, p. 53.
[2] Balukhaty, p. 130.

Introduction

It is a commonplace that Chekhov's text 'reads badly', but plays beautifully, and this book aims to recreate a stage sense of his drama in order to understand him.

It is hoped that this treatment will also incidentally illuminate the playing conditions of the nineteenth-century European theatre with and against which Chekhov was working. An appreciation of the task of the naturalistic dramatists of the period is essential in Chekhov's case above all. Since his remarkable preface to *Miss Julie* of 1888, Strindberg had been pleading for that licence to release the stage from its stereotypes of character and action; this release became an absolute necessity for the weaving of Chekhov's delicate webs. In arguing for an 'intimate theatre', Strindberg twenty years later was still attacking false, declamatory acting:

A declaration of love is bellowed forth, a confidence expressed like a call to arms, a secret of the heart whispered hoarsely from the bottom of the throat and lungs, and everybody on stage acts as if he were in a frightful temper and only interested in getting offstage.[1]

The story of Chekhov's own attack on such theatre and of his theatrical development are one and the same. It is also the story of his progress towards objectivity in his beliefs as in his art. 'My holy of holies are the human body, health, intelligence, talent, inspiration, love, and the most absolute freedom – freedom from force and falsity, in whatever form these last may be expressed. This is the program I would maintain, were I a great artist.'[2] The words are familiar in Chekhov criticism, but they reverberate into all corners of his life and work. Even at the time of writing *Ivanov* he was aiming for a new impersonality as a playwright.

Present-day playwrights begin their plays solely with angels, villains, and buffoons. Now, search for these characters in the whole of Russia. Yes, you can find them, but not such extremes as are necessary for a playwright. One is forced to squeeze them out of one's head, get into a sweat, and give it up ... I wanted to be original; I have not introduced a single villain nor an angel, although I could not refuse myself buffoons; I accused nobody, justified nobody.[3]

John Hagan rightly argues that this is not to be construed as a

1 August Strindberg, 'Notes to Members of the Intimate Theatre', trans. E. Sprinchorn in *The Chamber Plays* (New York, 1962), p. 208.
2 Letter to A. N. Pleshcheyev, 4 October 1888, in Hellman, p. 56.
3 Letter to Alexander Chekhov, 24 October 1887, in Koteliansky, p. 93.

declaration of neutrality, but as an ideal of the artist's truthfulness.[1] 'To chemists there is nothing unclean in this world. A man of letters should be as objective as a chemist.'[2] If Chekhov's plays are to deal objectively in true problems of human relationships and society, the artist in him can hope for no more than to engage the spectator's interest as honestly as he can. Happily, the drama is a form which insists upon objective representation: the good playwrights seem impersonal, their characters are seen obliquely, and they are encouraged to do on the stage what might seem perverse in other literary forms.

In sum, we can learn Chekhov's lesson, his 'governing idea', only by getting to grips with his stage method. Chekhov, in the actuality of his practice, teaches us by refusing to teach us. 'You ask what is life? That is just the same as asking what is a carrot. A carrot is a carrot, and nothing more is known about it.'[3]

It remains to touch on two technical matters. I have chosen to retain the well-known translation by Constance Garnett for my quotations in the text. In spite of its slightly period flavour, this sensitive rendering is held by many, including myself, in great affection, and that same period flavour seems right for a *fin de siècle* drama. It is a controversial issue whether or not the Russian convention of trailing dots, which Garnett largely retained, but which the crisply modern and colloquial version of Ronald Hingley eschews, should be exactly rendered in the English. In stage dialogue these notorious dots helpfully indicate, it seems to me, the pauses and hesitations which the playwright intended us to hear on his characters' lips. It has been well said that Chekhov is the poet of half-lights;[4] his scenes and his people are fragile by nineteenth-century standards. Since his pauses of suppressed feeling or uncertain reflection are implicit in the vitality of his lines, we should hesitate before eliminating them from the printed page.

The commentary begins with *The Seagull* and treats in turn the four major plays. *Uncle Vanya* gets the shortest treatment, and to *The Cherry Orchard*, the summit of Chekhov's achievement, it

---

[1] See 'Chekhov's Fiction and the Ideal of "Objectivity" ', *P.M.L.A.* vol. LXXXI, No. 5 (New York, October 1966), 409–17.
[2] Letter to M. V. Kiseleva, 14 January 1887, in Hellman, p. 20.
[3] Letter to O. Knipper of 20 April 1904, shortly before he died (Hellman, p. 386).
[4] By John Gassner in an address at Brooklyn College on the occasion of the centenary of Chekhov's birth in 1960.

seemed appropriate to give the most attention. The book is not a history of Chekhov production, but to each commentary there is added a brief introduction on matters of stage history and Chekhov's method and purpose.

The Seagull

A Comedy in Four Acts

1896

The Seagull

The story of *The Seagull*'s production reads like a fairy-tale.
Jottings in Chekhov's notebooks after 1891 suggest that the play
was a long time in conception. *Ivanov* (1887) had been an unexpected success in Moscow and St Petersburg; the more naturalistic
play *The Wood Demon* (1889), however, was a total failure in Moscow. The former was a success with the public because it was
more closely modelled after the kind of melodrama which was
common throughout Europe at that time;[1] the latter was a failure
because Chekhov had discarded too many of those theatrical
conventions the audience expected. Six years were to pass before
he settled to write a long play again, six years in which he could
debate with himself how far he dare press upon his audiences a
more realistic and objective theatre. Thus F. A. Korsh, the theatre
manager, could not believe that a man could shoot himself, as
Konstantin Treplev does, without first making a speech about it.
It is hard for us today to see what simple, but fundamental, issues
Chekhov had to face.

In 1895, at his newly acquired farm estate at Melikhovo near
Moscow, he began work on the new play. All of Chekhov's plays
are 'country' plays rather than city ones, and the last ones must
owe something to life on a country estate where people are forced
upon each other's company. It is said that he wrote the first draft
in four weeks and read it to the party at Melikhovo. Family and
friends listened to it dubiously, and Chekhov set about revising it
that winter.

His diffidence about the new play from the beginning is apparent in the tone of his correspondence. 'It is a comedy with three
female parts, six male, four acts, a landscape (view of a lake), lots

[1] This in spite of his attack on angels and villains (p. 3 above), which suggests
that Chekhov had it in mind to subvert the established theatre from the beginning.
But his words do apply increasingly to the major plays which follow *Ivanov*.

of talk on literature, little action and tons of love,'[1] he wrote in a letter to his friend Alexei Suvorin, the editor of the St Petersburg *New Times*, on 21 October 1895. There were four female parts in the final draft, but he continued to call it 'a comedy in four acts'. However, it was accepted for production at the Alexandrinsky Theatre, St Petersburg, on 17 October 1896. The report of the Alexandrinsky's literary committee had already anticipated the worst: its most biting comment was on the loose structure of the play, and it was particularly critical of what it called its 'symbolism, or more correctly its Ibsenism', which it found to be 'running through the whole play like a red thread'.[2] As it happened, the committee was right in being more critical of this element than Chekhov was himself.

The story of the first night has been told many times: it was the occasion of a notorious fiasco. The theatre itself was associated with popular, low-brow entertainment. The play was directed in a hurry by E. M. Karpov, otherwise a writer of successful melo-dramas, with only nine rehearsals.

At the sixth rehearsal Chekhov observed with dismay that several of the cast were absent, a few still read their lines from scripts, and only an assistant director was present to guide the actors. *The Seagull* was just another play to them, and it was clear that the limited Karpov, in his staging and instructions to the actors, had failed to understand the structural innovations of the play, its poetic mood and the tender and refined delineation of character. Shocked by the stilted, traditional intonation of the actors, their false emphasis in reading lines, and their lack of comprehension of the roles they were portraying, Chekhov frequently interrupted the rehearsal to explain the significance of a phrase or discuss the real essence of a characterization. 'The chief thing, my dears, is that theatricality is unnecessary,' he would repeat. 'Really unnecessary. It is entirely simple. They are all simple, ordinary people.'[3]

The leading actress E. I. Levkeyeva, famous for her comic charac-ter parts, had selected the play for her benefit performance. In the event, she did not appear in the play at all, but only in the comic after-piece, and an angry audience that had paid benefit night prices was ready to jeer at any opportunity. In spite of the fine performance of the young Vera Kommissarzhevskaya[4] as Nina

[1] Hellman, p. 189.   [2] Simmons, p. 365.   [3] Simmons, pp. 366–7.
[4] Vera Kommissarzhevskaya's brother, Theodore Komisarjevsky, one of the out-

Zaretchny, the audience found an early occasion for mockery in Nina's speech which opens Treplev's play, 'Men, lions, eagles and partridges . . .', and Chekhov's little joke about *avant-garde* theatre was turned into a joke against himself. Both author and character seemed equally to belong to the 'decadent' school. Treplev's entrance with a bandaged head and the use of the property seagull were found to be uproarious. Chekhov left the theatre in despair, and Karpov took the play off after eight nights. Here was a straightforward, almost narrative, form for a play, it seemed to the author, and he had been shown that it was meaningless. It had been made meaningless, of course, because it had been played in the convention of another age.

In later performances at the Alexandrinsky *The Seagull* was better appreciated. It was also successfully performed in the provinces. But it was not until two years later, in 1898, that the event occurred that was both to justify Chekhov's experiment and promote that final rush of dramatic composition by a dying man which gave us three more brilliant plays.

Vladimir Nemirovich-Danchenko, the novelist, playwright and director of the dramatic school of the Philharmonic Society, came together with Konstantin Stanislavsky, the most talented actor and director of his time, to create the Moscow Art Theatre and eventually share the direction of *The Seagull*. Still under the spell of the ensemble playing of the company of the Grand Duke of Saxe-Meiningen which visited Russia in 1890, these two wanted, like Chekhov himself, to alter the course of the conservative Russian theatre and to present plays as honest works and not as vehicles for self-display. The new aim was to play as a team and to remain loyal to the intentions of the author. Thus the director was to acquire the authority previously possessed by the star actor.[1]

standing European directors of the 1920s, describes her playing of parts like those of Nina and Sonya (in *Uncle Vanya*) as of great simplicity and sincerity, symbolizing the deepest feelings and longings of girlhood and womanhood. And he quotes Znosko Borovsky's *History of the Russian Theatre*: 'She always seemed, by some inexplicable magic, to be much more than merely the person she was representing. Her wide-open blue eyes looked at us questioningly from the stage, while her inimitable deep musical voice seemed to be making an appeal to something beyond the bourn of this material world as if promising to tell a wonderful secret which everyone of us longed to know' (*Myself and the Theatre*, New York, 1930, p. 70).
[1] The reader should consult Stanislavsky's autobiography, *My Life in Art*, trans. J. J. Robbins (London, 1924) and Nemirovich-Danchenko's *My Life in the Russian Theatre*, trans. J. Cournos (London, 1937) for a full account of the M.A.T.'s policy.

The Seagull

No policy could seem to accommodate better the plays of a dramatist who had himself dispensed with star parts.

Nemirovich-Danchenko knew Chekhov personally, and it was he who persuaded both Chekhov and Stanislavsky to try the rejected play. Their decision became more important than the success or failure of one play;[1] it was a decision about the future of the new theatre and the direction the new theatre movement would take. It affected the theatre of the Western world for half a century.

Stanislavsky gave the play twenty-six rehearsals, an unusual amount of preparation at that time, and himself played Trigorin to Olga Knipper's Arkadina. He describes the occasion of the first performance at the M.A.T. on 17 December 1898:

I do not remember how we played. The first act was over. There was a gravelike silence. Knipper fainted on the stage. All of us could hardly keep our feet. In the throes of despair we began moving to our dressing rooms. Suddenly there was a roar in the auditorium, and a shriek of joy or fright on the stage. The curtain was lifted, fell, was lifted again, showing the whole auditorium our amazed and astounded immovability. It fell again, it rose; it fell, it rose, and we could not even gather sense enough to bow. Then there were congratulations and embraces like those of Easter night, and ovations to Lilina, who played Masha, and who had broken the ice with her last words which tore themselves from her heart, moans washed with tears. This it was that had held the audience mute for a time before it began to roar and thunder in mad ovation.[2]

The M.A.T. recognized their debt to their playwright by adopting a seagull as their emblem.

Chekhov's major drama encourages us to see without distorting, to follow an ideal of truth without romanticizing, and to be detached without being clinical. With *The Seagull,* he achieves his first real success in communicating to an audience what it feels like to see with his eyes. On 27 October 1888, he wrote to Suvorin telling him he must not mix up two ideas, 'the solution of the problem and the correct presentation of the problem'. And he went on, 'Only the latter is obligatory for the artist. In *Anna*

[1] *The Seagull* was not the first play produced at the M.A.T., but it was mounted in the first season.
[2] Stanislavsky, p. 356.

Karenina and *Onegin* not a single problem is solved, but they satisfy you completely just because all their problems are correctly presented.'[1] The spectator watching the play is to be the jury, and make his own decisions about the solution if he will, and if he can.

Yet *The Seagull* was a compromise with nineteenth-century theatre practice in many respects. Although we see neither event, the young female lead is seduced and the young male lead does commit suicide. The play is still built upon several intense and potentially melodramatic relationships, which tend to distort the objective view by calling for an audience's empathy with characters in exhibitions of individual emotion. Chekhov has not yet fully managed to arrange his characters to undercut melodrama: the character patterns express the somewhat staccato rivalry of youth and age, particularly the jealousy of an older woman for a younger, and of a younger man for an older. If Chekhov suppresses some of these exhibitions, they remain the bigger for their silence. If Act I mocks Konstantin Treplev's passion as a creative writer, Act III invites a conventional response to the display of his feelings towards his mother.[2] Chekhov will improve on his technique in *The Seagull*; by the time he comes to write *The Cherry Orchard* he will construct a comparable scene (between Ranevsky and Trofimov in Act III) which side-steps all melodramatic implications. Although Treplev shoots himself offstage rather than in full view like Ivanov, the effect of an over-strong theatrical statement remains as potent; Chekhov has a better idea when Vanya fires at the Professor and *misses*. He is teaching himself to

[1] Hellman, p. 57.

[2] As conventional playwriting, Chekhov's third act quarrel between mother and son, started by the boy's distress over Nina and his jealousy of Trigorin, and by the mother's jealousy of Nina and her contempt for her son, yet with all these feelings heightened and controlled by the maternal and filial relationship, is superb of its kind. The scene's graduated development from sympathy to vituperation to reconciliation makes of it a prototype exercise in the acting style of a former age. Sir John Gielgud, who played Treplev at the Arts and the Little Theatres, London, in 1925, and Trigorin at the New Theatre, London, in 1936, finds that *The Seagull* is 'written in a more conventional manner than *The Cherry Orchard*. There are big acting scenes in every act, and the four principal characters carry the interest in a far simpler method of exposition than in the later Tchechov plays' (*Early Stages*, London, 1953, p. 103). He makes the same point in *Stage Directions* (London, 1963), p. 86: '*The Seagull* . . . seemed to me a more conventional kind of play, and I felt I understood it a little better, at least as regards the melodramatic side of the plot (the jealousies, quarrelling, and Constantin's suicide at the end).'

work for an effect of the objectively amusing which makes us think rather than suffer. Robert W. Corrigan makes the general point:

All the traditional ingredients of dramatic action – love, murder, suicide, revenge – are present in the Chekhovian drama, but they are used differently, used to serve different ends. They are not ends in themselves or plot devices to further the action but are used as indirect means of focussing our attention on the inner lives of the characters themselves.[1]

When in 1900 Chekhov saw Hedda Gabler's theatrical suicide, he declared to Stanislavsky, 'Look here, Ibsen is really not a dramatist.' Chekhov had by then declared against the artificial in drama.

Although *The Seagull* is today still a risky enterprise, a great deal was achieved by the experiment. Complaints of Chekhov's lack of purpose and informal plotting were heard again, as they were of *Ivanov* and *The Wood Demon*. For it was not readily seen that the play is not a story about the tragic love of two young people. Chekhov's joking remark was, we remember, that there were to be 'tons of love', and Dr Dorn, the *raisonneur* of the play, emphasizes the same point at the end of the first act: 'How hysterical they all are! How hysterical! And what a lot of love . . .' Indeed, nearly every character (even old Sorin the ex-civil servant feels he has missed something) is involved in one of four love triangles:

Treplev	Nina	Trigorin
Nina	Trigorin	Arkadina
Medvedenko	Masha	Treplev
Dorn	Polina	Shamraev

While it is true the stress is on the first two of these, Medvedenko's comic wooing of Masha and Polina's wish to cuckold Shamraev comically parallel and parody the agonies of the others. There is so much love that arguably there is none at all. Chekhov's introduction of so many situations tends towards an alienation effect in the audience which perhaps only Brechtian theory can identify: 'A representation that alienates is one which allows us to recognize its subject, but at the same time makes it seem

[1] In his introduction to *Six Plays of Chekhov* (New York, 1962) and reprinted in *Modern Drama: Essays in Criticism*, ed. T. Bogard and W. I. Oliver (New York, 1965), p. 80.

unfamiliar'.[1] It is Chekhov's first exercise in 'complex seeing'. The many 'plots' of *The Seagull* induce this anti-emotional perspective, and we are encouraged to judge Treplev and Nina as we judge the unfamiliar. This points to one of the director's problems: 'I keep on reading and rereading your play,' Nemirovich-Danchenko wrote to Chekhov on 31 May 1898, 'looking for *those bridges* over which the producer must lead the audience, avoiding the crude conventions it loves so much.'[2]

The humour that results is reflective and elusive, the pauses at the ends of the acts even investing it with a quality of amiable lyricism. But this brand of humour can inform the whole play in spite of the emotional exchanges.

The 'portrait-gallery' tradition of Russian comedy after Alexander Griboyedov's *Woe from Wit* (1824), in which magnificent roles for actors became at once almost proverbial in the language, the staple of the actor's art and the test-pieces of the schools, was Chekhov's inheritance.[3] Creating the group vitality which made the characters into a family was his legacy. Maurice Valency's recognition that Turgenev's characters are growing, vital creatures is closely relevant to our understanding of the new development in Chekhov.

For his people, life is a process of self-realization. They neither know themselves from the start, nor do they stumble upon themselves suddenly in the end. They discover themselves little by little, and are constantly surprised at the things they feel and do. The result is that we gain insight into their natures step by step as they do themselves, and are quite unprepared for the turns and contradictions in their behaviour. The effect of this kind of development is extraordinarily lifelike.[4]

Valency goes on to argue that this technique is one of exploration and not of definition. 'Each suggestion is offered as temporary and provisional', so that the characters retain 'the enigmatic quality of people'. Unhappily, the professional actor in Russia in 1896 was no more ready to characterize his part according to fragmentary impressions in the text than he had been for *A Month in the Country*. The process of character discovery, which of

[1] Bertolt Brecht, 'A Short Organum for the Theatre' in J. Willett, *Brecht on Theatre* (London, 1964), p. 192.
[2] Balukhaty, p. 53 (my italics).
[3] See Valency, ch. 1, 'Chekhov's Theatre'.   [4] *Ibid.* p. 45.

course is a theatrical illusion, is especially strong in Treplev, Nina and Trigorin in *The Seagull*, but Chekhov made matters no easier for the actors by having them reveal themselves only within the small community the play presents on the stage.

The group acting is only possible because Chekhov has first precisely conceived his characters as individuals, each with a life of his own. Each is self-regarding, each is to himself a hero: Treplev battling against his mother, and his own weakness, for self-esteem; Arkadina herself battling against the onset of middle-age to hold her lover; Trigorin, the weakest of villains, a 'famous author' in old shoes and checked trousers, jotting his thoughts in a notebook for fear of forgetting them, having all but lost the fight for his own soul; Nina, her pretty head filled with big artistic ideas. And so on: Sorin, Masha, Medvedenko, Polina – all are tragedy heroes to themselves in their disappointments, but each has forsaken his dignity. All are, like Masha, 'in mourning for their lives', young and old, pathetic and comic. As we discover them, we gain a sense of the deflation of all their pretensions.

It seems that each character is engaged in a lonely struggle: Arkadina talks herself back into her popularity; no one listens to Sorin's whining, or to Medvedenko's; Treplev does not pay attention to Masha, nor Dorn to Polina. Yet the character-weaving in this play is unlike anything in drama before. It is the first great experiment on the modern stage which demands 'orchestrated', 'symphonic' acting. The party scenes, the arrivals and departures, of which Chekhov grows fond after *Ivanov*, are prime examples of Chekhov's work for ensemble playing. If such scenes of social gathering seem a challenge to the director today, they serve the plays as a way of revealing people in the way that they do reveal themselves only in social groups. And they ensure that the social groups themselves remain at the centre of attention.

It is part of the same achievement that prompts the critics so often to return to the idea that Chekhov's dialogue merely makes parallel lines that do not meet. Chekhov's way is to supply a thousand details for his creatures to remain true to themselves while they also interact and reflect the embracing mood of the moment as a group. Even while Stanislavsky was still indifferent to the quality of Chekhov's writing in *The Seagull*, he set about composing the *mise-en-scène*, and after finishing it in three or four weeks he declared, 'To my surprise the work seemed much easier than I had anticipated: I both *saw and felt* the play.'[1] He recognized that such sequences as the management of the rebellious stage audience in Act I, the sudden quarrel over carriage-horses on the hot summer day of Act II, in Act III the unexpected call for attention to Sorin as he is struck by pain, in Act IV the daring anticlimax of the game of lotto, were all brilliantly written for a new kind of stage direction, that of scoring for an orchestra, for a group.

It follows that an understanding of *The Seagull*'s meaning is likely to come only through the experience of it in the theatre. Chekhov's stage method of juxtaposing individual attitudes within the group encourages the spectator to find the universal statement in the particular lives. Raymond Williams has recently diagnosed Chekhovian realism as 'a way of seeing the world in which it was possible to experience the quality of a whole way of life through the qualities of individual men and woman'.[2] All good drama takes this way in some degree; the theatrical problem is to supply the correct microcosmic presentation which is to stand for society at large. Williams adds, 'A whole group, a whole society, can be seen as victims. It is not a question now of the dramatic resolution of the fate of a single individual, but of an orchestration of responses to a common fate.'[3] The story of Treplev and Nina is not to be that of individual tragedy, but representative of a general comedy: the steady passing of their love points to the limitations of the love in all the others.

We are neither to like nor to loathe Chekhov's Treplev, Trigorin and Arkadina, but to hold them in what might be called his 'balance of sympathy' by which we are forced to come to some sort of judgment. Our contradictory responses to the particular people of the play hold the secret of the play's theme. It is deceptive to turn for guidance to the symbolism of the seagull itself.[4] Chekhov was interested in the symbolist movement, and especially in Maeterlinck, at this time: *The Seagull*'s qualities of lyricism and symbolism derive in part from him rather than from Ibsen.

[1] Balukhaty, p. 55. [2] *Modern Tragedy* (London, 1966), p. 139.
[3] *Ibid.* p. 143.
[4] The well-known story of the killing of a woodcock, the apparent source of the symbol, is told in Chekhov's letter to Suvorin of 8 April 1892. See the accounts in Hingley, vol. II, p. 337; Simmons, pp. 279 and 332–3; and elsewhere. *Chaika* in Russian means 'gull', embarrassing if exactly translated into English.

The Seagull

The seagull property strikes us today as too overt and defined a symbol for a naturalistic play, one which in any case would work quite well without it. It tends towards the static and inert by comparison with, say, the cherry orchard, in which the central symbolism remains organic and develops with the action. It jars when it is seen and when it is talked about. Moreover, the seagull's close delineation diminishes an essential dramatic activity on the part of the audience. The famous seagull is meant, no doubt, to be all-embracing, but it points too directly to Nina, only partly to Treplev, and hardly at all to the rest of the group. The seagull we take to be, at its simplest, an image of innocent life destroyed by human indifference. After Act II, the recurring reminder of it, verbal and visual, prompts the audience to try to give it a widening range of reference. Treplev, in shooting the beautiful, free young bird on the wing, threatens Nina that he will take his own life in the same way; obviously he sees himself as the seagull, and we may see him so too – a young, aspiring creature cruelly handled by his mother, a Hamlet misunderstood, a failure as a writer. But he kills it wantonly, and this reflects the violence in himself, just as in the play he becomes his own destroyer. When his mother will not appreciate his talent in the beginning, he flings a tantrum, and then the threat of his self-destruction is his blackmail of her. At the end, when he discovers that Nina is her own property, he carries out the threat. Treplev's seagull, therefore, as he lays it at Nina's feet in Act II, is part victim, part tribute and part threat.

In Act III Trigorin takes up the idea in his own way and applies it to Nina: it becomes the subject of the story he never writes, and our image of his mindless destruction of her. By Act IV we find Nina linking it strictly with her own sense of loss: she uses it as a signature on her letters to Treplev and repeatedly talks of herself as a seagull in her last moments on the stage. For her, it symbolizes her childhood attachment to her home and the lake, to which she naturally returns. But it also reflects the hold which Treplev and Trigorin both selfishly try to exert on her. Yet though the symbolism of the seagull is asked to generalize youthful lost illusions and to reflect such varying lights, it cannot stand for the general condition of the lives of *all* these unhappy people.

Chekhov's juxtapositions of character are far more successful in projecting his theme, and he does not repeat such mechanical symbolism in the plays that follow. The pattern of youth and age ensures that the image of the one has meaning only in the mirror of the other. Thus Polina's story is that of a woman unhappily married to a bore. She longs for the least attention from Dr Dorn. When, therefore, her daughter Masha, in despair at ever winning attention from Treplev, accepts as her husband the dull school-master Medvedenko, it is Polina who implores Treplev to be kind, and her striking understatement is, 'I know from myself' (Act IV). Polina and Masha project images of the same state at two stages of life. Or again, the patterning can be seen in the relationship, more submerged, between Sorin and Treplev. Old Sorin longs for his youth, would like to have had a wife and live in town, and even wanted to be a writer (Act IV); he is the one who can appreciate the boy's ambitions. For his part, it is Treplev who pleads with his mother to give his uncle the money to live in town. They too mirror each other. The famous author Trigorin also understands how Treplev is striving to create an identity for himself: 'Everyone writes as he likes and as he can' is his comment on the play of Act I. But his own life is that of a successful automaton, a mediocrity still struggling unsuccessfully to express his true self, for it is his devotion to his art which makes him inhuman in the way he uses Nina.

These and other echoing relationships persist while we are shown how experience can destroy innocence. The stronger ones, Arkadina and Trigorin, the one an unconscious sham, the other a conscious one, have the power to consume the weaker. Arkadina cruelly, Trigorin mindlessly, abuse the love and need of the boy and girl. But like Nina and Treplev, Arkadina and Trigorin are desperately seeking self-preservation. In particular, Arkadina knows she is fading, for her 'art' depends upon her looks, and she is not the sort of actress who can go on to play elderly women. She resists giving out too much human feeling because she is clinging to a mental precipice herself. When Chekhov was asked why Treplev and Nina perish and Arkadina and Trigorin triumph, he did not answer. He had no need to: no one triumphs. The 'tons of love' are tons of pain. Only Nina suggests a modicum of hope: what matters, as she says, is 'to bear one's cross and have faith' – a note that Chekhov is to strike again. Ironically we see her go off to a third-rate acting company, and we are left to surmise whether she is not an embryo Arkadina who in her turn will be corrupted by the pressures of her profession. Patterns thus become themes.

It is the total view of so many individual conflicts, so many people failing each other in their need, rubbing each other the wrong way, which grants us the Chekhovian comic perspective. It is a comedy, not of happy endings and other externals, but of the little pains of human pride and vanity. This total sense of the Chekhovian world is managed by particular detail, of tone, mannerism, mood, speech and silence, and these details we must now proceed to examine.

Act One

The curtain rises on a twilit stage for the most romantic setting
Chekhov ever provided. In the initial silence of the empty stage
the audience may examine Pyotr Sorin's lush parkland, with its
vista in the half-darkness of a wide avenue of trees and bushes in
full leaf, the sun setting behind them. This avenue is to suggest
the path to a lake, which will be painted in our imagination before
we see it better in the sunlight of Act II.[1] It is, as so often in the new
naturalistic perspective of the proscenium arch stage, the kind of
exterior set which is designed to pull us into its imaginary depth
as the eye follows a path or an avenue of trees, just as an interior
(the so-called box set) may include a door which beckons us
further into the house. But the illusionary romanticism of this
parkland setting is all to be undermined by the action which will
take place against it. Stanislavsky added to these visual suggestions the 'distant sounds of a drunkard's song, distant howling of
a dog, the croaking of frogs, the crake of a landrail, the slow
tolling of a distant church-bell . . . flashes of lightning, faint
rumbling of thunder in the distance'. He explains that these

[1] In 1906, Vsevolod Meyerhold, who was a member of the Moscow Art Theatre and
who was to become one of the greatest of Russia's directors in the post-naturalistic
manner, complained that Stanislavsky made the setting too literal. 'In the first
production, one could not follow the characters' exits during Act I: running across
a small bridge, they disappeared into a dark thicket, going *somewhere* . . . During the
revival of *The Seagull*, however, every corner of the stage was exposed. They built
a summerhouse with a real cupola and real columns. There was a ravine on the
stage, and one could see clearly how people went offstage on to it.' And he concluded, 'This striving to exhibit everything whatever the cost, this fear of Mystery,
of implication, turns theatre into a mere illustrator of the words of an author. "I
hear a dog howling again", says one of the characters. And without fail, the howl
of a dog is reproduced. The audience knows of a departure not only by the
retreating sounds of bells, but also by the hoof-beats on a wooden bridge over a
river. The patter of rain on an iron roof is heard. Birds. Frogs. Crickets.' (From
Teatr. Kniga o novom teatre. Sbornik statej, 1908, trans. J. C. Vining in Jackson, pp.
63 and 65.)

noises are to 'help the audience to get the feel of the sad, monotonous life of the characters'.[1]

It is almost a dream setting. It is a set for Konstantin Treplev, and its fancy reflects his young imagination. Among the trees he has had built a rough platform upon which to present a play, and thus Chekhov suggests *two* areas on his stage, which are to signify two opposing attitudes or ideas.[2] The audience sees the awkward incongruity of this erection, and after a moment hears a discordant and quite unromantic coughing and hammering backstage. The crude structure among its natural frame of leaves will give us some sense of Treplev's pretensions.

For all the dreamy twilight of the picture, the reality will be present in many ways. In a Chekhovian scene, the weather, the time of year and the time of day are always precisely known, and they are always meaningfully atmospheric. Here at the beginning of *The Seagull* the audience is quickly to learn that it is 'stifling' and that a storm is coming. The heat will be reflected in everybody's behaviour. Above all, the play begins with an attack in which comic distancing is immediately felt. Two characters emerge from the bushes, one whose chief task is more of factual exposition, and the other in a contrasting attitude whose function is to control for comedy our responses to what we see and hear, a plan Chekhov follows in *Uncle Vanya* and *The Cherry Orchard*.

In spite of the heat and humidity, Masha, the daughter of Sorin's steward, makes her entrance in a black and forbidding dress. She is followed by Medvedenko, her schoolmaster wooer, a man 'aged thirty-two with a grey beard'[3] and wearing white linen trousers.[4] He makes an unlovely suitor, for the two make their entrance bickering and quarrelling. We note also that

[1] Balukhaty, p. 139. Such effects, however lifelike, are questionable. The howling dog is justified by Sorin's speech early in the act, one of many of Chekhov's carefully selected sounds intended to focus an emotion, the sort of effect which culminates in the axe-stroke on the trees in *The Cherry Orchard*. But it might be thought that other evocative, but arbitrary sounds, not of Chekhov's choosing, are the equivalent of inserting actual lines of dialogue, colouring the scene for a romantic melancholy greater than the play asks for.
[2] This device, as for a play-within-a-play, Chekhov extends in *Three Sisters*, Act I, and *The Cherry Orchard*, Act III.
[3] In Chekhov's Notebook I. See Hingley, vol. II, p. 335.
[4] According to E. M. Shavrova-Just (Elena Shavrova), as reported in a letter from Chekhov to Nemirovich-Danchenko of 29 January 1899. See Balukhaty, p. 72.

Act I

Medvedenko *follows* the girl, as if she were trying to escape him. And when they sit on a bench in the moonlight they do not embrace.[1] They have come to see Treplev's play, having returned from an evening's walk, one which was hardly enjoyable for Masha. In the aggressive way of a man who bears a rooted grudge against life, Medvedenko has been telling her about his low salary as a teacher, and hectoring her as if she were one of his pupils. He is obsessed by money to the extent that he can measure the happiness of others only by their wealth.[2]

The girl is twenty-two, as Arkadina tells us in Act II, but she is incongruously wearing sombre, matronly colours. Her opening line, which has puzzled and amused many playgoers by the obliquity of its meaning, must immediately strike an audience as comic, in whatever tone it is spoken.

MEDVEDENKO. Why do you always wear black?
MASHA. I am in mourning for my life. I am unhappy.

In practice, Masha can speak the line only in what seems to be a 'theatrical' voice, both dramatizing and mocking herself at the same time.[3] Whatever an audience might have expected after viewing the fantasy of the setting, it was not this. It is as if Masha were trying to conclude a conversation abruptly, not start one. Her casual and pettish reply is a whimsically cruel stroke against her dull lover, although it may be justified by her unrequited love for Treplev, as will appear. When the audience later observes her addiction to snuff and brandy, we see it both as a symptom of her need for the stimulant Medvedenko cannot supply,

[1] Stanislavsky would have them stroll about as after dinner, with Masha cracking nuts and Medvedenko smoking, a point which Stanislavsky presumably deduces from his concern with the high cost of tobacco. But their dialogue may suggest a far less casual relationship beneath the appearances, and such details of 'external characterization' risk distorting an exact intention in the action of the scene.
[2] Chekhov had great sympathy with the lot of the poor village schoolteacher, hungry, crushed and intimidated, as Maxim Gorky's *Reminiscences* of 1905 prove. See also Chekhov's letter to Suvorin of 27 November 1894 in Simmons, p. 359, and short stories like 'The School-Mistress'.
[3] Reviewing Martita Hunt's performance as Masha in Komisarjevsky's production at the New Theatre, London, 1936, James Agate found it 'unholy joy': 'This exquisitely poised actress radiated glumness, hammered out a full-dress Hungarian rhapsody on a theme of Mrs Gummidge, and rightly convulsed the house ... Miss Hunt's tragic mask, wet with booby tears, made one cry with laughter' (*More First Nights*, London, 1937, p. 275).

and as an eccentric gesture of a woman's protest against her lot. While Medvedenko talks about his misfortunes, she reveals hers by hints which suggest a more deeply seated grief: 'It isn't money that matters. A poor man may be happy.' If Medvedenko is the practical one, Masha is at heart the romantic.

Medvedenko persists in whining about the cost of his pension, the size of the family he must support, the price of tea and sugar, as well as, in an afterthought, of tobacco: the whole catalogue of miseries. Masha in her boredom finally tries to change the subject with the remark that the play is soon to start. She has no success. The man adores to hear his own voice, and this reference to the play merely introduces the topic of its author's love for its young actress. The spectator will notice Masha's pained reaction to the mention of Konstantin Treplev and can understand the hidden reason for her indifference to the schoolmaster. It may not be so easy to understand her wish to inflict on Medvedenko the wound she feels herself.

Within a very short time of playing, Chekhov has started an ambivalence in the action. Already we are lightly alerted to the kind of comedy to which we must respond. The comic pathos of this unhappy affair, in which there is no point of contact between the lovers as they sit stiffly on the bench, opens the play with the kind of discord which will echo wittily through all the saltily mixed relationships of the play. As if to guide our response, Masha takes snuff, with the noisy and graceless gesture of sniffing. To cap the comedy, she offers her lover a pinch of it for himself. This he rejects with the serious, but throw-away, line, 'I don't feel like it.' The pause which follows speaks for the audience's amusement.

For a couple to quarrel over who had more right to be unhappy is perhaps a commonplace of married life; for an unmarried couple to quarrel in this way is to suggest their childishness. The humour of this notion is enforced objectively by the clarity of their distancing tones and mannerisms – the harping of the man and the eccentricity of the girl. What we may mistake at this stage is the real motive for their quarrel, Masha's unrequited love for Treplev. When she declares with conviction, 'To my mind it is a thousand times better to go in rags and be a beggar than . . .', her unfinished thought must be, '. . . than to love in vain'. Theirs will be the first of many images of the vanity of an abortive human desire. For Masha's reference to the heat, 'How stifling it is!', embraces both the weather and the state of all the characters.

Age and youth make their appearance: Sorin, the ex-civil servant gentleman-landowner, leaning on his stick as he shuffles towards the bench, and Konstantin Treplev, his nephew, in a sweat for the success of his play. They are talking at cross purposes – yet age has its sense of humour; youth has none.

Chekhov ensures that Sorin's rueful laughter[1] endears him to us, but his little vanities, like his beard-combing in this scene, slightly undercut sympathy with the old man. Sorin has retired at sixty, as we learn in Act II, and has returned to his country home. But he finds that he is withering away in the country: 'I shall never get used to it.' His clothes and his hair are untidy, as Treplev remarks. He goes to bed too early; he falls asleep too easily. He is worried by trifles: the dog will not stop howling (although, at least, we may think, if his sister Arkadina cannot sleep for the noise, he can). However, we observe that he complains equally about both city and country life. He is a character whom Chekhov has exactly particularized: an ageing man disappointed with his life, but who takes his pleasure in grumbling. He harks back every time to his unfulfilled past – 'Women never liked me' – until no one listens to him any more. Yet he can laugh at himself out of self-defence, and Chekhov has paired his genial good-nature with the over-earnestness of young Treplev, so that the humour of the older man must accentuate his nephew's self-concern. Naturally, Sorin's tone merely irritates the boy, who is thinking about other things.

For this scene is Treplev's, and *The Seagull* differs from the later plays in keeping a single character more in the centre of the action. But Treplev is not central in the traditional way, for he is no Byronic poet-hero, no Hamlet (in spite of the allusion in the dialogue). He is to be one of the new anti-heroes of the modern stage: the audience is to grow to understand but not admire him.

---

[1] Stanislavsky comments on Sorin's sudden outbursts of laughter, 'In my opinion Sorin's laugh is rather startling and unexpected. One moment he is talking quite seriously, then he suddenly bursts out laughing, and loudly, too.' (Balukhaty, p. 143). This surmise introduces into the characterization a touch of hysteria that is hardly appropriate to Sorin's years. Stanislavsky's other suggestion (p. 169), that Sorin always carries a rug to wrap round his legs in the evenings, which the others help him to do, seems right.

In his anti-heroic role Chekhov will use him to point to the selfish indifference of those about him. Thus, not by didactic statement, but by ironic demonstration, his case will define the general sickness.

The boy makes his entrance in a state of great excitement and nervous tension. That he is not really listening to Sorin's ramblings is proved by his abrupt treatment of Masha and Medvedenko when he catches sight of them. They have arrived too soon! Will they please go away until they are called? For Masha this is only another rebuff from the one she loves. And her disappointment must explain why, when Sorin asks her to tell her father to have the dog let off the chain, she snaps a refusal. She leaves, and we see that Medvedenko follows her as before, like a puppy.

Not unlike a repetition joke of the *commedia dell'arte*, Masha's sense of irritation as she goes off is passed on to Treplev. The workman Yakov, who has been intermittently hammering a nail backstage, calls to Treplev to ask whether he may take a swim, presumably in the romantic lake itself. Treplev glances at his pocket-watch – a gesture we are to see him make three times in the next few minutes – and reluctantly lets him go, calling after him testily, 'But don't be more than ten minutes.' The pressure of time and urgency for the young is casually introduced, introducing through Treplev a whirlpool of anxiety into a complaisant stage.

It is also time that Treplev's leading lady were here: this will be Nina Zaretchny, the daughter of a neighbouring landowner. Treplev is unable to take his mind off the events of the evening. He describes his riskily unorthodox stage arrangements to Sorin. The scene is to be lit by the real moon, a plan which only Bully Bottom could otherwise have conceived, and the backdrop is to be the mysterious lake itself, the ultimate in scenic realism. He goes over these plans with a breathless fervour as if trying to justify his concept of theatre. In his zeal, he is too self-occupied to hear, as we do, the empty encouragement of Sorin's hollow comment, 'Magnificent'.

At this point in the scene, Stanislavsky suggests that Treplev is so agitated that he excitedly examines the stage and jumps on to the bench, 'rocking it so violently that Sorin grunts and catches hold of the plank with both hands'. This piece of business might effectively distance the audience, and prepare us to be suitably critical of Treplev's play. But it must also be clear that its success

26

is dear to him, and Stanislavsky adds, 'It is not for nothing that he is in such a nervous state after its failure. The more jumpy and agitated he is now, the stronger will his mood of despair be after the failure of his play.'[1]

It is also soon evident that his repeated looking at his watch reflects his anxiety about the arrival of his most special audience. For it is more than the performance of the play that is preying on his mind. As the line, 'If Nina is late it will spoil the whole effect', suggests, it is more than his feeling for Nina too. When Treplev sits down at last beside his uncle, it is his mother, his guest of honour at the play, of whom he is thinking most.

The moment is an intimate one. With some familiarity the boy adjusts his uncle's cravat and begins to talk frankly about Mme Arkadin. In what he says, the audience can recognize the tug of his ambition for the future against the familial frustrations of the past. This is one source of tension in the young man. As Treplev thinks of his mother, a new pulse is felt in the action of this opening scene. Arkadina, it will emerge, is as self-centred an actress as her son is an author. In particular, it seems that her advancing years are worrying her, and the presence of a grown son of twenty-five is an unwelcome reminder of it. Thus Treplev, sensitive for her approval of his effort as a creative artist, has until now found it lacking. He tries to explain it as boredom, as jealousy of Nina, of whose youthful charm his mother may be jealous, and out tumbles the whole burden of his resentment against her: her vanity, her superstition, her meanness. In due time we shall judge the justice of this for ourselves; for the present we suspect his claim that he feels no envy of Trigorin, his mother's lover and his own most immediate rival as an author. These hasty vituperations tell us a little about Arkadina by way of exposition, but they tell us much more about her son, as Sorin's quiet comment suggests: 'You are already upset and all that.' In this way Chekhov skilfully, but obliquely, sets out his central situation, the method an invitation to us to re-appraise it.

As Treplev diagnoses Arkadina's theatrical conceit, he sits abstractedly pulling petals off a flower, doubtfully testing her love for him as might a lover or a little boy – both, indeed. By such touches of realism, Chekhov has us associate the gift of flowers

[1] Balukhaty, p. 143.

with the gift of self. As in other places in the play, the fragility of flowers represents a character's most vulnerable feelings.[1]

In discussing his mother's work in the theatre, Treplev reveals his own theatrical position, and it is curiously like Chekhov's. The modern theatre has become sterile:

TREPLEV. When the curtain goes up, and by artificial light, in a room with three walls, these great geniuses, the devotees of holy art, represent how people eat, drink, love, move about, and wear their jackets; when from these commonplace sentences and pictures they try to draw a moral – a petty moral, easy of comprehension and convenient for domestic use; when in a thousand variations I am offered the same thing over and over again – I run away as Maupassant ran away from the Eiffel Tower which weighed upon his brain with its vulgarity.

SORIN. You can't do without the stage.

TREPLEV. We need new forms of expression.

It is typical that Chekhov should bury his most outspoken public criticism of the contemporary theatre in such a context. Sorin is the sleepy auditor. The agitated speaker is a student, and a failure at that; and as a playwright he has yet to prove himself capable of writing one line of stageworthy dialogue. With his quickening speech and its emotional outbursts, and with his tense, even fidgety, behaviour, he presents an image of amateurishness, as comic as his pretentious play. Unlike Chekhov's, Treplev's talent is not backed by self-knowledge and self-discipline. However, it is not so much a mark of modesty that Chekhov should give Treplev these very genuine lines; rather, he is insisting once again that the spectator should judge for himself, and in the impartiality of his presentation he seems deliberately to be undermining his own case. Only Treplev's indifference to the outward success of Trigorin's writings offers in all this the truly Chekhovian needle-thrust of criticism: external appearances mean nothing in the true judgment of art. The audience is invited to see through fashion and discard the trappings of popular success or popular contempt. *The Seagull* itself, the whole play, will supply the evidence by which the jury must reach a verdict.

So Treplev is the counsel for the prosecution and for the

[1] Stanislavsky misses the point of the tearing of flowers when he has his Treplev tearing blades of grass as well (Balukhaty, p. 147). A visual signal as precise as Chekhov's may not be blurred.

defence. Sorin's quiet comment that he too wanted to be a writer seems sublimely irrelevant, but is ironically intended to underline the issue by a melancholy parallelism: our unthinking condemnation of the enthusiasm of this young man could produce as a result a disappointed old man like Sorin. Thus the exposition of the play is concluded, if 'exposition' is the appropriate term for such indirection. Within ten minutes, and with no sense of the mechanics of dramaturgy at work, we have received a wealth of suggestions for mood, theme, central character and central situation, and, as a bonus, a good-humoured hint of the author's purpose in writing.

Treplev has heard Nina's approach and run to meet her, and with her breathless, lively entrance the pace of the action increases. The spirited arrival of Nina and the warm greeting of these two young people is in obvious contrast with the cold relationship between Masha and Medvedenko just seen. In order to play for Konstantin, Nina has escaped from her father and stepmother, a glancing suggestion of her oppressive home life and another reflection on Treplev's. He welcomes her impulsively, his anxiety over the play mixed with his adoration of the girl. Only Sorin's beaming comic presence saves the moment from sentimentality. He also serves to lift the scene to one of general excitement as he goes off to call the others, his singing and marching with his cane like a soldier and his sardonic little joke about his unpleasant voice a foretaste of the kind of vaudeville regulation of the stage mood Chekhov practises with Charlotta and Pishtchik in *The Cherry Orchard*. But the tragic atmosphere is turned by several other gentle redresses, as when Nina responds immediately to Treplev's rapturous greeting with a pathetic questioning assertion that she is not late, or to his clumsy kiss with a query about the name of the tree they are standing under. And Nina, worried because the famous Trigorin will be in the audience, almost touches off a quarrel by lightly suggesting that his stories are 'wonderful' – unlike Treplev's play which has no action in it, 'nothing but speeches'. Her apt throw-away line as she goes behind the curtain is, 'To my mind there ought to be love in a play.' Nevertheless, the quick sequence of comic exchanges between the two young people retains a charm which is the necessary prelude to the distressing scene to follow.

Nina is not quite right about the lack of 'action'. Treplev's instructions to Yakov warn us that his play will include a sensational effect of burning sulphur to accompany the illusion of a pair of red eyes. But she is right about something else. Chekhov unexpectedly inserts a line which is designed to fix our attention with its strange and unlikely image: 'I feel drawn to the lake here like a seagull.' Like Rebecca West's sudden, 'They cling to their dead a long time at Rosmersholm', this is a symbolist's hasty technique to send the spectator's imagination soaring with a provocative but unanswered question.

It is with careful differentiation of character that Chekhov now introduces the remainder of the stage-audience for the play-within-the-play. First to appear are Dr Dorn with the steward's wife Polina at his heels, her subordination thus reversing the role of her daughter Masha. They make an unlikely pair. The Doctor, at the age of fifty-five, is one of Chekhov's realists, the sanest of all the characters in the play, a witness himself of their struggles, like ourselves; Chekhov repeatedly uses him to modify our sympathies with the others.[1] It is probably for this reason that Chekhov's motivation of Dorn is also the weakest: perhaps in self-defence, having as a physician seen too much of the misery of others, he has adopted an attitude of non-involvement, as his studied indifference to Polina's attentions throughout the play insists. This is unhappy for that lady, who would so much like to mother him if his light-hearted nonchalance did not constantly deny her the chance. Their entrance, therefore, like Masha's and Medvedenko's, is also marked by a quarrel. The Doctor should watch his health in the night air: it must strike us as a jest that Polina should think it is the Doctor who needs nursing. He has been attracted by Mme Arkadin, she thinks, and all women are attracted to *him*: her accusations grow wilder. All these fancies are humorously brushed aside, but together they nakedly reveal poor Polina's passion for him. More important, her lack of interest in the play they have come to see will make them innocently guilty of contributing to the disasters of the evening.

Chekhov is now about to bring the whole cast of the play on stage, and its organization during the sequence which follows is

[1] Dorn was possibly conceived as a *raisonneur* in the French tradition of Dr Remonin in *L'Étrangère* of Dumas *fils*. See M. Valency, *The Flower and the Castle* (New York, 1963), p. 79.

a challenging exercise for any director, for the text is a master-piece of controlled guidance of the spectator's interests and sympathies. The chatter on stage seems casual, turning lightly on things of the theatre as is appropriate to the occasion, but while we seem to have been prepared to concentrate on Treplev's 'new forms of theatre', Chekhov slyly refocuses our attention on the 'great' actress, Treplev's mother, and her professional world. By dividing our interest between Arkadina and Treplev's play, Chekhov gives us the direct sensation of Treplev's own sense of treachery in his audience.

Only Mme Arkadin, Shamraev and Trigorin are at this point new to us, and Trigorin, who is largely silent during this scene, remains an enigma until he is alone with Nina in Act II. The entrance of Arkadina is 'theatrical' in the traditional way, simply because it is habitual with her to come into a group of people with a flourish. It is important that we see her as a fine figure of a woman, still beautiful even though her looks are fading, a woman accustomed to the attentions of men. Her pose as she sits sur-rounded by her male admirers makes the visual point immediately. She is an improvised show in herself, a counter-attraction to her son's play, always playing the *grande dame*, wearing the 'gorgeous dresses of a fascinatingly vulgar woman'.[1] Her own show is already in direct competition with Nina's anticipated performance. And although they may all settle with their backs and shoulders to us and their faces turned away towards the stage as if they were going to be good, attentive spectators, this will obviously be a difficult audience for Treplev.

[1] Letter from Nemirovich-Danchenko to Chekhov, December 1898, in Balukhaty, p. 71. The range for the interpretation of Arkadina's entrance is within these broad limits. Sir John Gielgud contrasts the entrance of Miriam Lewes as Arkadina in the production of A. E. Filmer at the Arts and Little Theatres, London, in 1925, with that of Dame Edith Evans in Theodore Komisarjevsky's production at the New Theatre, London, in 1936: 'Nothing could have been more different from Miriam Lewes's striking performance, than the brilliantly poised, temperamental Arcádina of Edith Evans. Miriam played the part as a tragic actress. She stalked on the stage in the first act, angry and sullen, looking rather barbaric in appearance, dressed in a strange picture frock and pacing the stage like a tigress, violent in her rages, and moody and self-accusing in her griefs. Edith, on the other hand, dressed the part like a Parisian, with a high, elegant coiffure, sweeping fashionable dresses, hats and scarves and parasols. On her first entrance she was all smiles and graciousness, but one could see from the angle of her head, as she sat with her back to the audience watching Konstantin's play, that underneath all the sweetness she was a selfish woman in a very bad temper' (*Early Stages*, London, 1953, p. 294).

Shamraev the estate-manager is a conversational bore, over-whelmed by Madame and her world of theatre. There are strong elements of the classical comedy of cuckoldry in the presentation of this elderly, inadequate husband, and Shamraev manages to bore even Arkadina herself. She has no wish to have her juvenile successes and acquaintances recalled to mind, especially not by a man who can remember exact dates from as long ago as twenty-three years: 'You keep asking me about antediluvians. How should I know?' It is Dorn who tries to supply the balance to Shamraev's colourful generalities about the good old days, but although he tries to bring attention to the present occasion, he can do nothing to prepare an audience belonging to the past for a performance dedicated to the future. The failure of Treplev's play is a foregone conclusion.

By her impatience, Mme Arkadin makes us fear the worst. As we see Nina's shadow against the moon behind the curtain, the professional actress offers her immediate audience a preliminary comparison with the amateur by intoning a few lines from *Hamlet* in her most resounding voice. She speaks Gertrude's lines with a gentle mockery, and without real thought for their meaning, but Treplev replies in her ear with all the suppressed fervour of Hamlet's fierce indictment of his mother's incest:

> And let me wring your heart, for so I shall,
> If it be made of penetrable stuff.[1]

In the nineteenth century, Hamlet was well-known to Russian playgoers as the melancholy, introspective and over-sensitive young man, and by reminding his audience of Shakespeare's character, Chekhov is cleverly caricaturing his own hero. This allusiveness is a trick Chekhov will use several times in his mature plays, if less mechanically. In this scene the theatrical atmosphere just allows him to interpolate such theatrical lines without too obtrusively interrupting the natural flow of the dialogue, and they serve as a point of literary reference outside the play by which Chekhov's audience may recognize the comic scale of false feeling: for if the son is playing the Prince in good earnest,

---

[1] *Hamlet*, iii. iv. 35–6. In the Russian, Treplev speaks a paraphrase that is less ambiguous: 'And why did you yield to vice, and seek love in an abyss of sin?' See Hingley, vol. ii, p. 355.

the mother is no Queen of Denmark. Such incongruity helps to sustain our ambivalent attitude to the whole scene.

The amateur theatricals are about to begin. Treplev calls for attention, but Chekhov's '*pause*' suggests that he does not get it too quickly. The stage audience, sitting in the dusk, is restive and noisy with nervous tittering. Eventually, however, the general laughter and chattering dies down, and Treplev as producer pounds impressively with a stick and chants a dreamy prelude:

TREPLEV. '. . . let us dream of what will be in two hundred thousand years!'
SORIN. There will be nothing in two hundred thousand years.
TREPLEV. Then let them present that nothing to us.
MADAME ARKADIN. Let them. We are asleep.

Sorin's worry about his lost past and his short future probably makes his jocular intrusion the most sincere of the comments, but there is no mistaking the anticlimactic contrast of his tone with that of Treplev's. There is a note of anger in the young man's reply, and we hear the antipathy in the affected boredom of his mother's attempt to cap the joke. Are they going to damn the play before it begins?

A play-within-a-play, whether in Shakespeare, Sheridan, Pirandello, Anouilh, Genêt or Peter Weiss, has the effect of sharpening the meaning and reality of the play which is its context. This is effected by the comic contrast of the more remote manner of its verbal heightening and stylized playing. 'The Murder of Gonzago', or 'Pyramus and Thisbe', the one for tragedy and the other for comedy, make their ironic points by accentuating a difference in style from the general tenor of the scenes in which they fall. So it is in *The Seagull*. In the naturalistic world of the proscenium arch stage, Treplev's flamboyant play, and Nina's playing of it, serve to ridicule declamatory speech and acting. Such verbal parody appears in later Chekhov only in the more integrated sententiousness of Trofimov's or Gaev's silly speech-making in *The Cherry Orchard*, a platform manner which must seem ludicrously incongruous with the naturalism of the action suitable to the picture-frame stage. In *The Seagull*, Treplev's play is his unintentional burlesque of French poetic symbolism and German romantic drama, and deserves no more than its fate. It does not bear the marks of quality upon which Treplev was insisting to

Sorin just before. By it Chekhov intends to show his rejection of one direction of the 'new forms' to which Treplev had referred. If *The Seagull*'s first audience at the Alexandrinsky Theatre in St Petersburg took it at face value and saw it as the author's own hope for the art of the theatre,[1] they ignored Nina's early warning that Treplev's play had no action and supported no living creatures, and were unable to see that Arkadina's accusation of the play's 'decadence' must forestall their judgment of Chekhov as a decadent. They certainly did not see how adequately it presents the genuine comedy of pretentious young ambition, for Nina's big speech reflects more of Treplev's character and his poetasting than it does *avant-garde* theatre. Nor did they see how adequately the play scene also illustrates the impatience of age with the younger generation. As an ingredient in a scene which is itself one of Chekhov's own experiments with dramatic form, it fully justifies the naturalism of the style which surrounds it, making the family group seem more real than before.

Nina as the spirit of life sits majestically all in white on a mossy rock, lit only by the pale moonlight. She is a young girl brought up modestly in the country, now on the stage for the first time and, as Chekhov said,[2] suffering badly from stage-fright. Her speech is replete with overstressed clichés, trite bathetic effects and pompous repetitions, when these are not intended for hesitations and prompts by Treplev.[3] The words are difficult to speak aloud without sounding stilted and Nina's rendering must seem slow and amateurish. Add to this the affected and uncomfortable lighting effects, crude effects such as the best professional nineteenth-century theatre would have despised, then, quite to overstep the bounds of theatrical decorum, the smell of burning sulphur, a realistic device in an unreal play, and Nina stands no chance with either stage or theatre audience. For all her simple earnest delivery of the speech, her performance under these conditions is a disaster.

[1] The audience jeered Nina's speech.
[2] Commenting on Kommissarzhevskaya's overacting during the fourth rehearsal of Karpov's production at St Petersburg, in Balukhaty, p. 22.
[3] Probably at the repetition of 'all living things' and 'I' in the first part of the speech. It is important that at least the second part of the speech shall run through without hesitations in order that the theatre audience may be given the opportunity to listen to her words and gather some interest before the stage audience disrupts the performance finally. We must share some of Treplev's irritation.

Act I

The ill-mannered behaviour of the stage audience as it sits in silhouette before us guarantees her failure. Trigorin is doubtless watching Nina, but for the wrong reasons; but Medvedenko soon turns to watch Masha, and Polina her dear Doctor, and not the stage at all. Yet it is primarily Arkadina who matches the fidgeting of the theatre audience. She sits as far upstage centre as possible, a key figure in the group on the stage, and starts the deliberate disruption of her son's play. The turn of her head as she sits in the half-light takes the attention of both audiences, and her jealousy of Nina and the tension between mother and son are present in her tone when she speaks. Her contemptuous comment on the play's decadence at first draws Treplev's reproach. Next, with an affected little cough, she remarks on the smell of sulphur and, with a laugh to those about her, draws attention to what is obvious, that it is a stage effect, so that they must respond with half-suppressed laughter. No doubt the weightiness of Nina's high-flown address would have called for a release of tension in any case, but Arkadina's brittle speech is in painful contrast with Nina's elevated delivery.

Nina stammers a little and tries to pick up where she left off, her voice now more shrill. Suddenly, sitting to one side of the group, and oblivious to all that is going on, Polina speaks. Her words ring out and are clearly heard by everyone as she chastizes the Doctor for having taken off his hat in the night air, probably to mop his brow in the heat. Although Polina is not really interested in whether Treplev's play succeeds or fails, it is she who inadvertently completes the disruption. As all heads turn to look in her direction, the movement of white faces in the moonlight catches the eye, and as general laughter is about to erupt, Arkadina takes up the theme to her own advantage: she will be the chief performer yet. 'The Doctor has taken off his hat to the devil, the father of eternal matter.' It is not a good joke, but it is enough. Everyone laughs out loud. Treplev, who has been watching for his mother's reactions with single-minded zeal, in heat calls for the curtain and stamps out like a child in a tantrum. The pace, which Nina's delivery slowed almost to a halt, now accelerates. We, the theatre audience, have mixed feelings: we have been restless like Arkadina, but we share some sympathy with the performer and even more with the author as a result of inimical impressions received from the mother before the play-within-the-play began. When she and Polina speak and turn their heads, the aural and visual distraction is complete, and we have a double sense of the son's vanity and the mother's cruelty. The comic and the pathetic are mixed in as neat a piece of stagecraft as one can find in Chekhov. The audience can laugh freely at Treplev's play and at the same time feel the justice in his indignant, 'The play is over! Enough! Curtain!' To all this Stanislavsky added a touch that was this time well in keeping with the comic intention of the scene: 'Shamraev, not realizing what it is all about, shouts "Bravo!" in a deep bass (*à la* Silva) and starts clapping.'[1] He thus kept the embarrassment on the stage well balanced for humour.

But Treplev's and Nina's project is in ruins. If the boy and the girl were previously united in the preparation of the play, they are divided by its performance. What they want, and what they are capable of achieving, are two sadly contradictory things.

The contest of moods is now resumed by the people on the stage as they gather themselves after the performance. Arkadina is angry both with her son and with herself.[2] She moves apart and we feel her temporary isolation from the others. Sorin, Trigorin and Dorn from their places gently round on her. Sorin speaks from elderly experience about hurting the feelings of the young; Trigorin speaks on behalf of the sensibilities of all authors; Dorn displays his usual objectivity. Only Medvedenko the schoolmaster surprises us by coming to her aid; he has taken the play very seriously as an 'intellectual' should,[3] and starts to argue learnedly that spirit and matter may not be separable. However, Arkadina takes little comfort from this, for he quickly returns to his favourite topic and solemnly suggests to Trigorin that someone should write a play about the hard lot of the teacher. Although strong feelings continue to smoulder, this sublime irrelevance

---

[1] Balukhaty, p. 161.

[2] Stanislavsky saw Arkadina as 'in the habit of folding her hands behind her back when she is excited and angry, and it is in this pose that she is taking long strides up and down the stage' (Balukhaty, p. 163). This, one may think, does not display the composure of a leading lady well accustomed to holding large theatre audiences spellbound by her grace and deportment.

[3] Chekhov always mocks the dilettante intellectual. In an earlier version of *The Seagull*, he had a line for Medvedenko, 'The earth is round', which Dorn counters with, 'Why do you say that with so little conviction?' The complete passage is reproduced in Magarshack, p. 185, and in Hingley, vol. II, p. 342.

relaxes tension and leaves Chekhov free to pursue some of the hares he started in the first movement of the act.

To echo the quieter feeling, singing is heard from across the darkening lake. It helps to carry us back to a more untroubled time. Arkadina softens and tries to show her composure to Trigorin, whom she fears she may have offended by her treatment of a fellow author. Her language, too, is tempered as she talks of days past, the days of her youth and success as a young actress. Only the ripples on the surface of her speech hint that beneath the calm she senses her son's personal tragedy, and feels the touch of guilt. Where is he? She did not mean to hurt him. However, more than anyone Masha has shared his indignity, her long silence hiding and revealing the depth of her sympathy; appropriately, it is she who offers to find him, and she goes off calling his name. Her 'Konstantin! Aa-oo!' seems to echo ironically behind the first coy meeting between Trigorin and Nina which is to follow.

Attention is soon diverted to this other victim of the unlucky evening. Nina now emerges timidly from behind the curtain. Her audience cannot be as thoughtless a second time, and as if to compensate for their reception of poor Treplev's play, they shower fulsome congratulations upon his actress. The falseness of their praise will mark the beginning of her personal tragedy, just as the rebuff to Treplev, where a little approbation from his family and friends might have been expected, is the beginning of his. Sorin's 'Bravo!'s are like those of an old admirer for an appealing young girl. Madame's effusions are transparently a reflection of her nostalgia for her own early attempts upon the stage. Although Nina is a threat both to her love and her fame, in the circumstances Arkadina is very civil to the girl. 'With such an appearance, with such a lovely voice, you really cannot stay in the country; it is a sin. You must have talent. Do you hear? It's your duty to go on the stage.' But she is recapitulating her own decision: it was *her* duty not to stay in the country but to go on the stage. By this new parallelism, Chekhov renews our apprehension of the difference between youth and age, innocence and experience, as we regard the two women before us. With a blush, Nina accepts this advice from a great actress at face value, and Arkadina kisses her patronizingly.[1] Thus the sensibilities of the young become a careless playground for the old.

---

[1] This kiss is Stanislavsky's idea, not Chekhov's (see Balukhaty, p. 167).

Mme Arkadin even introduces her ostentatiously to Trigorin, a great moment that the trembling Nina has been waiting for. Again the seeds of personal tragedy are sown: Arkadina does not really doubt that the sober Trigorin's affection for herself is secure, and cannot see that Nina's adoration of the great man may feed his egotism in unexpected ways. All this is in the future. At this moment, Trigorin seems to show only the indifference of a celebrity for the rest of the world – or the numbness of a dead spirit for life itself. Chekhov, in this characterization, implies an ambiguity in Trigorin's motivation. He is not to be played as Stanislavsky first wished to play him, as the stereotype of an elegant, good-looking man of the world, but as the sort of man, Chekhov thought,[1] who would wear checked trousers and old shoes. If his fame might attract Nina, his negligent, easy-going manner would be less likely to frighten her.

There follows one of those deliciously strained conversations for which Chekhov became known: as two people fail to 'connect', their words run off at a tangent. Nina invites Trigorin's opinion of the 'queer' play, sensing his incomprehension and by the use of this unflattering epithet offering him a lead. He mouths a few embarrassed words full of contradictions: he did not understand the play, but he enjoyed it; Nina acted 'so genuinely' and 'the scenery was delightful'. With this his flat voice dries up.

[1] In a cryptic comment reported in Simmons, p. 483, and in Magarshack, p. 200. In Theodore Komisarjevsky's production at the New Theatre, London, in 1936, Sir John Gielgud tended to follow Stanislavsky's interpretation of Trigorin: 'I conceived the part of Trigórin, with Komis's help, as a vain, attractive man, sincere in his insincerity, but not a first-rate writer by any means, really attracted by Nina in a weak kind of way, but not the professional seducer at all . . . Many people complained that I was not enough the genius, that I was too smartly dressed, and that I was not passionate enough in the scenes with Nina. But Trigórin himself complains of his facile talent, says that he cannot really write first-class stuff; then he is obviously a social figure when Nina is so much impressed by him in the first two acts, and finally, his innate weakness is shown in the two scenes with Nina at the beginning and end of the third act, and by his passive attitude in the scene with Arcádina which comes between. The difficulty, as always in a play, is to know how much of the real truth Trigórin reveals in his speeches about himself. Surely if Tchechov had meant the man to be a genius he would not have drawn the clear distinction and contrast between Nina and Konstantin, both potentially brilliant but unsuccessful, and Trigórin and Arcádina, both successful but intrinsically second-rate. And what could be more second-rate than the existence of Trigórin, trailing like a tame cat at his mistress's heels – "Again there will be railway carriages, mutton chops, conversations – !" ' (*Early Stages*, London, 1953, pp. 297–8). Gielgud makes the point again in *Stage Directions* (London, 1963), p. 89, describing Komisarjevsky's view of the part as that of 'a smartly dressed, blasé gigolo'.

After an excruciating pause, he adds, 'There must be a lot of fish
in the lake' – one of Chekhov's aptly deflating lines, one which
marks his embarrassment and relieves ours. But in this way we
also learn that the great man loves angling, 'sitting on the bank
of a river in the evening and watching the float', a sign of
humanity beneath the sham.[1] Nina in the burning energy of youth
cannot accept that this can be true of an important artist. We
see the infinite distance between their ages and attitudes.
We also see that Arkadina is listening intently to their every
word.

The tension built up by the play scene is nearly broken, and
with Shamraev Chekhov now completes the break. In a loud
tone he drags up a typical reminiscence of his younger days about
an opera star whose voice was surpassed from the gallery by a
church chorister. It is quite irrelevant: his seeing Treplev's play
has set his mind wandering along channels of its own. There is a
comic silence; Shamraev's interpolation leaves them all at a loss
for words, and Dorn comments, 'The angel of silence has flown
over us.' In this interlude we may sense that the stresses between
the young and the old shift from the trial and judgment of creative
idealism to the strains of a more personal engagement, the unspoken passage of thoughts between Nina, Trigorin and Arkadina. Chekhov is adept at capturing such 'untheatrical' moments
of eloquent silence in which the spectator is hyper-sensitive to the
least flicker of an eye.

It is Nina who makes the first move to withdraw. All about her
seem immobile and trapped in their frustrating situation, Arkadina and Trigorin, Sorin and Medvedenko, Shamraev, Polina and

---

[1] This impersonal presentation of the character of Trigorin before his long self-
revelatory speeches to Nina later in Act II deftly suggests the balanced, unassuming
image of the man Chekhov wishes us to have initially. Kachalov, who played the
part for a few performances during the 1901–2 season, reported that Chekhov
intended this mild impression of Trigorin through his fishing to be the central one,
and the norm for the actor's performance. 'His fishing rods are home-made, you
know, all bent. He makes them himself, with a penknife. His cigar is a good one,
perhaps even a very good one, but he never removes the silver paper from it.'
Then, after a moment's thought, Chekhov added, 'But the chief thing is his fishing
rods.' (The quotation is from Magarshack, p. 201. See also Balukhaty, p. 84.)
Magarshack argues that this absence of vanity in Trigorin helps to explain his
success as a writer and Nina's love for him. It is true that his fishing is attractive in
expressing a genuine human wish and releasing him from his writing treadmill, but
in that it is *all* he wishes to do when he is not in the treadmill, it also seems petty
and a limitation.

Dorn. Only Nina as yet feels the freedom of an expansive future, although even that is not unrestricted. Her father expects her home, and we have another quick insight into her difficulties there. We are now better able to realize how closely parallel with Treplev's own case with his mother is Nina's with her father. Both parents are domestic tyrants, their children slaves who must revolt or perish. As always, Chekhov sustains each character in a completely consistent and thought-out environment. Nina kisses Arkadina and shyly extends her hand to Trigorin; then she shakes hands more quickly with the others and hurries off, a slender, naive figure.

Everyone unbends when she has gone. There is nothing now to keep them out in the park. Sorin remarks upon the damp, stretches his legs, staggers a little[1] and rubs his hands against the cold. So the 'stifling' weather has now changed and tempers are cooled. Indeed, a chill is in the air and the dog is faintly heard to howl in the distance, reflecting the general impression that all is not well as they move off towards the house. Arkadina takes Sorin's arm. Shamraev in a display of ill-appreciated gallantry offers his arm with a 'Madame?' to his wife Polina, who must leave her beloved Doctor behind. And so the little party leaves, Sorin still grumbling about the dog, Shamraev retelling his story about the chorister, Medvedenko asking his characteristic question, 'And what salary does a chorister get?' The event of the evening is over.

Only Dorn is left, and only he has a genuine word for Treplev's play. For in spite of himself he has been impressed by it. 'I don't know, perhaps I know nothing about it, or have gone off my head, but I liked the play.' Treplev comes in quickly, evidently trying to escape Masha, whose calls are heard again sighing through the trees. He is hurt to find only the Doctor there: 'They have all gone.' His sense of failure seems complete. Masha may have been calling for him 'all over the park', but he does not want her pity. He knows that she loves him, and so he suspects that her comforting words would be insincere. 'Insufferable creature she is!' Cruelty in this circle is a merry-go-round: everyone needs someone else and is denied.

The Doctor, 'the weak, clever, observant Dorn, who has ex-

---

[1] 'The first steps Sorin always takes rather hesitantly': Stanislavsky in Balukhaty, p. 169.

perienced everything',[1] with a warm generosity offers Treplev
his thanks. The boy must persevere: his play dealt in abstract
ideas, which was right, since 'a work of art ought to express a
great idea' and Treplev must write only of what is important and
eternal. One hears the echo of Tolstoyan teaching. As a doctor in
general practice, Dorn himself has not known 'the spiritual
heights which artists reach at moments of creation'. In all this,
Chekhov might be recounting his own story, and perhaps it is as
if he senses that he is introducing his own thoughts as a writer.
If so, it is unlike Chekhov to persist in this for long. It is not
enough that the play which prompted these sentiments was a
travesty of all his own practice, but he must also deflate the streak
of pomposity in Dorn's advice. Thus he provides the comic
distraction through Treplev. The boy has long since ceased to
listen. Rather late, it seems, he has thought of Nina, and he turns
to look at the sad little stage. Twice he interrupts the Doctor by
asking where she is, and eventually Dorn abandons his theme and
says that she has gone home.

Treplev is about to follow Nina down the path to the lake when
Masha catches up with him. Won't he come indoors? And lest he
think that she is the one who is anxious, she adds in an afterthought, 'Your mother wants you. She is worried.' When Masha
links Arkadina's desires with her own in this way, and with Nina
gone, Treplev feels that the whole world of women is tormenting
him. 'Let me alone!' – and his sweeping gesture takes in both the
girl who hangs on his every word and the good-hearted Doctor
who is solicitous for his welfare. He flings off, almost brushing
Masha aside. But she is used to such humiliation.

DORN (*with a sigh*). Youth! Youth!
MASHA. When people have nothing better to say, they say, 'Youth!
Youth!'

And she takes a pinch of snuff. But this gesture is hardly comic
now: the moment of pain, heard in the drop between the two
tones of voice, is not undercut by this business as it was before;
instead, we are surprised to see that in a sudden moment of un-
characteristic anger, Dorn flings Masha's snuff-box into the
bushes – 'That's disgusting!' The pause that follows is a moment
for him to savour the implications of his lapse and for the audience

[1] Nemirovich-Danchenko's comment to Chekhov, December 1898, in Balukhaty,
p. 72.

to recognize her degradation. Masha is the third young creature, we observe, who must pay the price of innocence. In the pause is also heard Stanislavsky's sound of a piano from the house. The tinkling notes and the tinkling voices of the family gathering mock Masha as she stands apart and neglected, an outlaw from normal social relationships, unable to speak her secret. She stands there as the light fades, representative of all the forlorn young aspirants to happiness. How can she tell her troubles to her father Shamraev, who lives in a self-contained world of the past? As Dorn turns away towards the sounds from the house, she decides that it is he who has the sympathetic ear she needs.

MASHA. Help me. Help me, or I shall do something silly, I shall make a mock of my life and ruin it . . . I can't go on . . .
DORN. What is it? Help you in what?
MASHA. I am miserable. No one, no one knows how miserable I am! (*Laying her head on his breast, softly.*) I love Konstantin!

Masha began the act in a farcical mode; she finishes it with pathos. We listen to her, however, with the compassionate ears of the gentle Doctor. It is he who channels our feelings with his quiet humour. For his comment on the whole fermenting cauldron of self-centred, troubled people, young and old, lightly identifies their malady and lifts our spirits. 'How hysterical they all are! How hysterical!' Lest this be taken as too harsh a view, Chekhov softens the criticism by adding, 'And what a lot of love . . .' The wry jest that follows is one against *The Seagull* itself: 'Oh, the sorcery of the lake!' Too many people seem to be in mourning for their lives. The Doctor gives us the perspective view of the over-laden stage, and gently returns the mood to comedy.[1]

[1] Stanislavsky underlined the melodrama of the moment, using conventional gesture and retrospective sound effects to excess: 'Masha bursts into sobs and, kneeling, buries her head on Dorn's knees. A pause of fifteen seconds. Dorn is stroking Masha's head. The frenzied waltz [from the piano in the house – J.L.S.] grows louder, sounds of the tolling of a church-bell, of a peasant's song, of frogs, of a corncrake, the knocking of the night-watchman, and all sorts of other nocturnal sound effects' (Balukhaty, p. 175). In this way Stanislavsky denies the Doctor his smile and the scene its comedy, and reduces the effect of 'fading away' at the end of the act, an effect Chekhov uses to suggest the continuity between his act-divisions and the sense of passing time.

Act Two

The sense of a revelatory aftermath is not easy to achieve without risking an anticlimax, and for *The Seagull* the aftermath of Act II is as important as its cause. It helps that the curtain rises on a change of setting.[1] In the way that Chekhov repeated in *Uncle Vanya*, the sequence of set changes leads us further and further

[1] Ignored in the first Moscow Art Theatre production: a second elaborately realistic outdoor set within two acts was asking too much of the stage manager.

It is interesting that Theodore Komisarjevsky's production at the New Theatre, London, in 1936 also used the same set for Acts I and II. Komisarjevsky was, of course, familiar with the M.A.T. production, but the decision disturbed Sir John Gielgud who was playing Trigorin: 'Komis's garden for the first two acts was a triumph of naturalism, and made a lovely and romantic background, with its paths and pillars, banks of flowers and rustic bridge. I was surprised, however, to find him putting both acts into the same setting, as we had done at Barnes in the earlier production [planned for Barnes Theatre, London; actually produced at the Arts and Little Theatres, London, 1925 – J.L.S.], with a neat little stage built for Konstantin's play, and a curtain drawn on strings to conceal it.

'Tchechov's stage directions are – Act I: A part of the park on Sorin's estate. Act II: Croquet lawn of Sorin's house. In Stanislavsky's book there is a fine description of the setting for the first act at the Moscow Art Theatre. Remembering this, I always imagined the scene taking place in a damp and gloomy corner of the park, with wet leaves underfoot and slimy overgrown foliage. Beyond the trees, a magnificent view of the lake, and, hiding it at first, a great flapping sheet hung between two trees. Here Arcádina must sit shivering in her thin shoes and evening dress, while Konstantin declaims his prologue, and then the sheet falls, disclosing the placid lake, and the figure of Nina, dressed strangely in some kind of modernistic costume, raised, perhaps, above the level of the onlookers on a clumsily contrived platform of planks and barrels. This is Konstantin's new theatre: so different from the conventional indoor theatre which he despises; the place where he can make love to Nina and lose himself in his romantic dreams.

'In the second act there should surely be a great contrast – the croquet lawn with its neat beds of geraniums, hoops, mallets, deck-chairs and cushions, all the ease and luxury of Arcádina's proper atmosphere. Here she is mistress in her own domain, laughing at the slovenly Masha and making scenes with her servants. Here Konstantin is ill at ease and out of place with his old suit and his gun and his dead seagull, while Trigórin, strolling on the lawn with his elegant hat and stick and notebook, is in his element, master of the situation, easily able to impress Nina with his suave talk of the beautiful view over the lake and the anguish he suffers in the achievement of his successes as an author' (*Early Stages*, London, 1953, pp. 295–7).

43

into the heart of the family as our understanding of its quality of life deepens. Add to this Chekhov's instinct as a naturalistic dramatist to try to counteract the loss of rapport between actor and audience resulting from the barrier of the proscenium arch and draw us into the scene, and the spectator now finds himself outside Sorin's house itself, beside a croquet lawn as elegant as Mme Arkadin herself. The lake is seen more clearly, and supplies our orientation for the new setting, but now all romanticism has been dispelled. We see part of the imposing façade of a wealthy home with a large verandah surrounded by neat flower beds. The whole scene is sunlit.[1] Treplev's solitary world of moonlit parkland has gone, and we are to be in Arkadina's bright social circle of friends, neighbours and admirers having tea. But the sun is both high and hot.

The brilliance of the scene after the dusk of Act 1 makes Masha's matronly black dress and unhappy looks seem more incongruously out of place than before. Her appearance is amusingly contrasted with that of the ageing Arkadina dressed in a light, youthful blouse. Arkadina is still playing the matinee idol, but in bright sunshine Masha has no hope of playing the tragedy queen, and we, like Arkadina, are prepared to a degree to mock her. Once again the dialogue seems caught in flight when the curtain rises, and, clearly, Arkadina has been criticizing Masha's behaviour to her face. 'Come, let us stand up. (*They both get up.*) Let us stand side by side. You are twenty-two and I am nearly twice as old.' Madame is parading herself again; Masha reluctantly moves into the great lady's aura. Arkadina appeals for a verdict from her immediate audience. This is the Doctor, whose open book on his knee suggests that he has been trying to read without success. 'Which of us looks the younger?' she asks, and the Doctor drily obliges her with the answer she wants: 'You, of course.' The comparison is not flattering to Masha, and this demonstration – however instructively meant – revives the theme of warring generations. Stanislavsky emphasized Masha's lack of grace by having her drink her tea noisily,[2] an uncouth mannerism in keeping with her drinking and snuff-taking. But the inelegant

[1] Such lighting changes made good use of the new electrical equipment at the M.A.T.; the exact communication of a naturalistic atmosphere became increasingly possible to Chekhov.
[2] Balukhaty, p. 179.

girl was never a match for the sophisticated actress, and Arkadina could afford to be more generous with her.

Arkadina, like many of Chekhov's materially 'successful' characters to come (Serebryakov the Professor in *Uncle Vanya*, Natasha in *Three Sisters*, even Lopakhin who buys the cherry orchard) offers advice from her place of eminence. Why is it that she looks younger? Because she *works* and never looks to the *future*. The audience has already had sufficient hints of Arkadina's superficiality to be alert for the irony in these easy sentiments. Her work is the constant selling of her self; and *if* it is true that she does not look to the future or think about her old age, it is because a woman who trades on her looks without other reserves of strength faces a spiritual death when she faces the reality. Thus she reveals her fear of the future, and under the apparent confidence there is turmoil. Meanwhile, in her own way, Masha is play-acting too. Measuring years by what she thinks of as experience, she feels she has been 'born long, long ago', has lived a lifetime. From his chair, the Doctor's quiet humming provides the sufficient comment, and lumps both women together, whatever their difference of age and occupation, into much the same category of foolishness. The song he is humming is 'Tell her, my flowers', a sly criticism of the whole love-sick pack, all sick of self-love.

Masha has sat down again. Arkadina, '*with her arms akimbo*', flaunts gracefully about the lawn like a player on a stage, talking and talking, in spite of the heat apparent in the lassitude of the others. It is as if silence for her were as terrible a fate as solitude, and so she talks insistently about the frivolous symbols of her sexuality, her dress, her hair. 'I could take the part of a girl of fifteen.' This is whistling in the dark: it may be true now, but for how long will it be? Again, Dorn's negative response is to pick up the book and say, 'Nevertheless, I shall go on.' Perhaps Arkadina knows she has overplayed her role, overstepped the mark with the Doctor: she takes the book from him and reads aloud herself. The book is Maupassant's collection of travel tales, *Sur l'eau*. As Chekhov's means of returning Trigorin to the centre of interest and of further exploring the nature of Arkadina's relationship with him, it is an awkward device of literary allusion, but it serves. Maupassant is saying that it is unwise for a French society woman to pursue 'an author whom she desires to captivate' by flattery. Oh, but that is not true of the bond between Trigorin and Arkadina: a Russian woman must be in *love* to do such a thing. The audience recognizes that in saying this Arkadina has missed the point and that it is Maupassant who is right. However, the entrance of Sorin does not allow the reading to proceed, and she is saved from giving herself away further. We, nevertheless, have had a fair hint of her need to rationalize her doubts about Trigorin.

Sorin hobbles in on his stick, Medvedenko pushing a bath-chair behind him; these personal properties make him seem older than before. The old man is talking to Nina as to a child, rather as Arkadina talked to Masha. Nina's father and stepmother have gone away for three days, and she is overjoyed. She embraces Madame with 'I am happy! Now I belong to you.' A poor exchange of parental authority, if Nina understood Arkadina's tyranny over Konstantin, and his over her. Like any young idealist, Nina is in the habit of dedicating her life spontaneously and in its entirety; although a hidden reason for her enthusiasm is hinted when she casts a glance towards the place where she knows Trigorin to be fishing in the lake upstage. After a perfunctory kiss, Arkadina dampens Nina's spirits a little by the tone in which she makes a quick enquiry of Trigorin's whereabouts: his distant behaviour is troubling her. The answer comes that he is fishing. 'I wonder he doesn't get sick of it.' Arkadina also wonders what is wrong with Treplev. Everyone seems to be disagreeable to her today. Masha, understanding more than the mother, snaps at her, 'His heart is troubled', and gets a little of her own back for Madame's previous condescension. Arkadina's silence after this betrays her double uneasiness.

In another tone, *'timidly'*, Masha asks Nina, her rival for Treplev's affections, to read something from his play. Masha is thinking only of him, his glowing eyes, his pale face, his fine mournful voice and his poet's gestures. But Nina, who has been looking over towards the lake again, has her mind elsewhere: 'It's so uninteresting.' The maturity of the famous author has already cast the young man's efforts into the shade. So as the three women sit on the lazy lawn in the warm sun, Chekhov by innuendo gently weaves the pattern of their affections, each distracted by a dream of human love in three different keys, and each more or less deserving our sympathy as we estimate the uncertain basis of each plea for help. Unspoken emotions, interlocking dangerously, lie beneath the smooth, urbane surface of this summer scene.

As yet the audience is not to be too concerned. Sorin has fallen asleep in the sun and his snoring punctuates and punctures Masha's adoring words about Treplev. The subsequent small-talk concerning his state of health offers the kind of dry illumination of character that Chekhov manages so well. Under pressure, the Doctor scornfully suggests his usual prescription, valerian drops, a tranquillizer that was the popular cure-all of the time. Madame proposes a trip to take the waters. Medvedenko appropriately declares that he should give up smoking, and to this Dorn adds drinking. Together they provide an effective diversion from emotional torments, and Masha and Nina sit there with their overwhelming feelings quite ignored. Meanwhile, poor Sorin, besieged on all sides by advice he does not want, attempts to defend himself with a frankness that reduces to ashes all their philosophy. He turns on the Doctor with his characteristic sardonic laugh.

It's all very well for you to argue! You've lived your life, but what about me? I have served in the Department of Justice for twenty-eight years, but I haven't lived yet, I've seen and done nothing as a matter of fact, and very naturally I want to live very much. You've had enough and you don't care, and so you're inclined to be philosophical, but I want to live, and so I drink sherry at dinner and smoke cigars and so on. That's all it comes to.

He at least speaks aloud what is on his mind. In his own clownish way, however, he might be the devil's advocate for them all. Only Dorn, everyone's counsellor, finds his grumbling 'frivolous', as he says, and calls him 'Your Excellency', a little to humour him and at the same time to remind him that his life has by no means been a failure. But Masha gets up and goes. Her spirits have been dashed, and her pointed departure indicates that their remarks on unhappiness mean nothing to her. 'My leg has gone to sleep', she says in Chekhov's seemingly irrelevant way. The physical image as she hobbles off defines the general ennui. The Doctor does not watch where she goes, but states simply that she will have a glass or two before lunch; he seems to be saying that at twenty-two she is already in Sorin's sad case.

The lazy day drags on. The whole first movement of this act constitutes an extraordinary exercise by Chekhov in communicating the deadening tedium of the life of this house. Except for Nina's continuing excitement, the voices drop and drone on, the direction of the conversation growing more and more arbitrary. Yet no character merely repeats another, and by now the attention of the spectator is alert to the hundred and one sparks of individual life each displays; at the same time he is aware of each buried relationship between this character and that, and of the kinship of everyone on the stage: they are all of a kind. Thus among the details surrounding Sorin, for example, we observe Dorn's touch of good-humoured sarcasm when the old man is heard to snore – 'Good night!'; and Sorin's defensive reply when Arkadina asks him whether he is asleep – 'Not a bit of it'; we see his petty annoyance when the Doctor will not give him a dose of medicine, refusing to satisfy his need for attention; and recognize his diagnosis of Masha's trouble as his own – 'She has no personal happiness', adding, 'poor thing', as if this were the kind of understanding due to himself; and we recognize that Sorin's is a rooted suspicion that Dorn is in a position to give him advice simply because the Doctor 'has all he wants'. When later Dorn calls Sorin an 'old woman' in his absence, he rather cruelly sums up our own findings.

The pace has slowed to one of imperceptible motion. Arkadina forgets her age and thinks about learning her part in a hotel bedroom somewhere, to which the unfledged actress in Nina responds with enthusiasm. For Arkadina, the hotel bedroom is her normal life, when she is not on one of these appalling holidays when everyone gets at her. Sorin dreams of an elegant life in town, with telephones and cabs 'and everything'. Dorn hums. Nevertheless, Chekhov has conceived this mood of extreme lassitude as the perfect prelude to the storm which is about to break.

In the heat of the summer sun, a perspiring, no longer affable Shamraev and his wife invade the calm scene. It is the cue for a rapid change of pace and mood. His voice rises: is Madame proposing to drive into town today? Then how is she to travel? The horses are all at work carting rye. Carriage horses? But where is he to get collars for them? Shamraev's mismanagement and Arkadina's stinginess must make things difficult on the estate, especially since part of the profit is sent to her regularly;[1] but it is

---

[1] Substantiated in an earlier version of the play. See Hingley, vol. II, p. 345.

ironic that the underlying discontents of the lovers first come to the surface through so trivial a matter as the supply of horses on the farm.

SHAMRAEV. Honoured lady! you don't know what farming means.
MADAME ARKADIN (*flaring up*). That's the old story! If that's so, I go back to Moscow today. Give orders for the horses to be hired for me at the village, or I'll walk to the station.
SHAMRAEV (*flaring up*). In that case I resign my position! You must look for another steward (*goes off*).

Such heightening of tension is commonplace in nineteenth-century drama, but always by some great confrontation as a means of pointing a crisis of jealousy or betrayal, and always tied inseparably to the central line of the plot. Chekhov teases us by having this silly quarrel erupt to no immediately apparent purpose; but the spectator has a fair notion that the issue is other than horses, and the access of emotion confirms that the calm of the scene was all deception. Thus, all in a moment, the sleepy stage explodes with hot words. Arkadina is on her feet. Sorin is roused to anger. Even Nina is indignant that 'the famous actress' is refused her wish. Polina's despair at her husband's ill-manners offers a glimpse of her married life. Only Dorn has not moved; humming and musing in his chair, he seems unaffected by the storm all about him.

Sorin is pushed off in his bath-chair, declaring Shamraev insufferable, intending to stop his sister from carrying out her threat. But she has already set off impetuously towards the lake to find Trigorin, and '*a moment later she can be seen entering the house*', with Trigorin on her heels with his fishing tackle. We may doubt her true intentions: she is actress enough to intimidate her manager by this display. Yet she may simply by using the occasion as an expedient to remove Trigorin from Nina and temptation.

It seems natural that the stage is left to Polina and her Doctor, since it was she who suffered the most from the upset. Dorn and Polina are one more sample of individual tragedy. They know, as we know, from Dorn's contented immobility as a bachelor and Polina's marriage ties, that their relationship cannot prosper. We are to watch the butterflies on the pin revolving like their words.

Dorn's first comment on Shamraev's exhibition of petty authority suggests what impractical farmers Sorin and Arkadina are, and that their manager is something of a scoundrel; but it also comforts Polina. 'Your husband ought to be simply kicked out, but it will end in that old woman Pyotr Nicolayevitch and his sister begging the man's pardon. You will see!' No doubt for Shamraev to leave and take his wife with him would be unthinkable for her. But she is still trembling from the incident and thinking of her burden: she cannot 'endure his rudeness'. When she quickly drops into another tone, she might have rehearsed the moment: she has probably, indeed, played such a scene many times before. She takes Dorn's criticism of her husband as a sign of personal sympathy with her position. She wants him to love her. Their time is passing. They are no longer young. Here once again the melancholy note is struck – ironically this time, since her words echo the graceless attitude towards time which Dorn had condemned in Sorin. Polina at last falls silent, waiting for the Doctor's answer.

The pause gives the audience an instant in which to recognize the crux, and to anticipate what Dorn will do about an embarrassing situation which is closer to himself and calls for more than valerian drops. He does not move a muscle, but says in a distant voice, 'I am fifty-five; it's too late to change my life.' His position is different from Sorin's: the older man is discontented and everlastingly grumbles about lost time; Dorn is not discontented. The audience is never to know whether he is resigned, or merely indifferent to the life he has chosen to lead. But does it matter which? Both Sorin and Dorn, each in his own way, are at the same impasse, except that Dorn's detachment is less fussy. Chekhov hardly takes us closer to the Doctor's position than this.

Whatever attitude Dorn may have decided upon for himself, Polina's situation is unchanged. She resorts to whining. She is jealous: a doctor meets other women; but he cannot run off with them all. To this Dorn responds as most men might to a similarly demanding challenge from the opposite sex, and mumbles a meaningless 'It's all right' as he turns gratefully to greet Nina who has just drifted into the garden[1] picking flowers upstage.

[1] Chekhov's characters often merely 'come in' – they do not 'make an entrance' in the nineteenth-century theatrical manner. However, first entrances are usually traditional for principals: Arkadina's first entrance was prepared by Treplev in Act 1; cf. also the first entrances of Vershinin in *Three Sisters* and Mme Ranevsky in *The Cherry Orchard*, but contrast that of Uncle Vanya.

Dorn asks Nina about the state of affairs in the house, and she reports that Arkadina is crying and that Sorin has an attack of asthma. The Doctor gets up to go to them: 'I'd better go and give them both valerian drops.' Whether he is impelled by his duty as a doctor, or by his wish to escape the imprecations of Polina, remains in doubt. If he speaks cynically of valerian drops as if they were sweets for a child, his good sense is suggested by the general prescription of a sedative.

Our last view of Polina in this scene is disturbing indeed. Nina hands Dorn the flowers she has picked, a pretty and quite impersonal gesture, and as Polina goes off with him she says, 'What charming flowers!' Her tone is too different from her strained voice of a moment before to be anything but false, and when they are near the house she adds *'in a smothered voice'*, 'Give me those flowers! Give me those flowers!' The shocking image of the middle-aged woman as she tears the flowers to pieces and throws them aside sharply accentuates her distress. In the irritating heat Polina is tearing to pieces all the other women in the world; by her action she is also trying to extinguish her distraught feelings and hopes. It is Treplev's earlier gesture inverted and grown petty,[1] and on reflection would be laughable if it were not horrifying.

Luckily Nina was not looking and does not see this destruction of the innocent flowers. Her thoughts are far away: she is transfigured by an emotion that is new to her, innocent as yet of the destructive side of human love. Innocent, she is puzzled that a famous actress could cry. She is also amazed that a famous author could spend the whole day fishing — 'and is delighted that he has caught two gudgeon'. Chekhov makes his point with delightful simplicity: famous people 'cry and fish, play cards, laugh and get cross like everyone else!' He uses a child to show the truth about people: greatness or littleness lies in the spirit, not in the status.

Nina's wide-eyed soliloquy is a classical preparation for the disillusionment of youth and the destruction of innocence. The tender story of Nina's love for Trigorin is about to begin. It will echo the pattern of Treplev's own loss of faith, and their two stories will be woven into the lives of the others. Filtered in this way through a subdued social scene, their emotion may not

[1] The incident with Polina mirrors that of Treplev's pulling the petals off a flower in Act I. See the comment on pp. 27–8 above.

overwhelm the delicacy of the comedy. Thus Nina and Treplev, too, must emerge from their crisis as but a part, a sample, of the complete social panorama.

Nina's story has a strikingly symbolic prelude, at this point in the play strictly visual and perhaps too subjective. Treplev lays at her feet a seagull he has shot.[1] This strong, obtrusive stage property is intended to grow in meaning to the end of the play. It gives its name to the play as a whole, and will draw together several of its threads. For the shooting of the seagull, which aptly prefigures the actual suicide of Treplev and the destruction of Nina's innocence, is also intended to reflect the disillusionment of all those who were at one time like these young people, but who now do not recognize the state of their spiritual mortality. In all his plays, this seagull is Chekhov's most pessimistic symbol of despair.

Nina picks up the bird and looks at it. We watch them both in silence. Treplev speaks after the pause and his voice is that of a hurt child: 'Soon I shall kill myself in the same way.' Nina seems to brush this aside as if it were a pretentious theatrical pose by a gesticulating young poet: 'I am too simple to understand you.' But she does not look him in the eye,[2] aware of his reproach. Instead, she sets the seagull on the garden seat, where it stays between them like an accusing chaperone.

Treplev gives a brief but harrowing demonstration of his condition after the failure of his play. He stamps his feet and his words grow wild. His semi-hysteria must seem to us juvenile and somewhat comic. 'Women' never forgive failure; Nina has grown cold; she considers him 'commonplace, insignificant, like so many others'. He curses his brain, and his pride. Then he sees Trigorin wandering aimlessly on to the stage, the aimlessness itself indicative of the casual way the new love affair will develop.

Here comes the real genius, walking like Hamlet and with a book too.

---

[1] It is interesting that the audience laughed at Treplev's entrance with the dead seagull, not only on its first night at the Alexandrinsky Theatre, St Petersburg, 1896 (see pp. 10–11 above), but also in A. E. Filmer's production in 1925 at the Arts Theatre, London (and probably in many other productions). Sir John Gielgud, who played Treplev to Valerie Taylor's Nina, does not, however, attribute the unwanted laughter to the play itself: 'On a very small stage it did look rather like a stuffed Christmas goose, however carefully I arranged its wings and legs beforehand' (*Early Stages*, London, 1953, p. 103). See comment on p. 18 above.
[2] As Stanislavsky suggests, in Balukhaty, p. 193.

(*Mimics*) 'Words, words, words.' . . . The sun has scarcely reached you and you are smiling already, your eyes are melting in its rays. I won't be in your way (*goes off quickly*).

But Chekhov has turned the *Hamlet* reference (II.ii.196) for a theatrical irony: Treplev is both the sarcastic Prince who mocks Polonius, and the comic Lord Chamberlain who spies on Hamlet. If the famous author is a poseur in Treplev's eyes, in ours Treplev is a young fool, and a potentially dangerous one.

The seagull remains on the garden seat throughout the ensuing dialogue between Nina the unwitting victim and Trigorin the rather less unwitting villain; he will pick up Nina as deliberately as he will drop her, and the seagull will remind us of the act of destruction.

At the mention of Trigorin, Nina lowered her eyes again; the audience is ready for their encounter. The final and most telling duologue in this short sequence of duologues must now inevitably be presented: everything has led to it. As between a young girl and an older man, this 'love scene' is fraught with the dangers of overstatement, and it risks plunging the play into sentimentality. The delicacy and judgment with which Chekhov conducts it is therefore important to the total effect of *The Seagull*. However, Nina can only be all wide-eyed worship, and the control of the scene turns on the handling of Trigorin's role.

Trigorin enters from the house and ambles downstage with a cigar in his mouth,[1] making notes as he enters. He is collecting 'copy', but from what he is muttering his notes are, significantly, *not* about Nina, but about Masha. The initial suggestion is that he is indifferently interested as an author in anybody he meets. The further suggestion is that he uses all experience as grist to the literary mill, regardless of the harm to himself and others. His greeting to Nina continues this impression of detachment with a perfunctory 'Good morning'. He announces that 'it seems' they are leaving unexpectedly today: 'We are not likely to meet again.' This clipped and unpromising assertion appears to be a dry and conclusive farewell, but it also suggests that he is not exposing himself riskily by being frank with her. He implies that his interest in her is merely professional.

[1] Chekhov to the actor Kachalov. See p. 39, n. 1, above.

I don't often get the chance of meeting young girls, youthful and charming; I have forgotten how one feels at eighteen or nineteen and can't picture it to myself, and so the young girls in my stories and novels are usually false. I should like to be in your shoes just for one hour to find out how you think, and altogether what sort of person you are.

Perhaps an affair with a young girl will remind him how one feels at eighteen or nineteen, and he will get it right in his next story.

How does Nina respond to this confession?[1] She is covered in confusion, but very much alert. She answers him honestly: she would like to be in his shoes to know how it feels to be famous. Wonder and admiration are in her eyes; she is enthralled. How she envies him his interesting life 'full of brightness and significance'! And she adds, 'You are happy.' The contrapuntal tones of their voices suggest that the truth about happiness lies somewhere elusively between innocence and experience.

It is important that Chekhov scotches the effect of warm sentiment in Nina's young enthusiasm. Trigorin has never thought about fame: perhaps he is too much of a machine to be so human. 'When they praise me I am pleased, and when they abuse me I feel out of humour for a day or two.' His implied question is, What has all this to do with *happiness*? He seems uninterested in whether his life is happy or not. Indeed, as he speaks he looks at his pocket-watch as if he is really wondering whether he can spare the time to talk about such irrelevances. If he is attracted by Nina's youth and beauty, he shows no emotion; the machine itself does not react, and there is no suspense. He is allowed to have no tinge of the seducer.

Nina's ready ear gives Trigorin his chance to talk freely as we never heard him speak with Arkadina. Or so Chekhov arranges it: it is necessary after gaining so many general impressions of the famous author from the others, coloured by Arkadina's possessiveness, Treplev's envy, Nina's adoration, to complete the picture of what this quiet, rather passive man is like from the evi-

---

1 Stanislavsky has extensive production notes on this episode. 'After Konstantin's departure Nina looks worried, but as Trigorin approaches, her face clears; she wants to go up to him, but cannot summon enough courage to do it. Pantomime. At last Nina summons enough courage and runs up quickly to Trigorin. As soon as she starts speaking, she is overcome with confusion. A pause. They look at one another. Nina is very embarrassed' (Balukhaty, p. 195). Chekhov's text suggests that Nina is more reticent than this, and also more independent and less naïve.

dence of his own lips. To date, our image is cloudy. He expressed sympathy with Treplev's feelings as a fellow playwright, while accepting without contradiction Arkadina's volatile judgments on her son; he seemed more excited by the thought of fishing in the lake than of spending time with either Arkadina or Nina. We wait for him to talk now of what Nina considers his splendid bright life.

He speaks at length, but an unbelieving Nina hears only of the drudgery of being an author. 'I am haunted day and night by one persistent thought: I ought to be writing.' He is 'excited' by being with her, he admits, but every moment he remembers his unfinished novel. When he goes off to the theatre or when he goes fishing, there is no escape: 'There's a new subject rolling about in my head like a heavy iron cannon ball.' The spectator can guess from the sincerity of his tone that here might be a little of Chekhov's own story; this is too frank to be false modesty. However, as Trigorin's voice quickens with the memory of his first enthusiasm as an author, we realize that his excitement is not caused by his interest in writing novels and stories, nor by his new relationship with this young girl, but by his self-absorption and his self-sympathy – like all the rest. We are all inescapably egotists. In this respect there is nothing special, nothing romantic, about Trigorin, only in Nina's worship of him.

He continues to explore his feelings. 'I feel that I am eating up my own life, and that for the sake of the honey I give to someone in space I am stripping the pollen from my best flowers, tearing up the flowers themselves and trampling on their roots.' The flower imagery, now less concrete and more elusive, widens to include the vulnerability of the creative mind. On the face of it Trigorin is conducting his life like a madman, and the more his friends heap praise upon him, the more it all seems a sham and their kindness an act of cruelty.

Suddenly in all this he illuminates the problem of the young. As a beginner, he found that writing induced the 'unmixed torture' of self-distrust.

A small writer, particularly when he is not successful, seems to himself clumsy, awkward, unnecessary; his nerves are strained and overwrought. He can't resist hanging about people connected with literature and art, unrecognized and unnoticed by anyone, afraid to look anyone boldly in the face, like a passionate gambler without any money.

I hadn't seen my reader, but for some reason I always imagined him hostile, and mistrustful. I was afraid of the public, it alarmed me, and when I had to produce my first play it always seemed to me that all the dark people felt hostile and all the fair ones were coldly indifferent. Oh, how awful it was! What agony it was!

As his thoughts grow transparent, we become aware that, like a chorus, he is explaining not only his own, but Treplev's and probably Nina's feelings too – the torments of all artists. In this way the inarticulate thoughts of the young people are explained in these intimate and natural terms, while at the same time the form of the play grants a foresight so that we may see in them a possible Trigorin and Arkadina to be. Chekhov distinguishes and yet identifies the two generations by working his magic with time upon our imagination.

With concrete detail, Trigorin recounts the unglamorous side of the creative process. There is happiness in the writing, in reading the proofs, but the torment soon follows. When the book is in print, all its errors become petrified. After the sweat and tears his readers offer simple judgments like 'charming and clever', but add that he is not as good as Tolstoy, or that he is inferior to Turgenev. This will be his epitaph: 'Here lies Trigorin. He was a good writer, but inferior to Turgenev.' And Trigorin laughs, the laugh of a man disillusioned with the empty forms of success, a laugh that offers no kind of relief to one who knows his life is a jest. Nina suggests that he has been 'spoiled by success'. *Is* this success, Trigorin wishes to know?[1] He loves nature, but he is not a landscape painter. He loves his country and his people, but the subject is too great for him. He can only describe scenes, 'and in everything else I am false to the marrow of my bones'. He says this with a fearful honesty. He knows he is second-rate, although it is not enough merely to know it. Is this consistent with Stanislavsky's smart, successful author? From such evidence of his spiritual humility, Chekhov was right to insist that Trigorin wear checked trousers and have holes in his shoes.

Trigorin speaks in tones of complete sincerity, but as Nina sits

[1] Chekhov's famous *obiter dictum* on success was written in a letter to Suvorin of 3 November 1888: 'Dividing people into successes and failures means looking upon human nature from the narrow, preconceived point of view . . . Are you a failure or not? Am I? Napoleon? Your servant Vasili? Where is the criterion? One must be God to be able to distinguish successes from failures and not make mistakes . . . I'm going to the ball' (Hellman, p. 62).

transfixed we also hear his words through her ears. She has not understood, and obstinately identifies herself with the idolizing public.[1] We are to understand, and be amused by, her gullibility, while Chekhov suggests her immaturity by loading her with grandiose clichés. 'If I were a writer like you, I should give up my whole life to the common herd, but I should know that there could be no greater happiness for them than to rise to my level, and they would harness themselves to my chariot.' She breathes her lines ecstatically, and Trigorin's flat reply, spoken naturally and conversationally, 'My chariot, what next! Am I an Agamemnon or what?', sets them in two different worlds of belief, the romantic and the realistic. With her head in the clouds, Nina will not be discouraged so easily. 'I would be ready to endure poverty, disappointment, the dislike of those around me; I would live in a garret and eat nothing but rye bread . . .' Coming as a crescendo to the scene, her lines marked by the ringing clarity of her voice, the audience may be forgiven for expecting that this will turn out to be part of Nina's very story.

In this 'love scene' there has been not a word of love, no protestations and prostrations, certainly no seduction. Strangely, however, and quite convincingly, the honest differences between the man and the girl have drawn them together; for Trigorin sees his lost ideals in her, and Nina sees the embodiment of her deepest wishes in him. As Arkadina's voice is heard calling Trigorin to her side, it is as if the realities of the present break into their lyrical mood. Suddenly they discover that they have Dorn's 'magic lake' in common. Trigorin does not want to leave it; Nina has spent all of her short life beside it. That is as near to the conventional love scene as Chekhov will allow here, so that the encounter between these two has been more a revelation of character than a study in sexual proclivities.

Chekhov has his trump card still to play. Only now does Trigorin see Treplev's dead seagull on the seat. Throughout the duologue we have been aware of it, representing Treplev's threat of suicide as it lies there, tarnishing the intimacy between Trigorin

---

[1] John Fernald argues that when Nina breaks her 'expressive silence', a pause will convey her 'unstated but clearly powerful sexual desire . . . Here is her moment of realization of dark impulses . . . It is here that she loses her innocence' (*Sense of Direction: The Director and his Actors*, London, 1968, pp. 45–6). But this is distracting: the importance of Nina is that she is genuine in her vocation.

and Nina. Now it changes its function, and its forlorn image is explicitly linked with the girl.[1]

Even the seagull, however, is copy for the author, as Nina may be too. For it seems a cold-blooded act when he writes a note in his notebook.

A subject struck me. A subject for a short story: a young girl, such as you, has lived all her life beside a lake; she loves the lake like a seagull, and is as free and happy as a seagull. But a man comes by chance, sees her, and having nothing better to do, destroys her like that seagull here (*a pause*).

Did we see Nina shudder slightly in that moment of silence? For the girl, dressed all in white, *is* the white seagull, and, unexpectedly, Trigorin seems to liken himself to the man who has nothing better to do. The story is wooden, for the second-rate novelist in him has dramatized his state into that of the unfeeling villain of the piece, although his view of his role cannot be either ours or Chekhov's. Neither the vacuity of 'having nothing better to do' (people destroy others because they are no better than they are) nor the malice of such destruction is appropriate to him. Trigorin will come near to destroying her, until she learns what is real for her, her acting. But Sophoclean irony is not in Chekhov's mind. In the brevity of Trigorin's notes, he has crudely epitomized the relationship, as a newspaper headline might, but we know now that such fictionalizing is too simple to account for the behaviour of two complicated people. Nevertheless, even if the seagull symbol makes it too simple and easy (the usual trouble with symbols), this outline serves to remove some of the mystery in the obliquely disclosed plotting to come, and the audience is left free to concern itself with the impact of the event on the whole group, rather than with the event itself.

The summer heat of this act seems to have rapidly brought on the sickness of Masha, Sorin, Arkadina, Polina and Trigorin. Individual issues have been cast into focus while the total perspective remains unchanged. Perhaps in Chekhov's suggestion of impending disaster for Nina, he risks bringing his second act to a close with the traditional 'strong' curtain, one that threatens to rob the other characters of their share of our attention and to

[1] To reinforce this idea, Stanislavsky had his Nina theatrically stroking the dead bird while Trigorin was speaking (Balukhaty, p. 205). This makes the symbol still more obtrusive, and the gesture hardly true to a Nina enthralled by Trigorin.

throw the play off balance. Yet happily, in suppressing Nina's story and leaving her position largely unresolved in nearly all of the two succeeding acts, Chekhov will practise a dramatic economy which will leave the other characters to hold the stage.

Thus before the curtain falls Chekhov manages to impart an essential plot line and at the same time to remind the audience that there are others involved.

(MADAME ARKADIN *appears at the window.*)
MADAME ARKADIN. Boris Alexeyevitch, where are you?
TRIGORIN. I am coming (*goes and looks back at* NINA. *To* MADAME ARKADIN *at the window*). What is it?
MADAME ARKADIN. We are staying.

(TRIGORIN *goes into the house.*)
NINA (*advances to the footlights; after a few moments' meditation*). It's a dream!   CURTAIN

Arkadina's words, although sweeter, are still those of one who gives the orders. Trigorin obeys them, but his glance back at Nina is not only an *au revoir*, but also a comparison between the two women. We see the amorous triangle anew. Madame has been persuaded to stay, rather a foregone conclusion. So Trigorin and Nina will not be so quickly separated, and what was begun in the garden will be given time to mature. Yet there can be no doubt that Arkadina is well aware of her rival as we see her in the house taking Trigorin's arm and leading him off. With this impression in mind, Nina's suppressed excitement is mildly amusing to us. 'It's a dream!' spoken quietly and slowly to herself, may suggest her joy that these famous people are going to remain, that her particular idol will be accessible, that with feminine intuition she has recognized in that glance a personal meaning and reward for herself. Even if the line means all these things, it is one of profound comic irony.[1]

[1] As usual, Stanislavsky marked this curtain by extra-dramatic effects. Nina sits 'with a rapt look on her face. She clasps her hands behind her head and, leaning against the tree, looks up at the sky . . . A pause of ten seconds.' As it happens, this excess of feeling in Nina cannot reduce the irony of the curtain. But he goes on, 'During the final pause of ten seconds it might not be a bad idea for the curtain on the platform to start swaying violently and flapping against the platform (as a hint of what is to be mentioned in Act IV). The danger is that it might produce a rather ridiculous effect. Shall we try it?' (Balukhaty, p. 207). Of course, Chekhov himself had intended no deserted inner stage to be seen in his second act, with or without an evocatively flapping curtain, and in the fourth he wisely leaves it entirely to the imagination.

Act Three

With the third act we have moved inside the house, where we find ourselves in a family room, the dining-room. It is almost midday, and the light is clear as for Act II. The immediate impression is of disorder, of parcels and boxes set about the stage haphazardly, with some pieces of furniture covered with dust-sheets. V. A. Simov, Stanislavsky's designer, attempted to contrast what he called 'the happy comfort of the genial and agreeable life in the first half of the play' with, here, 'the depressing emptiness, hollowness, and discord in the lives of the people in the play in the last two acts'.[1] The impression of confusion created by the luggage is set against the seated figure of Trigorin quietly having lunch among the muddle, a comic sight to meet the eye on the rise of the curtain. Masha is standing beside him swaying a little tipsily as she talks to him; she has been drinking.[2] When the curtain fell the audience was told that Sorin's visitors were staying; now we see the signs of their departure and we assume the time to be some days later; we soon learn that a week has passed. Once or twice Yakov passes across the back of the stage with trunks and cases. The stage is a restless one.

The audience is immediately interested to discover what has passed during the intervening week. Chekhov does not leave us long unsatisfied. He adopts a retrospective method of exposition in the Ibsen manner, and each character talks on the assumption that the previous 'events' have happened already. Since these are also the events that were anticipated in the first two acts, our sense of their actuality is redoubled and conviction is increased. In spite of this technique, for Chekhov this is a tiresomely formless act, one which is overplotted with too many facts to be established.

[1] Balukhaty, p. 65.
[2] For Stanislavsky, 'Masha, feet on the chair and elbows on the table, sits beside Trigorin, pensively tracing lines on the table-cloth with a fork' (Balukhaty, p. 211).

Act III

Did Treplev carry out his threat? No. He has wounded himself with a gun, but not seriously, it seems. This Masha and Trigorin reveal to us indirectly when she tells him she would have taken her own life if Treplev had died. Trigorin impassively eats on. However, Masha is determined to destroy her love for Treplev – she will marry Medvedenko after all: 'Anyway, it will be a change, you know.' Laughter: a desperate rationalization and a sad personal anticlimax. However, the careful preparation of Masha's seemingly fruitless liaison with the schoolmaster has been to some dramatic purpose: it allows the girl to take one unromantic step further towards futility. She pours Trigorin and herself another drink with a hint of bravado.[1] When Nina comes in, Masha speaks about her schoolmaster with a cynicism that her rival should perceive. She sways as she tries to justify what she has done. Medvedenko is not brilliant, and he is poor; but he is good-natured and 'very much in love with me'. And she adds, 'I am sorry for him. And I am sorry for his old mother.' Stanislavsky suggests that as she goes out it is as if she were really saying to Nina, 'Look what you have done to me!'[2]

She leaves Trigorin alone with Nina for a brief exchange, and their developing relationship is quickly touched in. The informality of their greeting is now striking. The subdued feeling which passed between them at their previous meeting has changed in quality. Their regard for each other is still shy, and it is as delicate as before; but that there is a new level of intimacy is apparent from a simple Chekhovian gesture. Nina unaffectedly stretches out a fist with something clasped in it. Trigorin looks up.

NINA. Odd or even?
TRIGORIN. Even.
NINA (*with a sigh*). Wrong. I had only one pea in my hand. I was trying my fortune whether to go on the stage or not. I wish someone would advise me.

[1] On the disclosure of her plan to marry Medvedenko, Stanislavsky visualized Masha's attitude and stance in detail. She pours vodka 'with an assumed air of gaiety. It can be seen from the way in which she fills the glasses that she is an expert at that kind of thing.' She has 'the devil-may-care air of a student'. He also adds several more notes for Masha along similar lines, as 'One arm akimbo, like a man, [she] clinks classes energetically, also like a man'; she 'empties her glass at one gulp and has a bite of something (she eats noisily), then slaps Trigorin on the back' (Balukhaty, p. 211).
[2] Balukhaty, p. 213.

The private game suggests a private language. Of course, she wishes Trigorin to tell her what to do: the real question is, should she stay with him or not? And of course, he cannot tell her what to do. Thus are great personal decisions arrived at by little signs. It is only after the business with the pea that, with some embarrassment, she gives him a small parting gift. It is a medallion bearing the intriguing words, *Days and Nights*. This is the title of his recent book, and beneath it a page and line reference is engraved. Is this then a token of farewell, or a gift of herself? We are left in doubt. Is Nina going on the stage, or will the new intimacy between them grow? And before she leaves, Trigorin reminds us of the dead seagull. We are not allowed to forget it, even when it is not on the stage, and both Nina's undetermined choice and her unexplained gift are associated with it. Nina's hopes both as an artist and as a woman in love are hazily coloured by its beauty in death. Chekhov supplies an important pause for the spectator to reflect on this, and the same pause also extends the actress who must convey Nina's troubled indecision.[1]

Now the characters seem to wander in and out, picking at the lunch table and eating on their feet to suggest the unrest of departure. They continue to drop hints which confirm established impressions and pursue changing relationships. In honour of his sister's departure, and obviously happy to have the chance to go into town at last without having to beg from Shamraev, Sorin makes a splendid appearance wearing *'a dress coat with a star of some order on it,'* a sign of his former importance, now a mockery. As Madame sits down exhaustedly, her glances tell us that she is fully aware of Trigorin's faithlessness.

Her scornful look after the retreating figure, the weary harassed

---

[1] Stanislavsky overworks this pause for a different subtextual implication: 'Another awkward pause. Nina jumps quickly to her feet and is about to leave the room, but Trigorin stops her by catching hold of her left hand. Nina stops without looking at him (she stands with her back to him, her eyes fixed on the ground). A pause. Trigorin puts her hand gently to his lips. A long kiss. Nina *gently* [Stanislavsky underlines this in ink – J.L.S.] frees her hand and walks away quickly. She stops at the stove, tracing something pensively on it with a finger, then she turns round quickly, goes up to Trigorin, finishes her speech rapidly without looking at him, and goes out at once. A pause. Trigorin follows her with his eyes and kisses the medallion' (Balukhaty, p. 215). There is no hint that Chekhov intends anything of this, or as explicit as this. He is already risking a scene of some sentiment in itself, and the text suggests that he wishes to keep it clipped and subdued, if not, on the surface, passionless.

manner in which she sank into a chair, suggested all that had happened to Arcádina since the second act – her fear of losing her lover, her jealousy of the young girl, her weariness with the details of running a house and packing to leave it, her perfunctory affection for her old brother, her longing for attention and flattery; above all, her dislike of being middle-aged.[1]

She apologizes to him for disturbing his tête-à-tête with Nina, and her slight sarcasm on her affectedly French *pardon* is pathetically inadequate. But Trigorin has his mind too much on Nina, or his own writing, to be affected by Arkadina's attempt at wit; he goes to check the girl's reference on the medallion.

Arkadina perversely tries to persuade her brother to stay at home and not come to town with her. He will risk catching cold. Let him look after Treplev instead. The hesitation with which she precedes this request suggests that it is really Treplev's condition of mind which is troubling her; she seems to agree with our findings from Act i that Sorin is one of the few who are able to speak to the boy with understanding. She does not know why he tried to shoot himself. She suspects jealousy, an emotion she can identify, we may assume, from her own current feelings, and names Trigorin. But again the doubt exists: we are left to guess whether Treplev's jealousy arises from Trigorin's success as a writer or from his success as Nina's lover. But one thing seems clear, that it is Trigorin's affection for Nina that is the reason for their leaving.

As Sorin eats and picks his teeth, he draws upon his own bitter experience to explain Treplev's action. He has no money and he has nothing to do. 'He feels he is superfluous . . . It's easy to understand, it's *amour propre*.' The mention of self-love diagnoses a malaise which is consuming so many of them. It is a deft stroke that the oldest member of the family, himself at one extreme of self-concern, should be the one to articulate the thoughts of the youngest. Before he is finished, Sorin also touches on a topic which Treplev raised when the two were together in the first act – Arkadina's stinginess. 'Just look at him,' he declares, 'he's been going about in the same wretched jacket for the last three years and he has no overcoat.' Just as Arkadina talked about her son's

---

[1] Sir John Gielgud describing the performance of Edith Evans in Theodore Komisarjevsky's production at the New Theatre, London, in 1936 (*Early Stages*, London, 1953, p. 295).

state of mind in terms that applied to herself and that she could understand, so Sorin explains him in terms that apply to himself and that he can understand. At the same time he gives his sudden laugh as if to disguise the attack on his sister. No matter; it is too late to save Arkadina's rising temper. She stops eating and protests angrily that she cannot afford it, and, as Treplev had shrewdly said she would, she bursts into tears like a spoiled child. She is an actress, she reminds him, and her dresses alone are enough to ruin her. Her passion when asked for money proves how much money means to her: giving it away will weaken her security like losing her figure and her looks.

The argument is cut short suddenly when Sorin staggers and clutches the table. 'I feel dizzy . . . I feel ill and all that.' Arkadina forgets her tears in a moment, calls her son, and he and Medvedenko run in. The focus on Sorin undercuts the theatricality of an entrance by Treplev with a bandaged head. The young man is not allowed to be a 'star', even temporarily. And the ominous moment passes quickly: 'It's passed off . . . and all that.' The old man's comic tag, 'and all that', helps to diminish the emotionality of a scene of mortal sickness. 'Don't be frightened, mother, it's not serious. Uncle often has these attacks now'; but the appendix to the boy's consoling words is more important for the shaping of the play as a whole. Stanislavsky argues that Sorin's fit should be frighteningly real to heighten suspense;[1] however, the scene is introduced less for such an undirected response than lightly to reintroduce the theme of death associated with both the young and the old, as well as to remind us efficiently of the passage of time. All these static lives must move towards such a moment of mortality. The threat passes quickly, and Sorin hobbles off to his room. 'But I am going to the town all the same.' He is not dead yet, and he is not going to let anything spoil his outing. Medvedenko helps him away, trying to cheer him up with a riddle – as might be expected, it is a 'chestnut'. We observe incidentally that the schoolmaster is in much better spirits than before: Masha must have made known to him her decision to marry him.

We have been allowed to scan the present scene, the scene before the departure, with a generalizing, associative eye, an eye for the group. The action now narrows to demonstrate more

[1] Balukhaty, p. 221.

specifically the relationship between Arkadina and her two men, the son and the lover.

Mother and son are alone together for the first time in the play. The episode that follows is rich with the subtleties of a most intimate human bond, and, coming in the middle of the play, it bolsters our sense of a flesh-and-blood solidity at the heart of the family situation. Treplev first makes use of Sorin's condition as his opportunity to raise an issue which has been rankling in his mind. 'It is not good for him to live in the country. He gets depressed. If you would be generous for once, mother, and lend him fifteen hundred or two thousand roubles, he could spend a whole year in town.' The boy is kind, but he is, in a sense, pleading his own cause too. Sorin asked money for his nephew; now the nephew asks money for the uncle. By having the audience recognize the irony in the echo, Chekhov is able to emphasize that both the oldest and the youngest in the family group suffer from the same kind of frustration. But Madame's answer is always the same for Treplev as for Sorin. Her curt reply marks the narrow inflexibility of her mind and her anxiety for her future: 'I am an actress, not a banker.'

Treplev asks his mother to change the bandage round his head, as if to pacify her and restore to her a maternal warmth: 'You do it so well.' The human touch, however, must reduce him in the spectator's eyes, especially since his stature has been shaken before. He cuts rather more of a comic than a pathetic figure, since to shoot oneself unsuccessfully is less than glorious: failure is a joke. Chekhov here samples an effect he is later to repeat with more control and more comedy when in *Uncle Vanya* the central character shoots and misses, but on stage in full view. For what was the boy's motive in trying to shoot himself? Surely the essentially childish sentiment of When I'm dead you'll be sorry! Treplev's aspiration to heroism is sapped even more as, calmer now, his mother dresses his wound and talks to him like a child: 'You won't do anything naughty again while I am away, will you?' The physical image, too, with Arkadina bending over her son, is that of mother and child. It must seem to him by now that the older generation always talks to him in this way, but he accepts her affection gratefully and her voice induces memories of his childhood. The scene increasingly brings out the baby in him. He recalls her clever hands. This is real, incestuous feeling, of a quite normal kind. Does she remember when she once washed her tenant's children in a tub? The audience finds this tale a little hard to swallow, but the relationship on the stage is suddenly electric. For her part, the lady does not wish to be reminded of humbler days, and her answer is a sharp 'No'. The short reply keeps the sentiment at bay, and the tension between mother and son increases sharply.

Oblivious of this warning, he spills out his heart to her. He wants to be dependent on a loving mother, and in the play he never breaks the cord, even though the adult in him sees through her weaknesses and is revolted by his dependence on her. He loves her 'as tenderly and completely as when I was a child'. Speaking less cautiously, he proceeds to reveal his antagonism towards Trigorin. Treplev has actually challenged his rival to a duel – a young man's bluster which Trigorin has naturally ignored. And then Treplev insists that both Arkadina and Nina are under the influence of the man. Arkadina reacts; she reacts not so much to the implication of her folly as to the mention of Nina and herself in the same breath and on the same footing. 'I' – she speaks carefully – 'respect that man'. But the quarrel has begun, and what started as a wistful, even endearing, scene grows rapidly until they are stripping naked each other's souls. The truths they tell each other are terrible.

Chekhov's lines suggest an increasing pitch and pace as the sentences become shorter, the tones shriller and the logic wilder. Arkadina asserts that 'people who have pretension without talent' attack real talent, and she regards him as a mediocrity. With this, Treplev tears the bandage from his head[1] as if he wishes at one stroke to renounce all his mother's care of him from his childhood days until now. Go and act in 'your paltry, stupid plays!' To which she retorts, 'You are nothing but a Kiev shopman!' With this barbed reference, dredged up from former days along with all her gall, she shows how much his undistinguished

---

[1] This is Chekhov's only violent stage direction in the play. Stanislavsky sees this scene, however, in far more tempestuous terms. 'Miss Arkadina, beside herself, flings the end of the rolled up bandage she was holding in her hand in Konstantin's face. She then walks away from her son. Konstantin, in a fit of uncontrollable fury, tears the bandage savagely off his head and almost screams at his mother . . . Konstantin throws the bandage towards his mother . . . Miss Arkadina sends the chair she is leaning against crashing to the floor . . .', and so on (Balukhaty, p. 227).

work and lack of status as an artist exasperate her, and recalls his
father's insignificance and her own struggle into the limelight. So
the scene advances to the crisis by two phrases which disclose the
woman's cheapness of spirit. 'You miser!' cries Treplev. 'You
ragged beggar!' cries his mother.[1]

The boy is the first to break and the first to come to his senses:
he sits down and cries quietly. Her last accusation – 'Nonentity!'
– is still pounding in his ears as she too collapses into tears. She
comforts him with kisses and asks his forgiveness. It is the
moment for the whole truth to emerge, and he confesses that he
is heart-broken over Nina. 'If only you knew! I have lost everything! She does not love me, and now I cannot write . . . all my
hopes are gone . . .' The pace has slowed almost to a halt, and the
scene is moving to a painful close when Trigorin appears with the
book he had gone to look for.

He has found Nina's reference in the text and is overwhelmed.
In a theatrical way which reveals the falseness of his art and
perhaps his own insincerity, he reads it aloud no less than three
times, and all within Arkadina's hearing. 'If ever my life can be
of use to you, come and take it.' It is the message of the medallion
and of the dead bird. At once the issue between himself and Nina
is in the open. He is too weak a man in his middle-age to resist
the opportunity of having a fresh young girl throw herself at him.
He pleads with Arkadina to stay on, to free him. It may be that
Nina's love is just what he needs. It is as if he feels he could
resolve his discontent by grasping now what he thinks he has
missed, by feeding on her youth. The man will be using the
woman, and the audience can perceive the evil in this vampire
attitude towards another human being; and yet we can fully
understand his impossible desire to recapture lost time.

If Arkadina, meanwhile, has not understood Trigorin's needs,
she has understood why he wants to stay. Every remark he makes
is a wound to her vanity. Nina's youth reveals to both of them
the loss of their own youth. Trigorin 'terrifies' Arkadina with the
implication that her life is finished when he claims his: 'You are

[1] James Agate's comment, after watching Edith Evans play Mme Arkadin at the
New Theatre, London, in 1936, was: 'Arcadina is a well-known actress; Trigorin
is a well-known novelist. The liaison is notorious and a good advertisement for
both. She has got used to him, at forty-three doesn't want the bother of looking
for somebody else, and is not going to have her nose put out by a ninny who goes
in for amateur theatricals' (*More First Nights,* London, 1937, p. 274).

the last page in my life.' With this kind of bombast she falls on her knees and grovels before him, clinging to his legs like an actress in an old-fashioned melodrama. After all that has been said by her son about staginess, it is supremely ironic that there should come this high point where the great actress, in genuine terror, can only resort to her 'art'. The whole scene, indeed, is tinged with burlesque. By such theatricality, it may be argued, Chekhov is, falling back upon the safe acting techniques of his time in order to force a crisis of emotion upon his audience. This is just possible; but we should not forget that Arkadina is herself in love with her youth as well as being an actress of the period – the time is 'the present' – and her manner on the stage suggests that she is putting on the performance of her life to keep her novelist. The abasement is real and horrible: he is her last hold on youth and she is desperate to keep him. She kisses him, embraces him, laughs and cries at once, flatters and cajoles him, while the poor man can hardly utter a word. And she wins. 'I have no will of my own,' he finally admits. Then in a controlled voice she adds, 'But, of course, if you like, you can stay.' When she sees she has dominated him, and says, 'Now he's mine!' so theatrical an aside is not Chekhov relapsing into the convention, but shows that she has regained confidence, is now really enjoying acting a part – 'I am an actress acting an actress who is acting a part in real life' – and can even permit herself a little game with the conventions. Her glance of triumph at the real audience both brings us into the play and is a gem of a Chekhovian alienation-effect by which the old convention is completely transcended. As if to confirm the suspicion that Arkadina was unconsciously play-acting all the time, Chekhov supplies an illuminating and explicit stage direction: she speaks to Trigorin *'in an easy tone as though nothing had happened'*, so that the final effect must transparently be mainly one of comedy.

At all events, Arkadina is triumphant, and Trigorin offers no resistance whatever. As if to confirm his defeat, he returns immediately to his humdrum routine of collecting notes, and mechanically scribbles a phrase in his ever-present notebook. Perhaps this whole episode with Arkadina and Nina will prove to be nothing more than material for more fiction. He has retreated again into his private world of fishing and fabricating. However, we may also suspect that his submission came too easily, and that the weakness of a will that can give way to Arkadina may yet give way to Nina. He may even be the predator of his own hapless volition and shoot his seagull.

The tensions between all parties are at their greatest when the time comes for the departure scene in this play. It differs from the departure scenes in *Uncle Vanya*, *Three Sisters* and *The Cherry Orchard* in that it has only the appearance of a traditional scene of decision and finality, and is illusory. However, there is none of Vanya's mood of waste and emptiness as he remains behind in the vacuum left by the Professor and his wife, or of the sisters' need for reorientation, and none of the inevitability of the loss of the orchard. The whole group will be seen again in Act IV. Nevertheless, the episode contains within itself the same quality of summary that is found in the other scenes of departure. It is as if the focus on Treplev, Arkadina and Trigorin is blurred in order that the audience may survey the family as a whole for a broader comic perception. The emotional storms of the last few minutes are adjusted to the total image when Shamraev, Polina and the rest come to say goodbye.

The estate manager is in the best of humours again. With his touch of shame, he is now more of a fool than ever: 'I have the honour to announce, with regret, that the horses are ready.' He seems to have been able to resolve the difficulty over the horses when he put his mind to it. In an attempt to revert to the easier conversation of that earlier day of Treplev's play, he does not omit to give his 'honoured lady' a commission to enquire into the present situation of an actor he remembered in his youth. And he adds a pompous joke about a muffed line in a melodrama he once saw. 'Izmailov had to say, "We are caught in a trap", but he said, "We are caught in a tap!" (*Laughs*) A tap!'[1] The stony silence which falls hardly relieves the feelings of the moment on the stage, and Shamraev must laugh at his own joke.

For her part, Madame is busy with her hat, coat, gloves and umbrella. In a touching gesture, Polina gives her a basket of plums for the journey and promptly bursts into tears. By his movements with the luggage, weaving between people and furniture, Yakov hinders any possibility of the family's coming

---

[1] Ronald Hingley provides a more plausible translation: 'We're caught in a trap' becomes 'We're trapped in a court' (Hingley, vol. II, p. 266).

together again as a unit. Sorin, looking pathetically like a lord,[1] exhibits an old man's anxiety over time, and hurries off to the carriage before his sister can change her mind about his trip into town. Medvedenko, proudly poor as usual, announces dully that he will *walk* to the station; but no one listens, and the hesitation in his voice as he expands the point with 'I'll be there in no time' suggests that he would still welcome an invitation to ride with the others. All the servants have assembled, and Arkadina, with a large gesture as if from a farewell performance, takes her leave of them: 'Good-bye, dear friends . . .' It is to be the grand exit. 'Don't forget me.' But Chekhov interposes one detail which cuts her down to size: she gives the Cook a coin with 'Here's a rouble for the three of you' and at the door she adds to Yakov, 'I gave the cook a rouble. It's for the three of you.'[2] This exit line spoils her whole performance. If there was sentiment in this departure, Treplev's absence and Arkadina's rouble has killed it.

As in his later plays, Chekhov gives his director the chance to organize evocative sound effects off. The stage is empty and the audience listens in silence to the noise of the departing carriage with the chinking harness of the horses: we feel that we too have been left behind in the vacuum. This is Chekhov's first instance of a stage emptied to create the meaning of departure.[3] The stillness of the stage is broken comically by the hasty re-entrance of the maid. She has returned to fetch Polina's basket of plums, which Arkadina, for all her thanks, neglected to pick up in the heady ceremonial of departure. Another truth to life which cements the character of Arkadina and with its laughter undermines possible sentiment. The tensions appear to have been quelled.

Nevertheless, the playwright has one more piece to fit into the

---

[1] Stanislavsky has him looking 'much younger' (Balukhaty, p. 239), but this mistakes the signs of his steady decline to the fourth act, especially after his alarming fit earlier.

[2] As a gesture, this stinginess is comic today, but in its own time it would have an uglier undercurrent; the middle-class sense of guilt towards household servants, that is, serfs not long liberated, would accentuate the meanness of her action. For Arkadina, however, the meanness again reflects her anxiety about her future: she is going to need the money when she gets no more parts. The student of Chekhov will contrast with this the generosity of Madame Ranevsky in Acts II and IV of *The Cherry Orchard*. See also p. 288, n. 1 below.

[3] He grows increasingly fond of using the eloquence of an empty stage in *Three Sisters* and *The Cherry Orchard*.

pattern, placed carefully so that the curtain must rise upon a final act. Trigorin comes back too, with an obviously loud, 'I have forgotten my stick.' He had prepared a final meeting with Nina by asking her for a last word, alone. For her part, she has been waiting for this moment, and simultaneously appears from the verandah. They are both in a state of great excitement, and both talk quickly.

Boris Alexeyevitch, I have come to a decision, the die is cast, I am going on the stage. I shall be gone from here tomorrow; I am leaving my father, I am abandoning everything, I am beginning a new life. Like you, I am going . . . to Moscow. We shall meet there.

So all was not as Arkadina, or Trigorin, or we, thought. And we observe that Nina has more courage than Treplev: while he is tied to his tyrant mother, she has the strength to leave her tyrant father. Moreover, as if Chekhov must interpolate a dozen hasty 'plot lines', we learn that Nina is going to Moscow, not only to go on the stage, but also to meet Trigorin. The curtain falls on their '*prolonged kiss*'.

A modern audience may find these nineteenth century theatrics tiresome, and it is appropriate to see from the abundant evidence of this scene that Chekhov in *The Seagull* is still sometimes writing for the conventional stage of Scribe and Sardou. But a more pertinent question for the understanding of Chekhov's development towards more understated relationships like those between Irina and Tuzenbach, Anya and Trofimov, and Varya and Lopakhin, is to ask why he does not end his play here.

It has been an act of stark revelations, especially of the feelings of the more central quartet of lovers. Emotions have run higher than in any other act in the play. With its several reconciliations, albeit shaky ones, the shaping of the action bears the hallmark of the grand climax of the *pièce bien faite*. Thus, indeed, the play could end here. Chekhov, however, intends to mould the image of his meaning and cast our responses less melodramatically. A final act is to create one great, thought-inducing *anticlimax* for the play, and Chekhov will yet turn the tables on his facile predecessors. The spectator is to understand that two years pass before the rise of the curtain in Act IV – an awkward expedient which Chekhov does not try again – two years which will tell a different story of Treplev and Nina, Trigorin and Arkadina. They are two years which indicate his intention of forcing us to see the family in a fresh way. The two years will have meaning in themselves, and time will be the final protagonist of the play. The daring passage from climax to anticlimax between Acts III and IV is to create in our minds a transparent 'before-and-after' consideration of the direction and value of their overheated passions, individual and collective. If now we find the situation between Trigorin and the two women somewhat unresolved, if satisfaction required that Trigorin's dream, Nina's new life and Arkadina's false hopes are not left in question, if we have remarked that Treplev was missing from the scene of his mother's departure, these are signs that final judgment should not yet be passed.

The Seagull Act 1

The Seagull Act III

The Seagull Act IV

Act Four

It is one thing to read in a programme note that 'two years have passed', another to find that the passage of two years is convincingly recognizable on the stage. To move furniture, to change costume and make-up is not enough. The previous assumptions of the audience about the characters in their situation must be taken into detailed account. Especially in the naturalistic theatre, the spectator checks every tone, every gesture against what he knew before. The slightest differences *make* the new image of the scene. The last act of *The Seagull* is more than an exercise in echoes and embellishments: in the shaping of the play, Chekhov must capture the exact details which will both contrast with the feverish condition of the previous action, and themselves seem the natural result of two years.

Although *Three Sisters* employs a comparable passage of time, there it is virtually continuous through the play. The break between Acts III and IV of *The Seagull* is exceptional in that sharp change makes us objectively aware of transience. The subject of the play becomes time itself when we watch the effects of its passing on the lives of the family. The designer, V. A. Simov, wanted the changed setting to bear 'the stamp of impermanency', and he reasoned that 'outside it is cold, damp, windy; but there is no warmth in the room, either'. The sense of middle-class prosperity has to give way to 'decay, affliction, and adversity', and the furniture must be arranged to obtain 'the effect of mental disequilibrium, so that one can see immediately how indifferent the person who lives in that room is to the way the furniture is arranged. If some piece of furniture is in his way, he moves it aside, and does not bother to replace it until someone else finds it is in *his* way.'[1] If this visual suggestion works, it will do so pervasively through the act.

[1] Balukhaty, pp. 65–6.

73

In spite of the restlessness in the setting, it is noticeably more intimate. From the busy dining-room with its packets and parcels, we are led into a bookish room, a room used as a study for Treplev. It is as if we have finally moved into the heart of Treplev's world. Books are everywhere, and the stage glows from a single lamp. It is an evening scene, the windows are dark and our impression of the garden outside is created by the protective watchman[1] whose tapping is heard between the melancholy gusts of wind in the trees. To this Stanislavsky added notes that 'the rain is beating against the windows, sound of rattling window-panes and frames . . . howling or distant barking of a dog.'[2] Like the storm in *Uncle Vanya* and the fire in *Three Sisters*, the storm outside induces a mood of foreboding in the blatant tradition of the nineteenth century, while the single lamp inside leaves the room half in darkness, hypnotizing the spectator with its patch of light. The constriction of the soul that grips all the characters is thus represented physically on the stage as a kind of visual claustrophobia. Senses alive, we listen to the broken sounds for a time, adjust our eyes to the half-light and see Medvedenko and Masha as the girl turns up the lamp. They are the two who opened the play in Act 1.

Their first words are rich with suggestion. As she comes in, Masha is calling, 'Konstantin Gavrilitch! Konstantin Gavrilitch!', but only the storm replies as if Treplev were a phantom. Against the noise of the wind, we learn from Masha that there are great waves on the lake, and from Medvedenko that Treplev's little stage of Act 1 is still standing.

How dark it is in the garden! We ought to have told them to break up that stage in the garden. It stands as bare and ugly as a skeleton, and the curtain flaps in the wind. When I passed it yesterday evening, it seemed as though someone were crying in it.

Chekhov evokes half mystical memories of the past as Maeterlinck might, and the imagination fashions the derelict stage better than any scene builder.[3] To the stage's bare skeleton and its flapping curtain we bring associations of Nina and Treplev; and that

---

[1] The watchman in this and the other plays was employed on an estate to guard the property from thieves. He announced his presence by beating with a stick on a board.

[2] Balukhaty, p. 247.

[3] Cf. p. 59, n. 1, above.

'someone crying' may be Nina or Treplev, or merely the suggestion of the loss of his young hopes.

In this way Chekhov uses two minor characters to paint the atmospheric background of the scene. He now shows what has happened to them. We may guess whether Masha has come to visit her mother Polina or to remain near Treplev, in whom, it appears, her interest has not waned. However, Medvedenko wants her to go home. In his flat, whining voice he asks her not to forget their baby boy. So they are married, and they have a child. But Masha's indifference to the baby – 'He has been three nights now without his mother' – tells us quickly of the shortcomings of their marriage.

MASHA. You are a bore. In old days you used at least to discuss general
  subjects, but now it is only home, baby, home, baby – that's all one
  can get out of you.
MEDVEDENKO. Come along, Masha!
MASHA. Go by yourself.
MEDVEDENKO. Your father won't let me have a horse.
MASHA. Yes, he will. You ask, and he will.
MEDVEDENKO. Very well, I'll ask. Then you will come tomorrow?
MASHA (*taking a pinch of snuff*). Very well, tomorrow. How you pester
  me.

So Medvedenko's state has changed only for the worse: he is still too poor to have a horse, and Shamraev and Arkadina are still too mean to give him one, but now he has a wife who does not love him. His sincerity may be granted: he merely wants the 'simple married life'. If only Masha's heart were not elsewhere.

However, in this passage the emphasis is on the new wife. Masha's desolation is now as great as her mother's, and the marriage to Medvedenko is a forlorn echo of Polina's marriage to Shamraev. Medvedenko is a bore and a pest, and with the baby Masha's chains are complete. The girl's irritation is balanced by the man's whining, his obsequiousness by her disdainful gesture of snuff-taking. Together they make up a picture of mutual wretchedness. Medvedenko awkwardly says goodbye; no one is interested.

Treplev and Polina have entered with bedding to make up a bed for Sorin in Treplev's room. The old man has declined from a figure with a walking-stick to one in a bath-chair to one in a bed, a steady progress towards extinction. Sorin cannot now live without his nephew, and the affecting relationship between the young and the old which we noticed before has grown closer. When we learn that Treplev has had some success with publishing, it is possible to feel that Sorin sees his own fulfilment in the boy, in a more healthy way than Trigorin hoped to in Nina.

All these elements overlap in the conduct of a continuous action. It was Polina who, with a shade of flattery, remarked Treplev's success as a writer. What degree of success we are not to know, for she had other ends in view. Now she adds, 'Dear, good Kostya, do be a little kinder to my Mashenka!' Masha is embarrassed and angry. Treplev turns and walks away saying nothing, and a moment later he is heard playing a '*melancholy waltz*', the extension of his mood, in another part of the house. 'A woman wants nothing, you know, Kostya, so long as you give her a kind look. I know from myself.' At once Polina's own unrequited love is slipped into the pattern of generations: one age is no different from another. So Treplev leaves the room, and a desperate mother and daughter watch him go. But lest we think that the Mashas of this world will learn nothing, her comment also reveals that she will try not to be trapped into playing her mother's unhappy game. Masha's husband has been promised a transfer, and she will tear the love for Treplev out of her heart. Love is nonsense – only avoid seeing Treplev and she will get over it. We may well ask whether Polina did not at one time speak in exactly the same way about Dorn, since, for all Masha's talk, the iron has not quite entered her soul. She listens too intently to his piano playing; in spite of her husband and child, she lingers in Sorin's house; and when Treplev comes back later, she cannot take her eyes off him.[1]

Chekhov's characters can say one thing and do another; this is his comedy of self-deceit. If Masha cannot break with Treplev, neither can Medvedenko carry out his threat to go home without her. After all his goodbyes of a minute before, we are amused to see him re-appear, assisting the Doctor to push Sorin in his bath-

---

[1] Stanislavsky has Masha wipe tears from her cheeks (Balukhaty, p. 253), but Chekhov's more subtle stage direction, '*dances a few waltz steps noiselessly*', designed primarily to show that she is listening to Treplev's playing, is also an indication that, while she has not resigned herself to his indifference, she is controlling her feelings. John Fernald makes the helpful point that the piano playing keeps 'the theatrical thread that Konstantin represents woven into the tapestry of the scene' (*Sense of Direction: The Director and his Actors*, London, 1968, p. 102).

chair. He talks as despondently as ever about his responsibilities at home: '. . . and flour is two kopeks a pound.' When Masha asks why he has not gone home, he explains that they would not let him have a horse; the lame excuse and the guilty tone, however, tell what his real intentions were. Equivocation over the small things points to the big lie upon which people base their lives.

The women and the Doctor sit beside Sorin, immobile in his wheel-chair with a newspaper. A permanent invalid, he is finally beyond the hope of going to Moscow, and his acquaintance with the world outside is reduced to the doubtful, vicarious pleasure of reading about it in the papers. From Sorin we learn that his sister has come to his sick-bed, and that at present she has gone to meet Trigorin at the station. 'I must be dangerously ill.' No one responds to this. More testily: 'It's a queer thing, I am dangerously ill and here they don't give me any medicines.' His reproachful, self-pitying glance at Dorn produces only a gentle sarcasm about valerian drops; all the comic battles between doctor and patient are compressed into this short exchange. So Sorin's thoughts pass from his new bed in Treplev's room to a subject for Treplev's writing.

I want to give Kostya a subject for a story. It ought to be called 'The Man who Wished' – *L'homme qui a voulu*. In my youth I wanted to become a literary man – and didn't; I wanted to speak well – and spoke horribly badly, (*mimicking himself*) 'and all the rest of it, and all that, and so on, and so forth' . . . and I would go plodding on and on, trying to sum up till I was in a regular perspiration; I wanted to get married – and I didn't; I always wanted to live in town and here I am ending my life in the country – and so on.

His sorry plan for Treplev's story summarizes all his regrets – his failure to write, to marry, to live in town. Again we notice the closeness of the parallel between the uncle and the nephew. Thus when we recognize how in his failure Sorin has become a comic butt whether to the family or to the audience, we may see in Treplev's tantrums what he too could become. As yet Treplev is an object of pathos and Sorin is on the point of death, the image of senile frustration; if we guess that the young man will not allow himself to descend to Sorin's state of despair, it will only underline the pathos behind the comedy of age. However, what is acceptable in the young may not be so in the old, and Dorn's sharp but realistic comment marks the difference between the two: 'To be expressing dissatisfaction with life at sixty-two is really ungracious, you know.' It is worse than expressing dissatisfaction at twenty-two. Yet is there a difference in despair?

Treplev wanders in slowly, and Masha looks up. The stage is still, and we listen to the rain. Chekhov turns the conversation casually to Nina, whose history remains unexplained. He is clumsy in passing information to the audience with another character as reporter, especially in the middle of the action. But after the two year lapse of time and in Nina's absence, it must be done and only Treplev can do it. This in itself is awkward, since his feeling for Nina requires his reticence, not his volubility. He tells of the new Nina at some length. Trigorin gave her a child, which has since died. When he left her, she went on the stage. Her appearances in the theatre were a disaster and her acting was tasteless. Finally, she returned to the lake, but her father and stepmother refused to see her. This sordid tale has been told in letters to Treplev, letters in which Nina always signed herself 'The Seagull'. Although Treplev says that she will not come to the house, we are told that she has been seen nearby, so that we are left to expect her coming.[1]

In two years, each character has remained what he was, yet has changed to become more conclusively what he *is*. Furthermore, we see more clearly the connections between one character and another, while Nina's history by its vivid suggestion of suffering accentuates the passive, futile suffering of the rest. The lives of the people of *The Seagull*, we see, are fixed, caught in a trap of their own making.

The melancholy story of Nina has depressed the spirits of everyone on stage. With a typical shift of pace and tone, Shamraev's loud laugh is heard, and Arkadina bustles in with Trigorin and Shamraev in tow. Madame flamboyantly tosses off her clothes, examining herself in a mirror; she is as much the actress as ever.

---

[1] Stanislavsky's device for emphasizing the general response to Treplev's speech is very satisfying: 'Konstantin props his head up with his hands, his elbows resting on his knees. His gaze fixed steadily at one point. Dorn is rocking himself in the chair and, as Konstantin's story grows sadder and sadder, his rocking grows slower and slower, until at last, at the pause, he stops rocking himself altogether. The whole scene proceeds like that. All of them are motionless, as though frozen' (Balukhaty, p. 259). Pauses filled with the sounds of the night outside punctuate Treplev's speech and underscore its importance.

Act IV

As he pulls off his galoshes and shakes the rain from his coat, Shamraev's elegant compliment to her is, in its transparent emptiness, relevant to our impression of the group as a whole. 'We all grow old and dilapidated under the influence of the elements, while you, honoured lady, are still young . . . a light blouse, sprightliness, grace . . .' Arkadina's affectation of youth is seen as the sham it is by her response to such an unsubtle piece of flattery. But while she does not for a moment question its truth, even she is apprehensive of the ill-luck such light comments may bring. The same shadow lies over them all.

The mood is only superficially gay, for when Trigorin enters to greet the family after his long absence, we with our new knowledge about his affair with Nina are in the position of being able to watch the attitude of each member of the group beneath the pleasantries. Trigorin asks after Sorin's health; Sorin makes no reply. He asks whether Masha is happy; Masha makes no reply. It is in doubt whether these responses are snubs, or merely signs of defensiveness; they are probably both. Trigorin speaks to Treplev more hesitatingly, even though Arkadina has told him that the boy is no longer angry; Treplev at least offers his hand in answer. In warm response, Trigorin reports that questions are being asked about the new author, and he hands Treplev a copy of the magazine with his new story in it. So is it a fact that Treplev is a success at last? Again the audience may not be sure of the truth of what a Chekhovian character says, and in this case our doubts are confirmed when Treplev observes later that Trigorin has read his own story, but not even cut the pages of Treplev's.

We could also put that down to Trigorin's egotism. He had made an embarrassed circuit of the stage, and when he finally sits down, he announces that he cannot stay long: he is in a hurry to finish his novel: 'It's the old story, in fact.' As if Chekhov is reminding us of the state of the weather outside, Trigorin adds that, if the wind drops, he would like to go fishing. His mind has run off at a tangent, and inconsequentially he remarks that a visit to the lake will help him to recollect the circumstances of two years ago. Ah! so he has feelings about Nina after all. But it is 'for a story'. For Trigorin, it seems, everything, however momentous, may be reduced to fiction.

On the other side of the room, Masha is pleading with her father to let Medvedenko have a horse to get home; as we may expect, he finds an excuse to refuse her. In his gloomy voice, Medvedenko says he can walk – 'It's only four miles'. Polina's comment, 'Walk in such weather', together with her sigh, mixes sympathy, disdain and finally indifference as she settles down to the card-table. So poor Medvedenko, with a suppressed reference to the baby, must make his adieux a second time; he leaves shamefacedly. We shall not see him again, and he takes with him his loveless marriage; he is a man whose future is blasted through nobody's fault, unless his own.

Meanwhile the older people have set up a game of lotto.[1] Characteristically, this trivial pastime will be the foil for the final tragedy of Treplev as well as Chekhov's medium for the final review of the attitudes of the family. If the game seems rather hastily contrived after Trigorin's recent arrival, it is possibly Chekhov's most astutely comic piece of writing in the play. By bringing people together in a spirit inappropriate to the central issue of the play, the device foreshadows others like the carnival in *Three Sisters* and the ball in *The Cherry Orchard*. It even shares a quality found in the use of the old nursery furniture in *The Cherry Orchard*, since the game for Arkadina, like the room for Mme Ranevsky and Gaev, nostalgically intimates how one generation repeats the characteristics of another: 'Look, it's the same old lotto that we had when our mother used to play with us, when we were children.' The story of Treplev and Nina in *The Seagull* is, we see, just an episode in a much longer story. However, Arkadina's attempt to resurrect the past is not wholly successful. Her Kostya walks off, offering *en passant* a kiss on her head, a sign of both spontaneous affection and obvious rejection, as he lays down the magazine on the writing table.[2] His rejection of the game is a rejection of her attempts at appeasement. A moment later, his melancholy waltz is heard again from the adjoining room.

So Arkadina, Trigorin, Dorn, Masha, Shamraev and Polina begin their frivolous amusement as the faint sounds of the music of tragedy are heard, their voices in ugly contrast with its feeling. They play a complete hand, and as the excitement of the draw increases the tempo of the action, we hear the dissonance. Arkadina

[1] Lotto is a game of chance played almost universally. As in a *lottery*, numbers are drawn at random and players accordingly cover the squares on a grid. Known also as keno, bolito, house, bingo, etc.

[2] Stanislavsky had him throw it down (Balukhaty, p. 269).

speaks gaily, Masha with false abandon,[1] Dorn indifferently, Shamraev heatedly. Just as Gaev of *The Cherry Orchard* will be called upon to utter his series of billiards' terms, words meaningless in themselves can be full of significance for the way in which they are spoken. Between the calls, the passion of the melancholy piano and the storm outside makes its ironic comment on the shallow lives of those on stage.

Madame nominates the stake; we observe that littleness of spirit in her again when we see how the great actress likes to play for money. Moreover, in the same breath she asks Dorn to place her stake for her. As banker, Masha draws the numbers, and with a gaiety of affected indifference calls them out faster and faster – 'Eight! Eighty-one! Ten!' – so that her father must ask her to slow down. Arkadina, hardly concentrating on her card, suddenly speaks of the reception she received in Harkov, the ovation, the flowers, the wreaths, and the gift of a brooch, which she lays on the table. This brooch is a momentary distraction from the game, and the practical Shamraev is impressed by its value. But Masha and her numbers call them all to order: 'Fifty!' Polina seems to have been having no luck, and as she waits she remarks Treplev's piano and echoes its mood when her thoughts stray to herself and her Mashenka: 'He is depressed, poor fellow.' Whereupon Shamraev adds that 'he is awfully abused in the newspapers': is this, then, nearer the truth about his success as an author? Trigorin seems to confirm our idea that he was lying before by his comment on the boy's work, 'There is always something queer and vague, at times almost like delirium.' And he adds, 'Not a single living character'. We notice that he echoes Nina's first judgment without knowing it. However, it is just like Trigorin to talk shop and take a purely technical view of writing without much thought for the writer. So the game goes on, each player speaking casually, while his words reveal that he is really talking for himself alone. Here is a stage image of community and separation, of triviality and tragedy, in a simple, unified composition. Chekhov's well-known observation is apt to the intentions of this episode: 'It is necessary that on the stage everything should be as complex and as simple as in life. People are having dinner,

[1] Stanislavsky suggests a 'bored', 'monotonous', 'dead' voice for Masha, but the evidence of the speed of her calls belies this.

and while they're having it, their future happiness may be decided or their lives may be about to be shattered.[1]

A grunt from Sorin, and we look to see that he has fallen asleep. His snores, together with the notes of the piano, the rain at the window and the calls from the table, make up a regular cacophony. After an interval of time, Dorn in an afterthought speaks in support of Treplev's writing: 'There is something in him! He thinks in images . . . The only pity is that he has not got definite aims.' Dorn is a neutral judge. By now we may have concluded from the two writers' respective approaches to their art that it is Trigorin who has no confidence and Treplev who has too much. In the play, these moments of complete seriousness from the Doctor supply a quiet island of normality in order that the audience may assess the ineptitude of the rest; they also extend his general position, that a work of art ought to express a great idea (Act I) and that human life must be treated seriously (Act II). So he arrives at the particular point: is Arkadina glad that her son is a writer?

MADAME ARKADIN. Only fancy, I have not read anything of his yet. I never have time.
MASHA. Twenty-six!

Masha's cry comes like an ironic laugh – the lady has time enough for lotto. At the same moment, the audience notices that the music has stopped and Treplev has wandered in. Did he hear his mother's crushing remark?

In his blustering way, Shamraev unwittingly aims another blow at the pale, silent young man. On his last visit two years before, had not Trigorin asked Shamraev to have the shot seagull stuffed? Trigorin ponders a while; 'I don't remember! . . . I don't remember!' The effect is neat. This seagull, we recall (Act II), was to be the kernel of the story he wanted to write about Nina, a point he had so carefully noted in his book, the very essence of that day at the lake he now wishes to revive. Yet he has forgotten it: as casually, it is suggested, has he forgotten Nina's young life and ruined her happiness. For such a man, the minutes matter too much, while the days are forgotten. Again Masha's call falls like a criticism, and Treplev breaks his silence as he opens the window and the weather beats in: 'I don't know why I feel so uneasy.' At

[1] Quoted in Magarshack, p. 118. Also in Jackson, p. 73.

this point, the game stops short, for Trigorin has won: 'The game is mine!' Trigorin wins the games of chance or love; he makes no effort, nor does he care.[1] If Arkadina is piqued, it is amid a chorus of 'Bravo!'s that they wake Sorin and all troop off to supper. Treplev is left alone at his desk, aware of the world's indifference.

In a corner of the stage, Treplev scratches a moment or two with his pen, and then reads to himself what he has written. We listen to the noise of hollow chatter at the supper-table offstage. We understand the boy's isolation as we share his solitude. In the nineteenth-century way, Chekhov is preparing us for a soliloquy, for it is no part of the playwright's intention to keep us in suspense over the final stage of Treplev's feelings about his mother, Trigorin, Nina and his own career. The soliloquy falls quite naturally as he discusses the manuscript before him in dialogue with himself, and if Chekhov's first audience expected an onset of melodramatic flourishes from the hero before the curtain fell, it may have been surprised at the dramatic understatement it got. The young man merely goes over his new piece of writing, scratching out the clichés, screwing up a page, attempting to control loose thinking. Treplev's agonizing at his desk supplies the visible image of Trigorin's account to Nina of his creative pains in Act II. There the older man saw himself 'eating up my own life . . . for the sake of the honey', and 'stripping the pollen from my best flowers, tearing up the flowers themselves and trampling on their roots'.[2] Here the younger man demonstrates how one must destroy to create, and reject to accept. The business of living must involve choice and loss. Soon we shall see him *'tearing up all his manuscripts'*. Emotionally, the stage is quiescent, and the sequence offers the actor a delicate, thoughtful mime from which his speech arises smoothly.

I will begin where the hero is awakened by the patter of the rain, and throw out all the rest. The description of the moonlight evening is long and overelaborate. Trigorin has worked out methods for himself, it's

---

[1] In his production at the New Theatre, London, in 1936, Theodore Komisarjevsky saw Trigorin more kindly, as reported by Sir John Gielgud: 'In the last act Komis saw him as a tragic figure, aware of the disaster he has brought about, sorry for Konstantin (whose talent he recognizes as more important than his own), rather ashamed of his own return to Arcádina, and genuinely moved and horrified by the death of her son at the end of the play' (*Early Stages*, London, 1953, pp. 297–8).
[2] See p. 55, above.

easy for him now . . . . With him the broken bottle neck glitters on the dam and the mill-wheel casts a black shadow – and there you have the moonlight night, while I have the tremulous light, and the soft twinkling of the stars, and the far-away strains of the piano dying away in the still fragrant air . . . . It's agonizing (*a pause*).[1]

It is as if Chekhov himself were saying, Do not assume my character's state of mind to be a theatrical stereotype, an overelaborate cliché; my Treplev is as individual and particular as he tries to make his ideas. The struggle to create is the struggle to recognize the aptness and strength of individual people and particular behaviour, for only these can speak persuasively to an audience. As for the author, whether novelist or playwright, he must 'write because it springs freely from his soul'; the truth cannot run to a formula, and one's philosophy of literature is essentially no different from one's philosophy of life. However, there is one more trial awaiting Treplev. He hears a tap on the window and he peers into the garden, while the wind gusts in and howls with new vigour.

As the company in the next room laughs and shouts (an effect partly comic, partly harrowing, which Chekhov employs again with more subtlety in *Three Sisters*, Act I, and *The Cherry Orchard*, Act III), the long-suffering Nina is to be presented for a last time. She has presumably come in the half hopes of testing her own feelings for Trigorin by being near him, even of testing *his* feelings

---

[1] Chekhov is reproducing material he used in his story *The Wolf*, published on 17 March 1886 (see D. Magarshack, *Chekhov: A Life*, London, 1952, p. 422), and explained in a letter to his brother Alexander of 10 May 1886:

'In my opinion a true description of Nature should be very brief and have a character of relevance. Commonplaces such as, "the setting sun bathing in the waves of the darkening sea, poured its purple gold, etc." – "the swallows flying over the surface of the water twittered merrily" – such commonplaces one ought to abandon. In descriptions of Nature one ought to seize upon the little particulars, grouping them in such a way that, in reading, when you shut your eyes, you get a picture.

'For instance, you will get the full effect of a moonlight night if you write that on the mill-dam a little glowing star-point flashed from the neck of a broken bottle, and the round, black shadow of a dog, or a wolf, emerged and ran, etc. Nature becomes animated if you are not squeamish about employing comparisons of her phenomena with ordinary human activities, etc.

'In the sphere of psychology, details are also the thing. God preserve us from commonplaces. Best of all is it to avoid depicting the hero's state of mind; you ought to try to make it clear from the hero's actions' (Friedland, pp. 70–1).

Although this passage is about writing stories, it closely characterizes Chekhov's technique in the writing of dialogue for characterization on the stage as well.

for *her* one last time. She has come through the garden from the lake, and she has seen Treplev's stage standing derelict, a melancholy reminder of their young ambitions and of what they shared before they separated. She sobs on Treplev's breast, afraid that anyone should discover her until he props a chair against the door that divides them from the family, afraid that Treplev may reject her as her parents have. In a strange state of distraction, a mood that lends a strangely unnatural air to the scene, she quotes Turgenev's lines on the pathos of the homeless. In an obtrusive passage, rather mechanically managed by Chekhov, she repeatedly speaks of herself as a seagull, and repeatedly rubs her forehead with a 'That's not it', almost like a symptom of mental derangement, or semi-delirium. Tomorrow she must go as an actress to Yelets, a small provincial town two hundred miles south of Moscow, travelling 'third-class . . . with peasants'. There she will be pestered by the 'local business-men'.[1] She is the picture of despair at this point: she seems less of a great actress like Arkadina than he an author like Trigorin. But in spite of Treplev's pleas as he smothers her hand in kisses, she prepares to go, giving him no answer. It is one of the most affecting moments in Chekhov.[2]

When Nina hears Trigorin's laugh from the next room, her distraction grows worse. She now knows there is nothing to hope for from him, and that there is no point in staying. But knowing that he is in the house leads her to tell her version of life with the great man. 'He did not believe in the stage.' This reveals to us, at least, his emptiness. She speaks like a dead thing, and we may make our estimate of her unhappiness and his integrity as a practising playwright from this. 'He always laughed at my dreams and little by little I left off believing in it too . . .' So she lost her ability to act. However, since Trigorin left her, she has been recovering her faith in herself: 'In our work – in acting or writing – what matters is not fame, not glory, not what I dreamed of, but knowing how to be patient.' With experience can come wisdom, and Nina's story in the end is the least pessimistic of them all.[3] She offers a muted hope. She will be like Arkadina again in the sense

[1] Hingley's translation, vol. II, p. 279.
[2] Cf. Stanislavsky: 'Nina wipes her tears with a handkerchief and smothers her sobs. Konstantin stands motionless, glass in hand, leaning against the lamp-post, staring lifelessly at one point. This is where he really dies' (Balukhaty, p. 279). Arguably, 'where he really dies' must come when Nina says that she still loves Trigorin.
[3] And in danger of being treated as a lesson in courage and optimism in later M.A.T.

that she is determined to be a success if she can, but she also has been purified by the experience of the play and has reached a more disinterested dedication to her vocation.

Chekhov, however, will not allow the end of this affair between Nina and Trigorin to be conventional; nature will still play its tricks. So we are surprised when Nina declares that she still loves Trigorin: 'I love him passionately, I love him to despair.' Explain that if we can. For Treplev, this is the last blow, but in Nina herself it is a sure sign of depth and sincerity. In telling him, she means it kindly, to make him shake loose; for in the last two years he has attached to her some of his dependence upon his mother. So she wants him to be a man and tells him she is beyond his reach; and it kills him. Chekhov, with his simple, familiar image, recalls where the real values lie in the relationship between the sexes: the man and the girl had 'feelings like tender, exquisite flowers'. Nina is now a mature woman, even though we see her still as a victim of the predatory needs of another. Chekhov makes the point in neat, theatrical terms by having her recite the opening speech from Treplev's play; we remember that in shame she had refused Masha her request to quote from the play two years before. Now, although sometimes struggling with her emotion in recalling the occasion, Nina speaks the lines spontaneously and with an assurance we did not hear on Treplev's stage in Act I. It is a new Nina. Before, her simpler, hesitant, mechanical rendering reduced the words almost to nonsense; now, the 'cycle of sorrow' matches her experience as well as our sense of Chekhov's mood, and, astonishingly, Treplev's supernatural portrait of a desolate world rings true.[1]

Treplev's 'Won't you stay and have some supper?' is his last hope of keeping her. But she has no intention of playing the role of mother to him; she is her own woman, and she has already made her decision. Stanislavsky had her speak the whole of her last speech standing at the open French window, so that her recital of

revivals (see G. Tovstonogov, 'Chekhov's *Three Sisters* at the Gorky Theatre' in *The Drama Review*, vol. 13, no. 2, New York, Winter 1968, p. 148).

[1] James Agate, reviewing the production at the Little Theatre, London, 19 October 1925, regarded Nina's recital of the lines from the play as an echo of a former 'rehearsal' the two young people might have had. 'Disaster has come upon her, and upon him is the full sense of failure; yet for a moment they touch something for which there is no name – a recollection of earlier happiness' (*The Contemporary Theatre, 1925*, London, 1926, p. 86).

Treplev's words from the play was spoken with an eerie finality against the howling wind and the rain. To this is added the same distant tolling of a church-bell his audience heard during the performance in the garden in Act I. As Stanislavsky's Nina left, the window slammed violently, and at the same time he had a pane of glass smash to mark the culmination of a highly charged scene. To this he also added the laughter from the next room, and, still not content, he had Treplev let fall the glass of water from his hand.[1] From the paucity of his stage directions, one might think that what Chekhov really intended was an understatement to counterpoint the highly wrought feelings of the young people.

Nina's strength emphasizes Treplev's weakness. When she has gone, he stands a moment in silence. 'It will be a pity if someone meets her in the garden and tells mother. It may upset mother . . .' This is spoken, not in sarcasm, but in concern. The lines are a final confirmation of his obsession with his mother and his need of her love, even in death. It is as if Treplev, unlike Nina, has not grown taller from his experience of suffering. In silence he *'spends two minutes'* tearing up his manuscripts, an exceptionally long time on the stage for such business, but no doubt Chekhov intends us to see this tearing up of his precious writing as the echo of the tearing of flowers.[2] The violence of the act suggests his old childishness. His writing was to have won admiration, or to prove something about himself, but no one shall have it now. Did he ever have intrinsic respect for it? He leaves through the door in the set that has not yet been used; he has first to unlock it, and by this Chekhov means us to see that he is not returning to the piano.

The stage is painfully empty for a space, while we guess what the boy is doing. Then we hear Dorn struggling briefly at the barricaded door, and when he finds the chair there, he seems to know what has been going on. So the family returns from supper bringing their drinks, talking gaily, keen to resume the game of lotto. The action will seem to run on as before, with the same reminiscences, the same triviality. Unexpectedly, however, Shamraev takes from the cupboard the seagull he has had stuffed

[1] Balukhaty, p. 283.
[2] During the long pause, Stanislavsky has Treplev tearing up his work with great deliberation and then burning the scraps in the stove and watching the flames rise. He returns to his desk and also burns a bundle of letters. All this before he 'ponders for a second, looks round the room once more – and walks out thoughtfully, unhurriedly' (Balukhaty, p. 283).

and shows it to Trigorin – and to us.[1] The beautiful bird now looks appallingly dead. Trigorin looks at it, and repeats those terrifying words: 'I don't remember it . . . I don't remember.'

The long expected shot is heard offstage. As if he has been aware of the meeting between the boy and the girl and of its meaning, the Doctor allays the fears of the others by suggesting that one of his medicine bottles has exploded. It reminds Arkadina of Treplev's previous attempt on his life. Like the guardian of their well-being, Dorn leaves to find out what has really happened. He comes back humming. With seeming nonchalance, he turns over the leaves of a magazine while taking Trigorin aside downstage; Trigorin is the only person he can trust. He whispers to him to take Arkadina away: 'The fact is, Konstantin Gavrilitch has shot himself.' Treplev destroyed his manuscripts and has now destroyed himself. He wants to hurt his mother intolerably: it is the childish threat finally carried out. Perhaps he had been only playing the first time, expecting to be snatched back and bandaged. Now he will really give pain. The curtain falls slowly just as Masha is preparing to call the numbers for a new hand of lotto. The understatement is complete.[2]

'Well, I have finished the play,' wrote Chekhov in a letter to Suvorin.[3] 'I began it *forte* and ended it *pianissimo* – contrary to all the rules of dramatic art.' The death of the white seagull, free and happy by its lake, has prefigured the pattern of destruction and is intended to reflect on them all. Treplev dies; only Nina lives on in hope, but with the burden of her memories; Arkadina, Trigorin and the rest embody a death of the spirit – is there a difference? We may decide whether the only 'cure' is valerian drops.

[1] It is not clear from Chekhov's stage directions whether the audience is intended to be aware of the stuffed bird in the cupboard throughout the act. Nor does Stanislavsky clarify the point. Its visible presence would add an irony to the activities at the card-table before supper, and a special poignancy to the parting of Nina and Treplev, although it would add also to the artificiality and obviousness of the symbol.

[2] From an extreme example of misinterpretation, Sidney Lumet's film of the play (1969), in which David Warner played Treplev, ended with a sight of his bloodstained corpse floating in the lake.

[3] 21 November 1895, in Friedman, p. 146. Also in Hingley, vol. II, p. 334.

Uncle Vanya Act I

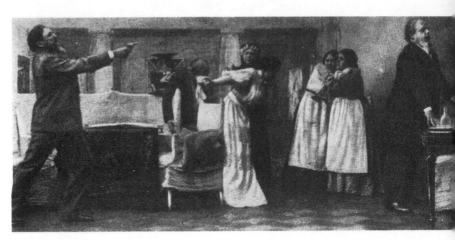

Uncle Vanya Act III

Uncle Vanya Act IV

Uncle Vanya

Scenes from Country Life in Four Acts

1897

Uncle Vanya

ಐಐಐಐಐಐಐಐಐಐಐಐಐಐಐಐಐಐಐಐಐಐಐಐಐಐಐಐಐಐಐಐಐ

There is a clarity of vision in *Uncle Vanya* not present in *The Seagull*. The broad divisions between the generations in *The Seagull* invited moral judgments too easily; in *Uncle Vanya*, Chekhov risks the comfort of his audience in teaching them to understand his characters without sentimentality, to recognize individuality. He pursues this purpose with a precision and honesty which subjects him as a playwright to a fiercer discipline, and his dramaturgy to a radical reform. The uncertain response of the first Moscow audiences to the play testifies to the extremes to which Chekhov now goes in reducing conventional theatricality.

Working over his own material in *The Wood Demon* of 1889, Chekhov deliberately evokes a tawdry, provincial world, with mostly trivial, mediocre people living in it. It is rural Russia again, but this time wholly without glamour. Chekhov subtitles his play *Scenes from Country Life*, a title borrowed from Alexander Ostrovsky. In fact, *Uncle Vanya* in 1897 takes a big step towards realizing the naturalistic ideal of drama as documentary, one which neither Ibsen nor Strindberg chose to take. In letting actuality seem to speak for itself, Chekhov also makes a clean break with the Russian tradition of didactic purpose in writing for the stage. Unlike *The Seagull*, the play has no obvious centre in a great actress or a famous novelist or a would-be poet; in *Uncle Vanya*, Chekhov appears to adopt the role of social historian of his times, presenting a general picture of the absentee middle-class land-owner and his dispossessed counterpart (Serebryakov and Telyegin); he seems to criticize the intelligentsia of late nineteenth-century Russia as academic and effete (Astrov, Serebryakov and Mrs Voynitsky); and refuses to romanticize the household peasantry (Marina the nurse). Thus some of the sources of unrest in the unhappy reign of Tsar Alexander III up to the revolution of 1905 appear in this play, as in *The Cherry Orchard*, to be Chekhov's target. Needless to say, to think like this about the play is to belittle its real achievement.

The appearance of 'actuality' on the stage calls for a specially acute creative activity, designed to exhibit monotony without being monotonous, to work through finely particular details without losing the generality of statement. If the playwright aims to present the truths of a soul-destroying rural life, he must find a way to have the spectator discover them for himself. In the particular world Chekhov creates, *Uncle Vanya* all but completes the nineteenth-century movement towards naturalism in the theatre, and at the same time starts the trail of twentieth-century drama which leads to the many major sub-Chekhovian comedies like *Heartbreak House, Juno and the Paycock, The Iceman Cometh* and *The Glass Menagerie.*

The date of the play's composition is uncertain, and it may have been planned, even written, before *The Seagull*, although no doubt it profited from the stage experience of this play. Soon after it was published in 1897, it had several productions outside Moscow,[1] but it was first produced by the Moscow Art Theatre in 1899, after the long-established imperial Maly Theatre, to which Chekhov had promised it, had asked for changes to be made. The official literary committee which read all plays to be performed in a state theatre like the Maly had criticized it on grounds that, among other things, the longer speeches of Astrov and Sonya were boring and some of the scenes lacked realistic motivation. This criticism offers us some measure of the contemporary failure to understand what Chekhov was doing. The committee had its own notion of realism, and could not understand why Vanya should want to shoot the Professor in Act III: they considered that for Vanya to chase after him with a gun was 'irresponsible' and refused to see the play's internal necessity for such an explosion of feeling. The committee was applying social and not artistic standards of judgment.

When the Maly threw out the play, Chekhov was pleased to be able to gratify Nemirovich-Danchenko,[2] who had asked for a successor to *The Seagull* for the M.A.T. It had its first Art Theatre production with Stanislavsky playing Astrov and Olga Knipper (later to become Chekhov's wife) playing Yelena. At the M.A.T.,

[1] See Hingley, vol. III, p. 303.   [2] See Nemirovich-Danchenko, pp. 199–200.

the play did not have the immediate success of its predecessor, but Nemirovich-Danchenko reports that its popularity grew with the second season. It went into the permanent repertory of the theatre and became one of the best-loved of Chekhov's plays.

The Wood Demon had misfired ten years before at the Abramov Theatre in Moscow, and Chekhov had never allowed it to be published. It was a melodrama in which the Vanya-character (George Voynitsky) had shot *himself*, not the Professor, with fair theatrical panache in Act III (the action takes place offstage, but the family responds with running, shrieking and fainting). *The Seagull* had brought down its curtain with another offstage suicide. With *Uncle Vanya*, however, Chekhov had decided that 'in life people are not every minute shooting each other, hanging themselves, and making declarations of love. And they are not saying clever things every minute. For the most part, they eat, drink, hang about, and talk nonsense; and this must be seen on the stage'.[1] In a scene of farce the new Vanya shoots at the Professor, but he *misses*. In *The Wood Demon*, the actors and actresses were conventionally paired off before the final curtain. In *Uncle Vanya*, Sonya wants Astrov and is rejected. Vanya wants Yelena and does make a declaration of love, but is also rejected. At the curtain, nobody is allowed the oversimple satisfaction of death or marriage. These important changes point directly to the new qualities in *Uncle Vanya* as drama. Anticlimax and the denial of expectations become a finely tempered technique by which the audience's sense of truth to life is fostered and its objective frame of mind sustained. The refusal of theatrical sensationalism in the shooting episode and in the 'love scenes' is a way of indicating something beyond the theatre itself, a motioning towards an anti-romantic basis for the honest assessment of a real situation. *Uncle Vanya* is in fact made up of many scenes of comic perspective, scenes in which the audience is forced to react in self-contradiction. It is a great comedy of anticlimax.

The effect of anticlimax in the theatre denies, too, the propensity of the stage to preach at us, persuade us and comfort us with a sermon. *Uncle Vanya* instead taunts us with its maddening state of affairs, and then refuses to pass direct comment on what

---

[1] Quoted in Jackson, p. 73. Hingley helpfully lists the decline in the scenes of violence between *Platonov* and *The Cherry Orchard* in vol. II, pp. 2–3.

should be done about it. The future the playwright leaves to us. So when Vanya, the central character of the play, shoots at the man he loathes, the apparent source of all his woes, and misses him, the sensational non-sensationalism becomes a blatant way, not only of emphasizing the ineffectual conduct of Vanya, but also of testing the integrity of the audience watching him.

The feel of life results from such an inconclusive treatment of the action. Romantic Dr Astrov, taken from the title role of *The Wood Demon* (in which he appears under the name of Khrushchov) is moved aside from the centre of attention. Nor does he repeat the role of Dr Dorn of *The Seagull*. Although Astrov serves at times as *raisonneur*, and although his presence tends to redress the balance of comic sanity in scenes to which he is a witness, he, like the rest, is oppressed by thwarted ambitions that Dorn knew nothing of. More important, the clownish figure of Vanya ensures that at the heart of life in the play is someone quite mundane, average and mediocre, far less romantically charged than Konstantin Treplev. Hence we do not ask whether or not Vanya will win the lovely Yelena – we know from his first aggrieved words to her that this is dramatically impossible, and the thought never enters our heads – but we do ask *why he wants her*. We are permitted an understanding of him without sympathizing with his motives or desiring his success. He is altogether an uncomfortable anti-hero who offers no definitive values of right or wrong in the conduct and direction of a human life. Neither Astrov nor Vanya in the new arrangement, therefore, allows the audience to dwell in a world of romance.

If Chekhov recognized that his play could not convey a mood of frustration, claustrophobia and loneliness by theatrical sensationalism, the problem still remained to pass the experience of such desperation on to his audience. And so in *Uncle Vanya* he works towards his statement in a manner of which he had proved himself a master: through a host of unemphatic details. We shall see how, in the opening scene, for example, the heat of the day, the click of an old woman's needles, the peculiar pacing of a man, his broken speech, the mixture of the urgent and the trivial in his words, the tensions in a pause, are together able to make an impact of comic exasperation in the auditorium.

Tolstoy was quick to point out that it was Chekhov's fleeting impressions rather than the force of character or plot which did his work for him:

Chekhov, like the Impressionists, has a style all his own. At first glance it seems as if the painter h·.s merely daubed his canvas with any colour that came to hand, using no discrimination, so that his strokes do not appear to have any relationship. But as soon as one steps back and looks from a distance, one gets the remarkable impression of a colourful, irresistible painting.[1]

Doubtless Chekhov's early training as a writer of hundreds of short stories for the St Petersburg weekly *Fragments*, for which its editor N. A. Leikin insisted upon a maximum length of a thousand words, forced him into the brevity of a highly selective impressionistic method.[2] Just as Treplev in Act IV of *The Seagull* wanted to prune his flowery language,[3] Chekhov was constantly advising others to adopt a simple, glancing style of description: 'To emphasize the poverty of a beggarwoman it is not necessary to speak of her miserable appearance, it is enough to remark *in passing* that she wore an old rusty cloak . . . A single detail is enough.'[4] Thus in *Uncle Vanya*, the Mother's preoccupation with her pamphlets, or the Nurse's concern for her samovar, tell us much of the routine of these good ladies' lives. In turn, such trivialities tell us how insufferable is the environment of Vanya and Sonya. Multiply these a hundredfold, and we have a measure of the quality of the country life in Chekhov's portrait.

Yet moodiness tips easily into melodrama, and having worked hard for a many-faceted precision in the dominant state of mind of his group, Chekhov finds also that he must hold the balance against over-emotionality. His protests to Stanislavsky against over-acting increase, and their reiteration is in part a confession of failure to ballast his vehicle adequately with elements of comedy. The outstanding instances of this are the scenes of parting between Yelena and Astrov, and Sonya and Astrov, in Act IV.[5] Seven years later, in *The Cherry Orchard*, he has less need to insist that the true tragedy of an individual occurs internally, not externally, and by the time of this last play he has learned the art

[1] Quoted in M. Slonim, *From Chekhov to the Revolution: Russian Literature, 1900–1917* (New York, 1962), p. 74.
[2] See Valency, p. 53.   [3] See pp. 83–4, above.
[4] Letter to I. L. Shcheglov, quoted in Valency, p. 61.
[5] See pp. 134–6 and 138–9, below.

of reducing emotionality by juxtaposing incongruous actions, and thus inducing the detachment of his audience. 'One ought not to be afraid of the farcical in a play, but moralizing in it is abominable.'[1] Here and there in *Uncle Vanya*, Chekhov can be found inserting into his text elements of control characteristic of farce, as when Vanya, clutching his bunch of roses in Act III, comes upon Astrov in an embrace with Yelena. This interruption of a stolen kiss is in the best tradition of Labiche and Feydeau. But in *Uncle Vanya*, he has not yet altogether made the delicate distinction between the laughter of the ridiculous and the smiles of satirical irony.

Although one still finds in *Uncle Vanya* a tendency to structure the action upon a series of duologues as in *The Seagull*, upon 'contests' between characters, Chekhov is beginning to show his unique ability to *pattern* those characters so that by groups they suggest the forces acting upon individual lives: we look beyond their differences to what they have in common. Circumstances overwhelm all the characters in this play and they all reveal weakness of personality and an inability to cope with circumstances, displaying a terrifying average of failure in work or in love. Yet together the characters supply a full dramatic life for the stage because each *group* is discernibly pulling in opposite directions. The main characters are clearly opposed as forces affirming and denying human vitality. In areas of personal power and sexual domination, of material and emotional tyranny, the Professor and his wife – without in any way becoming stereotypes of male and female villainy – are destructive in their selfish inertia. They bear down upon Astrov, Sonya and Vanya, the only ones with a desire for redemption, and deny them their birthright. The dichotomy between such negative and positive forces is as yet too tidy, but the presence of the more passive group, the unlovely chorus of Maman, Waffles and the Nurse, blurs at the edges the moralism implicit in the contrast.

The tragic undertow of this dramatic patterning is not finally allowed to endanger the comedy, with the exception of the pathos in Sonya, which Chekhov surprisingly leaves undiluted. Through our mixed response to cynic and buffoon, our sympathies are kept

[1] Reported by A. Gurlyand and quoted in Simmons, p. 190.

at bay, and by retaining the constant interplay of discords in the life of the family, which had proved itself well as a dramatic method in *The Seagull*, Chekhov asserted an active theatrical principle of humorous comedy. Every discord is the author's ironic nudge to invite a wry smile. At the crisis, when the Professor proposes to sell the estate, each member of the family is facing in a different direction, each is in pursuit of his own ends, and coming from the whole group, the mixed reactions to the shocking announcement are more amusing than painful. Maurice Valency offers the intriguing theory that N. A. Leikin's requirement of only light and humorous stories for his weekly paper trained Chekhov early in his career to transmute even his sad and serious ideas into comic ones:

He taught himself to look for what was humorous in the pathetic, for the grotesque in the tragic, for the wry comment with which one could redeem a lapse into sentiment. In this stern school, his tales acquired a characteristic outline, and for the rest of his life, brevity, humour, and self-restraint defined his style. In after years he was often surprised to find that what he thought was funny was considered by others to be tragic: this discrepancy in attitude was the source of infinite misunderstanding when he came to deal with such resolute intermediaries as Stanislavsky and Nemirovich-Danchenko.[1]

This ingenious argument, however, suggests that Chekhov's ambivalent attitude to life was no more than a characteristic of style, and is too simple an explanation of his complexity.

In the end Chekhov leaves the spectator's own insight to unify the disparate elements of the piece. By comparison with *The Seagull*, *Uncle Vanya*'s plotting is uncomplicated, and a simple arrival-and-departure structure again provides a framework for the action. But this simplicity does not lend the play any quality of conclusiveness, and it is very much in doubt whether, as some have maintained,[2] Vanya, Sonya and Astrov are seen to grow from ignorance to self-knowledge. It is more true to say that it is the spectator who receives his education at their hands: the inconclusive ending calls for completion in the mind of the audience.

[1] Valency, p. 54.
[2] See E. R. Bentley, *In Search of Theater* (New York, 1954), p. 347. Bentley had seen the Old Vic Company's production of John Burrell at the New Theatre, London, in 1945.

For Act IV closes on a wholly reflective curtain, anticlimactic in spirit, one belonging to *'an autumn evening and very quiet'*. After the explosion of Act III, this tone is maintained throughout the act, and Sonya's final assertions, far from being a prophetic, optimistic and uplifting expression of hope and faith, are shot through with the implicit doubts of one who seeks to console herself for her servile mortality with the merest intimations of immortality.[1] In a context of Chekhovian irony, broad moralistic assertions, like those of Vershinin, Tusenbach and Trofimov later, are always deliciously suspect. In *Uncle Vanya*, Act IV, the weight of the play denies Sonya her faith before she opens her mouth. Chekhov offers us only a final quizzical portrait of waste and frustration, and refuses to resolve the problem he raises. As Vanya buries his tears in his account books, and Sonya repeats her refrain, 'We shall rest', we also see and hear their environment as it was in the beginning, indifferent to their troubles: the watchman tapping, Waffles strumming on his guitar, two old women knitting and scribbling; and the Russian winter has returned. When Vanya weeps, he is reflecting Sonya's despair *in spite of* the fine words she is uttering. Chekhov's 'scenes from country life' are more than an economic and social survey of rural Tsarist Russia, more than a moralistic documentary on the salvation of the soul; rather they are an appallingly intimate study of the chasm that may at any time open up between human hopes and the naked reality.

[1] See Magarshack, pp. 223–5, and Simmons, p. 487, for the opposite view on Sonya's curtain speech. The impact of this speech is further discussed on pp. 139 ff. below.

Act One

A sultry garden by a ramshackle old house sets the scene. The thick atmosphere will hang heavily about each character as he is introduced. A table is set for tea, and the time of day is thus proposed, but the table and its samovar lack all human animation. *'Not far from the table there is a swing'*, but the swing, too, is waiting for someone to grace it, and it hangs there like an unfulfilled promise. Straining against the silence on the stage, the audience also waits.

There is suspense in the waiting, but, unlike the opening of *The Cherry Orchard*, it is a suspense without excitement; indeed, this opening smacks of *anticlimax*, for the action progresses towards no evident objective. Two people are moving, but moving quite monotonously. Marina, an old nurse, is knitting beside the samovar, and in the silence we may hear the click of her needles, regular, unhurried, finally irritating. Marina was not present in *The Wood Demon*, and she is introduced into *Uncle Vanya* for a reason. She in part embodies the concept of the idealized *muzhik*, the peasantry, 'the people', with their mystical ability to endure all vicissitudes and to sacrifice themselves and above all 'to love' (*lyubit*). We shall see how Marina's passivity and constancy in affection in this play are set against the educated, 'Westernized' intellectuals like Professor Serebryakov, Uncle Vanya himself and, here, Dr Astrov with their inability 'to love'. At the same time, the old Nurse is not the dear old soul, the romanticized peasant, of a hundred stories and plays of the period, but *a heavy old woman*, slow of body and thick of head. In her colourless grey dress and with her humped figure, she is the visual representation of rural Russian lassitude. Chekhov modifies the sentimental image by stressing her negative piety. She knits on with her fat fingers.

Slowly pacing the stage before her is Dr Astrov, his hands thrust in his pockets or clasped behind him to suggest at once his

99

torpor and his suppressed vigour. By the knitting and the pacing, Chekhov ordains the sluggish tempo of the overture to his act, and asserts its peculiar tension. This tension is stretched until, without a word, Marina at last stops her knitting, pours a glass of tea and invites the Doctor to drink it as if she were comforting a child. By this action, the servant does her duty and the tense man finds an excuse for speech, even if it is heard only by her dull old ears.

For the audience it is a deflationary opening indeed. Astrov takes the glass reluctantly, for his thoughts are on matters more profound and he is not interested in drinking anything. Immediately Marina mistakes the reason for his reluctance, and, evidently knowing his habits, offers him vodka instead. Their broken remarks prepare us for the question which plumbs his thoughts. 'Nurse, how many years have we known each other?' This sudden utterance has a middle-aged ring. Time, its passing, growing old, nothing to show for his labours – weighty matters like these have been troubling him, and while the old woman fumbles uncertainly in her memory as old people do, Astrov is too ready with his next question: 'Have I changed much since then?' But he is not ready for the cruel honesty of her answer. 'Very much. You were young and handsome in those days, and now you have grown older. And you are not so good-looking.' Nobody wants to hear this kind of truth. However, its frankness matches his mood, and he accepts it. With no more prompting than this, he plunges into his most morbid sentiments.

Astrov's first major speech is like a prologue, embracing all the major themes of the play. In a personal, not abstract, way, however, it runs over the dry business of living, the shock of change, the misery of blunted ideals and the mortification of un-satisfying human relationships. All this is particularized by Astrov's experiences as a country doctor. His acid comment on life as 'tedious, stupid, dirty' expresses the vexation of a man who admits to having been turned into 'a queer fish' by disgust at his sordid work. No doubt Chekhov is recalling his own life as a country doctor in the district near Melikhovo, the farm he bought in 1892, and the account of Astrov's weariness – always on his feet, always being dragged out of bed by a patient – smacks of actuality. The epidemic of typhus at Malitskoye, the filth and stench in the village huts, people and cattle living together, the death of a patient under chloroform and Astrov's sense of guilt as the doctor responsible, are all accurate reporting.[1] But we know from the style of Astrov's complaints that they are symptoms only of a greater malaise, and his blunted feelings are a result of a lack of a particular objective, indeed, the lack of human love: 'There is ... no one I am fond of.' This confession is both climactic and bathetic together. Chekhov's familiar double ironies are at work again. No audience can receive so early an outburst of *taedium vitae* at face value. The breaks and hesitations which precede its delivery also diminish its force as truth. When at the height of expressing his feelings of disgust with life Astrov twists his moustache and notices with self-mockery the neglected growth of drooping hair on his face, it is as if a silly thing like a moustache can take on an animation of its own like an object in a play by Harold Pinter. The Doctor's monologue, moreover, becomes surprisingly real for the triviality of the detail, and the spectator is delighted to spy a little of the clown behind this morose man, and a sly sense of humour in his flash of self-amusement.

We shall learn more about him than he can tell us. If Astrov is a failure, he had the makings of something better. He is superior to Vanya, and it is significant that Yelena has her head a little turned by him and that the sensitive Sonya loves him. He works hard, is intelligent and has genuine ideals. His is a case of what provincial life can do to a man who might flourish in another setting. If he could have loved Sonya, they could have been happy; that he cannot love her is an example of the pure arbitrariness of life.

As a monologue, we may think Astrov's speech somewhat old-fashioned upon the new naturalistic stage. But it works easily just because the Nurse is present as an apparent listener. The heaviness of the afternoon seems to draw out a confession, and the old woman seems a suitable substitute for an imperturbable confessor. The presence of Marina also ensures that the spectator hears

[1] M. Slonim describes the years preceding the composition of the play: 'Of nine million peasant households, two and a half million did not possess so much as a horse. A great many of the poorer peasants were slaving as farm hands at very low wages, or struggling on their tiny holdings. The agrarian crisis was aggravated by the drop of prices on the world wheat market, and the low level of husbandry turned droughts or poor crops into catastrophes for vast regions. In 1891-2 a famine spread over an area with thirty-five million inhabitants. Hundreds of thousands of peasants perished from starvation and epidemics of typhus and cholera.' (*From Chekhov to the Revolution: Russian Literature, 1900-1917,* New York, 1962, p. 13.)

Astrov's exasperation through her imperturbable ears, and sufficiently completes the circuit of comedy to modulate the impact of his overwrought speech into laughter. In addition, the poignancy of his complaint against life and the passing of time is neatly turned by the Nurse herself. She will be no audience for him, as she quickly makes clear. His longing for human affection is comically greeted with, 'Perhaps you would like something to eat?' Astrov may love her as a child loves its old nurse, but he has no wish to be pacified like a child. He becomes conscious, as we do, that he is dramatizing his despair too much, and this impression is confirmed later when he makes more positive speeches. His egotism is deflated, and he knows it. The vehemence of his fear that most human effort will in the end be forgotten is killed by the apathy behind the dried religious fatalism with which the Nurse comforts herself: 'God will remember.' This is the sentiment which will be echoed by Sonya with comparable irony at the end of the play. Astrov half glimpses the old woman's comfort, and entertains it for a moment: it almost comforts him. But he is not to be a tragic hero, and his now toneless voice betrays the hurt in his reply: 'Thank you for that. That's a good saying.' Amen.

The Wood Demon was named after the Astrov character, but *Uncle Vanya* is named after a far less stable hero.[1] That 'hero', Ivan Petrovitch Voynitsky, now makes his entrance. However, Vanya's is anything but a star entrance; rather, it is a deliberate hit at one of the theatre's most cherished conventions. '*He has had a nap after lunch and looks rumpled*', reads Chekhov's naughty stage direction. His irritable, yawning posture as he slumps in the chair in front of Astrov with legs spread-eagled, accurately reflects in one gesture the mood already established, but it adds to it a comic element only hinted at before by Astrov's moustache, Marina's knitting, her glasses of tea and her simple piety. Vanya is the picture of a bungler and a buffoon, without being unbalanced by a distortion of feature or behaviour. He must of course be something more than a fool, or his story will not hurt, and what he says identifies immediately the source of his irritation. 'Ever since the Professor and his wife have been here our life has been turned topsy-turvy.'

[1] 'Chekhov deliberately drops from his masthead the evocative *demon* in favour of the utterly banal *uncle*. If the name Vanya sounds exotic to non-Russian ears, one has to know that it is the equivalent of Jack.' (E. R. Bentley, *In Search of Theater*, New York, 1954, p. 349, footnote.)

Noticeably, his instinct, like Astrov's, is to make a comparison with the old days. What things are today are never what one hoped they would be. Yet again Chekhov slants the sentiment towards laughter with the help of the old woman whose ministrations at the samovar, part of her own sedate routine, have also been upset. Nevertheless, Vanya's vexation is real enough to him, and expresses itself in a sarcasm to Astrov and a growl at Marina.

So ends the play's moody prelude, shot through with subversive elements of mockery as it is. A 'scene from country life' has begun, and more will follow. It seems at first glance that it is to be a study of men incapable of coping with their work, of 'superfluous men', in the contemporary Russian jargon; but are Astrov and Vanya in the tradition of Goncharov's Oblomov, men who have lost sight of the point of living?[1] Astrov and Vanya think they know what they want, only the appositeness of their desires has yet to be decided.

The stage fills with new figures, and as they pass from the garden to the house, we have only a brief time to study them. We are quickly aware of the ill-matched couple of Professor Serebryakov and his lovely young wife Yelena. In spite of the heat the Professor is wearing a heavy overcoat like a hypochondriac, as if to protect himself from contamination by the peasants, wearing it almost like a uniform to distinguish him from rural ignorance, while in the height of city fashion Yelena glides fluttering gracefully across the lawn from the trees with her sunshade. Sonya, the Professor's unmarried[2] daughter by his first wife, follows with her godfather, the comic hanger-on Telyegin with a pock-marked face,[3] otherwise affectionately known as Waffles because of this disfigurement. An oddly assorted group, and their first five speeches sound a fair range of discordant notes.

The Professor's lofty comment, 'Exquisite views!' is spoken with that kind of false enthusiasm for the countryside which a retired professor of art (of all things!) might think the proper response; it is also the response of a city-dweller and a philistine,

---

[1] See Slonim, *From Chekhov to the Revolution*, p. 65. Marc Slonim distinguishes Chekhov's characters as 'moody men', victims of their environment and too weak to rebel against it.

[2] Sonya wears her hair severely plaited to mark her status.

[3] A characteristic also of Dyadin, Telyegin's original in *The Wood Demon*.

and of a man who cares nothing for what he sees. He praises the estate to which Vanya has devoted his life, but the praise has a cruel irrelevance to the practical concerns of Vanya's management. Vanya says nothing, does not rise from his seat, nor alter his lazy attitude; for the moment he is in control of his feelings, but his silence borders on insult. The simple Waffles as always smells trouble early, and tries to pacify their antagonism; family dissension frightens him, and although Chekhov's hints on social status are always delicate, we are intended to recognize his fear that a quarrel between the owner and the manager of the estate might undermine the security of his position, one of complete financial dependence. Sonya takes up Telyegin's theme, and with sweet politeness presses her father to go the next day to see their plantation, perhaps to show him some of the real work of the estate. For his part the Professor says nothing – he has no wish to walk another foot; no doubt he is content with 'exquisite views'. So Vanya ends this abortive conversation piece with a gruff 'Tea is ready!' Yet even tea will be a bone of contention, since the great man will take his tea in his study, as if the walk has been a waste of his precious time. He stresses his superiority to the rest by having them wait on him.

Marc Slonim notices that Professor Serebryakov is very like Belikov, the teacher of Greek in Chekhov's story 'The Man in a Case' (1898).[1] Belikov is a mediocrity as a man, and mediocrity has turned him into 'a living caricature'. Whatever the weather, Belikov wears his overcoat collar turned up, a muffler round his neck and goloshes on his feet; and he always carries an umbrella. Serebryakov is almost his double, as Vanya describes him: 'It's hot, stifling; but our great man of learning is in his greatcoat and goloshes, with an umbrella and gloves too.' He is protecting himself from the actualities of life, wrapping himself up in the self-love of the hypochondriac, burying himself in his studies. Vanya's verdict is that he is 'an old dry-as-dust, a learned fish'.[2] And, like Stepanovitch, the professor of medicine in 'A Dreary Story' (1889), Serebryakov also has a family with whom he lives like a stranger.

The audience sees the Professor only in his family circle; in fact,

---

[1] See M. Slonim, *From Chekhov to the Revolution*, p. 64.
[2] Translated by Ronald Hingley as 'an old fossil . . . a sort of academic stuffed trout', vol. III, p. 22.

we know nothing for certain about his merits as a scholar; but within the framework of the play his function is only to ruffle the others. Thus, as so often in Chekhov's family groups, attitudes are constantly at odds, and the spectator quickly senses the tensions between people on the stage, tensions which flow from the presence of temporary irritants like Serebryakov and Yelena. Neutral himself, the spectator cannot avoid viewing family dissension with an objective and comic eye.

The handsome wife and the plain daughter have followed the Professor into the house, Sonya calling after him pathetically, 'You will be sure to like the plantation.' We see him often with a little tail of women. The disgruntled Vanya is left to grumble to the Doctor. He expresses both his loathing of the Professor as a person and his envy of him for his beautiful wife. Strangely, Vanya's stronger passion is jealousy. Maurice Valency argues, 'Into the seemingly stable lives of these country people, there is suddenly introduced a disturbing element, in the nature of a catalyst, and almost at once the whole little world begins to seethe and fume.' He goes on,

Obviously, Chekhov did not choose Elena's [Yelena's] name at random. He had in mind, doubtless, that other Helen who set the world by the ears and who, after much travail, returned in the end to a husband she despised. The difference is that Chekhov's Helen has no Paris, no Troy, no adventure, and no epic.[1]

Her passivity in this role, while alarming in its effect on the others, nevertheless makes her character something of an enigma throughout the play.

Waffles at the samovar senses further discord and attempts to interpose his own watery philosophy in that comically sentimental language we begin to expect from him. 'I feel unutterably joyful. The weather is enchanting, and the birds are singing, we are all living in peace and concord – what more could one wish for?' Vanya ignores this bland optimism completely, for he is ruminating on the annoyingly successful career of his enemy. The Professor is a sponger. An academic charlatan. He is a Don Juan. His new wife has sacrificed her youth. So it goes on. Waffles offers his simple remedy: he, at least, has been faithful in love, and even

[1] Valency, pp. 182–3.

when his wife deserted him – 'on the ground of my unprepossessing appearance', so he believes – he kept his *pride*. Vanya protests in irritation, and we are left to assess the real value of a pride like Telyegin's, and to question a virtue which now demonstrates itself in such abject deference to those about him.

The sultry atmosphere works on each man individually, and each begins to quicken in anger; only Yelena, who has returned with Sonya, seems unaffected by the climate, God's or man's. She arranges herself prettily upon the garden swing. With its slender ropes and its lazy motion, it seems a perfect extension of her person, of both her beauty and her lassitude. The gentle swing of the pendulum is amusingly out of key with the feelings on the stage, and set to one side, Yelena's presence on the swing lightly comments on the heated emotions of Vanya and Astrov. Waffles's ineptitudes have incensed Vanya, and Yelena reports that the Doctor's services are no longer required by the Professor. However, Astrov – with a glance at the young wife – will stay the night. Sonya's eyes brighten at the news, as we observe, but Astrov betrays some annoyance over his fruitless journey. Even Waffles loses his composure and speaks sharply to Yelena for addressing him wrongly. So the pace accelerates. Then a fresh irritant is introduced upon the scene as an older, unsmiling woman in black, trailing behind the girls a little, settles herself into the best chair. This is Marya Voynitsky, mother of the Professor's first wife, and of Vanya himself.

Vanya's mother is for him 'my old magpie', babbling about the rights of woman, always with her head buried in a learned document, complacently admiring the Professor's dry academicism, out of sympathy with her son's practical labours. Her contribution to the conversation offers a cameo of her pedantic mind.

MARYA. I got a letter today from Harkov, from Pavel Alexeyevitch . . . he has sent me his new pamphlet.
ASTROV. Is it interesting?
MARYA. It's interesting, but it's rather queer. He is attacking what he himself maintained seven years ago. It's awful.

Vanya, who has kept a brooding silence for some time after Waffles's unusual outburst, suddenly turns on his mother as if in her person she epitomizes all the narrow views of her dear professor. But Marya retaliates in kind. 'You used to be a man of definite principles, of elevated ideas.' She has touched his tenderest spot. Once more the image of the past, with its lost idealism, presses on his mind, and all his grievances find their seat in what might have been. He is forty-seven; he has wasted the time when he might have had everything – everything for which he is now too old. He might, of course, have had a Helen.

So the quarrel mounts, until Sonya's intervention leaves Vanya and Marya silent but fuming. Yelena, relaxed upon her swing, surveys the scene with cool indifference and remarks upon the weather.

(*A pause.*)
YELENA. What a fine day! It's not too hot.
(*A pause.*)
VOYNITSKY. A fine day to hang oneself!

As Waffles tunes his guitar, the Nurse is heard calling to a hen: 'Chook, chook, chook!' A bothersome, nagging and finally intolerable sound like that of a fly buzzing round one's head, one that evokes at once the monotony and the triviality of their arid lives. It is also heard like a mocking laugh, and it releases the tension felt in Chekhov's tormented pauses. In the silence which follows, the vestiges of vexation are dispelled by Waffles, who strikes up a jolly polka as if, again, to mollify all hot tempers.

The present reality enters in the shape of a workman looking about him in embarrassment and anxiety. Can the Doctor come to the factory? 'Well, I suppose I must go. What a nuisance, hang it!' None of the physician's idealism here. The audience feels Astrov's sense of dull resignation through the song he mumbles and the vodka he calls for. And Sonya's plans for a dinner party with the Doctor at her side are spoiled. There seem to be no satisfactions to be had. Unhappily also for Sonya, Astrov's parting remarks are all for Yelena, and Sonya's glance shows us clearly, if we did not see it before, that his interest is in the more attractive woman. 'If you ever care to look in upon me, with Sofya Alexandrovna, I shall be truly delighted.' In his hastily interpolated phrase, poor Sonya is very much an afterthought. He goes on to invite them to see his 'model garden and nursery', where he indulges a passion for forestry.[1] Astrov seems to be on the point of

---

[1] This echoes Chekhov's own enthusiasm for his Melikhovo estate. He had moved

leaving, but in fact Chekhov has led us casually to the surprise of his second major thematic speech.

The Doctor hovers, and the mention of trees produces a Chekhovian discord of comment. The elegant lady is mildly astonished that a doctor, a man therefore of some local standing, could be interested in 'nothing but trees and trees'. Vanya knows at first hand the ill-paid slavery of forestry by necessity and not as a hobby, and throws a curt sarcasm to show Yelena that he is unconvinced – he knows that wood is for fuel and for building barns. Only Sonya echoes Astrov's enthusiasm, although the warmth of her tones tells us that it is not forestry alone that is exciting her: 'If you listen to him you will agree with him entirely.' In *The Wood Demon*, Sonya was a fine girl of good looks who received the conventional reward of marriage; in this play, she is plain and unsophisticated, and constantly betrays her feelings for Astrov. Can he possibly have mistaken her intentions? She offers reasons for the preservation of trees with such aplomb that we suspect she has made it her business to study the matter. Even Vanya shows surprise in his mocking 'Bravo, bravo!' – but he absolutely refuses to accept such fantasies about beautiful forests begetting beautiful people. If the whole act till now has been a sorry negation of good human values, Astrov's moment centre stage strangely represents a positive position we could not have expected. Fired by the discussion of his favourite subject, he gives us a simple, luminous statement of a major theme in the play. 'Man is endowed with reason and creative force to increase what has been given him; but hitherto he has not created but destroyed.' It is a weakness in the play that Chekhov should need to use a spokesman, but in the playing, Astrov is carried along by his excitement until the audience knows he is talking not of trees, but of his own soul and its salvation. He remains in character, the same doctor who was worried by his ragged moustache at the opening of the act. The vodka he wanted appears with the workman almost as a reminder of the reality, and he is stopped short. With a self-deflating quip about his own eccentricity, he takes his leave, and a saddened Sonya is the one who shows him out through the house.

there in March 1892, and his doctor did not order him to Yalta and its kinder climate until October 1898. His time at Melikhovo therefore spans his work on *The Seagull* and *Uncle Vanya*.

Act I

The departure of Astrov and Sonya provides the cue for one
more relationship to be advanced. Yelena, who from her swing
has been listening to their idealistic talk like a magnificently
remote bird in its fine plumage, walks idly across the stage and
mildly reproves Vanya for his behaviour. All Vanya's frustrations
now centre upon her, the ease and comfort of her life, the indifference she shows to his problems, her phlegmatic acceptance
of his love for her. 'You are too indolent to live!' She is more than
this: her characteristic silence and stillness are partly a painful
self-control. However, these are hardly the words of the conventional lover. His fury demonstrates his jealousy of the old
husband and his desire for the young wife. But Yelena seems to
him quite undemanding and infuriatingly content with her
marriage; at least, she certainly does not want Vanya's attentions.
Unfortunately for him, she finds the Doctor's single-mindedness
about trees more of a challenge to her as a woman than all of
Vanya's storming. Moreover, as the spectator may observe,
Sonya's obvious interest in Astrov makes him more interesting
to her than ever Vanya could be. So Uncle Vanya's blandishments
are brushed aside. The audience has the impression that he has
plagued Yelena on more than one occasion. She leaves in some
embarrassment and his misery deepens.

The curtain of Act I falls as Waffles again strikes up his silly
polka, and Maman makes notes in the margin of her pamphlet.
Mrs Voynitsky has been witness to the scene between Yelena
and Vanya throughout. Her negative gesture is slight, but enough
to show us her complete lack of concern for her son's problems.

Now we have met them all, the old and the young, the em-
bittered and the indifferent, the masters and the slaves, and those
who are still resisting their thraldom. We may dislike Serebryakov,
puzzle over the indirection in Yelena and Astrov, feel sorry for
Sonya, laugh a little at Vanya. As yet there is no call at all to see
them in the light and shade of simplistic moral judgment. As the
brittle polka on the guitar advises us, we reserve our position.

Act Two

With the new scene we have moved inside the house, and although it is not the same sultry day, the same summer heat persists, and the tensions in the action will continue to develop as the storm offstage blows up. The time, however, has changed: it is just after midnight. The scene is hushed, even more still than before, and the irregular tapping sounds of the watchman's stick[1] in the garden accentuate the motionlessness on the stage. Professor Serebryakov is dozing fitfully in his chair, and his wife is dozing beside him. The spectator assimilates the stillness and the incongruity of the picture.

The old man wakes with a grunt and a start. Seeing his wife beside him, he acts the part of the domestic tyrant more than necessary: 'I am in unbearable pain' – yet not so unbearable that he was unable to sleep. The young wife dutifully ministers to him while the mind of the old egotist flits from notion to notion: the heat, the time, the book he wants, his health, his age. Did Turgenev get his angina from gout? This could be Serebryakov's trouble too. His self-pity becomes laughable, and so remote an association with the great adds to the comedy of pompous, irascible age. 'And, of course, it is stupid of me to go on living. But wait a little, I shall soon set you all free. I shan't have to linger on much longer.' Nothing, we imagine, is further from his thoughts. 'I am the only one enjoying life and satisfied. Oh, yes, of course! . . . Well, suppose I am disagreeable, egotistic and tyrannical – haven't I a right, even in my old age, to think of myself?' The thoughts of this shallow man veer about as irritability replaces empty humility. The speech rumbles on, broken only by Yelena's short, exhausted protests, the watchman's low singing and the banging of the window in the rising wind. It is clear that the Professor distrusts his wife and dislikes his family,

[1] See p. 74, n.1, above.

probably because of his very dependence upon them. And we may guess that he turned Astrov away because the Doctor must know too much of the truth about his ill-health.

Another underling has come in, and the Professor is quick to find a task for her. 'Sonya, fetch me my drops from the table . . . Oh, not those! It's no use asking for anything!' Sonya has joined Yelena in the unrewarding vigil; Vanya and the Nurse appear a moment later. The picture of domestic tyranny becomes almost caricature. We learn that Serebryakov's first wife also used to stay up with him 'night after night'; it is evident that he likes the attentions of all these women. He has, however, less use for the men, unless, like Vanya, they can earn his living for him. Vanya above all irritates him with his incessant demands, and just by thinking about his manager the Professor works himself up into a frenzy which only Marina with her mothering can appease. The old woman's warmth is mindless, but genuine, and the old man responds. She and his daughter finally take him to bed, leaving Yelena and Vanya exasperated and worn out.

This ugly prelude to the act sharply demonstrates one source of their discontents, and the development of the hidden fever of those on stage may now proceed apace. The growth of the storm echoes their feelings. By a series of naturally interpolated comments from his characters, Chekhov reinforces the reality of the noises from the wind and rain machines, and of the effect of a flash of lightning. It is almost as if Chekhov is mocking the crude pathetic fallacy of the nineteenth-century *scène à faire*. But in this suffocating atmosphere Vanya can exhibit his smouldering passion for the young wife, and on the naturalistic stage the weather justifies an explosion of feeling without making it grotesque. Yelena, in her remote position as a beautiful goddess, has herself not been left unaffected by the demands of the night, perhaps by the years in which her devotion to her husband has worn down her young idealism, and she expresses her dislike of this 'dreadful' house; everyone is angry with someone else in this unhappy family. Why does not Vanya try to reconcile some of these quarrels? In her desire for an unruffled existence, however, she has underestimated the depth of the wounds and knows nothing of their causes. Vanya's comment, 'Let us drop this moralizing', makes the point simply; what can she know of his feelings? Her admonitions are nothing to Vanya. But there is a contribution she *could* make. He tries to take her hand, and clumsily finds that it is not there when he bends to kiss it. He wants to fall at her feet; his personal salvation is in her hands; his past life has been 'stupidly wasted on trifles'. This bizarre behaviour is evidently his idea of *la grande passion*.

The pathos in all this is not allowed to grip the spectator. For Vanya has begun to harangue Yelena around the stage, and in her frills she makes absurd attempts to escape his embraces. The goddess looks very like an ordinary girl in an ordinary predicament. Once more Labiche and Feydeau have crept in. In any case, not only is Yelena the wrong sort of woman to sympathize with Vanya's self-pity, but, as we increasingly suspect, she is incapable of love herself. Of course, in refusing his advances, she is doing the right thing, but it is what suits her temperament. Moreover, she is tired from sitting up half the night with her husband, and shows it. She clearly does not believe what he is saying, and as a last resort she looks him in the eye and says, 'Ivan Petrovitch, you are drunk!' Perhaps he is. Nevertheless, how is she to get rid of him? 'Go to bed! You bore me!' But he has gone too far to hear her insults, and in his final assault upon her he looks the fool he frequently is.

VOYNITSKY (*kisses her hand*). My precious . . . marvellous one!
YELENA (*with vexation*). Don't. This is really hateful (*goes out*).

So at last she manages to escape – to escape both Uncle Vanya and commitment. The lady remains aloof, leaving her vassal more abject than before, now without a shred of pride, speaking in maudlin soliloquy through his sleeplessness.

Why am I old? Why doesn't she understand me? . . . Oh, how I have been cheated! I adored that Professor, that pitiful gouty invalid, and worked for him like an ox . . . My God, and now! Here he is retired, and now one can see the sum total of his life. He leaves not one page of work behind him, he is utterly unknown, he is nothing – a soap bubble! And I have been cheated . . . I see it – stupidly cheated . . .

There is truth as well as self-pity in this. The scene has progressed from the Professor's tyranny in physical particulars to his tyranny over Vanya's heart: for the spectator as for Vanya, they are of a kind. Now Vanya wants Helena as a reward, and as a revenge, for his slavery.

Act II

The hour is late, the storm is at its height, the atmosphere still thick. The mood of Vanya's despair is broken by the entrance of the Doctor. Like Vanya's love, Astrov's appearance borders on the grotesque. He is '*in his coat, but without waistcoat or tie; he is a little drunk*'. He turns to Waffles who is at his heels and tells him to strike up. Chekhov is pushing his midnight scene as far as he dare towards the absurd, and the signs of desperation are ominous.

ASTROV. Play something!
TELYEGIN. Everyone is asleep!
ASTROV. Play!

Λ sense of panic and madness descends upon the theatre as the Doctor strikes an attitude and sings in a cracked voice. Suddenly he picks up a handful of the Professor's medicine bottles. 'Medicines! What a lot of prescriptions! From Harkov, from Moscow, from Tula. He has bored every town with his gout. Is he really ill or shamming?' The vodka has loosened his tongue and he joins in the attack on Serebryakov. Then as he rolls round the stage he turns on Vanya, who is huddled in a chair thinking of his humiliation. Is he in love with 'the Professor's lady?' Vanya grows angry, but is in no state to parry the repartee. In a moment, Astrov's cynicism grows sardonic and self-critical, and the pace temporarily slows to a halt. When he is drunk, he explains, 'I don't think of myself as a crank at such times, but believe that I am being of immense service to humanity – immense!' In his individual key, he has taken up Vanya's own theme of wasted endeavour. Then, drunkenly amused by his own desperate sense of humour, he calls for more drinks.

Sonya has heard the noise, and Chekhov rearranges the partners in duets of discontent once more. Her entrance sends Astrov scuttling off with the explanation that he is not wearing a tie. In the early hours he might be excused this immodesty, but obviously it is Sonya's presence that troubles him.

Uncle and niece are now briefly alone together for the first time. If we expect evidence of their common grievance and their mutual sympathy, we shall be disappointed. The audience perceives immediately that the girl is the stronger character, concerned with the practical, the all-important business of the unfinished hay-making and worried by her uncle's drinking and dreaming. Vanya for his part reacts with tears to her mention of the hay rotting in the rain. But they are not tears shed for an unlucky harvest or a bad crop. Vanya kisses Sonya and says nothing about the hay. Instead, we hear, 'You looked at me just now so like your dear mother.' His tears are for the past. So he struggles off to bed: their common grief has been too great for words; it has not needed talking about.

Still largely structuring his scene as a sequence of abortive duologues, as if each of the relationships must be established in the spectator's mind before the combined assault of one party upon another in Act III, Chekhov next pairs off the Doctor and his devoted Sonya.[1] Sonya and Yelena will follow, although the pairing of Yelena and Astrov must wait for a later, more critical time in the shaping of the play, since the more positive feeling of Astrov for Yelena and of Yelena for Astrov will, by the comparison, show us how thin are the hopes of Sonya and Vanya.

We see Sonya for a moment hesitantly alone. She knocks timidly on the door through which she saw Astrov go, and the form of her words signifies the way her desires are moving. 'Mihail Lvovitch, you are not asleep, are you?' He emerges slowly and rather sheepishly '*with his waistcoat and tie on*', and mouths a doubtful, 'What can I do for you?' The pace is again at a minimum, and with this the tension rises somewhat: will Astrov accept her love? Sonya searches for a topic of conversation. He is not to let Uncle Vanya drink. Astrov readily agrees at least to this. 'Very good, We won't drink any more (*a pause*). I am just going home. That's settled and signed.' As if to offer every logical reason, he adds that 'It will be daylight by the time they have put the horses in.' Sonya must now play for time. 'It is raining. Wait till morning.' Then, 'Won't you have something to eat?' Then, 'I like eating at night.' Astrov's weakened defences collapse before this pathetic assault, and when he spies some cheese in the sideboard, he settles for that.

Cheese is now the laughable medium through which Sonya conducts her lame love scene. They both stand awkwardly at the sideboard, mouths full, conversation limping. In the pause while Astrov drinks, he decides to speak his mind, and thoughtlessly uses the helpless but willing girl as his confessor, like the Nurse before her. But there is a difference. He has sensed that Sonya is

[1] This may be seen as a trial run for the delicately ambiguous love scene between Varya and Lopahin in the last act of *The Cherry Orchard*.

the only one who will listen to him, the only sensitive person among them all.

The long monologue from Astrov which follows points, like his first speech in Act I, to a theme of the play. The character, although speaking between mouthfuls of cheese and wine, and still rather drunk, is, next to Sonya, the one whose words we have come to accept as the least distorted, and which represent values as untarnished as any in the play. Moreover, the long speech spoken to an enthralled Sonya comes at a place of rest in the play: the storm outside is passing and the storm in Vanya's mind has temporarily abated with his tears, while the crisis for them all is yet to come. The storm has served to accentuate all their eccentricities and reveal innermost feelings. Now Astrov chorically summarizes and evaluates the situation of the family. 'There is no one here and one may speak frankly.' His words are intended to touch everyone in the Moscow audience.

He refers explicitly to the atmosphere in the house (how everyone seems so well aware of it!) and the melancholy ego-centricity of each of them. In particular, he is torn by the contra-lictions which Yelena represents in his mind – and perhaps in the spectator's too. His anger with Yelena suggests that he is certainly not indifferent to her. Without sensing in her stepmother a rival, Sonya pays special attention to these remarks. Yelena is a paragon of beauty – as such we hear her praised through the ears of plain Sonya – and she fascinates everyone with her good looks, but her life is one of idleness. She is like the disease which infects them all, a criticism Astrov is to repeat to her face in Act IV. His own dissatisfaction with 'everyday provincial life in Russia', for all its charm, is a dissatisfaction with its purposelessness. For all the work he does, he despises himself because he lacks vision. 'You know when you walk through a forest on a dark night, and a light gleams in the distance, you do not notice your weariness, nor the darkness, nor the sharp twigs that lash you in the face.' The Doctor has stopped the restless movement which accompanied his distraction over Yelena. The stage is still. The speech has passed from the particular to the general and in this moment of repose the play has moved into poetry and becomes a lyrical lament for lost ideals.

Sonya is the perfect listener, and Astrov is encouraged to

return to the particular and diagnose the weakness in his own life. He repeats what he said in Act I: 'It is years since I cared for anyone.' Sonya is again alert, and with a faint bashfulness in her tone prompts him further: 'You care for no one at all?' Astrov misses the innuendo. No, neither the peasants on the one hand, nor the educated people on the other, have anything but limited, petty, stupid ideas and feelings. As it would the words of any chorus, the audience measures what he says against what it has seen of the family itself, and finds it largely just.

Sonya is still hanging on every word that Astrov says. When in the heat of his utterance he reaches for his glass to refill it, she stops him. It is a sudden, maternal impulse. 'You always say that people don't create but only destroy what heaven gives them. Then why do you destroy yourself, why?' To Sonya, Astrov is 'beautiful', the very word he has applied to Yelena.[1] But the plain girl sees beauty elsewhere than on the surface.

As if she has touched his conscience, he rather hastily agrees to stop drinking. He has no wish to blunt his feelings. He still loves beauty. And so his thoughts wander back to Yelena. But, emphasizing abruptly the division in his mind, he unexpectedly *'covers his face with his hands and shudders'*. 'In Lent one of my patients died under chloroform.' This has the sharp sting of reality, and Chekhov has revealed one source of the Doctor's distraction of mind. Empty lives on the one hand, ugly death on the other – both are equally destructive of 'beauty'.

Sonya hastens to turn the conversation back to his thoughts on love, and probes as far as she dares. If she had a sister – a younger sister – who loved him, what then? Again he misses her meaning and says flatly that he could not respond to her love. And Sonya seems to have gone too far this time, for, uneasily, he decides he must go, and quickly slips away. Did he realize what she meant? Neither she nor we can know. Standing dazed in the centre of the stage like a child lost in a wood, Sonya speaks one of those naturalistic soliloquies of Chekhov's which go to the heart of the character. Astrov said nothing, yet why does she laugh with

---

[1] Chekhov's word is *prekrasny*, a word of more general application than the English 'beautiful'. While it may be used of a woman's physical attributes, it can also be used of a man's mind, meaning 'fine', 'excellent'. Hingley translates: 'You're a really fine man' (vol. III, p. 39), but loses the effect of the echo. Sonya is modulating the word for a more spiritual connotation.

happiness? Because after all this time she found the courage to convey her feelings to him. Like Viola's in *Twelfth Night,* hers is the pure happiness of having loved selflessly, without requital. In her state of high excitement, Sonya next dips into despair. If only *she* were 'beautiful'! Like Yelena? – we savour the bitter-sweet irony of this.

The scene's series of exploratory duologues has not been the most inventively structured sequence in Chekhov. Yet by the device of the duologue the spectator is enabled to test the re-action of one character to another and arrange them in pairs of the compatible and the incompatible, like so many guests at dinner. Sonya has not truly confronted Yelena so far, and then only in the first act to contradict her views on the significance of trees, when they were seen together in acute contrast as the provincial and the city girl. At the end of this second act, the two have been brought together again, the storm over, fresher air circulating, friendship between them.

They come together naturally, since they are of an age – but not as equals. Yelena's superiority does not arise from her married status or her position as Sonya's stepmother; rather, the audience knows that she has a superior power in her beauty, and, more subtly, an apparent strength in her cool indifference to the anxieties of those about her. But Chekhov refuses to allow the beauty and indifference of a Helen to petrify her as a person. When in 1903 an actress who had been cast for the part of Yelena wrote to Chekhov to ask whether the character should be interpreted as a woman incapable of thinking or loving, the author replied, 'It may be that Yelena does seem incapable of thinking or even of loving, but that wasn't my idea when I wrote *Uncle Vanya.*'[1] When Sonya cries, Yelena cries too, and we warm to her. When, mistaking the reasons for Sonya's upset, she confesses that she married the Professor for love, albeit mis-takenly,[2] we warm to her again. This Sonya can appreciate also.

---

[1] Letter to M. F. Pobedimskaya of 5 February 1903, quoted in Hingley, vol. III, p. 302.

[2] Perhaps as Masha in *Three Sisters* married her schoolmaster Kuligin, out of an adolescent 'crush'. In *The Wood Demon* her counterpart sacrificed herself in marrying an old man. But in *Uncle Vanya,* Chekhov does not fill in the background to Yelena's marriage: 'I was attracted to him as a learned, celebrated man' is all we have. To say more would dispel her mystery. She certainly lacks the depth of the Dorothea who married Casaubon out of idealism in George Eliot's *Middlemarch.*

And Sonya understands when Yelena says, 'You must believe in everyone – there is no living if you don't.' In this way, Sonya's sympathy directs the spectator's, and Chekhov directs both. But we may yet suspect that Yelena is rationalizing: trust and belief is not her way, nor will be.

Sonya has now relaxed, and she turns to Yelena in the faith that the married woman is the only one who can sympathize with her in her affection for the Doctor. But she has taken Yelena's trust too literally and she speaks unthinkingly. Her question, 'Do you like the Doctor?' is unguarded and clumsily ambiguous. Sonya means only to reassure herself that her admiration for Astrov is justified, and she is quite unable to see anything else in Yelena's positive, but generalized, answer. The audience makes the comparison between Sonya's simple tones of infatuation in a line like 'His voice trembles and caresses one', and Yelena's non-committal admiration. Perhaps she sees another Serebryakov in him.

My dear, you must understand he has a spark of genius! And you know what that means? Boldness, freedom of mind, width of outlook ... He plants a tree and is already seeing what will follow from it in a thousand years, already he has visions of the happiness of humanity. Such people are rare, one must love them ...

In having the question put to her like this, Yelena seems suddenly to acquire an awareness of Astrov's virtues. Sonya's love for him has touched a chord in Yelena too, almost competitively. Certainly she speaks with such unaccustomed fervour that an audience must suspect her personal feelings for him. However, she collects herself, kisses Sonya and wishes her happiness.

In wishing Sonya happiness, Yelena reminds herself of her own situation. As she paces the stage, she is 'very, very unhappy'. Sonya, for her part, cannot forbear laughing. She is 'so happy ... so happy!' If Yelena, the girl who has beauty, is unhappy, it is because she does not know what it is to be in love. Sonya, the girl without beauty and who is no longer young, knows, like Viola, the happiness of being in love, and her craving to be loved is more genuine. Sonya guides us to the belief that love is an active and a creative passion. As she buries her face in her hands in her ecstasy, she is a radiant lesson in the meaning of unselfish devotion, and beside her Yelena looks bogus.

The playwright's last impressions in the scene are designed to bring us back to present realities, back to life with the Professor. In case the spectator should interpret Yelena's lovelessness as a sign of heartlessness and frigidity, Chekhov adds another clue to her personality: she is not only young and lovely, she likes music and is also a pianist.[1] Any facile judgment on Yelena is inappropriate. She may be as much entitled to her self-pity as Vanya is to his. 'Do play something!', cries Sonya; but no one can lift a finger without the great man's permission, and so Sonya goes off, still joyful, to ask Serebryakov whether Yelena may play the piano.

As we watch an agitated Yelena alone on the stage, we hear the watchman tapping as he did when the act began, recalling her devotion to her husband. The watchman's stick, and his whistling and calling to his dog, is a gentle naturalistic reminder of the working world outside, carrying on as before, ignorant of personal sufferings, however momentous they may seem. Yelena tells him to go away and not disturb the master, and as we hear his whistle fading away, we sense the tedium of life on the estate. No audience can avoid feeling something for Yelena's lonely wretchedness.

Sonya returns unwillingly with her message from the Professor, and Yelena looks across the stage hopefully. May she play? The answer has been curt, and Sonya's tone is flat: 'We mustn't.' For a second as the curtain falls we see the girls as two of a kind, victims of their sex.

[1] Again we may compare Masha of *Three Sisters*, whose husband suppresses her desire to perform at a concert, and denies her creative ability.

Act Three

The third act conveys a quality of clarification, a clearing of the air in every sense, not only in the way the set refreshes us with broad daylight after the night and a sweeter atmosphere after the storm, but also in that the characters speak more freely. It is the drawing-room, and we have passed further into the house. Now almost all the cards are down.

Vanya and Sonya are seated, their restlessness for the present abated. Only Yelena in her boredom is moving listlessly about the stage. Chekhov comes straight to the point, and in Vanya's most sarcastic tone of voice we hear, 'The Herr Professor has graciously expressed a desire that we should all gather together in this room at one o'clock to-day (*looks at his watch*). It is a quarter to.' In the familiar pattern of Chekhov's plays, we are to witness a crucial family gathering before Serebryakov and his wife leave, and in preparation for this the playwright has already begun to dispose his creatures in their several roles. However, he specifies a fifteen minute period of anticipation, and a lot will happen in that interval of time.[1] All the principals except the Professor himself will have suffered an unsettling experience before the announcement is made. In the long hot summer, time seemed to have stopped, but suddenly we are challenged with the clock and feel an unaccustomed urgency.

By her movements, Yelena's boredom becomes the occasion for comment. The practical Sonya offers her own simple solution – work. That is her anodyne against pain and the knowledge of emptiness. Yelena could help with the estate, teach the children, look after the sick, go to the market, sell the flour. As she poses

[1] 'The "fifteen minutes" prove to be extraordinarily paced with action and everything that happens in this brief interval prepares and strengthens the explosion which takes place at the conference' (V. Yermilov, *Dramaturgija Chekhova*, Moscow, 1948, trans. E. Henderson in Jackson, p. 115. See pp. 115–17 for a discussion of this sequence).

elegantly, Yelena's reaction to these suggestions may be guessed. Thus the play's immediate subject again comes into focus: useful work and a purposeful life was Astrov's solution to their problems too. Yelena protests her ignorance. 'It's only in novels with a purpose that people teach and doctor the peasants.' A hit at Tolstoy, maybe, but Yelena's line also subtly suggests that in this environment of unrewarding effort she is living a fictional life of her own. This appalling limitation to human growth, the possession of merely second-hand knowledge about the realities of living, has been hinted by Yelena before, when she declared in her confession to Sonya at the end of the second act, 'In music and in my husband's house, and in all the love affairs, everywhere in fact, I have always played a secondary part.' We remember that her love for Serebryakov was 'not real love'. She had made it all up, 'but I fancied at the time that it was real'. Through Yelena, together with her husband, the play has introduced a dialectic on the nature of real living and true values. It will be, however, a dialectic of human feeling.

Sonya extends the discussion to indicate shrewdly that Yelena's ennui is only symptomatic, for her stepmother's affliction is one whose cause infects them all. Sonya herself has grown lazy; Vanya follows Yelena about 'like a shadow'; Astrov neglects both his patients and his forestry. And Sonya looks wryly at Yelena and says, 'You must be a witch'. She is joking, but, indeed, we see how she haunts the minds of the two men, and seems to embody their loss of purpose.

Vanya's eyes have been following Yelena all the time, and now his desire comes quickly to the surface. At the same time he offers her *his* cure for her sickness: he advises her, 'Let yourself go for once.' He is suggesting that she be herself, that she break with social convention, and fall in love – with him. Yelena responds in anger, and to mollify her the romantic Vanya, in some alarm, offers to bring her 'autumn roses – exquisite, mournful roses'. So it is autumn already; but how autumnal of Vanya to make this gesture!

Sonya and Yelena are alone together again, and Sonya is eager to talk and talk about her new sensations. The audience has almost forgotten the announcement to come as it is stunned by a new feature of Yelena's elusive character. In the episode which follows, Chekhov will again use this woman to have us recognize another symptom of the provincial malaise. Motherless Sonya, for the first time finding a person whom she thinks a soul-mate of her own generation, tells of her torment of love for the Doctor. She has loved him for six years, and everyone knows of it except the man himself.

SONYA. . . . all the servants know I love him. Everybody knows it.
YELENA. And he?
SONYA. No. He doesn't notice me.
YELENA (*musing*). He is a strange man . . .

The ambiguity of Yelena's response to Sonya's misery must strike the audience. For all that Yelena is sympathetically stroking Sonya's head as it is pressed to her bosom like a child's, these are not words of sympathy. Her thoughts have wandered away, and her mind is working over a new idea. She will discover Astrov's true feelings about Sonya. She will speak to him 'carefully', of course; she will only 'hint at it'; she will question him 'so tactfully that he won't notice it'. The point is reiterated both to reassure Sonya and to make it impossible for the audience to forget. 'All we want to find out is yes or no (*a pause*). If it's no, he had better not come here, had he?' Sonya's unspeaking nods are sad to watch. Why is Yelena forcing on her so coldly rational a decision? Is it merely to achieve a quick death for her uncertainty? We may feel that, foggy as it is, there is another motive to Yelena's mind. Sonya herself half questions the wisdom of finding out the truth: if one remains in ignorance, 'one has hope, at least'.

Our supicions about Yelena's motives are partly confirmed when she is alone. Her soliloquy is one of Chekhov's less successful uses of the device, but it seems necessary for a woman both secretive and confused to make a confession at this point, in order that the scene with Astrov which follows may be sufficiently charged with comic irony. Chekhov implies from the beginning of her speech that she realizes already that Astrov is not in love with Sonya, although this does not preclude a good match for her in the Doctor. Yet while Yelena may wish to discover whether there is still a chance of marriage for Sonya, her thoughts weakly lead her to consider her own feelings for the man. She speaks of Sonya's problem as a woman in her own condition might think of it.

I understand the poor child. In the midst of desperate boredom, with nothing but grey shadows wandering about instead of human beings, with only dull commonplaces to listen to, among people who can do nothing but eat, drink and sleep – he sometimes appears on the scene unlike the rest, handsome, interesting, fascinating, like a bright moon rising in the darkness . . .

Her starting point is her own 'desperate boredom', and so she is talking of her own troubles as well as Sonya's. When she adds, 'I believe I am a little fascinated myself', therefore, we are not to see her subsequent theft of Astrov's affections as deliberate malice, but as part of a slow, all but unconscious, process. And, since she admits that she feels a pang of guilt at the way her thoughts are going, her decision cannot appear cold-blooded. She lacks fulfilment as Sonya does, and by the time Astrov appears, Yelena has forgotten her. Nevertheless, this revelation of her feelings makes it clear to the audience that her love is unlike Sonya's defenceless humility. Yelena may have need of Astrov, but she will merely use him to ease her ennui in a mindless, negative way.

If we have doubts about Yelena, they are certainly not fully resolved when Chekhov hurries Astrov in with his chart. He immediately plunges into an involved analysis of a favourite topic, the deterioration of the land.

The audience only half listens to his long account. No doubt we recognize that his description of the thoughtless destruction of the forests recapitulates in broadly symbolic terms the sickness which afflicts Vanya's family. 'This degeneration is due to inertia, ignorance, to the complete lack of understanding . . . Almost everything has been destroyed already, but nothing as yet has been created to take its place.' The social concern behind Chekhov's writing in *Uncle Vanya* here expresses itself in yet another way: the agents of the destruction and creation of natural beauty are people.

However, the other half of our attention is upon the silent figure throughout his lecture. Our eye tells us another story, as so often in Chekhov, and the generalizing and perspective view of this scene, of the fierce intent of the man and the relaxed composure of the woman, is touchingly ironic at Astrov's expense. For Yelena has not been listening to a word, as Astrov eventually sees and she admits. We see in her evasive gesture and careless attitude a visual demonstration of the train of thought she was following before Astrov came in. Could she, should she, love him? In the man, standing beside this willowy creature, first bending earnestly over his charts and then flailing his arms oratorically, Chekhov provides an image of the contradictory forces in the play. And we feel the impact of the contradiction in the particular sexual tension through which these forces are represented.

The tension is increased as Yelena shocks us by broaching the subject of Astrov's feelings for Sonya. For she does it in as direct a way as seems possible, with, 'Does she attract you as a woman?' This, after she promised so tactful an investigation! Sonya's unattractiveness 'as a woman' is what is most painful to her. We find ourselves blushing for her, and recognize that such a direct question is the one which Yelena would ask only for her own satisfaction, not Sonya's. When, after a moment's consideration, Astrov denies any feelings for Sonya, Yelena concludes her 'examination', as she lightly calls it, as peremptorily as she began it, by stating that Sonya is 'unhappy' and that the Doctor must stop coming to the house. Oh, Yelena! Do you urge so extreme a measure out of a wish to avoid a commitment of your own? Worse still, your coaxing tones sound as if you want to thwart Sonya even though you cannot have Astrov for yourself.

Astrov is not as shaken as he might have been by the flattering news of Sonya's interest in him. Again we wonder, did he know of it all along? Perhaps in his constant concern for his dulled senses, perhaps somewhat confused by the vodka he has drunk, he has been unaware of the sensibilities of those about him. He is embarrassed, but, faced with the idea that he must go away for good, he is reminded of Yelena, not Sonya. That must have been Yelena's intention in the first place. He begins to smile, and with a *savoir faire* of which Vanya would have been incapable, he '*looks into her eyes and shakes his finger at her*'.

You are a sly one! . . . (*laughs*). Sly! Suppose Sonya is unhappy – I am quite ready to admit it – but why need you go into it? . . . Please don't try to look astonished. You know perfectly well what brings me here every day.

In saying this, Astrov seems to support our doubts about Yelena's motives for speaking out in the way she did. Nevertheless, her amazement at his laughter suggests yet another possibility. Even if she cannot admit his charge, Yelena may simply not understand her own feelings, so that her first instinct is to repress them by asking Astrov to go away.[1] Of course, with Astrov mocking her, calling her 'a beautiful, fluffy weasel', terms which reflect the contradiction of attraction and repulsion in him even in her presence, she is shocked into recognizing her own social position. Yelena's reluctance to be unfaithful to her husband, and what it represents,[2] may not be easily dismissed. But she is also torn as a woman.

There follows a powerful scene, wild with unfocused and unacknowledged feelings. The Doctor's laughter suddenly changes to a wild exhibition of passion we could hardly have expected from so cynical a man. Yelena tries to escape, but he chases her to the door and bars her way. The zany scene between Yelena and Vanya is repeating itself. He seizes her hands and kisses them. He puts his arm round her waist and kisses her on the lips. And we watch Yelena change her mind again and again: passing from an attitude of self-righteous indignation, she allows the kiss; then after acquiescence, she struggles in his arms; following a moment of resistance, she lays her head on his breast; after a pause of ecstasy and repose, she breaks away in fear. For such a woman, yes means no and no yes, we may think, and Yelena is getting her deserts. But in her way she is also a victim of Serebryakov's tyranny and inadequacy as a husband.

As for Astrov, he is behaving like an adolescent, not the figure of maturity and moral respectability we took him for. In his desperation, his forestry is one dream, and kissing someone else's wife serves for another. The audience is now in a position to assess his hopes for a creative future. In this crazy exhibition, so out of key with the rest of the scene, we see again the pattern of action in which a sharp explosion can erupt beneath a smooth surface, and this peculiar dramatic rhythm, like that of a quiescent volcano, having been felt before, will be felt again.

[1] Valency maintains that Yelena is behaving virtuously and dutifully in this scene, and that for Chekhov this was a sign of 'lack of vitality' in the woman and a 'fundamental romanticism' in the man: 'For Chekhov, it was immoral above all to thwart nature, and worse than immoral to do so under the guise of moral obligation' (Valency, p. 188).

[2] 'Let the wife fear her husband' is the injunction written into the Russian Orthodox marriage service, although the dogma was debated with disapproval by the intelligentsia.

But Chekhov has another subversive stroke to play. Whatever sympathy we may have felt for the Doctor in his extremity is promptly reduced by a grotesque stage trick. '*At that instant* VOYNITSKY *comes in with a bunch of roses and stands still in the doorway.*' These are his mournful autumn roses, and he stands clutching them while he listens to fully two speeches from Yelena and Astrov: 'Spare me . . . let me go . . . No!' 'Come to the plantation tomorrow . . . at two o'clock . . . Yes? Yes? You'll come?' These are the astounding words that strike Vanya's ears. His entrance is a cliché of the theatre, the triangular confrontation seen in a hundred mawkish dramas and a hundred stereotyped farces. Here Chekhov is using it with his tongue in his cheek, and Vanya's delicious entrance douches the feverish emotions of this clumsy trio with our laughter. Vanya's roses puncture two love affairs, Astrov's and his own. There is to be no *grande passion*, no noble love, only bathos, in this silly confusion of their petty desires. Yet we are also sorry for all three in their pain.

The scene immediately dips into near-farcical hysteria. Yelena, not knowing where to hide her face, goes to the window. Astrov fills the moment with a gabble of anticlimactic words about the weather, the topic reserved for those who have nothing to say; then he hastily rolls up his map and leaves. Vanya places his roses on a chair in a daze, as if he were laying his hopes into their grave, and wipes his face and neck with his handkerchief. 'Never mind . . . no . . . never mind . . .' This is his moment of awful understanding. Still rooted to the same spot, he is far more agitated than Yelena, and in his position upstage centre it is he whom we watch. The loss of this young, beautiful woman shows him how hollow his life is, and gives him a vision of his empty years ahead.[1] Yelena turns and goes up to Uncle Vanya. She must leave

---

[1] Valency draws attention to Chekhov's story 'The Beauties' (1888), in which Chekhov describes the encounter with beauty and its 'indefinable sense of loss' (see pp. 183–4). In the presence of a lovely young Armenian girl, the story's narrator feels her beauty in a strange way: 'It was not desire, nor ecstasy, nor enjoyment that Masha excited in me, but a painful though pleasant sadness. It was a sadness vague and undefined as a dream.' He feels that everyone in her presence 'had lost something important and essential to life which we should never find again' (*Select Tales of Chekhov*, trans. C. Garnett, London, 1949, p. 370). In the same story, the sight of a station-master's daughter calls up the same response in a wrinkled, beefy-faced guard, who 'wore a look of tenderness and of the deepest sadness, as though in that girl he saw happiness, his own youth, soberness, purity, wife, children; as though he were repenting and feeling in his whole being that that girl was not his' (*ibid.* p. 375).

the house today. Chekhov's moment of farce has deeply tragic implications.

Into this tumultuous, ludicrous scene comes the husband himself, oblivious to all that has happened, unaware of his responsibility in the matter, insensitive in any case to the feelings of others, incapable of anticipating the explosion about to take place. He is looking for the family, looking for his audience, and he rings the house-bell in irritation. So begins one of Chekhov's most celebrated and delicately prepared comic-pathetic sequences.

Using Telyegin and Yelena, the playwright in a few strokes first gives another neatly accentuated portrait of the Professor and his self-importance. Waffles, calling Serebryakov 'Your Excellency' and complaining of his poor health, is ignored completely. The Professor calls for the Mother and for his wife, giving his orders as to the world at large in a loud voice. At his side, and in a quiet voice, a trembling Yelena says submissively, 'I *am* here.' The effect is amusing.

Our eyes are, however, partly on Sonya, who slips in and approaches Yelena nervously. She asks in a whisper whether the Doctor said he would not come again. Yelena nods slowly. We feel the earth shake for Sonya, and the girl retires into her grief for almost the remainder of the scene, all but indifferent to anything her father has to say.

The Professor continues to organize the gathering like a class of his students. Will they sit down, please? – he is all politeness. Waffles goes timidly to one side; the Nurse sits down and '*knits a stocking*', like a revolutionary waiting to watch the heads roll at the guillotine. Finally Maman makes her distinguished entrance, and the meeting may begin. Only Sonya does not hear the word of command, and Vanya, still overwhelmed by his glimpse of Astrov and Yelena in each other's arms, wants only to leave. At the moment of crisis, the two who have most to lose are in another world.

The Professor coyly addresses his subject. With the little cough of the formal orator and a preparatory joke as if to a public assembly, he begins. 'I have invited you, gentlemen, to announce that the Inspector-General is coming.' No one laughs and he starts again: 'But let us lay aside jesting.' He re-assumes his authoritative pose. He asks for their advice, and adds sternly, 'I hope to receive it.' He muffles the tone of command in these words by a quick appeal to sympathy in a gesture of false modesty: he has 'never had anything to do with practical life' – a remark whose hypocrisy will be apparent when he goes on to argue about percentages of profit. In his most honeyed tones he looks about him for flattery, to Vanya, to Waffles, to Maman. Vanya is barely listening to this meaningless preamble; Telyegin with a vacant smile on his face sits wondering what is coming; while Maman, the one with least experience of 'practical life', nods earnest assent.

It is quite a performance. With a schoolmasterly Latin tag spoken in a sober tone, he says he must settle the family affairs before he dies. And although he adds, 'I am not thinking of myself', it is to himself that he returns: 'It is impossible for me to go on living in the country.' So, with the family, we learn by degrees that he wishes to return to town,[1] and live on the income from the sale of the estate.

Our estate yields on an average not more than two per cent on its capital value. I propose to sell it. If we invest the money in suitable securities, we should get from four to five per cent, and I think we might even have a few thousand roubles to spare for buying a small villa in Finland.

A practical notion indeed, but his diffident approach to this bombshell – he has 'the honour of submitting' the measure for their 'consideration'; he only 'proposes' that the estate be sold – hardly lessens the momentousness of the announcement. We look at the assembled group, sitting tensely before the speaker. Every member of the family receives the news differently, and the spectator's scanning eye embraces the differences.

Vanya is the first to come alive. 'Excuse me . . . surely my ears are deceiving me! Repeat what you have said.' In his insensitiveness, the Professor has not realized that he has upset anyone. Nor perhaps would a Russian of property in 1897 find his action too unreasonable, since landowners at the end of the century were making decisions very like Serebryakov's. But in terms of the play, what is to become of Vanya, and Mother, and Sonya? And does not the estate belong to Sonya? Has not Vanya worked like a slave for twenty-five years? Has he not paid off the mortgage,

---

[1] I.e., Harkov. See Telyegin's comment at the opening of Act IV.

conscientiously sending the Professor the money? Is this his only thanks? Has he not sacrificed his life to the Professor? To a man who is nothing more than an impostor! The play itself must condemn the old man in the eyes of any audience. Vanya's speeches build up his anger to a point of hysteria, and with no sense of what wild things he is saying, his voice reaches its pitch. 'If I had had a normal life I might have been a Schopenhauer, a Dostoevsky . . . Oh, I am talking like an idiot! I am going mad . . .' The man he has idolized all these years has feet of clay.

Serebryakov parries these thrusts as best he can, apparently astonished at the storm he has brought about his head. The Mother, wholly without sympathy for her son, three times reproves him for speaking to her favourite in this way – 'He knows better than we do what is for the best.' And when Vanya's last pitiful appeal to his mother is rebuffed, her indifference to his feelings is felt as a stroke of intense cruelty.

The quarrel about the proper use of the estate for a while centres on Sonya, its rightful owner, and both Vanya and the Professor have addressed themselves to her. But Sonya is unmoved: the extent of her personal tragedy is measured by her appalling silence during the scene. Lost in panic-stricken thoughts of the awful finality of Astrov's departure, she crouches in silence beside Marina, oblivious to the collapse of the real world about her in her horror at the collapse of her hopes and illusions. Her only gesture is to turn in grief to the old Nurse while the angry words of those she loves fly over her head.

Telyegin for his part is in a state of utter consternation. His panic arises because the sale will leave him homeless, and because further dissension between Vanya and Serebryakov can only make his future position worse. He begins a long, deferential circumlocution of an address to the Professor, going to ridiculous lengths to make his appeal, drawing upon his brother's wife's brother's master's degree as evidence that he cherishes for learning 'not simply a feeling of reverence, but a sort of family feeling'. His intention, presumably, is to soften the impression of any criticism of his benefactor, but he is not allowed to complete his comment. Vanya stops him in exasperation, and the Professor was not listening anyway. After three further attempts to heal the rupture, he staggers out '*in violent agitation*', and remains to the end completely and comically ineffectual.

Yelena, too, finally explodes. Holding her head in her hands, she screams, and cries that she is 'going away from this hell this very minute'. The audience may notice with some amusement that this outburst comes from her immediately after Serebryakov has in his rage told Vanya to take the estate and do what he likes with it. We know, of course, that she has her own reasons for protesting, mixed as they are – she refuses to suffer a further shock to her composure; she is troubled by her feelings for Astrov, and she wants to avoid the embarrassing attentions of both her admirers; she is anxious to return to her natural habitat, the sophisticated city, in spite of her dreadful life with Serebryakov; she may be capable of seeing the injustice of his proposal, but when she asks her husband to restore peace, it may also be out of fear that they will lose their income. For all her agitation, this butterfly remains largely unaffected by the real issues thrown up by the shattering announcement: she is too concerned with herself.

The joy of experiencing this sequence in the theatre turns upon receiving this calculated concatenation of sights and sounds. The comedy of Serebryakov's upstanding pomposity is set against the pathetic earnestness of Uncle Vanya, itself set against the indifference of the two droll old women and the equally droll self-concern of Waffles. Sonya's silent suffering in turn points Vanya's erratic outbursts and Yelena's self-centred display. The pace of this string of contradictory attitudes increases the scene's wild discord until Vanya rushes out on the line, 'I know what I must do!' Will he kill himself?[1] The stage is in frenzy, Yelena screaming, the Professor bursting with indignation, and even Sonya on the floor pleading for his mercy. A moment later, everyone has rushed out after Vanya and only Sonya and the Nurse remain, the busy stage rigidly still in its suspense.

Marina has not stopped knitting her stocking. We now hear the croaking from the old woman as she tries to soothe the distraught girl at her knees. 'Never mind, child. The ganders will cackle a bit and leave off . . . They will cackle and leave off . . . A cup of lime-flower water, or raspberry tea, and it will pass . . .'

'It will pass.' The phrase summarizes her ancient and apathetic

---

[1] Desmond MacCarthy, reporting on the performance of the Stage Society, London, 16 May 1914, was the first to note the ambiguity in the line and the mistaken expectation in the audience; thus the outcome is doubly ironic (*Drama*, London, 1940, p. 129).

view of these 'children' and their problems. For Marina above the battle, as for Firs in *The Cherry Orchard*, everyone else is a child who has yet to grow up to learn acquiescence. For her, every difficulty will be resolved by time. The lull gives us leave to assent or dissent.

If this scene appears from one point of view to be one of high drama, it also seems upon reflection to be a wild parody of itself. For the lull also precedes the crowning joke of its climax. A shot is heard off-stage, then a shriek. Has Vanya shot himself after all? But the Professor, quite without his former dignity, runs stumbling in. His agility when faced with a gun is a neat comment on his illness. Where can he hide his miserable body? He is about to duck behind a chair when we see Yelena struggling to hold Vanya in the upstage door-frame. Vanya bursts past her, flourishing a pistol like a maniac, looking wildly about him for his foe. He fires again.

Bang! (*a pause*) Missed! Missed again! (*Furiously*) Damnation – damnation take it . . .

What killer at large ever said 'Bang!'? Like a child, Uncle Vanya is over-dramatizing a moment of which perhaps he has dreamed since he first saw Serebryakov for what he was. This travesty is something out of fiction, something straight out of the boulevard theatre. And what murderer ever missed his aim like this? What villain of the piece ever '*flings the revolver on the floor and sinks on to a chair, exhausted*'?

In this curtain scene, Chekhov surpasses himself as a comic playwright. He combines a riotous climax of noise and movement, not unlike that in one of his own vaudevilles, but mixed of wit and pain, with a superb anticlimax of farcical dimensions. He at once ridicules the overweening Professor of Art and mocks Vanya's last pathetic demonstration of his vitality and individuality. In this crucial instance, Uncle Vanya is not permitted his gesture of heroism. Thus an audience can understand, and yet need not respect, the martyr's condition.

Act Four

In the comic structure of *Uncle Vanya*, a play of anticlimaxes, the last act is all anticlimax; in the affective development of the theme it reaches its full climax. Yet the two patterns of thought and feeling react upon each other and are inseparable. The effect is to compel the audience to an emotional response to a ludicrous situation, and to a cool response to a pathetic situation. If at one moment we are tempted to characterize this last act as flat and dull after the excitement of preceding events, at the next we find ourselves stimulated into an intensely thoughtful activity.

The scene has moved progressively from the garden, through the dining-room to the drawing-room, from more to less public places; at the last it has passed into the unhappy heart of the house, into Uncle Vanya's own room. These are his bed and his personal effects. The room is cluttered with marks of his life's work: '*a big table covered with account books and papers of all sorts; a bureau, bookcases, scales*'. The room also smacks of Astrov's interests, his '*paints and drawing materials . . . a big portfolio.*' We also see two other quasi-symbolic properties, a starling in a cage and a useless and incongruous map of Africa, suggestive of the vague and muddled horizons of Vanya's thinking.

As so often in a Chekhov finale, this is a going-away scene, with all that this can lend the drama. The audience shall feel the regrets both of those going and of those left behind, two kinds of sadness; except that, as in common experience, the regrets of those left behind are the more poignant – most conveniently for the stage and auditorium, which must remain behind as well. Thus going-away scenes are in their nature reflective, evaluating the events of the play which led up to the departure. There is, too, a lively sense of decision about such scenes, which forces on our attention the motives and the consequences, the rights and wrongs, of the decision. Like the stage convention of marriage, it suggests a theatrical finality, while in practice it can persuade us that it is a return or a new beginning or merely a readjustment of forces, so that its image lingers in the mind longer than the event itself would seem to justify. It caps and concludes a mood, while perpetuating it.

This departure begins in stillness and silence, with the Nurse winding wool in her unhurried way on to Telyegin's outstretched hands; this is about all they are good for, and they both look suitably silly. Marina must have finished one stocking and is preparing to start on another. Winter is coming, and, as any peasant knows, warm stockings must be ready. But Chekhov places his curtain-raising emphasis on so trivial an occupation in order to mark so momentous a fact as the quarrel between Serebryakov and Vanya. In impatience, Waffles at last points out that time is short; but these two continue nevertheless to talk over the shocks of the morning.[1]

The old Nurse is particularly pleased that the intruders are leaving. 'We shall live again in the old way, as we used to. We shall have breakfast at eight, dinner at one, and sit down to supper in the evening; everything as it should be, like other people . . . like Christians.' There the old woman represents to us her vegetable self, consigning to oblivion so vital a conflict, showing her indifference to sensitive feelings; a picture of self-centred age at its most negative. Waffles, too, is his old self again, content that the status quo has been preserved and his position secured. As a precaution, he has hidden Vanya's pistol in the cellar. Slaves to their condition, Telyegin and Marina are happy and selfish. They wind their wool.

Vanya comes into his room like an over-dramatic *tragédienne*, telling everyone to leave him alone. Waffles tiptoes away as from an overwrought child, and the Nurse indulgently shuffles off after him. Astrov more intently follows Vanya into the room, anxious, as we learn later, to take a bottle of morphia from him. For Vanya has been contemplating suicide. He attempted murder and yet no one sent for the police. He says this, angry at a perfidious world, as if he sought his own execution. If they think he is mad, well, he is mad. Astrov listens calmly to this outburst and with a bedside

---

[1] It is not explained what Telyegin and Marina are doing in Vanya's room: perhaps avoiding the bustle of departure. But the arrangement is obviously convenient for the stagecraft.

manner clinically reduces the emotional temperature of what Vanya is saying.

You are not a madman: you are simply a crank. A silly fool. Once I used to look upon every crank as an invalid – as abnormal; but now I think it is the normal condition of man to be a crank. You are quite normal.

'You are quite normal' – unwelcome words to Vanya, and perhaps to any member of the audience who has offered him his sympathy too readily. Yet the audience will not mistake Astrov's brusque tones for Chekhov's. If we have been thinking Vanya a joke, or a special case of neurosis (and neither view excludes the other), Chekhov wants us to recognize that Vanya's condition is very like our own. Nevertheless, Vanya is shattered by the Doctor's judgment, and, sitting at the table, he collapses into his hands. If only he could forget the past, begin a new life!

For Astrov, the idea of beginning a new life is as romantic as killing oneself. The only hope for these people is that, when they are asleep in their graves, they 'may, perhaps, be visited by pleasant visions'. In this thought, Astrov echoes Marina and foreshadows Sonya. With such cold comfort, the Doctor again asks Vanya for the morphia. If he insists on dying, let him shoot himself instead. 'It will be quite enough for me to have to make your post-mortem. Do you think I shall find it interesting?' But Vanya still refuses to hand over the morphia, and Astrov appeals to Sonya, who has just come in, to help him retrieve it. 'Be patient!', she pleads, and we notice that in response to the more tender overture from the one who is closest to him in pain, a more passive Vanya hands over the bottle. He and Sonya will work, they agree, in order to distract themselves. We may well put the question, Is 'work' the panacea for ills of the soul and spirit like theirs?

Yelena reports that her husband wishes to see Vanya, and Sonya persuades her uncle to go with her to make up the quarrel. Thus Yelena and Astrov are left alone for a last time. However, the warmth and romance of their parting has already been undermined by the previous love scene in which Vanya came upon them with his wretched bouquet. The love scene cannot repeat itself without parody.

This last encounter begins with stammers and hesitations: both of them are about to go their separate ways. Each was attracted

to the other for equally personal, all but selfish, reasons, Astrov
to redress a loss of purpose in life, Yelena to dispel her ennui. In
this ephemeral process, each dashed the hopes of another votary:
Astrov's kiss had shocked Vanya into a dizzy recognition of a
truth, that he was what he always was; Yelena put an end to
Sonya's longings, and she returned to her mouse-like humility.
Yelena and Astrov may have thought they were in love, but now
they both realize that it was an idle fancy and that they are at
a hopeless impasse,[1] that neither can satisfy for the other the
demands of an insatiable wasting disease. Yelena is the more
resigned to the parting, and speaks with quiet emotion; but it
remains questionable to the end whether her true feelings are
really engaged. But Astrov's cynical teasing of the lady betrays
a more deeply seated trouble. His suggestion to Yelena that she
should give way to her emotion in his poetical woods is strangely
out of character. The Doctor is no seducer, and Eric Bentley
argues the matter thus:

When Yelena arrives, he leaves his forests to rot. Clearly they were no
real fulfilment of his nature, but an old-maidish hobby, like Persian
cats. They were *ersatz*; and as soon as something else seemed to offer
itself, Astrov made his futile attempt at seduction. Freud would have
enjoyed the revealing quality of his last pathetic proposal that Yelena
should give herself to him in the depth of the forest.[2]

Upon her refusal, Astrov speaks more soberly. Without in fact
making an accusation against Serebryakov and Yelena, Chekhov
again uses Astrov to underline the symbolism in the structure of
characters. Yelena and her husband have obsessed the family all
summer long. 'The two of you have infected all of us with your
idleness . . . wherever you and your husband go, you bring destruction everywhere . . . Well, go away. *Finita la commedia!*' The
strangeness of this diagnosis and its medical image suggests that
Chekhov himself is hard put to explain the forces of extinction
he has posited in the play. Nevertheless, it may be enough that he
has had us know that life-destroying agents are always at work,
and that we should discover what the true values are before it is
too late. Astrov at least has decided that Yelena, and what he

[1] At the end of Chekhov's story 'The Lady with the Little Dog' (1899), it is realized
that having an affair means 'a long long way to go, and that the most complicated
and difficult part of it was only just beginning'.
[2] *In Search of Theater* (New York, 1954), p. 349.

imagined to be his love for her, cannot answer his needs, as his casual parting from her implies.

> While there is no one here – before Uncle Vanya comes in with a nosegay – allow me to kiss you at parting . . . Yes? (*Kisses her on the cheek*).

Chekhov criticized Stanislavsky's emotional reading of these lines when he was playing Astrov at the Moscow Art Theatre in 1899.[1] The joke about Vanya and the peck on the cheek make it clear that Astrov has not succumbed. Chekhov has no need of Vanya to undercut the romance a second time: Astrov's own hint is enough to recall to mind that vision of Vanya at the door with his roses, and to puncture the second love scene also. However, while Astrov is still the cynic we are used to, it is an unusually reckless Yelena who '*embraces him impulsively*' as if he were *her* last hope. Perhaps he is. Perhaps the embrace is a tribute to his qualities: it might have been a match if she had been free, but now they will never meet again. Yet she is almost play-acting, still living at second-hand, doing only what the world seems to expect of her. They draw apart, and the painful hesitation with which they listen to the family approaching from the outer room signals again that quality of regret for lost opportunities which the play has captured.

Chekhov brings everyone on, Sonya and Vanya with the Profes-

---

[1] The exchange of letters between Chekhov and Olga Knipper (who played Yelena) tells the whole story. Olga Knipper to Chekhov, 26 September 1899: 'I am disturbed by a remark of Stanislavsky's about Astrov's last scene with Yelena; according to him, Astrov behaves to her like a man passionately in love, catches at his feeling like a drowning man at a straw. I think that if that were so, Yelena would have gone to him and would not have had the spirit to answer: "How absurd you are!" . . . On the contrary, he talks to her extremely cynically and even seems to be jeering at his own cynicism. Is that right or not? Tell me, author, tell me at once.'

Chekhov to Olga Knipper, 30 September 1899: 'At your command I hasten to answer your letter in which you ask me about Astrov's last scene with Yelena. You write that Astrov behaves to Yelena as a man passionately in love, "clutches at his feeling like a drowning man at a straw". But that's not right, not right at all! Astrov likes Yelena, she attracts him by her beauty, but in the last act already he knows that nothing will come of it, that Yelena is disappearing for ever, and he talks to her in that scene in the same tone as of the heat in Africa and kisses her quite casually, to pass the time. If Astrov takes that scene violently, the whole mood of the fourth act – quiet and despondent – is lost' (Garnett, p. 26. See also Hingley, vol. III, p. 302). In 1900, Chekhov gave a further hint to Stanislavsky: 'Uncle Vanya weeps, but Astrov whistles' (*Chekhov i teatr*, ed. E. D. Surkov, Moscow, 1961, p. 259). See also Hingley, *op. cit.*, and cf. Stanislavsky, p. 366.

sor, and even Maman, although we may notice that in slight irritation she keeps her finger in the leaves of her book to mark her place. As in the last act of *The Cherry Orchard*, he fills the stage to empty it again and in the contrast focuses upon those at the suffering heart of the situation. The stage is alive with farewells and embraces, each one betraying that certain falseness of public display which ironically illuminates the true relationship explored earlier. The Professor gives Vanya three formal kisses on both cheeks, 'perfunctory as the stropping of a razor'.[1] He feels confident that all is now well; bygones are to be bygones; and Vanya assures the old man that 'Everything shall be as before.' The spectator knows that nothing can really be as before, and thus may measure the bitterness of Vanya's show of resignation. He may also judge the pretension of the Professor's sentiment that he 'could write a whole treatise on the art of living for the benefit of posterity'. He who can, does; he who cannot, teaches.

Yelena embraces Sonya, but the two girls say nothing. By this time, Sonya has recognized the kiss of death in this creature's friendship, and Yelena knows it. But there is no hatred: both also know the future is bleak, and they part more like sisters. The Professor kisses his mother-in-law's hand, and she asks that he send her a photograph of himself. Her adulation remains intact. Waffles interpolates awkwardly a humble 'Good-bye, your Excellency!' Serebryakov kisses his daughter, and although he is about to speak, he can find nothing to say to her. And, shaking hands with Astrov, he leaves the company with a final thought, heavy with irony in Vanya's ears: 'You must work, my friends! you must work!' This echoes the sentiment heard from Vanya and Sonya a few minutes before, but hearing it again from the lips of this petty tyrant, we listen to it like a mockery. So the Professor bustles off importantly. With suppressed emotion, Vanya kisses Yelena's hand and forces from his throat the cliché, 'We shall never meet again.' Then they have gone.

The episode is one long anticlimax, but the simple act of saying good-bye has become complex for the weight of feeling it bears. Everyone is a hundred years older for the summer visit, and yet everyone is unchanged. As Yelena floats out, leaving Vanya and Astrov alone in the claustrophobic room, together with a starling

---

[1] Desmond MacCarthy reporting on the production of the Stage Society, London, 16 May 1914, the English premiere (*Drama*, London, 1940, p. 129).

in a cage and a hazy Africa on the wall, they both watch their desire slip gracefully away. Astrov is the first to move, but Vanya stands stupefied. When he sees the Doctor purposefully collecting his things together then he blindly *'rummages among his papers on the table'*, declaring, 'I must make haste and occupy myself with something . . . Work! Work!' The mockery of his own notion is heard again, sounding the more grotesque because this time he seems to be parroting his enemy. The silence has prepared the audience for listening, and that 'Work! Work!' reverberates against the jingling harness bells of the departing carriage horses. Together they sound a forlorn note of finality.

As the bells die away and the leave-takers return to the stage, Chekhov tries another medley of discords. The simple sentence, 'They've gone', is repeated four times, but each by a different character in a different tone of voice. Sharply from the Doctor: 'They've gone. The Professor is glad, I'll be bound. Nothing will tempt him back.' Thinking of Yelena, Astrov is anticipating his own departure: nothing will tempt *him* back. 'They've gone': we hear it again, and Astrov's sarcasm is capped by Marina's indifference as she settles herself down with a yawn and begins knitting that new stocking, thinking of bed, secretly pleased that things will be normal again. Sonya's grief, on the other hand, is genuine, and as she wipes her eyes, her muffled 'They've gone' is barely heard. The Mother comes in slowly – as if she too felt some untoward emotion stirring inside her – but her curt 'They've gone' is a rejection of feeling, for she promptly *'becomes engrossed in reading'*. Thus, in little, Chekhov reviews his microcosm of rural society now that the disturbing influence has passed on. Yet is the situation changed? There remain the sensitive and the insensitive, some who will suffer less, some more.

Astrov is still waiting for his horse, and conversation is made as it is made when the guest has said his adieux, but still waits for the taxi. Already Sonya and her uncle have buried themselves in the accounts, and both are writing in silence. A strained hush falls on the room. 'How quiet it is! The pens scratch and the cricket churrs,' says Astrov as he continues to gather his maps. The audience is compelled to see in all its dull particularity the rural life which has previously been only the object of talk. Sonya and Vanya work on, their lowered heads hiding their feelings.

As Astrov takes his leave, Sonya speaks her last cheerless words to him: 'When shall we see you again?' She is timid, fearing the blow in the answer that she has been led by Yelena to expect. But the Doctor, too, is timid: 'Probably not before next summer.' A suitably vague, but kindly, response to a woman in love; and their relationship remains much as it was. So Astrov lingers uncomfortably in this laden atmosphere, until the Nurse offers him a glass of vodka as she did in Act I. He hesitates: in Act II he had promised Sonya never to drink again. Now his 'Perhaps' is shattering. It is a last rejection of Sonya, and in the pause we know that both the man and the woman know it too. The irrelevance of 'My trace-horse has gone a little lame' is conclusive: he has no more to say to her. This end to their abortive relationship is more than un-romantic: it is anti-romantic. There is to be no sudden revelation of 'beauty' in Sonya's soul, or in Astrov's mind.[1] He will pass her by.

'I suppose that in that Africa there the heat must be something terrific now!' Astrov looks up at Vanya's madly incongruous map on the wall, and his idle comment on the heat suggests, not that he is burning with suppressed passion or that his thoughts are far away, dwelling on Helens and forests, but that the vagueness of his present mood, in its triviality, is a criticism of the general waste of human life. The future for the Doctor is as bleak as for those working at the table.

The Doctor goes, and the embarrassing problem of Sonya is left behind him. Once again Vanya burrows in his books, the symbols of his old life, counting the beads of his abacus like a bizarre rosary. He is writing aloud: 'February the second, Lenten oil, twenty pounds. February sixteenth, Lenten oil again, twenty pounds. Buckwheat . . .' Coping with February's bills in September seems to say that the past is always heavy on the present, and can be as real. Moreover, we are quietly reminded that the Russian winter is almost upon them. With his counting, once again the bells are heard mournfully receding into the distance. And once again Chekhov plays the game of chiming words upon the line, 'He has gone', the audience hearing in the changing tones a feeling-pattern of the rural life. In this repetition of his repetitive

---

[1] Valency makes this point, p. 186, and in adding that this ending would be 'normal in sentimental comedy' supports the idea that Chekhov is again flouting contemporary convention.

device, however, the tempo must go more slowly. 'He has gone', says Marina comfortably from her chair. 'He has gone', says Sonya as she comes in from seeing Astrov off, despair and the resignation of despair in her voice. And the Nurse yawns a perfunctory imprecation to an unseeing Deity, 'Lord have mercy on us!'

Meanwhile Vanya continues to count his figures, moving his mouth mechanically, and Sonya joins him. Waffles *'comes in on tiptoe, sits by the door and softly tunes the guitar'*. Chekhov is not ashamed to call up a wistful sound-effect to frame the final image of his play. The scene of vegetable life is as it was in Act I, and the play might begin again from here, a recurring cycle of wasted living, its illusions growing more dim at each revolution.

It is Sonya who is used to make the play's last assertions, Sonya who is the most ingenuous character of them all. She speaks with an almost choric emphasis, yet still within the naturalistic mode of the play. However, the formal staging of her monologue, with Sonya standing centre-stage beside Vanya,[1] distinctly detracts from Chekhov's naturalistic intentions, and seems to insist that she speaks as her author's mouthpiece. Unaffected she may be, but she speaks in her own voice, not Chekhov's. We as an audience must remain at liberty to judge what she says as a statement by a character subject to the limitations of its personality and its situation; more important yet, we must be invited by the stage to judge the statement in context, in the light of the evidence of the rest of the play. She is a pious girl, young by comparison with her uncle, and in the young it is natural to hope. Thus we hear her prayer in the way that we see Vanya's moving the counting beads, as if it were a sedative. For such reasons, and because of its carefully ambiguous wording, Sonya's curtain speech is punctured by our intrinsic and extrinsic doubts about the validity of what she is saying.[2]

[1] As found in many major productions, including Sir Laurence Olivier's with the National Theatre Company at Chichester in 1963 (transferred to the Old Vic Theatre in 1964).

[2] For an opposite view of this curtain, cf. Simmons, p. 487: 'Sonya's wonderful speech at the end to Uncle Vanya is filled with the courage born of defeat, a spiritual symphony of the undying hope that is to be found in lives dedicated to work and service to others.' But he does not go on to examine the implication of that interesting '*to* Uncle Vanya', that is, that ours is the choice between them. Cf. also Magarshack, who insists that the Russian *otdokhnyom* suggests 'not the horror of the rest in the grave, but a serene and happy rest after a task well done' (p. 224).

Act IV

'We must go on living!' Sonya speaks as she sits with her pen poised in her hand. After a pause in which she and we consider the nature of her decision, she reaffirms it with, 'We shall go on living, Uncle Vanya!' She is, we soon realize, however, thinking of life after death.

We shall live through a long, long chain of days and weary evenings; we shall patiently bear the trials which fate sends us; we shall work for others, both now and in our old age, and have no rest; and when our time comes we shall die without a murmur, and there beyond the grave we shall say that we have suffered, that we have wept, that life has been bitter to us, and God will have pity on us, and you and I, uncle, dear uncle, shall see a life that is bright, lovely, beautiful. We shall rejoice and look back at these troubles of ours with tenderness, with a smile – and we shall rest.

After this, a reiterated 'We shall rest' is spoken, not in ringing tones, but *'in a weary voice'*, as if Sonya has abandoned rational argument.[1] Chekhov's choice of verbal imagery in 'We shall hear the angels; we shall see all Heaven lit with radiance' indicates that we are to take this as a romantic, almost childlike, fantasy, which Sonya learned at her mother's – or Marina's – knee. The flighty tone is not unlike that of Vanya's to Yelena: 'You are my happiness, my life, my youth!' and so forth. Sonya is kneeling with her head in Vanya's hands,[2] this pair of soul-mates, the saint and the jester, caught in the same trap. Vanya is now in tears, not of joy, but of grief because he recognizes his niece's despair: we note that he cannot say a word to disillusion her.

Sonya's vision of work, work, endless work reflects Serebryakov's empty notions on parting, 'You must work, my

Nevertheless, Magarshack's characterization of the speech as one of faith and courage ignores the ironies an audience readily perceives. For political, religious or philosophical reasons, critical opinion has been sharply divided on the issue, and I owe to J. J. Moran a 'poll' of critics who interpret Sonya's optimism literally and those who do not. The literalists: H. W. L. Dana, John Gassner, Phyllis Hartnoll, David Magarshack, André Maurois, E. J. Simmons, K. Stanislavsky, M. N. Stroyeva, Raymond Williams, V. Yermilov. The non-literalists: Eric Bentley, W. H. Bruford, Robert Brustein, Rose Caylor, Ilya Ehrenburg, Elisaveta Fen, Francis Fergusson, William Gerhardi, Maxim Gorky, F. L. Lucas, Henry Popkin, Michel Saint-Denis, O. M. Sayler, Leon Shestov, B. O. States, N. A. Toumanova. Still others are non-committal; Russian-speaking critics appear in all groups. Chekhov's objectivity surpassed itself.

[1] In the Olivier production at Chichester, 1963, Joan Plowright as Sonya spoke her last 'We shall rest' with a break in her voice.
[2] And she does *not* rise to her feet in elation, as Chekhov makes clear.

friends! you must work!' Indeed, her thought echoes lessons learned from the Nurse, like the lame sentiment in Act III, 'God is merciful!' In another key, it also pursues Astrov's acid advice to Vanya earlier in this act, spoken half to criticize and half to pacify him: 'There is only one hope for you and me. The hope that when we are asleep in our graves we may, perhaps, be visited by pleasant visions.' That put the matter more bluntly.

So we conclude with Eric Bentley, 'This is not Chekhov speaking. It is an overwrought girl comforting herself with an idea. In *The Wood Demon*, Astrov was the author's mouthpiece when he replied to Sonya: "You are trying to distort your life and you think this is a sacrifice." The mature Chekhov has no direct mouthpieces.'[1] The speech is lyrical and seems to invite an intoned rendering – indeed, it has been set to music by Rachmaninoff[2] – but it is worth remembering that Chekhov himself was an agnostic. Sonya is only his ironic puppet.[3]

Vanya and Sonya, the two of them, hug each other in their misery. Like the chopping of the trees in *The Cherry Orchard*, the tapping of the watchman going about his business outside continues to the fall of the curtain. Nor are Vanya and Sonya alone on the stage: there are five persons in all, and if two are crying, three are not. A front-centre delivery of Sonya's speech must, like a close-up on the television or cinema screen, blot out the total stage picture Chekhov intended. For the curtain image is a perfectly balanced one: Waffles is playing softly on his guitar; Maman takes our momentary attention by writing something in the margin of her pamphlet; the Nurse works away at her second stocking. In this way, the three make their monotonous and melancholy comment on the last moving impression of the play, as they have done in several previous scenes. The trivial business of life is the same as at the beginning, but our understanding of these people has advanced. Such minute reminders of life as it is on *this* earth, comic with the pain that belongs to mockery, slowly bring down the curtain.

[1] *In Search of Theater* (New York, 1954), p. 361.
[2] See H. Popkin, *The Three Sisters* (New York, 1965), p. 14.
[3] The early play *Platonov* undercuts similar sentiments from Sophia, who speaks optimistically about the new life she will have with Platonov, by having her kill him in the last act. Uncle Vanya has no need to resort to so theatrical a gesture as murder. Cf. pp. 232 ff., below, in which Olga's curtain speech in *Three Sisters* is also aesthetically distanced.

Act IV

All the despair of the petty and trivial life, of work without purpose or reward, of an existence without dignity, is expressed in this mutedly ironic ending. *Uncle Vanya* is not a better play than *The Seagull*; it is only more daring. Chekhov said that any idiot can face a crisis; it is the day-to-day living that wears you out. Thus *Uncle Vanya* is a human portrait which is critical and satirical, while at the same time moving and compassionate. These people are the victims of themselves and of their relationships with others, and it is through our intimacy with them that we get a glimpse of ourselves and of the human condition.

Three Sisters

A Drama in Four Acts

1901

Three Sisters

This play shows a concentration and ordering of detail in all departments of theatre only equal in Chekhov's playwriting to *The Cherry Orchard*. It was his strong alignment with a particular playhouse and company of actors which encouraged this development, and this was the first play he had written in its entirety with a fair confidence in how it was going to be handled in the theatre. Nemirovich-Danchenko commented, 'Chekhov did something in his play that is usually censured by the shrewdest dramatic critics: he had written a play for definitely designated actors.'[1] But to satisfy so exact a skill as Chekhov was acquiring, we may rather praise than blame him for using the tools he knew.

The coming together of Konstantin Stanislavsky and Vladimir Nemirovich-Danchenko to found the Moscow Art Theatre in 1898 was an event of major importance for the modern theatre. The happy accident of a dedicated theatre's finding its own playwright when the time was ripe for the new realism meant that Chekhov could establish his style and experiment within it with effects of oblique humour and submerged feeling which only he could conceive. Stanislavsky and Nemirovich-Danchenko, having eliminated much of the older tradition of 'projected' acting and self-exhibition in their direction of *The Seagull*, had turned a failure into a success by maintaining a quality of theatrical honesty and a loyalty to the intentions of the play as a whole. Never had a dramatist more needed this kind of sympathetic treatment.

Chekhov was urged by Nemirovich-Danchenko to write his new play for the still struggling M.A.T., and by November 1899, he had decided its theme. By March 1900, he was still, as he wrote in a letter, 'nibbling at the bait'.[2] By August, he announced that he had written a good deal of the play, and hoped that it would be ready for the season of 1900–1. But both his increasingly poor

---

[1] Nemirovich-Danchenko, p. 211.
[2] To Nemirovich-Danchenko, 10 March 1900. See Hingley, vol. III, p. 305.

health and the detail and complexity of the work[1] proved to be unexpected obstacles, and in September it was still unfinished. Finally, in a letter to Maxim Gorky of 16 October, he wrote with relief that it was done.[2] The first version was read to the company in Moscow, and its author saw some early rehearsals while he was still revising the text, a favour he had never been granted before. In December he sent off the revised acts to Nemirovich-Danchenko one by one, and followed these up with letters containing additional corrections. (In the light of performance, he continued to revise the play during its second season.)

Thus *Three Sisters* had its birth. It was first produced at the M.A.T. on 31 January 1901, with Olga Knipper as Masha and Stanislavsky as Colonel Vershinin. Vsevolod Meyerhold was originally cast for Baron Tusenbach.[3]

Three Sisters, today the most frequently revived[4] and longest-running play in Russian theatrical history,[5] was only coolly received on its first night. Literary and dramatic criticism was a political act in Russia, then as now, and Chekhov's portrait of a soul-destroying provincial life was unwelcome. Stanislavsky writes,

[1] See his letters to Olga Knipper: 'It is not a play, but a sort of tangle. There are a great many characters, – perhaps I shall get in a muddle and give it up' (14 August 1900 in Garnett, p. 40). 'Although it's rather tedious I think it is all right, it is intellectual. I write slowly; that is something unexpected' (30 August 1900 in Garnett, p. 44). 'One of my heroines has gone a bit lame. I can do nothing with her and I am cross' (8 September 1900 in Garnett, p. 47). 'Writing *The Three Sisters* is very hard, harder than my earlier plays' (this to his sister Maria, 9 September 1900, in Hellman, p. 275).

[2] 'Can you imagine – I have written a play; but as it will be produced not now, but next season, I have not made a fair copy of it yet. It can lie as it is. It was very difficult to write *The Three Sisters*. Three heroines, you see, each a separate type and all the daughters of a general' (16 October 1900, in Friedland, p. 156, and Hellman, p. 277).

[3] 'Meyerhold is not liked. He lacks buoyancy, strength, life – he's dry!' So Olga Knipper wrote in rehearsal to Chekhov on 7 January 1901. Alexander Vishnevski confirmed the impression that Meyerhold was not playing for comedy: 'Meyerhold is very sombre . . . the play and his own role require that he be full of high spirits. Stanislavsky and Nemirovich-Danchenko did everything in their power to get the tone right for this part, yet, as everyone knows, they were unable to achieve this until the role was taken over by Kachalov, who, according to his own words, played "an optimist, in love with life" ' (12 January 1901. See Stroyeva, pp. 58–9).

[4] Notably by Nemirovich-Danchenko at the M.A.T. in 1940 and Georgii Tovstonogov at the Gorky Theatre in 1965.

[5] 'In Moscow they have a way of describing an evening at *The Three Sisters*: they speak of "visiting them", as if they were actually going to spend an evening with the Prozoroffs' (John Fernald, *Sense of Direction: The Director and his Actors*, London, 1968, p. 140).

At the end of Act One . . . there were about a dozen shattering curtain-calls. After Act Two there was one. After the Third Act only a few people timidly applauded and the actors could not appear, and after Act Four they got one very thin curtain-call . . . It took a long time for Chekhov's art in this play to reach the theatre-goer.[1]

Nevertheless, the play remained in the repertory, and its audiences left the theatre in an unusual state of thoughtfulness. It improved with playing and with seeing. 'When you read it,' V. M. Lavrov wrote to Chekhov, 'it seems an excellent literary work, but when it's interpreted on the stage things which had not been visible emerge brightly, in sharp relief and with merciless inevitability.'[2]

Three Sisters was a renewed attack upon romanticism, for boredom and waiting are in essence anti-romantic. This assertion calls for immediate modification, however, for it is a play which is closely knit and finely balanced. Its balance is such that it lends itself to un-Chekhovian overplaying and emotionality; at this extreme it can be morbid and repelling. Underplayed, its characters can seem anaemic and its object to lack incisiveness. *Three Sisters*, therefore, risks its life in its challenge to actor and spectator; but once the delicate circuit from stage to auditorium is closed, the play is irresistible in its realism and demands to be seen again and again.

However, the image of Chekhov as the singer of the woebegone and hopeless derives, if anywhere, from this play. Tolstoy declared, 'I could not force myself to read his *Three Sisters* to the end – where does it all lead us to?'[3], a view echoed in the beginning by Desmond MacCarthy, who described the girls as 'forlorn, ineffectual young women'.[4] Yet this insistence does not do justice to their various energies and efforts, whose failure makes us ask whether the wrong is in these people or in people as a whole, in their society or in society as a whole. It is helpful to know that Stanislavsky saw the play as a critical study of an environment, and Nemirovich-Danchenko outlined the structural design of the play as one showing the crushing growth of social triviality:

Here is the substance of his first act: a birthday party, the spring, gaiety, birds singing, bright sunshine. And of the second act: triviality

[1] Quoted in Hingley, vol. III, p. 316.
[2] Letter of 1 February 1901, in Hingley, vol. III, p. 316.
[3] Quoted in Magarshack, p. 15.   [4] *Ibid.* p. 19.

gradually takes into its hands the power over sensitive, nobly inclined human beings. Of the third act: a conflagration in the neighbourhood, the entire street is aflame, the power of triviality grows intenser, human beings somehow flounder in their experiences. The fourth act: autumn, the collapse of all hopes, the triumph of triviality.[1]

And if this play depicted only one disconsolate young woman, we might have reason to feel its pointlessness; the fact that Chekhov does not allow one character to dominate the stage with her emotions, that the chief characters are arranged as a group of three, makes this a thinking play with a satirical edge of social comedy. In *Patience*, W. S. Gilbert, like Sheridan in *The Critic*, also recognized that one forlorn young woman is pathetic, but that two or more can be something else. Nemirovich-Danchenko reported that when the M.A.T. had a first reading of *Three Sisters* in Chekhov's presence, he 'fought with his own embarrassment and several times repeated: "I've written a vaudeville piece!" '[2] In *The Seagull*, Treplev was all but a minor tragic hero, a dark shadow in the background of the comic scene; in *Uncle Vanya*, the title part was central, but Vanya was more of a buffoon and was grouped with two other losers in Sonya and Astrov; *Three Sisters* projected for the first time the image of a family, itself a microcosm of society, placing it at the centre: a plan that leads directly to *The Cherry Orchard*. The three sisters, their brother, their lovers, husbands and wives behave as a *group*; and to this group, caught in a controlled pattern of social events, built into a preconceived design,[3] we attend.

If in the theatre we get to know this family as if we were part of it, it is the design, not the characters, which controls our responses as an audience. In lieu of a 'plot', Chekhov substitutes a pattern; for a focus, he offers a family, even a community, no longer a central character to whom things happen. Without its observation of human behaviour under certain familiar stresses, *Three Sisters* would indeed be on the fringe of being a sociological study, if one of great personal and human interest. The play's only 'action' in the traditional sense consists simply in showing the departure of a regiment from a small provincial town after an interval of three and a half years. And although each of the sisters

---

[1] Nemirovich-Danchenko, p. 207. [2] *Ibid.* p. 209.
[3] Chekhov wrote, 'If an author boasted to me of having written a novel without a preconceived design, under a sudden inspiration, I should call him mad.'

in the family is individualized and longs for Moscow in her own way, it is not the non-fulfilment of this wish which holds the interest of an audience: we know that the dream of Moscow is unreal, like the hope of saving the cherry orchard. The failure of the sisters to make an active protest, or of Lyubov or Gaev to lift a finger to save their orchard, shifts attention from ends to means; it at once shows us their limitations as people and compels us to scrutinize the fabric of their lives. The old, relentless pressure of 'plotting' becomes of no account, since in a static situation we examine the sources of inanimation and not its outcome. Chekhov had been writing stories for years in which hopes were set ironically against realities,[1] and now on the stage it is the co-existence of several people living the same situation in different ways which creates the action of the drama, so that the hopes are real to us.

Thus it is the detailed individual definition of loose notions like happiness, hope and despair which provides the design of the pattern. Moscow on the one hand, but, more concretely, the officers of the regiment on the other, induce and accentuate these feelings. For the officers are partly of the family, but partly out-side, and always with an avenue of escape denied to the sisters – the regiment can move on. Irina reveals herself as she thinks at length of a life with the Baron, and we may guess that, even with-out love, she would have a predictably colourless, invertebrate future with him; when he is killed (by a brother officer, we observe, and not on the battlefield), things are not changed for her. Masha is able to settle for a dry, illicit affair with a marrowless colonel whose integrity is questionable from the start; when he is moved on, things are not changed for her either. Olga has no officer and she has no hope of marriage; her role is to mother the family while the off-duty life of the regiment revolves round her house, and thus, when the sisters are isolated at the end, she may only share their void.

Certainly, provincial life has its blessings; Chekhov knew this from his own experience. Only we, the audience, see the degree of happiness which is present, but which these women do not see for their Moscow blindness. Our response to their feelings is ambivalent throughout, and we remain critical to the end. We are

[1] Such well-known stories as 'The Kiss' and 'Happiness' are typical.

even more critical when we see the sisters as distorted reflections of each other: the older Olga who, desperately, would marry *any* man if he asked her; the younger Irina painfully fastidious about saying 'yes' because of her romantic preconceptions of love; the already married Masha who made a doubtful choice when she accepted Kuligin, but who is unwilling to compromise with her own mistake. 'Three heroines . . . each a separate type', we remember Chekhov writing.[1] But each is afflicted with the same malady, which the most unassuming member of the audience can diagnose: like impartially sympathetic doctors, we watch the sisters turning on their sickbed. We may not laugh, but we do not cry.

In order that the spectator can arrive at a balanced judgment, Chekhov keeps the family life and the family itself in sharp focus for all four acts. Some details are carefully understated and outside pressures are kept impersonal and of less importance to the audience. Thus Chekhov wisely denies us a sight of the powerful Protopopov who steals Andrey's Natasha from him, increasingly controls Andrey's work with the town council and eventually buys the sisters' house from over their heads. Irina's lover is shot offstage, and by the ambiguous figure of Solyony: in many ways an ugly character, quick of temper and jealous of a rival, a man with a reputation for duelling, he is nevertheless presented with some understanding as a misfit who is awkward and quarrelsome in company, and it is he who in the first two acts gathers as much laughter as anyone. His more sinister possibilities, like Protopopov's, emerge only after we have taken his presence for granted.

The evil in Natasha is of another kind, and Chekhov keeps her moving across the scene and has us watch how the poison spreads from the beginning. With her single-minded drive, her repulsive social climbing, her infidelity to Andrey, her petty cruelties in the household, her insidious domination of the family as a whole, Natasha would be the villain of the piece, were it not for the fact that her narrowness of spirit makes her the most satirically comic character in the play. What, after all, is her villainy? It is her way of life, part of the routine of the sisters' household, and it is never allowed to strike us as overwrought and melodramatic. Natasha

[1] See p. 148, n. 2, above.

is a character who is threaded through the lives of the whole family and only near the beginning and the end of the story is she required to 'hold the stage'. We remember what Chekhov had written to his brother Alexander of *Ivanov*: 'I have not introduced a single villain nor an angel though I could not refuse myself buffoons; I accused nobody, justified nobody.'[1] Nor is the conflict in *Three Sisters* a melodramatic opposition of the weak and the strong. Natasha is only symptomatic of those little pressures of destructive self-interest present everywhere, part of the cruel nature of life which fragile people like the sisters are unable to withstand. She is symptomatic of the petty frustrations which crowd in and render the strong weak and the weak weaker, and her frightening normality stresses the ineffectual gentility of the well-born sisters. The audience finds Natasha's vulgarity so familiar that it is laughable.

If the true comic tone and balance in the details of the play as a whole are achieved, none of these dangerous forces will be felt as anything other than the sort of human hazard we all expect to meet from time to time. They are equivalent to the indeterminate order from some military headquarters which moved the regiment elsewhere in the last act.

This tone and balance is found everywhere in the play. When we say that the focus is on the family as a whole, we are claiming that every detail of an immensely detailed play is relevant to our understanding of the family's immediate condition. In Act I, whether it is Natasha's scrubbed cheeks (her naive and primly Victorian attempt to attract brother Andrey's attention) which disgusts them all equally, and guides us to an understanding of their sense of their own superior social class; or whether it is the squeaky sound of Andrey's lonely violin reminding them of his failed ambition to be a university teacher (one more hope of Moscow destroyed); or whether it is the teasing mixture of pride and shame with which Andrey receives in front of a stranger Irina's unthinking praise of the picture-frame he made her – of a thousand touches, everything in the last analysis illuminates their predicament. Yet the profusion of such naturalistic details, from a major visual and aural sensation like Tchebutykin's smashing of the mother's clock to the merest inflection heard in Masha's soft

1 See p. 3, above.

whistling, is distracting unless subtly arranged also to add consistently to the play's meaning. Once the spectator is paying intense and close attention, he will tolerate no false clues: *Three
Sisters*, characteristically, has none.

Everything is 'as complex and as simple as in life.'[1] The play's
statement, emerging through an abundance of details, is as complex as the details themselves seem simple. Masha's '*amo, amas,
amat*' to her husband when he declares his love for her neatly
measures with an icy sarcasm what she thinks of the kind of love
marriage to a teacher of Latin has offered, or can offer. At the
same time it suggests what new views of love, even less real but
rather magical, she is harbouring as a result of her introduction
to Vershinin; and after we have heard the Colonel speak airily
and mechanically, we may well ask whether the one love is not as
unlikely as the other. As we assemble the pieces, we look beyond
the characters. We look beyond the retort delivered to Kuligin to
the muddle of tensions in Masha's head, and we look beyond her
thoughts to her contribution to an audience's impression of the
lives of these lovelorn girls, and of the inhibitions and hindrances
that prevent their fulfilment as ordinary people. The audience's
response becomes expansive.

Yet against all this, Masha and her sisters *are* ordinary people,
and their situation in provincial Russia in the late nineteenth
century is nothing unusual. Stanislavsky was right to find that the
sisters, like other mortals, try to put on happy faces and do not
sulk. On the contrary: 'It turned out that they were not dragging
around their burden of sorrow but were really looking for
gaiety, laughter, animation; they want to live and not just
vegetate.'[2] Therefore, when an audience sees on the stage their
discordant attempts to revitalize an existence which has been
deadened by the philistinism of Natasha and Protopopov en-
croaching upon their happiness, feelings in the theatre must be
poignantly ambivalent. A theme emerges, one which has to do
with the values of living in the face of social change.

This does not make *Three Sisters* a play prophetic of a new
society, but rather a play critical of the old society and its forms.
Nor does the play urge a tragic view of human life if the crescendo of discords is heard objectively, for in its special detachment an audience cannot be as emotionally adrift as the sisters

1 See p. 82, above.   2 Stroyeva, p. 57.

themselves. Is *Three Sisters* then a comedy? Chekhov called it 'A Drama in Four Acts', and does not refer to it as a comedy in the title, as he does *The Seagull* and *The Cherry Orchard*.[1] But as 'drama' it induces sympathy with criticism, and promotes the most inclusive of truly comic attitudes, that of human understanding.

[1] When Chekhov insisted to the M.A.T. that he had written a 'vaudeville', by the use of this inappropriate word he was undoubtedly trying to correct their tendency to play it heavily.

Act One

With Chekhov confidently in command of his medium, the sisters Olga, Masha and Irina are presented immediately on the rise of the curtain, and the audience is aware of the characters before it is aware of the room they are in. In the next minute or two we receive a complete, but already complex, exposition of the characters' situation and mood, many of the similarities and differences between them, and the possible direction of the scene.

The spectator is early struck with a sense of 'family'; excepting *The Cherry Orchard*, this is to be the most 'family' of all the plays, and silences between people and the conjunction and disjunction of comment will define the relationship of sister to sister (and, later, sister to brother) and convey much of the vital life of the group. Here we first see Olga, at twenty-eight the oldest, talking and walking and marking exercise books. Irina, at twenty the youngest, is standing still, listening and not listening. Masha, the more enigmatic middle of the equation, sits reading without moving a muscle. The familiarity of one girl with another is taken for granted; each is different, and yet each belongs to the others. Thus intensely naturalistic and specifically ensemble acting is expected from the start. At first glance this is a quick vignette of general family life: a table upstage is being laid for lunch, one person is still working, some are at leisure, and there is an air of waiting for others to arrive. It is a 'group' which is untheatrically not a group. For these people, if not entirely relaxed, are at home.

We partly attend to the home itself as Olga talks. Their large first-floor drawing-room, flooded now with cool spring sunshine, is impressive. The design and furnishing of the room, with columns separating it from another large room upstage, suggest comfort, wealth and style, even if it seems in the faintest way shabby. For we are to learn that the father was the general in command of a brigade,[1] but that he died a year ago; things have not been so comfortable during the last few years. One sister, Olga, has been working as a teacher for four years with a sense of drudgery, and we might wonder why she is correcting her exercises on Irina's saint's day: her work must seem to contradict the apparent status of the family. By degrees it is suggested that their situation is not all that they could desire. In a letter to Maxim Gorky,[2] Chekhov indicated that they are living in a provincial town many miles from Moscow, perhaps like Perm, an industrial town in the Urals, then with a population of 45,000. Luckily, the town supports an artillery barracks, so that the higher social and cultural life of the place is supplied largely by its officers, and has found a centre in the home of their late commanding officer. Conveniently, General Prozorov had three daughters to keep the tradition alive.

The elaborate preparations by the servants in the farther room mark this as a special occasion. Chekhov is again symbolically expanding the frame of the proscenium arch without disturbing the realism within it. Technically, the divided set draws the eye into the first room, and when from the second room the ear catches male voices raised in laughter, the house, together with its life and spirit, is granted a new dimension. A contradiction in the atmosphere of the home is quickly felt.

We look back at the sisters, and make our first comparison between the two who are on their feet, the one moving and the other still. Olga is wearing *'the dark blue uniform of a high school teacher'*, and its severe lines and colour are set against Irina's white, easy party dress: the dark and the light reflect the stages in development of their hopes and moods, and mark the difference of eight years at a crucial time in a young woman's life. At first the focus is on Olga talking; we have to wait for the first reluctant reply from Irina. Olga's manner, agitated, a little martyred, hints that she has been mothering the family, thinking for them, responsibly earning their living. We learn later that their

---

[1] 'In order to underline the breaking down, the growing shallowness of the sisters' lives [Stanislavsky] deliberately "demoted" them in "rank". Nothing in their home suggests that they are the daughters of a general. On the contrary, the house is "most ordinary, with cheap furnishings". (Simov [the designer at the M.A.T.] recalls that Stanislavsky asked him to design the house as if they were the daughters of a captain)' (Stroyeva, p. 57).

[2] 16 October 1900, in Hellman, p. 278.

mother died before they left Moscow, more than eleven years ago, when Olga was nineteen. And mother and Moscow are implicitly associated with one another. But the response of Irina, and especially the absence of verbal response from Masha, does not leave an audience uncritical of Olga. She asks largely unanswerable questions.

For a minute Olga seems to talk alone. This seeming soliloquizing is perhaps a Russian character trait, but in the theatre, and even when spoken in English, it does not seem inappropriate to the general spirit of reverie with which the play opens, and is here entirely acceptable as a method of semi-naturalistic 'exposition'. She could be half talking to the others, who, because of their preoccupations, are only half listening. Olga's 'monologue' is especially workable because the fact that her sisters do not speak compels the listener to judge its limited relevance to the total situation; Masha's refusal to concur, again, indicates particularly that much more could be said. Thus we listen also to what is unspoken.

Olga's talk is nostalgic and its pace is generally slow. We learn that today is not only Irina's saint's day, but also that it is the anniversary of the father's death. So there is every reason for ambivalent feelings in the speech itself. The bright midday sunshine streams through the window; the stage is alive with the spirit of springtime. Stanislavsky's prompt book makes this point firmly, if with characteristic over-emphasis.

'Branches with buds barely turned green' peer into the windows 'which have just been opened after winter'. Irina is preparing feed for the birds; one can hear their 'chirping outside beyond the bay window'. 'Andrey, full of spring feeling, is playing some melodious sonata off in the wings' . . . There are lots of flowers on the stage and from time to time one hears music, loud laughter, joyous exclamations.[1]

But Olga is also thinking of the cold sleet and snow of a year ago – a very particular memory, a great shock at the time. Now they 'can think of it calmly'. Or can they? Olga in her voice and movement is tense, the others are silent. As the sun started Olga's first train of thought, now the clock striking twelve (the lengthy

[1] M. N. Stroyeva, '*The Three Sisters* in the Production of the Moscow Art Theatre', trans. R. L. Jackson, in Jackson, p. 122. Stanislavsky is emphasizing these joyful effects presumably in order to sharpen the conflict between the buoyancy of the characters' hopes and their deadening environment.

'*pause*' for this effect and after it gives an idea of the slow pace of
the opening) is a time for feelings to well up as the strokes
themselves prompt further memories, memories of the military
band playing the funeral procession to the cemetery; and at the
end of the play such a military band will again be associated with
death. All the same, 'there weren't many people there': once an
important man, a general no less, transferred to a provincial
command, he had been buried in the rain and sleet miles from
anywhere and largely forgotten. Now even the memory of him
is fading. The clock struck the noon hour, and time is the subject;
from this moment everything is a decline to the end. Olga's
harping on the past begins to be unhealthy, as the sudden retort
from Irina suggests: 'Why recall it!' As with the contradictions
in the tone of the openings of *The Seagull* and *Uncle Vanya*,
Chekhov is directly introducing ambivalence into his audience's
response.

Olga needs the past. For her the present is dead and the future
unthinkable. Her tone brightens as she recalls the Moscow they
left behind. In Moscow with its earlier spring, it would be warm
in early May, while here the trees are bare of leaves, barren like
the lives of the sisters. But Moscow! – that is the place for
warmth and sunshine and blossoms! And that is the place to
revive the special happiness of the past. Olga's repetitions are
those of one who is consoling herself with memories, and as if
Masha knew it, her only response is a soft whistle of criticism and
boredom.[1] We see that it is springtime, a time for hope. At the
end it will be autumn, the time for reflection, although Olga's
spirit will be hardly different.

At this whistle, Olga's tone changes again, sharply. She stops,
turns, and with a sudden flare of schoolmistressy irritation she
says, 'Don't whistle, Masha. How can you!' All the anger of one
who works felt for one who does not is turned upon poor
Masha. Then the '*pause*' allows Olga time to control herself once
more, but too late to stop herself being dragged back, unhappily,
into the present. In her voice now is the spiritless tone of one

---

[1] Chekhov wrote to Olga Knipper on 2 January 1901, when she was rehearsing the
part of Masha, 'Don't make a mournful face in a single act. Angry, yes, but not
mournful. People who have borne a grief in their hearts for a long time and are
used to it only whistle and often sink into thought. So you may often be thoughtful
on the stage during conversations' (Garnett, p. 67). Nemirovich-Danchenko also
recalls this injunction, p. 209.

who also suffers day after day of unsatisfying drudgery. She talks aloud of her long hours, of her sense of growing old. All her thoughts are on the passing of time, and her Chekhovian, reductive comment on brother Andrey's fat and her own lean suggests that she is still thinking of how they used to be before, particularly the older ones. Olga is twenty-eight at the beginning of the play and thirty-three at the end, but she suffers from the delusion that she is ageing too quickly.[1] Even her optimistic remarks on Irina's youth and beauty and Masha's good looks – even on Andrey's too, had he not grown fat – are a reflection on her own hopeless spinsterhood. Although she is only twenty-eight, her chances of marriage are throughout the play never considered.

It's all quite right, it's all from God, but it seems to me that if I were married and sitting at home all day, it would be better (*a pause*). I should be fond of my husband.

This last quiet thought, directed, no doubt, at the married Masha, reaches out to us in its poignancy. She has dwelt on the notion of another life for herself, it seems, and the conditional 'I should be fond of my husband' tells the whole sad story of a woman who has sacrificed herself too long for others. However, she would be fond of her husband only if he were one she could be fond of. It is a characteristically theoretical statement, and Masha's marriage is the answer to it: the aspiration could be frustrated in various ways, and it is almost self-deception.

The mood is nearly all of regret. The bright sun lighting the room accentuates Olga's dark dress and her dark, submerged feelings, and her tones belie her thoughts even when she speaks more cheerfully of Moscow. She lives in the memory of Moscow, and when for the second time her thoughts return there, we note that Irina finishes her sentiment with striking alacrity.

OLGA. . . . only one yearning grows stronger and stronger . . .
IRINA. To go back to Moscow. To sell the house, to make an end of everything here, and off to Moscow . . .
OLGA. Yes! To Moscow, and quickly.

On this issue she and Irina are at one. Even the youngest, who must have left Moscow when she was no more than a child, is

[1] See also Act III, where she says, 'This night has made me ten years older.'

feeding on the same memory, although for her the future holds more hope. Irina has heard the same tune a hundred times, and Moscow has become a myth. Masha, however, still does not speak: she continues to whistle.

Irina's unresponsiveness to memories of the father, but ready acceptance of the Moscow dream, suggests that for her the tensions between the past, present and future are of a different order. Her Moscow is not an echo of Olga's, but a radiant expectation. And when Andrey is a professor, he will go there too. Irina's mood is entirely optimistic, and on her name-day she thinks of Moscow as she thinks of her childhood with her mother. All in white, young, spirited and attractive, we link her with the spring itself and the fulfilment of every maidenly promise.

'The only difficulty is poor Masha.' Masha's damaging silence spoils their unanimity as a group: she has still said not a word. She is almost as young as Irina, only twenty-two, but she is dressed heavily in matronly black. She sits as if buried in her book, but with her hat on her knee as if she were also on the point of leaving. Her light whistling under her breath strangely echoes the tenor of the seemingly irrelevant noise and laughter from the men in the farther room, and is as strong a comment as Chekhov needs to have her make. Two of the sisters are in accord, the third is not. At this stage, Masha's different circumstances must be guessed, for she is the one sister who is married. Moscow means little to her. She is trapped. She cannot leave, although Olga has the idea that she could spend the summer with them in Moscow every year. Such a notion is answered by a whistle from Masha as if to say that Olga does not know much about husbands, and perhaps babies. The dream of Moscow can serve as no artificial stimulus to her, it seems, and she has resorted to reading fiction as her only possible escape.

In another letter to Olga Knipper on the subject of Masha, Chekhov wrote that when playing the part she should 'look younger and more full of life. Remember that you are given to laughing and being cross'.[1] Just as the whistling is a symptom of a deep-seated discontent, so are her outbursts of laughter and anger. But there is also, indeed, something of the social nonconformist in a married woman who will whistle, and we noted

[1] Letter of 20 January 1901 (Garnett, p. 73).

Olga's reproof. We shall see in Act III how, unlike Yelena in *Uncle Vanya*, she is prepared to reject convention completely for the sake of an affair with Vershinin. In the light of this, it is helpful to record that a comparison between the earliest manuscript of the play and that in the keeping of the M.A.T. indicates that Masha had first been conceived as a 'slightly vulgar "daughter of the regiment".'[1]

The audience must gain the sense that if Olga is living in the past and Irina in the future, Masha, the realistic one, is inescapably rooted in the cruel present. If as an audience we are set at a distance from the turbulent feelings of Olga and Irina in this episode, it is because, in spite of Masha's long silence, we increasingly see them through her clearer eyes. As an inner witness, with her choric whistling, she makes of her sister's performance a play-within-a-play. Of greatest importance, she is aligned in our minds with the seeming indifference of the gentlemen who are joking in the room upstage.

The presence of these gentlemen, the officers, is slowly felt in the auditorium with increasing point. They impress us also as real, and except for Tchebutykin the army doctor, living very much in the present. Chekhov was careful that his picture of army life should be exact. He saw to it that a colonel was present at rehearsals in the M.A.T. to advise the actors on the authentic appearance and behaviour of officers of artillery. In particular, Stanislavsky reported, he wanted no heel-clicking stage caricatures.[2] They are to be *real* soldiers, and their genial but masculine

---

[1] According to A. R. Vladimirskaya in *Literaturnoye nasledstvo: Chekhov* (Moscow, 1960), quoted in Hingley, vol. III, p. 310. Hingley comments that the new Masha is made more genteel, though her dialogue retains its racy touch.

[2] 'Chekhov had left a viceroy in the person of a lovable colonel [Colonel V. A. Petrov: J.L.S.] who was to see that there should be no mistakes made in the customs of military life, in the manner and method of the officers' bearing in the play, in the details of their uniforms, and so on.' Stanislavsky also mentions rumours that the play was written in criticism of the army: 'In truth, Anton Pavlovich always had the best opinion about military men, especially those on active service, for they, in his own words, were to a certain extent the bearers of a cultural mission . . . coming into the farthest corners of the provinces' (Stanislavsky, p. 374). Again from Stanislavsky, 'He wanted us to play simple, charming, decent people, dressed in worn, untheatrical uniforms, without any theatrical military mannerisms, throwing back of shoulders, bluff remarks and the like' (quoted in Hingley, vol. III, p. 315, from *Chekhov i teatr*, ed. E. D. Surkov, Moscow, 1961, p. 279). Nemirovich-Danchenko also remarks the presence of 'a colonel in the artillery' for the sake of verisimilitude (Nemirovich-Danchenko, p. 209).

presence in this feminine world of dreams is the sharpest criticism that their author provides in this opening of the play. They behave in an easy, familiar way among the sisters as if they have been in the house many times before, but their speech is brusque and immediate, and, by contrast with the tones of the ladies, even mildly uncouth. This distinction in voice is strongly stressed by Chekhov's use of the divided stage, by which he precisely counterpoints every remark about Moscow with a distracting, but obliquely relevant, irrelevance. After Olga's expression of longing to go home, we hear them laugh.

TCHEBUTYKIN. The devil it is!
TUSENBACH. Of course, it's nonsense.

The men are not speaking other than to themselves, but with simple efficiency their casual freedom of tone sets them, and us, apart from Olga and Irina.

So the family Prozorov is introduced with the gentle admonishment of satire. Satire, because Olga and Irina continue in the same vein of futile longing, but, undercut, their woes reach our less sympathetic ears. Their song is of Moscow, Moscow the cosmopolitan centre of culture, opportunity and the full life, at once the romantic source of their memories of happiness and their reason for loathing the dreary present. 'Moscow!' – when the voices of Olga and Irina chime on the word, pace accelerates and hearts flutter. But we smile.

The two groups, three women and three men, join forces in the main playing area. As if he had done it many times before, one of the officers sits at ease to strum on the piano; it is the ugly little lieutenant, the Baron Tusenbach.[1] As if he were taking up a conversation that was broken earlier, he says, 'I forgot to tell

---

[1] The Baron's plain looks are important to dispel some of the possible romanticism the theatre at this time might have assumed him to have as the 'juvenile lead'. In the M.A.T. production of 1901, Kachalov played him in spectacles and with a spotty face (*Anton Pavlovich Chekhov in the Theatre*, ed. N. Gorchakov, Moscow, 1955, p. 45). In the production at the Barnes Theatre, London, in 1925, John Gielgud played Tusenbach and reported that the director Theodore Komisarjevsky 'cut all references to the Baron [*sic*] being an ugly man – which is Tchechov's reason why Irina cannot love him – and made me play the part in a juvenile make-up, with a smart uniform and side-whiskers, looking as handsome as possible. I have never been able to discover why he did this – but I have a suspicion that he felt that a juvenile love-interest was essential in any play that was to appeal to an English audience. He persisted in casting the part in this way in every subsequent

you . . .', and casually introduces the first element in the forward action of the play: Colonel Vershinin, the new battery commander, is going to call on the Prozorovs.

Lively interest is immediately shown by two of the sisters; only Masha, married and in chains, still does not speak. Olga is happy to widen her modest *salon*, but Irina's first question is to ask whether the Colonel is 'old', and on hearing that he is 'forty or forty-five at the most', in a shade less ardent tone she asks whether he is 'interesting'. Tusenbach replies without unkindness that he has been married twice, and no more is heard from Irina on the subject. The ripple of excitement in the room passes quickly.

In the Baron's few words about the Colonel, the audience learns a good deal without prompting; indeed, in spite of Tusenbach's obvious sympathy with him, we put another interpretation on the evidence. First, 'he talks a lot'. Second, he tells everyone about his difficulties with his wife. However 'nice' Vershinin may be, we anticipate a slight lack of poise, even a mediocrity, in the man. His wife 'frequently attempts to commit suicide, evidently to annoy her husband'; for his part, he 'puts up with her and merely complains'. The details might be those of tragedy or of farce, and the audience must take them as a warning that, when he appears, this Colonel may be neither romantic nor all that he seems. His wife is a cross which he bears with some credit, but when later in the play Masha finds him attractive, the spectator's suspicions about him will provide the measure of her emotional need, and be the test of values when assessing her attitude in searching for sensation in a drab life.

One officer has all the appearance of being a romantic hero, but not for long. A fiercely Byronic-looking captain of artillery, Solyony, has followed Tusenbach into the room, talking loudly of his physical strength. He too will not be all he seems. As we piece together the disturbing facets of his character, we shall find him an entirely self-centred man of the type who callously enjoys exerting power over others. Maurice Valency argues[1] that he is

revival of the play' (*Early Stages*, London, 1939, p. 107). However, for John Gielgud's company at the Queen's Theatre, London, in 1938, Michel Saint-Denis did not feel this necessity and had Michael Redgrave return to the first conception of the part and play Tusenbach as ugly and comic (see John Gielgud, *Stage Directions*, London, 1963, p. 87).

[1] Valency, p. 21.

modelled upon the hero of Mikhail Lermontov's romantic drama *The Masquerade* (1835), but with more comedy. In *The Masquerade*, Eugene Arbenin is a proud man who hides a cruel demonism behind an offhand, distant manner. The dark, Satanic love that Solyony reveals later for Irina, the young girl in white, is very much in the nineteenth-century tradition of melodrama. Valency also offers a psychological explanation for this enigmatic type and his actions: 'The disease of the spirit gives way to love. It requires – in the absence of a qualified psychiatrist – the services of a pure girl to relieve its misery. But, unlike the heroes of romance, these characters are inclined by nature to be suspicious and vindictive, and are incapable of a healthy sexual relationship. In these circumstances it is chiefly the girl who suffers.' Valency is too literary here. Solyony wants love, but anticipates, through self-knowledge mixed with fear, that he is unlovable. He then exaggerates this unlovability as if to spite the world and prove it right. He will destroy Tusenbach in order to take his revenge on the world and deprive him of the love he cannot have. He is very true and very frightening, and Solyony provides the only occasion outside the stories when Chekhov shows the destructive potentialities of malignant failure.

With Solyony is an army doctor, the last of Chekhov's sceptical choric doctors, but one very different from Dorn and Astrov before him. This Doctor has become the complete cynic, to cover a real glimpse of chaos. It is as if Dorn had lost his nerve, taken to drink, neglected his professional duty and grown coarse. Dr Tchebutykin wearily ambles in, reading a newspaper: he is never seen without one. He reads aloud. 'For hair falling out . . . two ounces of naphthaline in half a bottle of spirit . . . to be dissolved and used daily.' He writes this earth-shaking piece of information in a small notebook. The joke also hints at the Doctor's sense of loss: he is another who is conscious of growing old, losing his vitality, losing his hair. As a physician, too, he is so out of touch with professional practice that he resorts to collecting titbits from the popular papers. Tchebutykin's sorry little notebook is the mark of his failure as a doctor and as a man. He completes the audience's first impression of Chekhov's army: with the exception of the Captain, an ordinary, if somewhat dismal, one.

The group is joined and the stage is full. For five minutes before the entrance of Vershinin, the conversation seems to ramble and take on that deceptive, Chekhovian quality of inconsequence by which the central mood of the whole group is filtered through a hundred details of the characters' speech and behaviour. Irina greets the Doctor affectionately: we observe the special link between the oldest and the youngest in the gathering, just as between Sorin and Treplev in *The Seagull*. But Tchebutykin's liking for Irina will be seen as far more functional than Sorin's for Treplev.

A mock-Tolstoyan sentiment is heard from Irina, one heard from Vanya and Sonya before her: 'A man ought to work, to toil in the sweat of his brow.' But unlike Sonya, Irina does not lift a finger in work and toil for two more acts, and when she does, the experience is wholly distasteful to her. 'How delightful to be a workman who gets up before dawn and breaks stones on the road, or a shepherd, or a schoolmaster teaching children, or an engine-driver . . .'[1] But Irina, as Olga tells us, lies in bed 'at least till nine', and the comment is a sufficient deflation of this innocent nonsense. Olga's laugh, however, is also embarrassed: she is concerned for her youngest sister's future. Humourlessly, the little Baron echoes Irina's thoughts on work, even though he too, as a nobleman, has never done a stroke in his life.

The time is at hand, an avalanche is moving down upon us, a mighty clearing storm which is coming, is already near and will soon blow the laziness, the indifference, the distaste for work, the rotten boredom out of our society. I shall work, and in another twenty-five or thirty years everyone will have to work. Every one!

Again the comic deflation comes, this time from Tchebutykin: 'I am not going to work.' Yet Tusenbach's speech, which seems to some today prophetic of the communist revolution, is as much Chekhov's hit at the talking malaise of the intelligentsia of the period. There are other places in Chekhov where the routine of work is shown to be either an anodyne or a treadmill; it is hardly the answer to all that is wrong in society. According to their

[1] One is naughtily reminded of the elegant Lady India in Jean Anouilh's black comedy *Invitation au château*, Act III. Dancing a Mexican tango with her lover Patrice Bombelles, she declares that it would be wonderful to be poor: 'Moi j'adorerais être pauvre! Seulement, je voudrais être vraiment pauvre. Tout ce qui est excessif m'enchante. Et puis, il doit certainement y avoir une grande poésie dans la misère, n'est-ce pas, Patrice? . . . Tu travaillerais dans une usine . . . Tu rentrerais le soir harassé de fatigue et sentant très mauvais. Ce serait délicieux!'

lights, Tusenbach and Irina are sincere in their idealism, and
later they try to put their ideas into practice, but their solution is
inadequate, as the play proves. The tirades on work, spoken by
a light-headed young girl in a dainty party dress and by an
awkward young nobleman in officer's uniform, must be played
dead-pan for humour and not passionately for prophecy.

The ambiguous mood, which sets what we see against what
we hear, and purpose and hope against the reality, is extended.
Solyony cruelly takes up Tchebutykin's mournful comment and
with a cold straight face tells him that he will be dead in a couple
of years, or else 'I shall lose my temper and put a bullet through
your head, my angel'. The remark is half-jocular, half-serious,
and adds to the disconcerting uncertainty of the general tone,
especially when it is made as he takes from his pocket a bottle of
scent and '*sprinkles his chest and hands*'. The audience is to see this
aristocratic gesture many times until it is familiar, but, although
casual, it cannot be lost in the larger picture of the stage. As a
neurotic habit it catches attention from the beginning and lends
force to our suspicions of the Captain, colouring whatever he
seems to say in joke. Surprisingly, the old Doctor agrees with a
laugh that he is useless: since he left the university, he has not
read a book. If the ridiculous element in this is impaired when he
adds that he does not care either, the moment of apprehension
has passed.

Tchebutykin leaves the stage in answer to a knock on the
floor from below (we learn that Chekhov's stage houses have lower
rooms too!), and it is remarked that he is bringing Irina a present.
It seems almost defiant that Masha should get up to go home at
such a moment, but in this way Chekhov again stresses her
separation from the rest. And her first words, even then, are a
few evocative and haunting childhood lines from Pushkin's
mock-heroic romance *Ruslan and Lyudmila* (1820). These she will
repeat like a theme in music from time to time. They tell us of
her varying states of mind by the tone of voice she uses and the
almost imperceptible humming that goes with them, like Gaev's
tags from the imaginary game of billiards he perpetually plays
with himself in *The Cherry Orchard*. Here Olga interprets for us
explicitly that Masha is melancholy: Chekhov implies that it
takes a sister to know what a sister means by such cryptic signals.
Masha puts on her hat; she is going home. Neither Tchebutykin's

present nor Vershinin's arrival seem of consequence to her, and all in the group on stage are shocked that she should leave her sister's party. But Masha, unlike her namesake in *The Seagull*, is no child, and in her tragic black, *'laughing through her tears'*, she generously implies that it is better to take her depression off with her. 'In the old days, when father was alive, we always had thirty or forty officers here on name-days; it was noisy, but today there is only a man and a half, and it is as still as the desert . . .' Her proposal is like a cold douche of water on their efforts to work up the party spirit, and again the tenor of the scene wavers. Irina is annoyed, sentimental Olga is sympathetic, Solyony is offensive. The motivation of every character is consistent, and even after so short a time, Chekhov can smoothly run off a wide variety of individual reactions so that each is different while together they still suggest the contrary feelings that hang like a cloud over Irina's party.

Solyony's sarcasm on woman's attempt to philosophize had produced a sharp, tetchy quip from Masha: 'You terrible person.' He answers her in kind with a quotation, this time from Pushkin's more light-hearted older contemporary Ivan Krylov.

> He had not time to say 'alack',
> Before the bear was on his back.

By this he exactly catches her short manner as she flashed at him, and turns her thrust aside with a joke. This quotation, too, is to echo in the play,[1] and the abundance of such literary references in *Three Sisters*, unlike the other plays, appropriately suggests the level of culture of the group of officers and ladies. But Chekhov is careful to exploit these allusions in a variety of styles and tones as another indirect, but naturalistic, means of revealing submerged feelings. Masha here takes the point, and, in a typically Chekhovian chain-reaction, transfers her anger to Olga, whose excessive expression of emotion has irritated the person who for the most part has learned to suppress her own: 'Don't blubber!'

---

[1] Krylov was a writer of comic fables, and the quotation is from *The Peasant and the Farm Labourer*. The lines are a moment later also associated with Protopopov, whom Masha calls Mihail (dim. *Mishka*, 'bear'). Magarshack discusses the punning, p. 235, arguing that Masha, the most sensitive member of the family, is the one who feels something ominous about Protopopov.

Act I

Anfisa the aged nurse[1] ushers in deaf old Ferapont from the council office: 'This way, my good man . . .' A comic duo of old age, which relieves the tension a little. The old clerk brings a cake from 'Mihail Ivanitch Protopopov', giving his master his full, formal title. The part Protopopov has to play in *Three Sisters* begins here in this modest way. He is evidently a man of some importance, but one whom we are never to see in the play. His pervading presence behind the scenes will be increasingly felt, and we are immediately struck with a warning that he is a man to distrust.

MASHA. I don't like that Protopopov, that Mihail Potapitch or Ivan-itch. He ought not to be invited.
IRINA. I did not invite him.
MASHA. That's a good thing.

The hint is that he is a local man of wealth and official position, not of the sisters' class or culture, but, like Natalya Ivanovna later, trying to ingratiate himself with the General's family. So, subtly, Chekhov introduces a black knight unobserved among the pawns.

Tchebutykin with unaccustomed excitement brings in a soldier with his gift for Irina. Is the party spirit rising? Everyone on stage stops still and looks with astonishment at what he has brought. It is an impressive silver samovar. Then follows '*a hum of surprise and displeasure*'. The audience looks at Tchebutykin's idiosyncrasies enlarged through the eyes of the tiny audience on stage. From Olga we hear, 'A samovar! How awful!', and as she walks out upstage a new chill is felt in the room. For a samovar is an inappropriate present to an unmarried girl; it is the traditional Russian offering from a husband to his wife on their twenty-fifth anniversary of marriage. The Doctor is making the anniversary of the father's death and the daughter's name-day into one of his own, an anniversary for the dead mother. In giving a samovar to the girl, he is making a most elaborate gesture, one both pathetic and offensive, of undying love for the woman he never married. He sees himself as carrying a torch for her to his grave, and perhaps it is this that impels him to play the possessive father to Irina – certainly in Act IV he is indifferent to the death

---

[1] Chekhov gives her age as eighty, and she is an interesting foreshadowing of the ancient Firs in *The Cherry Orchard*.

169

of her lover the Baron. Perhaps he sees Irina as the image of her mother, and perhaps the spectator is also to see her image in this young girl – thus again through an older person Chekhov brings the sense of generations to the immediacy of the stage. At all events, Tchebutykin defends his action by saying that the girls are all he cares for, and the best that Irina can do in her embarrassment is to evade the point and say that the gift is too expensive. The audience is, by this mystery, quietly alerted to a new complexity in the family pattern, and uneasily feels again the demands of the past on the present.

Saving all their faces, old Anfisa announces that a colonel has just arrived at the house. But before we see him, Chekhov touches again the theme he has just introduced. As if Anfisa were Irina's mother, the old woman tells her that she must watch her manners. By such a hint, Chekhov delicately keeps alive the picture of the sisters' Moscow childhood in a house which was always receiving distinguished guests, and as the girls compose themselves to receive Vershinin, the dead mother is again brought like a ghost into the room.

Colonel Vershinin's introduction into the play is mildly cataclysmal, but falsely so. Chekhov introduces into a known group an unknown factor, and seems theatrically to offer promise of a new dramatic departure; but when the subsequent upheaval he causes has died down, the little community is rather worse off than better, and we see it with greater clarity. The Colonel makes an impressive entrance – he likes to make his presence felt. He is all blandishment and striking pronouncements. But as time goes on, they sound more and more the repetitive, empty phrases of a somewhat hollow man, and the processes of the play steadily belittle his romantic figure.[1]

Irina is at first merely polite, until Tusenbach points out that the Colonel has come from Moscow. At the mention of the name, new life enters the room as if someone had waved a magic wand. Irina is all ears, and in a flutter calls Olga to come. Meanwhile Vershinin, trying his best to recall the little girls he had

---

[1] According to Sir John Gielgud's estimate, all the great directors of *Three Sisters*, Stanislavsky in 1901, Komisarjevsky in 1925 and Michel Saint-Denis in 1938, emphasized the romantic, not the comic, side of the character of Vershinin (*Early Stages*, London, 1953, p. 108).

seen years ago, chooses the attractive Masha for the courtesy of
the non-committal 'Your face, now, I seem to remember'. It is
their first encounter, but Masha's slowness of response suggests
that she will not easily be moved to expressions of enthusiasm:
she has been hurt before. Irina and Olga are the ones who set
upon the man who seems to hold the secret to their wildest
dreams.

IRINA. . . . What a surprise!
OLGA. We are going to move there, you know.
IRINA. We are hoping to move there by the autumn.

And they both '*laugh with delight*'. In the end, Masha, too, catches
the fever. 'Now I remember! Do you remember, Olya, they used
to talk of the "love-sick major"? You were a lieutenant at that
time and were in love, and for some reason everyone called you
"major" to tease you . . .' Evidently Vershinin's proclivities were
apparent in his youth. And it is Masha who returns us to the
theme of time when she adds through tears that he looks so much
older. Vershinin mournfully agrees; he is forty-two. But, Olga
insists, he is not an old man: 'You haven't a single grey hair.' We
may suspect that his gentle appeal for sympathy from the ladies
is not quite justified by the facts; as if we were meeting a stranger
ourselves, we make a quick assessment of the man, but, with the
advantage of seeing him through both Chekhov's and the sisters'
eyes simultaneously, we are granted a more objective view.

The three girls and the older man reminisce happily. They
have lived in the same street, known the same barracks. Meanwhile, Chekhov intermittently touches in Vershinin's character.
He used to walk to the barracks over a gloomy bridge, and he
reflects, 'It makes a lonely man feel melancholy (*a pause*)', couch-
ing the thought of suicide in such a way that past and present are
enticingly confused. And on another sobering note, he tells them
that he knew their mother. The earlier chill is felt again in the
room, and the ghost stirs again. Irina and Olga remember her
burial; Masha confesses in a tone of sudden panic that she finds
it difficult to remember her face.

As in *Uncle Vanya*, the fearful theme of ephemeral human life
is taken up again. They will be forgotten. How can we know
what people in the future will think of as important, or as absurd?
wonders Vershinin. The tortured uncertainty of a sceptical age,

unable to resolve the conflict between idealism and doubt, is heard in his words. He articulates for the sisters their most profound unease. One day their way of life may look stupid, 'perhaps even sinful . . .' Vershinin holds the stage imposingly for his speech, and at first Chekhov seems to be passing a moral judgment on the life of the family; but the tentative form of the Colonel's words, which roll rather freely from the lips of a slightly pompous and certainly loquacious man, does not allow them to carry the force of a final evaluation. If this episode in the play appears to be a sample of discussion drama, its dialectic remains naturalistic and accordingly suspect. Tusenbach is used to ensure that we take as balanced a view as possible.

Who knows? Perhaps our age will be called a great one and remembered with respect. Now we have no torture-chamber, no executions, no invasions, but at the same time how much unhappiness there is! . . . The unhappiness which one observes now – there is so much of it – does indicate, however, that society has reached a certain moral level . . .

The Baron is the sanest man in the room, but even his optimism is undermined by chicken-chucking noises from Solyony, a silly joke from the Doctor and indifference from Vershinin, who, having so much to say for himself, does not listen to other people. So the conversation winds on, its lack of direction echoed by the wavering strains of Andrey's violin played offstage.

When they hear the music, the talk changes to the brother and his fortunes. Andrey is the clever one: 'We expect him to become a professor.' Olga and Irina also take pleasure in telling their guests that he is probably 'a little in love', a further extension of their wish to see the world in a romantic glow. Married Masha, the experienced one, however, expresses doubts about the sincerity of the affair, and refuses to believe that her brother could choose Natalya Ivanovna of his own free will. Natasha dresses in pathetically bad taste. And she scrubs her cheeks – to make them rosy, like any cheap creature in search of a husband. Their brother has better taste than that. Masha has heard that Natasha is going to marry Protopopov anyway: 'And a very good thing too . . .', since, presumably, they are two of a kind. The spectator must wait to see this Natasha in order to make a just estimate of the snobbery in Masha's words. We have also yet to see Andrey himself, the fourth member of the family. Masha calls him in, and to the visitor from Moscow introduces a homely figure in old clothes, rather overweight and with tormented eyes.

The relationship between the sisters and brother Andrey offers one of Chekhov's most neatly managed insights into their family life. His sisters need to respect their brother as they respected their father, but like their dream of Moscow he constantly has trouble living up to their image of him. From his early remark that they will let Vershinin 'have no peace', we guess that he gets no peace from them himself: for he is their ticket to Moscow. Did he choose his academic career because he could not see himself in his father's shoes? Can this irresolute man before us achieve his object? Has he chosen the first girl who comes along as a way of escape from the demands of the family? For the answers to all these questions we have only the evidence of the sister's concern for him, and we concentrate on this. They insist that he is 'good all round', and draw attention to his accomplishment as a violinist: we remember it as painfully amateur. They praise his skill with a fretsaw: the ironic point is neatly made when Irina shows the Colonel a small picture-frame Andrey has made for the occasion, and in embarrassment Vershinin can mouth only, 'Yes. Quite something, isn't it?',[1] not knowing what to say. Immediately the sisters' adulation of their brother is laughable. When Andrey *makes an impatient gesture and moves away*, we see his predicament in a flash. It is not merely his own weakness of character, but also their ambition for him that is destroying his spirit, the same fantasy-making that could destroy their own. He pleads that he is not feeling well; he did not sleep last night. In haste lest this should be taken to mean that he is love-lorn, he adds that he is anxious to translate an English book into Russian. So he knows English? politely enquires Vershinin. The form of Andrey's answer tells much of the story of their life with the General: 'Our father, the Kingdom of Heaven be his, oppressed us with education'; but since the father died, Andrey has been putting on weight. Little by little we piece together the strict regimen of the home and examine the results on the son. Poor Andrey embodies the hope of the whole family, a role he can never live up to.

Vershinin is not at all interested in this brother who makes

[1] Ronald Hingley's translation, vol. III, p. 83.

picture-frames, and soon takes over the conversation again. He pontificates and prognosticates. In a dull town like this, he says sagely, they will be 'lost in the crowd'.

You will have to give in to it. Life will get the better of you, but still you will not disappear without a trace. After you there may appear perhaps six like you, then twelve and so on until such as you form a majority. In two or three hundred years life on earth will be un-imaginably beautiful, marvellous.

Part of this is true, that in this town the sisters are defeated in advance. But the 'two or three hundred years' is hazy and of small comfort when the girls are counting the days before they see Moscow, 'by the autumn'. Vershinin cuts a melancholy figure, but is he a prophet or a dreamer? The audience looks to the others on stage to prompt its response to his idealism, for the speech produces at least four immediate reactions, all personal and all contradictory. Tchebutykin continues to read his paper: perhaps he has not listened to a word of it. Andrey *'has slipped away unobserved'*: he cannot stand such specious reasoning. The Baron, however, largely agrees with Vershinin's sentiments: he daydreams somewhat like the Colonel himself. Irina wishes someone had written it all down: the bookish fancies of the young are visible in her eyes as she sits listening in a trance. Masha *'takes off her hat'* and announces that she is going to stay to lunch after all: the Colonel's ardour, or his visionary speech, or both, have caught her interest. As for Vershinin himself, he immediately loses his interest in what he is saying and turns to admire the flowers in the room.

Among other things, the Colonel expresses his distrust of the married state, and as if to illustrate his argument, Masha's husband makes his first appearance. Kuligin is a minor triumph of characterization for Chekhov in this play. His primary function is simple: with his pomposity as a schoolmaster and his limitations as a husband, he justifies the sensitive Masha's discontent as his wife. We learn later from Irina that at the age of eighteen Masha had married him out of admiration for his learning – as her con-temporaries would have said, she had a 'crush' on him. Yet Kuligin must not be such a Victorian stereotype that Masha's sad tale is merely tragic. Indeed, a case is made for Kuligin himself. He is *The Seagull*'s Medvedenko given far more charm,

and a pathos all his own. His performance in the play will scale
Masha's pretensions to martyrdom.

It is with a great display of affection that Kuligin now goes
straight to Irina to greet her on her name-day, and his speech
embraces a superb set of Chekhovian insights into his character.

Dear sister, allow me to congratulate you on your name-day and with
all my heart to wish you good health and everything else that one can
desire for a girl of your age. And to offer you as a gift this little book
(*gives her a book*). The history of our high-school for fifty years, written
by myself. An insignificant little book, written because I had nothing
better to do, but still you can read it. Good morning, friends. (*To*
VERSHININ) My name is Kuligin, teacher in the high-school here. (*To*
IRINA) In that book you will find a list of all who have finished their
studies in our high-school during the last fifty years. *Feci quod potui,*
faciant meliora potentes (*kisses* MASHA).

This is humour, not caricature. One might point to his genuine
warmth towards his young sister-in-law, and to his pleasure in
being one of the family. No audience can deny him his good
heart, and all other characters acknowledge it. He is a thoughtful,
if blinkered, man. However, along with these better qualities
goes that touch of schoolmasterly morality for a girl not long out
of school herself – 'and everything else that one can desire for a
girl of your age'. Then his gift, the history of the school, besides
indicating that there is no money to spare at home, sets his social
values squarely before us: the high-school – and he reiterates the
words – must be recognized for its importance in the town, and
they should congratulate themselves that they have made an
alliance with a man of some distinction. But as he stands there
stiffly in his school uniform, a far from impressive figure, his
hint of modest pride, 'Written by myself. An insignificant little
book' has a pleasing pathos. His announcement of his rank to
the man of rank he now meets follows naturally from the pleasure
he takes in himself. When he rounds off his address to the company
with a Latin tag about modest endeavour, we may assume that
he is a teacher of the classical languages, appropriately dead.
Finally, to conclude his speech in the best platform manner, he
kisses his wife with conscious propriety. Kuligin is the complete,
self-contained man of petty affairs, and in his own eyes the
perfectly conducted husband. His self-satisfaction is his moral
and intellectual death.

No doubt Irina's knowledge that the book contains all the names of the last fifty years conjures up for her a vision of the next fifty years and a similar procession of frail little ghosts, all duly congratulated with a Latin tag and sent into the world. It is she who pricks the bubble when she points out that he has given her a copy of the book before. Yet his embarrassment is only momentary. With a short laugh, he confidently passes the book to the Colonel, and the stranger, dazed by the assault of words, takes it automatically.

Every line Chekhov gives his Kuligin to speak is a gem of comic precision. He hurries on, addressing the gathering, addressing his class, addressing Masha like a student. For him, life has only to be orderly to be agreeable. He enjoins them all to enjoy themselves. They will roll up the carpets for the summer, but they should not forget the moth-balls. The embodiment of triviality, his mind constantly returns to the classroom. The Romans knew how to work and how to play: 'Their life was moulded into a certain framework.' If we found the family undirected in their thinking before, we may well ask whether this kind of moulding is not worse. Kuligin's sense of order must be driving Masha to despair. In the middle of this, he has time to squeeze his wife's waist, tell them all that he is happy, give advice on the curtains and carpets, and announce a headmaster's outing for the staff and their families at four o'clock. This is the first mention of Kuligin's famous headmaster – 'a splendid man' – Masha's own offstage chimera of trivial, but tyrannical, influence upon her life. She is frantic, but she cannot wriggle out of the arrangement, since the trip is to be followed by an evening at the headmaster's house. Then, with laughable finality, Kuligin concludes by remarking that their clock is seven minutes fast.

Nearly everyone in the muddled circle of the Prozorovs has been introduced. They drift casually upstage to the lunch table in the next room, Kuligin still talking, Tchebutykin thinking of Olga's pie and combing his beard, Masha bemoaning her lost evening, Solyony with his chicken noises teasing Tusenbach, Olga testily calling Andrey from his violin.

Irina and the little Baron have a moment alone before they too leave the main stage. The youngest ones are isolated from the crowd, and we might expect the traditional declarations of affection. The new intimacy in their tone does indeed reveal that they share an amorous secret, but the relationship is anything but straightforward. Irina is troubled: 'I don't like that Solyony of yours, I am afraid of him.' Her intuition clarifies our sense of unease, and spoken to Tusenbach it links Solyony's malignity with their courtship. Ironically, the man with whom the Baron now sympathizes will be the one to destroy him. When he confesses his love for her – 'How many years have we got before us . . .' – she dismisses it as if she wishes to see the future only in her own terms, as if her dream excludes the present actuality. The Baron will again be the victim. From her own experience she cannot believe that life holds beauty for them, and the panacea is 'work'. We have heard this before; we shall hear it again. Echoing round this indolent community trapped in its own misty fantasies, the call for work is amusingly ironic.

The last minutes of Act I introduce the audience to the ambiguously prepared Natasha. It was she whom the sisters resented as an intruder into the family and whom Masha despised for her vulgar taste in dress and her dubious reputation with the other sex. We are now to try to judge for ourselves whether Natasha deserves their spite, but Chekhov teases us with a few deft strokes of further equivocal evidence.[1]

Natalya Ivanovna has been hurrying. Upon her entrance, she pauses nervously ('I am late') and then *'steals a glance at herself in the glass and sets herself to rights'*. Is this the sign of a girl out for her own ends, or an appropriately feminine gesture? When she sees Irina, she *'gives her a vigorous and prolonged kiss'*. Is this gesture excessive and ingratiating? Did Irina flinch? Or should we feel that this is a special occasion, after all, for a display of affection between young girls of similar age? She comments on the presence of guests, and adds, 'I really feel shy'. Would a truly shy person have the courage to say that? and repeat it when Olga comes to greet her? Yet in a strange house of superior status,

---

[1] It would be to oversimplify Natasha's image if her actress modelled herself on the character of Aksinya in *In the Ravine* (1899), but Valency (p. 223) offers the suggestion that Chekhov's description of the upstart servant might be helpful in casting her. Aksinya had 'naive grey eyes which rarely blinked', a 'little head on a long neck' and a 'snake-like' shapeliness (*Select Tales of Tchehov*, trans. C. Garnett, London, 1949, p. 67). Against this it is proper to argue that Andrey must credibly fall in love with her, and that such bold definition of character would prejudice the development of the part as Chekhov traces it.

with a young girl about to meet a group of army officers, it is understandable. While on the one hand the spectator remains in doubt about the evidence Natasha presents in her own person, on the other hand Olga, '*in an undertone, in alarm*', draws attention to the green sash Natasha is wearing with her pink dress: 'My dear, that's not nice!' Bad taste, perhaps, but Natasha responds tearfully, as well she might at Olga's way of upsetting her self-confidence before so important a party. Olga's feline cruelty reflects less credit on the hostess than on the visitor. The sympathy we feel for Natasha is the same that is aroused in Andrey later, sufficiently to draw from him a declaration of love and a proposal of marriage. It is one of Chekhov's little jokes about life that the sisters who so disliked the idea of having her in the family should be the ostensible cause of her becoming their sister-in-law.

There follows a mature Chekhovian effect, the first of a number of aural-visual experiments with an empty stage to occur in *Three Sisters*. Olga leads Natasha into the dining area. The main stage lies deserted and the audience only partly sees and hears those at the lunch-table. This device has the curious effect of providing a prolonged '*pause*' in the action, sufficient for our assimilation of the total of ambiguities which the author has created round each member of the party. The hiatus occurs without interrupting the naturalistic flow of life within the proscenium arch. It is also as if Chekhov encourages a physical widening of our aesthetic distance from the many individual concerns of the group. Snatches of trivial conversation filter through to us, spoken casually, but always in character and relevant to what has gone before. Indeed, in the gay confusion of voices, at whose identity we must guess, even if not always with success, the life of the group is extended and mingled into a single impression for as long as the main stage does not visually direct our thinking.

Kuligin believes Irina should get married, and so touches a sore spot we can now understand. Tchebutykin thinks Natasha should marry too, and touches another sore spot for the sisters. Masha tries to change the conversation by declaring that she wants to make a speech.[1] She '*strikes her plate with her fork*', having

[1] The early manuscript of the play discovered in 1953 has Masha asking for 'a little glass of something' on this line. See Hingley, vol. III, pp. 307–9. On reflection Chekhov had no wish to push the part into that kind of melodramatic cliché.

assumed an unaccustomed gaiety in the presence of Vershinin. Kuligin's jolly remonstrance, 'You deserve three black marks for conduct' is in his mock-schoolmaster's voice, although it also suggests his *petit bourgeois* anxiety about decorous conduct. Vershinin congratulates Olga on her wine, speaking as the man of the world he imagines himself to be, and perhaps surprised to find good wine in so out of the way a place. Solyony's interpolation that it is made from black beetles is the sort of cynical remark everyone has come to expect from him. Tchebutykin teases Andrey with a line from a popular love-song. And Andrey is appropriately irritated by it.

Two second lieutenants, Fedotik and Roddey, momentarily distract the crowd as they run in to the upstage room with flowers and a camera on a tripod. Fedotik promptly calls the whole party to attention and a silence is sustained amidst titters while he takes two snapshots; a burst of noise and laughter follows this restraint as the newcomers are welcomed uproariously to the table. Again the main stage is empty, while the conversation bounces along to reach a higher pitch than before. In it we hear Masha's lines from Pushkin repeated as if she cannot get them out of her head, for she is still feeling uncertain of her new lightness of spirit. And with a nicely reductive irony, Kuligin in jest announces that there are thirteen at table. If it is true that the happiness of people may be decided and their lives shattered while they are having dinner, the high spirits of the family Prozorov must be tempting providence.

The final impression of this rich first act is arranged in order to lead straight to the opening of the second.

KULIGIN. If there are thirteen at table, it means that someone present
    is in love. It's not you, Ivan Romanovitch, by any chance? (*Laughter*)
TCHEBUTYKIN. I am an old sinner, but why Natalya Ivanovna is
    overcome, I can't imagine . . .
    (*Loud laughter*; NATASHA *runs out from the dining-room into the drawing-room followed by* ANDREY.)

Natasha has run away to escape their taunts, it seems. Again we puzzle over her motives: is she really upset by their mockery, or is her embarrassment a pretence designed to stir Andrey's sympathy and entice him from the table? She comes downstage and stands a solitary figure on the empty stage until Andrey joins her. Was the glance over her shoulder made in order to see whether Andrey was following her? She *'covers her face with her hands'*. Beneath them, is she crying or smiling?

Andrey attempts to comfort her, leading her to the window where they cannot be seen from the table. He at least has no censorious eyes for the green sash on her pretty pink dress: 'Oh youth, lovely, marvellous youth!' He has capitulated, whispering breathless confessions of love to her, believing her show of shy resistance is because she is afraid of being seen. Finally she hears, 'Be my wife!' and at once permits a kiss. Brother Andrey, at least, achieves his immediate end, and perhaps Natalya Ivanovna has achieved hers too.

While Natasha and Andrey embrace, two more officers arrive in haste for the party. As in a farce, they stop short and stare in amazement at what they see. The audience is released, the curtain falls and Chekhov ends his act on a broad laugh.

Act Two

For once Chekhov decided to keep the same set for a second act, and even in the half-light an audience will recognize the room at once, now empty of people. However, if the scene is the same, the mood is utterly different, and part of the dramatic exercise is to disclose and discover the changes. The vivacious scene with its birthday mood is replaced by realities that before lay beneath the surface. The fugitive sounds of a concertina in the street outside recreate the banality of provincial life; to these Stanislavsky added 'the bells of a troika driving by in the street, drunken shouts and . . . far away the drunken song of a passing reveller'.[1] The darkness of a winter evening has replaced the morning sun of springtime.

The changes are those of many details, some due to time, some to the hand of Natasha. Stanislavsky aimed to characterize the new state of affairs long before a player was seen:

It is dark in the living room, the fire is almost out, there is only a streak of light falling from the open door leading into Andrey's room. Now and then Andrey's shadow cuts across the band of light as he walks up and down in his room, thinking aloud back over his lectures. You hear Andrey's steps and his low monotonous voice, an occasional cough, sigh, his blowing his nose, and the creak of chairs being moved about. Silence. He has stood still by the table and is leafing through some blank notebooks. Rustle of papers. There is a sound suggestive of weeping, then again he blows his nose, you hear his steps, his low voice, and see his shadow move.

In the dining room the lamp is almost out; it flickers, then dies down. The windows are frozen tight. There is snow on the roofs . . . Outside it is snowing. A blizzard.[2]

The melancholy mood is capped with 'the monotonous tick of

[1] Stroyeva, p. 48.   [2] Stroyeva, p. 47.

two clocks', while 'the wind howls in the chimney' and the storm 'lashes at the window panes'.

Stanislavsky also had a sharp eye for signs of Natasha and her new baby. The piano stood in front of the bay window; there was a child's blanket tossed over the divan and toys were every-where; pieces of material, scissors and a towel were on top of the piano. If this visible disorder is not true to the officious Natasha we come to know, Stanislavsky was right to fill the room with the spirit of the busy mother and the petty house-wife.[1]

It is appropriate that Natasha should lead us into the changes in the family circumstances, and even without Stanislavsky's display, in Chekhov's text she is quickly provided with all the suggestions needed for us to appreciate her new role. She enters in a dressing-gown: she is indeed one of the family. Looking about her, she fussily moves across the stage with a candle in her hand: very much the behaviour of a suspicious custodian. She stops by Andrey's door, through which we dimly perceive his figure humped over a book, and delivers this revealing first line. 'What are you doing, Andryusha? Reading? Never mind, I only just asked . . .' The possessive tone, the obviousness of the enquiry, tell us immediately, and with a familiar humour, that this is a wife addressing her husband. It also implies that Natasha has something else on her mind, belying her 'I only just asked'. Like Andrey, we wait to discover what.

Natasha's speech, like Kuligin's in the first act, shows Chekhov's brilliance of revelation by innuendo. It entirely discloses the progress of her relationship with Andrey and the sisters; it entirely resolves the uncertainties lingering after the curtain of Act I about the sort of person she is; and it entirely justifies Masha's distrust of her. It speaks much more besides, prompting forebodings of the family's future when it is in the grasp of this sly, determined, self-centred schemer. It is impossible in words to do justice to the mincing tones, the well-timed wheedling implied in her phrases as she works her will upon the defenceless Andrey.

[1] Before Natasha's entrance, Stanislavsky also had old Anfisa in her slippers drag her ancient body across the stage to take Andrey a pitcher of kvass. The audience should see that she had changed too: she had become 'shrunken and pale'. Looking exhausted, she went down on her knees to pick up some toys, and on Natasha's entrance she put the toys away in a fright.

Act II

Knowing his young wife has more to say, he comes in wearing his slippers,[1] reluctantly closing his book in the knowledge that his pleasure in reading is for the time being at an end.

As Andrey waits patiently, Natasha goes about the room opening doors, checking whether any member of the family has left a light burning. Or so she says: it may be that she is merely curious to know who is in and who is out of the house. She is evidently running the establishment.[2] She announces that the unmarried sisters are still at work, 'poor dears'. She speaks, of course, from the superior position of a married woman, who must keep track of them all. She incidentally reveals that Irina's desire for purposeful labour has resulted in only a humdrum job at the telegraph office (a nice contemporary detail to make the action more immediate for the audience of 1901). 'I was saying to your sister this morning, "Take care of yourself, Irina darling", said I. But she won't listen.' This remark speaks volumes for the irritation Irina must feel towards the intruder.

Natasha comes to a stop in her travels and finally names 'our Bobik'. She and Andrey have been married long enough to have a baby. She proceeds to use the child as a stick to beat Andrey into submission. Bobik, she says, is not well; she is worried. The poor man tries to fend off the big blow that is to come. But she persists until she makes her purpose clear: she does not want a carnival party that evening in the house. Andrey protests that they have already been invited, but Natasha continues to talk incessantly of the baby until she again arrives blithely at her verdict: 'So I shall tell them, Andryusha, not to let the carnival party come in.'

Again Andrey protests. It is for his sisters to give the orders. Nevertheless Natasha retorts, 'Yes, for them too.' She has secured her first objective. So she is on the point of going, but feels her advantage too good to lose, and is immediately off on another

---

[1] According to Nemirovich-Danchenko, p. 209.

[2] Henry Popkin makes a plausible case for a theme of a hidden class struggle in Chekhov's handling of Natasha: 'The sisters belong to that most precarious branch of the nobility, the military aristocracy, precarious because their place in the world depended on their father, the general.' As in Ibsen's *Hedda Gabler* and Strindberg's *Miss Julie*, a military tradition that is bequeathed to a daughter 'is an inheritance, and yet it is not an inheritance'. Thus the sisters have 'no secure basis for their way of life'. Referring to Natasha, Popkin adds, 'A kind of modified class warfare takes place in the play when a daughter of the local *bourgeoisie* invades the home they love and forces them out' (*Anton Chekhov: The Three Sisters*, New York, 1965, p. 18).

tack. Andrey is too fat, and is to have junket for supper: his personal indulgences are no longer for him to choose. Then, as a parting thrust, Natasha tries her strength and uses the child for a *coup de grâce*. With even more sugar in her voice, she points out that the little tyrant's room is cold, and that he should have Irina's. 'She is never at home anyway, except for the night.' In Act III we find indeed that Irina has been displaced, and that another hold has been gained by the sister-in-law. Finally, after a pause, she coos his most intimate name: 'Andryusantchik, why don't you speak?' What can the man say?

Natasha has gone, but, we observe, leaving behind her own candle burning. Andrey stands in a daze after the whirlwind until deaf old Ferapont from the council brings in a book of old lectures and some official papers from the Chairman. The unseen hand of Protopopov is not far away. Following the sinister, if humorous, comedy of Natasha, Chekhov lightens the tone with the broader comedy of deafness. Andrey attempts to read what is given him, while Ferapont's repeated 'Eh?' compels him to say everything twice, and louder each time. Yet, against this farce, what is said also serves to disclose that Andrey has become Protopopov's secretary on the council: his dreams of a career at Moscow University are already fading. It is as if Andrey is speaking in monologue, but quite naturalistically, for Ferapont is with him, even if he cannot hear, or understand if he did hear. In any case, there is no use in Andrey's talking to anyone else, since 'My wife does not understand me. My sisters I am somehow afraid of – I'm afraid they will laugh at me . . .' It is touching, but nevertheless it is one of Chekhov's wry jokes that Andrey should pour out his heart to an old man who is deaf.

Andrey shares his sisters' desperate dream of Moscow, and again Chekhov designs a deflationary tactic. The old man has never been out of the district, and all that he knows about Moscow is the story of a man who died of eating forty or fifty pancakes. Life in Moscow, it is implied, is as pointless as life in the provinces. But in his turn, Andrey is not listening to Ferapont. They are both off at a tangent, the young and the old, the cultured and the ignorant, equated in a ludicrous trick of dialogue. Their 'conversation' concludes,

ANDREY. . . . . Have you ever been in Moscow?

Act II

FERAPONT (*after a pause*). No, never. It was not God's will I should (*a pause*).[1]

The older man is piously content; as long as the younger clings to his dream he will suffer the more. Its sad decline is traced and the Moscow myth is exploded once again through the marriage and misery of brother Andrey. He stretches himself and wanders slowly back into his room, while we catch the sound of a lullaby sung offstage to Bobik. Andrey's future is decided.

What of the sisters in their new circumstances? The spectator will first see the younger ones, Masha and Irina; Olga will not appear until the end of the act. Before we see them, the stage remains empty and the continuing sound of the lullaby begins its work of suggesting the maternal tyranny of Natasha's régime and of signifying the sisters' discontent, as it does on occasion throughout the act. Now it also plays in Masha and Vershinin, with Masha in the high spirits she had acquired at the end of Act I. Their conversation lifts the tone from that of Andrey's morbidity, and to match the new mood a servant lights a lamp and some candles. Stanislavsky, keen to sustain the ambivalence of the action, had their 'love scene' undercut by interruptions, inventing offstage business for Andrey in order to remind us of the realities behind the exhilaration in the high-flown words of those on stage. Thus from Andrey's room is heard first the 'extremely mournful wail of a violin' followed by 'the sound of someone sawing – apparently Andrey turns from one thing to another out of a sense of hopeless yearning, but everything drops from his hands'.[2]

The intimacy of Masha and the Colonel has developed to the point where the once-silent Masha is talking freely about the family and herself. Her chatter also smacks of flattery for Vershinin: the military are the most civilized people in town. At one time she thought her schoolmaster husband important; now the company of her husband's colleagues, with their lack of refinement, makes her 'quite miserable'. In this scene we see the other side of the secretive Masha, as well as some of the charm she had as a young girl.

Vershinin responds obliquely with the same tempting mixture

---

[1] The same terms of pious resignation spoken by Marina in *Uncle Vanya* and by Firs in *The Cherry Orchard*.
[2] Stroyeva, p. 48.

of confession and assurance. Why is everyone, he asks flamboyantly, 'worried to death' by his wife and children? Masha blossoms almost imperceptibly at these words. Vershinin and his wife
have had a quarrel, and he has walked out.

I never talk about it. Strange, it's only to you I complain (*kisses her
hand*). Don't be angry with me . . . Except for you I have no one – no
one . . . (*a pause*).

His attraction to and for Masha is understandable, but a man who
is ready to broadcast his troubles with his wife, in spite of his
blatantly untrue disclaimer, 'I never talk about it', would be
suspect in most eyes. This is the talk of a thousand restive husbands, although to us Vershinin is humorous without being ugly.
To Masha he seems beyond suspicion, and in the pause that follows, we know that Masha has been won. No doubt she finds herself in a romantic predicament; to the spectator she is a creature
at the same time both melodramatic and amusing. She gracefully
avoids answering his praises, and moves away with a laugh,
savouring every word. 'What a noise in the stove!' It is humming quietly in the silence.[1]

   Irina and Tusenbach join them. The Baron has walked the
tired girl home from her work at the telegraph office. It is worth
noticing that Chekhov does not allow us to see Irina's first
happiness at the prospect of doing useful work at last. He shows
her only when she is already bored by her job and looking for a
change. For on this day she has been short-tempered with a cus-
tomer, and she is full of the complaint that she cannot stand the
drudgery. Work in itself, it seems, is not enough: 'It is work
without poetry, without meaning.' And she flops into an armchair.[2] The Baron, however, is delighted that this development

---

[1] In her letter to Chekhov of 16 December 1900, Olga Knipper reported that
Stanislavsky added the sound of a mouse to the sound of the stove: 'He put in
something of his own, of course – a mouse scratches in Masha's scene with Vershinin' (Garnett, p. 62). Stanislavsky tells how during a late night rehearsal the
company sat in despair until 'someone was nervously scratching the bench on
which he sat with his finger-nails. The sound was like that of a mouse'. This noise
recalled to him a previous experience in the Proustian way, one which corresponded exactly with the mood he wanted for the scene, and the rehearsal was able
to continue (Stanislavsky, p. 373).

[2] In this lull Stanislavsky reintroduced his scratching mouse to match Irina's despair,
and, emphasizing the reality of everyday, he had Vershinin pick up one of Bobik's
toys, a clown with a cymbal: 'He holds the toy in his hands and from time to time

may increase her dependence upon him in the future. The pace is slow. Fragment by fragment the depressing picture of the last few months emerges.

It is so quiet that Tchebutykin has knocked on the floor from below, presumably to find out whether anyone is at home. His presence reminds Irina that he has been taking Andrey to the club and losing money heavily at the gaming table,[1] a thoughtless act of the Doctor's. Andrey has escaped into gambling, just as he did into his books and his violin. If only he lost everything, Irina says, they might have to leave the town: but what a desperate expedient and sad reversal after Irina's self-confidence in Act 1! 'Natasha must not hear of his losses', from Masha, reminds us that Natasha will control Andrey's movements, and therefore the family's, whether in or out of debt.

Only Tchebutykin appears to be unchanged. He comes in yawning and combing his beard from an after-dinner nap, and in his customary way settles to reading his newspaper. He is the picture of inertia. Nevertheless, the others find him a joke, and although their laughter lightens the atmosphere on the stage, one suggestion may trouble us: he calls Irina over to him and declares paternally that he cannot do without her. We sense that if his apathy could help to damage Andrey, some mindless action in the future could harm Irina too. The audience does not laugh at him as easily as the characters do.

The company lapses into general conversation, with the Colonel in his usual way at the centre of the group. Nevertheless, the discussion is of central importance. Like the melancholy dreamer he is, Vershinin will have them talk about life 'in two or three hundred, perhaps a thousand years'. The vagueness is characteristic, and is repeated to meaninglessness.[2] But Vershinin's views on the future do not match Tusenbach's: 'It is clear we do not understand each other.' For the pessimistic Colonel, conscious of his age, and speaking like a man who has written off this life,

makes the clown clap the cymbals, providing a kind of ironic accompaniment to Irina's words' (Stroyeva, p. 49). In the invention of such detail Stanislavsky shows his special ability to recreate the tone of a scene by stage business, even if here it suggests unnecessary emphasis.

[1] Stanislavsky's Vershinin tinkled the toy again.

[2] Stanislavsky accompanied this philosophizing by having Tusenbach casually turn the handle of a music-box of Bobik's which emitted vague, mournful little sounds (Stroyeva, p. 49).

the timeless future will bring 'a new, happy life . . . and that alone is the purpose of our existence'. Vershinin, the older man, speaks with the casual persuasion of the uncommitted, and the contradiction between theory and actuality is unmistakable.[1] The optimistic young Baron, on the other hand, thinks something can be done, for it is pointless just to wait and hope, even if the same problems always exist. In these lines he shows more realism than his superior officer: 'Life will remain just the same, difficult, full of mysteries and happiness. In a thousand years man will sigh just the same, "Ah, how hard life is", and yet just as now he will be afraid of death and not want it.' Yet he insists that he is happy; it seems that this dull, bad world is enough for him. In this dialectic of impressions and feelings, Tusenbach seems to strike a balance between idealism and melancholy, but finally Chekhov leaves the audience to choose its own position. Who is the realist? Where is the reality? The problem will remain as unresolved at the end of the play. There, transfixed as if in Tusenbach's eternity, the sisters will stand motionless, and Irina will say optimistically that one day 'there will be no mysteries', while beside her Olga will say, 'If we only knew!'

At the height of Vershinin's peroration, a simple device has the spectator glance at Masha: she laughs, a response out of key with the tenor of the discussion. She too is happy. Actuality tests abstract argument, and Masha is absorbed in her new sensations of love. Stanislavsky deciphers her laugh as a psychological subtlety: 'Masha's laugh is really nervous; she might cry, so she quickly puts out both candles.'[2] An audience, however, perceives that by her laugh she dismisses this talk of the purpose of life as idle, and when Tusenbach asks her what the matter is, she does not care to explain what does not need explaining. What matters to her is the present. In any case, Tusenbach goes on to offer his own explanation in a moment: people, he says, are like the birds

---

1 It is interesting to note that Stanislavsky underlines two contradictory comments written against these lines. First, 'It is very important to arouse the audience here, to be buoyant, lift the tone.' Then, 'The distant sounds of an accordion and drunken voices purposely recall the fact that all that Vershinin is talking about is far away in the future' (Stroyeva, p. 49).

2 Stroyeva, pp. 49–50. Stanislavsky has the rest of the scene played without lights, using only moonlight and the glow of lighted cigarettes. This certainly suits Masha's romantic mood, but somewhat ignores the anti-romantic elements in the scene to come.

which fly south in the winter: they will always fly on and on, whether they know why they do it or not. And he makes a gesture at the snow outside: 'What meaning is there in that?' Masha's present joy exists, she feels it, and that is all that can be said.

The officers Fedotik and Roddey have come in and have been singing softly to the guitar, echoing the dreamy talk. Irina sings a snatch also. Tchebutykin reads his newspaper and makes a note, announcing to the world at large, apropos of nothing, the titbit of information from the paper that Balzac was married at Berditchev. The empty remark falls as flat as the desultory conversation about the future of mankind, and the whole question, important as it is, dwindles into nonsense. Chekhov has Irina repeat the Doctor's words sleepily, partly to suggest that she is thinking that she herself might marry in as out-of-the-way a place as Berditchev, and partly to prolong the trivial rhythms of the action.

The talk meanders on in Chekhov's seemingly purposeless way, little by little building up the picture of the new phase in the family life. The Baron lets drop that he has resigned his commission: he means to do some real work and fall into bed at the end of the day exhausted like a labourer. Fedotik has bought Irina some crayons and a penknife as a present; she protests that she is not a child, but nevertheless takes them with childlike pleasure. Roddey teases the Doctor. Fedotik plays patience. Anfisa and Natasha prepare the samovar for tea. The Doctor offers the further news that there is smallpox in China. Natasha makes the mistake of telling Solyony about Bobik, and receives in return the blunt reply, 'If that child were mine, I'd fry him in a frying pan and eat him.' A moment later it is discovered that, like a child himself, he has eaten all the chocolates. The slow pulse of a winter's evening in the family circle is precisely captured. There are moments of boredom, moments of laughter; but the scene is spiritless.

How sluggish dare a dramatist allow the tempo of his stage to grow in the cause of verisimilitude? The mood of torpor and nostalgia all but halts the action. It is into this vacuum that Chekhov inserts a literary device of thematic importance. When Masha remarks that if only she lived in Moscow she would not care what the weather was like, it is Vershinin who replies with a parable.

The other day I was reading the diary of a French minister written in prison. The minister was condemned for the Panama affair. With what enthusiasm and delight he describes the birds he sees from the prison window, which he never noticed before when he was a minister. Now that he is released, of course he notices birds no more than he did before. In the same way, you won't notice Moscow when you live in it.

The point is well taken by the audience: it confirms what they already feel from their experience of this languor and mood of vague regret on the stage. The real enemy is a self-induced delusion about the actualities of life, not life itself. And such a notion comes all the more ironically from Vershinin, a man composed of such delusions. So the mood reaches bottom, and if it were not for the parable, the stage at nearly the mid-point of the play would be dramatically dead.

Chekhov chooses his moment to engineer dramatic stimuli which subtly intensify the mood and accelerate the pace. Vershinin is handed a letter. His wife has taken poison again, and he must go immediately. Masha is all attention, well aware of the conflict in the man's mind, but she can do nothing to delay his departure. Herself married to a person who exerts emotional pressure upon her, Masha must suspect Mme Vershinin's motives. At all events, the would-be mistress sees the wife succeed in reclaiming her Colonel and leaving her rival alone for the evening. In a sudden huff, Masha turns on the old Nurse when she complains that he has left his tea.

MASHA (*getting angry*). Leave off! Don't pester, you give one no peace . . . (*goes with her cup to the table.*) You bother me, old lady.
ANFISA. Why are you so huffy? Darling! (ANDREY's *voice*: 'Anfisa!')
ANFISA (*mimicking*). Anfisa! he sits there . . . (*goes out*).

Like a repetition joke from the *commedia dell'arte*, with one character giving another a cuff in sequence, the old woman relieves her gall on the unwitting brother.

The chain reaction of flaring feelings continues. Masha has angrily jumbled Fedotik's cards, Irina has criticized her and Tchebutykin has teased her. Masha turns on the Doctor: 'You are sixty, but you talk rot like a schoolboy.' And it is Natasha who next chimes in.

(*Sighs*). Dear Masha, why make use of such expressions in conversation? With your attractive appearance, I tell you straight out, you would be simply fascinating in a well-bred social circle if it were not for the things you say.[1] *Je vous prie, pardonnez-moi, Marie, mais vous avez des manières un peu grossières.*

With her society French, Natasha presumes to score a point of social manners at the expense of the General's daughter. *Vis-à-vis* Masha, she now evidently finds herself in the comfortable role of the good wife confronting the bad one. The Baron suppresses a laugh.[2]

Within a moment the placid atmosphere has been ruffled, but as Masha subsides once again into her more customary silence and Natasha trots off primly to attend to the baby, the former calm temporarily returns. Not for long, however.

Tusenbach offers Solyony a glass of brandy. In his open, friendly manner, the Baron has incautiously taken up his fellow officer and tried to sympathize with him. Now he feels he must reconcile their differences. But 'Why make it up? I haven't quarrelled with you' is the short answer from Solyony in his aggressive manner. Prompted, perhaps, by the Baron's warmth of feeling and his assertion that he likes him in spite of their quarrels, the Captain in a new voice confesses that he is awkward in company. Ominously, he likens himself to Lermontov: 'I have the temperament of Lermontov. (*In a low voice*) In fact I am rather like Lermontov to look at . . . so I am told', and he sprinkles more scent on his hands. This comparison with the Russian poet does not appear in the first version of the play,[3] and Chekhov has introduced it in order to give the audience an alarming premonition of events. His insistence that the name Lermontov should be spoken in a special tone of voice to indicate Solyony's self-dramatizing[4] would ensure

---

[1] Cf. p. 162 and n. 1, above.

[2] Stanislavsky turned this into a whole 'laughing scene' in order to raise the mood to one of gaiety before the general exit. At Natasha's French phrases, 'some laugh scornfully, others rock with laughter and roll on the sofa'. This business was continued after Natasha went, when Tusenbach out of relief 'begins to sing, to dance a little waltz downstage' and played the piano. At this Masha 'jumps up, begins to dance', first alone, then with Roddey. When Natasha sent them all packing, they made a 'comic, happy departure' (Stroyeva, p. 50).

[3] See Hingley, vol. III, p. 311.

[4] According to Chekhov's letter to J. A. Tikhomirov on 14 January 1901, 'Solyony actually believes he looks like Lermontov; but of course he doesn't – it is silly even to consider a resemblance. He should be made up to look like Lermontov. The

that the point would not be missed by a Russian audience. Lermontov, besides being one of the great romantics, was also a duellist who was himself killed in a duel in 1841, and to link him with Solyony increases the sense of fateful death that surrounds him. Chekhov clearly intends the Captain to contribute to the general feeling that there are partly unexplained forces at work directing our fortunes. Like Protopopov and Kuligin's headmaster, Solyony, too, will exert a destructive influence on the lives of others.

Meanwhile the brandy which makes Tusenbach gay has only made Solyony more aggressive. Against the noisy singing and dancing of the Baron with the Doctor, who had wandered in talking about food, and in contrast with Andrey, who had slipped in quietly to read a book, the vestige of his academic ambitions, Solyony tries to pick an argument, first about onions with Tchebutykin, then about the number of universities in Moscow with Andrey. The gaiety seems forced when the gap between ill-temper and high spirits is so marked. But Tusenbach is at the piano, and Masha is waltzing about the stage; there is general anticipation of the arrival of the carnival party, and on the surface all is noise and laughter and movement.[1] Chekhov is preparing his second act curtain with an aural and visual switchback of contrasting moods.

Chekhov begins an exquisite exercise in anticlimax, one which passes through several phases. The audience, of course, expects Natasha's arrival at any moment, like Malvolio's, to put a stop to the celebration. Sure enough, at the height of the fun she stumps in angrily, surveys the happy scene and then whispers to the Doctor.

IRINA. What is it?
TCHEBUTYKIN. It's time we were going. Good night.

likeness to Lermontov is immense, but only in the opinion of Solyony himself' (Hellman, p. 281).

[1] Olga Knipper's letter to Chekhov of 13 December 1900, best suggests Stanislavsky's final plan for this episode: 'Tusenbach pounces upon Andrey, sings, "My porch, oh my new porch!" All begin dancing, even Irina and Tchebutykin. Afterwards when Tusenbach is playing the waltz, Masha flies out and begins dancing alone, then Fedotik seizes her, but she pushes him away (he can't dance), while Irina dances with Roddey, and it is this uproar that brings Natasha in' (Garnett, p. 62).

Act II

TUSENBACH. Good night. It's time to be going.

IRINA. But I say . . . what about the Carnival party?

ANDREY (*with embarrassment*). They won't be coming. You see, dear, Natasha says Bobik is not well, and so . . . In fact I know nothing about it, and don't care either.

IRINA (*shrugs her shoulders*). Bobik is not well!

MASHA. Well, it's not the first time we've had to lump it! If we are turned out, we must go. (*To* IRINA) It's not Bobik that is ill, but she is a bit . . . (*taps her forehead with her finger*). Petty, vulgar creature!

Natasha has succeeded in using Bobik to assert her will over the whole company. The guests have no choice; the sisters are distinctly annoyed; Andrey is helpless to the point of repeating his wife's own pretext in the face of Irina's accusing stare. So the group disperses; the noisy stage grows quiet; Anfisa and a maid put out the lights; voices offstage fade to silence. The room is unnaturally still and dark after the festivity. At this point, the baby's nanny is again heard crooning his lullaby like a musical *leit-motif* of the day-to-day mediocrity of their lives.

In the gloom, Andrey and the Doctor, wearing outdoor clothes against the snow, enter softly. These two, as has been hinted, have struck up a friendship in hopelessness, and each lonely man has found a natural companion. The audience may wonder whether this unholy alliance of old and young despair can bring anything but disaster in its train. They are going to the club to play cards, and they must hurry before Natasha catches them. In Andrey's 'I am afraid my wife may stop me', the future course of his marriage is again foretold. Even as they leave to take their pleasure, the spectre of Natasha dogs them, Andrey with a conscience saying that he will only sit and watch. He adds that he does not feel too well – he gets out of breath; as we might expect, the Doctor cannot suggest a remedy.

The stage is empty again for another pause in the slowing action. After a moment, voices and laughter are heard outside, and the door-bell rings. It is the carnival party at last. As we sit looking at the darkened stage, listening to the sounds of happiness, it seems as if the dull house is duller still.[1] The bell rings

---

[1] An effect of sound on vision which was to be exploited to its fullest at the end of *The Cherry Orchard*. Stanislavsky surprisingly missed the point and had the mummers visible in their colourful costumes, introducing a whole lively episode on stage in order to make the contrast with Natasha's deadening authority. But, although the

three inviting times while Irina makes up her mind and then tells Anfisa to say that there is no one at home. As the old woman does as she is bid, the young girl, alone on the stage, is explicitly linked with the dreary atmosphere of the house. All this is in preparation for a further shift in mood and a new focus on Irina's unhappiness.

Chekhov is about to create a ripple of shock through the theatre. Irina is surprised by Captain Solyony, who comes in wondering where everyone has gone.[1]

SOLYONY. . . . Are you alone here?
IRINA. Yes (*a pause*). Good night.

Her uneasiness in Solyony's presence transmits itself to us. And it is justified, since he loses no time in fiercely declaring his love for her. We are as alarmed as she: he speaks in a wild, melodramatic language which is startling in its sudden vehemence, and which one takes to be his idea of Lermontov's tone. But she receives his declaration coldly, and in a moment he shows his demonic side. 'There must be no happy rivals . . . There must not . . . I swear by all that is sacred I will kill any rival . . .' And he adds incongruously, 'O exquisite being!' His love is possessive and dangerous, and once again this eccentric figure in their midst is explicitly linked with death. We, like Irina, know who the rival is.

Chekhov promptly diverts our attention from such morbid thoughts with comedy, a technique which will be used again and again in *The Cherry Orchard*. He scores a direct hit with a neat irony, as Natasha crosses the stage looking through all the doors as she did in the beginning of the act – all the doors except, this time, Andrey's. 'Andrey is there. Let him read. Excuse me, Vassily Vassilyitch, I did not know you were here, and I am in my dressing-gown . . .' This time she will not disturb Andrey: she has another object in view. And the joke is the more delightful because we know he has already escaped her! She is surprised to find Irina alone with the Captain, and must get rid of them, but

party is seen, it is not allowed to enter: 'Silence falls. All the jollity evaporates. Someone whistles. The laughing spirits of the crowd are dampened. In fact they are rather embarrassed' (Stroyeva, p. 50).
[1] James Agate recalled with pleasure a clever touch in Komisarjevsky's 1926 production at the Barnes Theatre, London, in which Irina is discovered on her own and frightened out of her wits by Solyony dressed in mummer's guise as a dancing bear (*More First Nights*, London, 1937, p. 192).

with complete aplomb she finds the 'polite', if not the prudish, way to dismiss him: 'I am in my dressing-gown.' So he goes with a growl, to Irina's relief, and Natasha immediately insists that Irina is tired and should go to bed. The schemer is laying her plans.

At the same time, she uses the moment to raise the matter of Irina's bedroom. Irina stands astounded as Natasha practises her pretence of motherliness. Bobik is such a sweet little fellow! How can anyone refuse him her room? If from this display we had any remaining doubts about Natasha's true qualities as a mother, they are swiftly resolved. A troika is heard driving up to the house, and the door-bell rings once more that evening. Rather too promptly, Natasha suggests that it is Olga; but the maid comes to whisper in her ear.

Protopopov? What a queer fellow he is! Protopopov has come, and asks me to go out with him in his sledge (*laughs*). How strange men are! . . . (*A ring*) Somebody has come. I might go for a quarter of an hour . . . (*To the maid*) Tell him I'll come directly.

The presence of Protopopov is felt again. In a moment, Natasha's tone has changed from that of anxious mother to that of coy maiden. She is the consummate second-rate actress. She will go out with Protopopov in spite of Bobik's health, in spite of the lateness of the hour, in spite of having put a stop to the visit of the party and to other people's pleasure. She hurries off to get herself ready.

This is the situation when Olga at last arrives home, followed by Kuligin and Vershinin. The audience has been given a complete insight into the cross-currents of life in a house with Natasha, and is finally to see how it strikes the newcomers. They all look in astonishment at the empty room, with Irina sitting miserable and alone in a corner. Where is the party? They too sit down and share her desolation. Olga complains about a headache, and reports that everyone is talking about Andrey's gambling losses. Vershinin has pacified his wife and, presumably with some excuse, has returned expecting to find Masha waiting for him. Even Kuligin was looking forward to a jolly evening, and can manage only a weak joke in Latin. Chekhov's anticlimax is almost complete. The visitors leave again, and the outrageous Natasha, dressed in her best fur coat and hat, hurries out after them, leaving her precious candle still burning.

Thus Irina is alone on the stage again, and we share the desolation of the house in our response to her isolation. In the silence we faintly hear a fading concertina, recalling the world outside and its retreating carnival, and at the same time leaving Irina abandoned. With it, contrapuntally, we hear the nurse's lullaby, symbolic of the rule of Bobik and Natasha. When with intense longing she speaks the magic words, 'Oh, to go to Moscow, to Moscow!',[1] we feel what she feels.

After the springtime elation of the party in Act I, the whole of Act II has been a slow, finally crushing, anticlimax. This design, however, does not leave the scene shapeless: spirits rise and fall, rise and fall again. But no 'plot' is advanced by what is seen, unless it is in the growth of Natasha's chilling egotism. Add to this the senseless corruption of Professor Andrey by Tchebutykin and the self-centred threats of Captain Solyony, and this transitional act amply creates its impression of the deceptive evil present in everyday living. At the same time, the picture is not wholly bleak: Masha and Tusenbach have found a new, if uncertain, happiness as well. Irina's forlorn cry for Moscow, like a sigh in the wintry trees, epitomizes her condition with both its frightening purposelessness and its flutter of hope.

[1] Stanislavsky had Irina lean and put her head on the piano as if in pain. The lamp burns low and flickers. The nibbling mouse is heard. The clock's pendulum swings Her voice is a sigh and a groan (Stroyeva, p. 51).

Act Three

Upon the rise of the curtain for the third act, we see and hear another new situation immediately. The scene is Olga's room, and Natasha has managed to have Irina move in with her older sister as she had planned. Screens have been set up to provide some privacy, but the limited space, cluttered with beds and other furniture, suggests the physical discomfort to which the sisters are reduced. The family now awkwardly holds court in this small room, but, as in *Uncle Vanya*, shifting the scene to a more personal *sanctum* deeper within the house has brought the audience closer to the heart of things. At the same time, moving into a smaller room gives a visual impression of the process of dispossession which is under way. Life is closing in on them.

These impressions are quickly overlaid by others. In contrast with the slow drift of the previous act, Chekhov now works to establish a feeling of exhaustion, tension and hostility. Stanislavsky, alert to this, made the observation,

Wherever possible in this act the tempo should be nervous. Pauses must not be overdone. The crosses, all movement, should be nervous and quick. Now it is no longer a question of a gnawing mouse, the speaking sounds of a music box, or the distant sounds of drunken revellers which create the 'mood'.[1]

The sisters are to be seen looking strained and anxious in the early hours of the morning. Yet no one is in bed or even undressed; only a tired Masha is lying on a couch.

Above all, Chekhov in this act has added an offstage 'event' of major proportions, not for its own sake or as part of any narrative, but as a dramatic image of dispossession which is to run parallel with the sense of exasperation the family feels at this stage. For against the quiet of the scene is heard a church bell ringing in the distance as an alarm to rouse the town: the town is on fire, no less.

[1] Stroyeva, p. 51.

And when the old Nurse hurries in with Olga to tell the story, we gather that the house and yard are full of refugees from the fire.

At the time of the first production of the play, there was doubt about the kind and degree of effect that Chekhov intended by his fire. Stanislavsky added to the author's directions with his customary theatrical overstatement, 'All during the act one hears with increasing frequency the insistent sound of a fire alarm . . . the engines roar by the house carrying the firemen, there is a red glow from the windows which falls in streaks across the floor'.[1] Stanislavsky evidently took Chekhov to be calling for a startling sensation after the quiet of the previous curtain. Justifying this, Nemirovich-Danchenko reported that Chekhov 'insisted that the sounds of the conflagration off the stage should be extremely verisimilar'.[2] But when Olga Knipper wrote to Chekhov after the rehearsal that Stanislavsky had 'created a terrible hullabaloo on the stage with everyone running in all directions and getting excited',[3] Chekhov replied,

Of course the third act must be taken slowly on the stage, that it may be felt that they are exhausted and sleepy . . . How could a noise come in? There are stage directions where there should be ringing.[4]

Again he wrote,

Why noise? There should only be noise in the distance behind the scenes, a confused hollow noise, but here on the stage all are exhausted, almost asleep. If you spoil the third act, the whole play is done for, and I shall be hissed in my old age.[5]

In spite of this dissension, there is no doubt from the rest of the scene that sleepiness is only on the surface, and that at this

---

[1] Stroyeva, p. 51.   [2] Nemirovich-Danchenko, p. 209.
[3] Letter of 11 January 1901, quoted in Hingley, vol. III, p. 314.
[4] Letter of 17 January 1901 (Garnett, p. 72).
[5] Letter of 20 January 1901 (Garnett, p. 72). Stanislavsky in *My Life in Art* gives a somewhat different account of the matter: 'On returning from abroad Chekhov was satisfied with us and only regretted that during the fire we didn't make the right noise when ringing the bell and sounding the military alarm signals. He was continually worrying about this and complaining to us about it. We invited him to rehearse the noises of the fire himself and put all the stage apparatus at his disposal for this purpose. Chekhov delightedly took on the part of producer and went at the thing with great enthusiasm, giving us a whole list of stuff which was supposed to be got ready for his noise experiment. I wasn't at the rehearsal as I was afraid of being in the way, so I don't know what happened there' (from *Chekhov i teatr*, p. 262, quoted in Hingley, vol. III, p. 315).

point the author wishes to introduce a special heightening of tension. The bells anticipate the clashes of attitude and temperament to come. Tempers are to grow shorter and things are to be said which could only be said at two or three in the morning when people are over-tired and very worried. The new tension first serves to accentuate the differences between those characters who care and those who do not.

Masha does not care. She does not move as Olga rakes through a wardrobe for old clothes to give to the homeless. Olga still cares, although her remark at the sound of the fire engine, 'How awful it is!', is not without a tinge of exasperation in its tone, and this is extended by 'And how sickening!' and again, later, by 'I am tired, I can hardly stand on my feet': even Olga, who seems to have taken charge in the confusion, is not to be seen as a saint. The Vershinins have been burned out, and they are all in this very house; which is probably the reason why Masha is here too. However, the melodrama of the situation is reduced when old Ferapont makes a joke about the burning of Moscow in 1812.

The one person who could have organized relief and attention for those hurt and distressed by the fire, and who indeed had a specific duty to perform in this emergency, is Dr Tchebutykin. But he does not care, for he is 'helplessly drunk'.

Into this state of confusion the old Nurse introduces a new problem.

ANFISA (*wearily*). Olya darling, don't send me away; don't send me away!

OLGA. That's nonsense, nurse. No one is sending you away.

ANFISA (*lays her head on* OLGA's *shoulder*). My own, my treasure, I work, I do my best . . . I'm getting weak, everyone will say 'Be off!' And where am I to go? Where? I am eighty. Eighty-one.

OLGA. Sit down, nurse darling . . . You are tired, poor thing . . . (*makes her sit down*). Rest, dear good nurse . . . How pale you are!

With such small cruelties as this threat of eviction to an aged woman who has been with the family for thirty years, Natasha is continuing her acts of dispossession; together with the old Nurse, she will have Olga and Irina out of the house in Act IV.[1] The episode points to the wider issue of the sisters' insecurity, and its nastier aspects are about to be demonstrated.

[1] The sequence of details in this dispossession is recounted by R. Brustein in *The Theatre of Revolt* (New York, 1962), pp. 158–9.

At first Natasha seems to care, but her mask is soon removed. She bustles in, putting on an officious performance as self-appointed mistress of the situation. They should 'form a committee' for the relief of the refugees. The self-important do-gooder of all ages is apparent in her attitude: 'One ought always to be ready to help the poor.' Nevertheless, she is afraid that the outbreak of influenza in the town will be dangerous with so many strangers in the house. She has in her mind her own children – Bobik, and now 'baby Sophie'. Andrey has evidently become a much married man in a very short time, although we may doubt the paternity of Sophie with the mysterious Protopopov about. Chekhov continues his portrait of the hypocrite with characteristic brilliance: a tiny domestic detail does the work for him. As Natasha talks about the danger to the children, she glances at the bedroom mirror, and she is promptly concerned with her own appearance, a trait we observed before on a more appropriate occasion, that of Irina's party in Act 1. 'My hair must be untidy' and 'They say I have grown fatter . . . but it's not true! Not a bit!' We estimate how real is her concern for the plight of others.

Worse is to come. Natasha sees Anfisa sitting where Olga has gently put her, and immediately the *hausfrau* flares up in anger. 'Don't dare to sit down in my presence! Get up! Go out of the room!' Her voice rises to a scream that is almost hysterical. Doubtless Natasha, like the others, is over-tired, but her pettiness shocks Olga, and shocks us too, as Chekhov intended. We see with a rare clarity both the sham and the tyranny of the woman. Even Natasha, as her temper cools, knows that she has gone too far, and she attempts to excuse her action: 'I like order in the house!' But it is evident that she has been threatening Anfisa before this, and when the old servant appealed to Olga a moment before she was indeed afraid for her future.

In this scene Chekhov is in some danger of making his Natasha a figure of loathing.[1] He is more careful to forestall an impression of villainy in Lopahin, the dispossessor in *The Cherry Orchard*, and thereby reduces the risk of having the audience place the blame for the disasters that befall the family exclusively upon him. But Chekhov intends this painful episode over the old peasant to extend the social reference of his play. The theme of class dif-

---

[1] See the discussion of Natasha's role, pp. 152–3.

ferences was absent from *Uncle Vanya*; it will be more central in
The Cherry Orchard; it is only incipient in this play. Masha is
beside herself with anger, and, taking a pillow, walks out of the
room. Olga is stunned, and Natasha tries to soothe her with
flattery, stroking and kissing her and calling her 'our headmistress'. But Olga cannot be mollified: this rudeness to an old
woman of a lower class is unforgivable in the eyes of a girl
brought up in the aristocratic idea that it is one's responsibility to
care for the peasants. To Natasha the *petite bourgeoise*, Anfisa is
not only a mere servant like the nanny and the wet-nurse and the
cook and the maid, but one who has outlived her usefulness.
Natasha is of the new ruling class who will adjust the old order of
master and serf to the new order of rich and poor, a more heart-
less régime.

We must come to an understanding, Olya. You are at the high-school,
I am at home; you are teaching while I look after the house, and if I say
anything about the servants, I know what I'm talking about; I do
know what I am talking about . . . And that old thief, that old hag . . .
(*stamps*), that old witch shall clear out of the house to-morrow! . . .

Natasha's character emerges with all its attendant cruelty, and
Chekhov places his family in an exact social situation. It is an
ugly scene, and at least one critic finds that it reflects as badly on
the sisters as on the sister-in-law.[1] We could have wished that
Olga and Masha had done more to defend their old nurse. Their
failure to make a stand must reduce our sympathy for them and
also point to their weakening authority as a class.

During all this, the audience is not to forget the events offstage:
while Natasha is full of her petty self-importance, the town is on
fire. Another fire-alarm has been sounded, and when Kuligin
comes in exhausted and looking for his Masha, he reports the
progress of the disaster. However, the fire is now dying down and
the threat to the town is passing. He flops into a chair, but with
that charming touch of childish humour we see in him at other
times, he jumps up to hide in a corner in mock horror at the
drunken Tchebutykin as he comes in. In the event, Kuligin's
joke, as usual, falls flat; everyone is too tired to laugh. The

[1] Mary McCarthy's notion after watching Ruth Gordon's Natasha in New York in
1943. See *Mary McCarthy's Theatre Chronicles, 1937–1962* (New York, 1963), p. 59.

Doctor walks in with the careful tread of a man unsure of his feet, and washes his hands at the washstand. He begins his longest monologue, and again it is naturalistically acceptable, this time as the kind of soliloquy to be expected from a drunken man. While he mumbles almost to himself, Olga and Natasha go off, and Kuligin stands unnoticed.

Tchebutykin's life story is emerging little by little. As in Chekhov's tale of Professor Nikolay Stepanovitch in *A Dreary Story* (1889), the Doctor feels that his life has been wasted. He is entirely self-aware; there is not a jot of deception about him, only a complete and appalling cynicism.

They think I am a doctor, that I can treat all sorts of complaints, and I really know nothing about it, I have forgotten all I did know, I remember nothing, absolutely nothing. The devil take them. Last Wednesday I treated a woman at Zasyp – she died, and it's my fault that she died. Yes . . . I did know something twenty-five years ago, but now I remember nothing, nothing. Perhaps I am not a man at all but only pretend to have arms and legs and head; perhaps I don't exist at all and only fancy that I walk about, eat and sleep (*weeps*). Oh, if only I did not exist!

This detail about the woman's death at Zasyp, echoing Astrov's story in *Uncle Vanya*, was introduced in the revised version of the play, and serves not only to suggest Tchebutykin's incompetence, but also to give the audience a premonition of the danger and destruction his attitude to life represents. The thoughts of being an inadvertent murderer have driven him to drink, and he convinces himself that his life is a pretence. He stands there, mechanically combing his beard, the picture of misery; he would dampen the flagging spirits of everyone, but only Kuligin is present to hear him. And the spectator, of course: for Chekhov juxtaposes Natasha's extreme performance with Tchebutykin's, a grim scene with one grimmer still, in order to show that every attitude is relative to every other. Thus he invites us to decide whether Tchebutykin's nihilism is not worse than Natasha's selfishness.

It is already three o'clock in the morning, and still no one has gone to bed. Chekhov contrives to bring the whole cast into Olga's bedroom eventually, without its seeming too unnatural. Irina now brings in Vershinin and Tusenbach,[1] ostensibly to

---

[1] Chekhov wrote to Olga Knipper, playing Masha, 'I hear from you that in the third act two of you lead Irina in supported on each arm. What's that for? Is that in your

escape from the crowd of people elsewhere in the house. In the exceptional situation, we do not ask, however, why gentlemen are in a lady's bedroom. The Colonel wears his service-dress jacket[1] and the Baron *a 'fashionable new civilian suit'*, but both men are dirty from the fire. Tusenbach has been true to his word and resigned his commission; unhappily, as Olga tells us later, he looks even more ugly out of uniform: we see him suddenly reduced to the level of an unglamorous provincial townsman like Andrey or Kliugin, and envisage him as an equally mediocre husband. We are to miss no significant phase in the demise of the Moscow myth and all that goes with it. The visitors add to the sense of suppressed hysteria in the scene, and prepare the stage for a further series of explosions of feeling.

The Baron has been asked 'to get up a concert for the benefit of the families whose houses have been burnt down'. The short sequence that follows surveys and accentuates another petty tyranny, that of Kuligin over his wife. 'Marya Sergeyevna plays the piano splendidly, to my thinking', Tusenbach suggests. This is a surprise to the audience, since we have taken her to be a somewhat withdrawn, suffering creature. Yet the musically accomplished Baron should know. With the note of pride in his voice that we heard before when something reflected his own achievement, Kuligin gladly concurs in the judgment: 'Yes, she plays splendidly'; but Irina's voice is cold when she points out that her sister has not played for three or four years. Kuligin recognizes that he is being attacked on all sides, and to defend himself adds feebly, 'I am very fond of her.'

TUSENBACH. To be able to play so gloriously and to know that no one understands you!
KULIGIN (*sighs*). Yes . . . But would it be suitable for her to take part in a concert? (*a pause*) I know nothing about it, my friends. Perhaps it would be all right. There is no denying that our director is a fine man, indeed a very fine man, very intelligent, but he has such views . . .

The Baron stares Kuligin in the face as he speaks his lines, making

mood? You ought not to leave your sofa. And can't Irina come in by herself? Why these innovations?' (letter of 24 January 1901, in Garnett, p. 74). He evidently mistook Olga Knipper's meaning here, since Masha is offstage at this time.
[1] According to a letter from Chekhov to A. L. Vishevsky, 17 January 1901, in Hingley, vol. III, p. 313.

as direct a criticism of the husband's attitude to his wife as so mild a man is capable of. Kuligin's *'pause'* is taken up with his silent appeal to the company for approval; he looks around at each person, but they only turn away. Everything he says serves only to condemn him more. Kuligin's unseen headmaster has a lot to answer for, and again the pressure of an outside force is felt upon these simple lives. After Kuligin's own pompous self-appraisal, and for all his *bonhomie*, the episode reveals his true stature as a man.

Vershinin relieves the embarrassed tone of the conversation, only to detonate a bombshell of his own. The brigade may possibly be transferred elsewhere: 'Some say to Poland, and others to Tchita'.[1] To the antipodes! Exile! But if this is bad for the military, what of the Prozorov circle should the brigade move out? 'The town will be a wilderness then.' Masha is offstage, but the audience recognizes in a flash what the loss of her colonel might mean to her. Irina in her innocence cries, 'We shall go away too', but we have grown used to such a reflex response, and remain sceptical.

Another shock follows hard upon the last. There is a crash on the other side of the stage, where Tchebutykin, with a tortured expression on his drunken face, has picked up a fine porcelain clock to look at it. On Irina's line, 'We shall go away too', he drops it. The departure of the regiment means, perhaps, his separation from his beloved Irina, from the living image of her mother. The smash takes everyone's attention, while the Doctor merely stands looking vacantly at the havoc he has wrought. 'To smithereens!' is all he says. Everyone is shocked, waiting for an explanation. Kuligin moves to pick up the pieces with 'I should give you minus zero for conduct!', able with his quip to show his relief that he is no longer the outcast in the group. Irina protests that it was their mother's clock, and we gather that this act of destruction represents more than Tchebutykin's repudiation of his pointless existence; almost an expression of the severing of the family bond and the loss of the sustaining vitality of the dead mother. The unexpected noise of the shattering china, like the breaking string in *The Cherry Orchard*, has that sense of finality and hopelessness with which Chekhov wishes to embrace the

[1] A town which is today in the Buryat Republic, almost in Mongolia and some three thousand miles from Moscow.

family as a whole – two marriages foundering, the purposeless labour of Olga and Irina, the fruitless yearning for a lost home and the irretrievable Moscow past. As for Tchebutykin himself, he is in the abyss, the black depths of despair. 'Perhaps I did not smash it, but it only seems as though I had. Perhaps it only seems to us that we exist, but really we are not here at all. I don't know anything – nobody knows anything.' He stumbles off, singing a tune from a popular operetta, while the glow from the fire, symbolic of destruction, flickers across the floor behind him.

The Colonel pursues his own thoughts, and tells his story of the night. What struck him most was the fear on the faces of his two small girls; why must there be this unhappiness? He thinks of war, of looting and burning, and before long he is off on his favourite theme. One day, in 'another two or three hundred years' (a vague gesture with his arm), their way of life will seem stupid, but eventually, 'Oh, what a wonderful life that will be – what a wonderful life!' (his head drops on his chest). Against the background of a fire still raging through the town, his words strike us as utterly barren.

However, Masha has heard his voice and comes in clutching her pillow, her hope of sleep, and is the only one prepared to listen to his ramblings. Indeed, Vershinin and Masha are the only ones in the sad gathering in the muddle of the cramped bedroom who are happy.

MASHA. Tram-tam-tam!
VERSHININ. Tam-tam!
MASHA. Tra-ra-ra?
VERSHININ. Tra-ta-ta! (*Laughs*)[1]

The tones of their voices articulate their feelings in a secret language which no one need translate. They communicate their love like two children playing a game, while not perceiving that they are lost in an indifferent world. And they laugh.

---

[1] Chekhov wrote to Olga Knipper, playing Masha, how to inflect the next lines of this unusual dialogue: 'Vershinin pronounces "tram-tram-tram" by way of a question and you by way of an answer, and that seems to you such an original joke that you utter your "tram-tram" with a little laugh, you call out "tram-tram" and laugh not loudly, but just audibly. You must not make the sort of face you do in *Uncle Vanya* [as Sonya – J.L.S.], but look younger and more full of life' (letter of 20 January, 1901, in Garnett, p. 73).

But hysteria is still in the air. Their gentle mood is broken by the wild entrance of Lieutenant Fedotik. He dances round the room like a madman, laughing at the top of his voice: 'Burnt to ashes! Burnt to ashes! Everything I had in the world.' Everyone laughs too. The effect is correctly sick, one of frenzied farcical tragedy.

This burst kindles a last renewal of energy in the scene. The audience is constantly reminded of the fire by noises off and reports of developments which come with each new entrance, and is aware of what is boiling beneath the false gaiety of the characters. Only Masha and Vershinin, self-regarding and perhaps self-deceiving, seem content in their private cocoon.

Fedotik's exuberance is cut short as Captain Solyony storms into the bedroom looking for Irina. The girl turns on him angrily: 'You can't stay here.' Why, then, he asks, is Tusenbach in the room? His jealousy of the Baron is now unmistakable as he sprinkles himself from his sinister bottle of scent, recites a mocking tag from Krylov and leaves the room with an insulting 'Chook, chook, chook!' at Tusenbach asleep in a chair. The Baron remains oblivious of his threat, which teases us the more. He has been dreaming, dreaming of a job at the brickworks, and he takes a tender leave of Irina with this in his mind: 'Come with me; let us go and work together!' If the shadow of Solyony's recent aggressive visit is not cast over these impractical notions, Irina's tearful silence casts its own, for she has not relinquished *her* dream. She persists in refusing the present compromise for the deluded happiness of the future. Her longing for a lover is confused with her longing for Moscow, and only in the Moscow of her dreams does she expect to meet her true love. The two young people are separated by an invincible ghost, while Solyony's scent lingers about them.

Kuligin is roused by his wife and stirs himself with a grunt; he too should go home. He agrees and makes a gesture of affection towards her. A mocking '*Amo, amas, amat . . .*' is all she returns, attempting a Latin joke after his own fashion. She does not intend it kindly, but whether he is blind to her indifference to him, or whether he smothers his doubts by playing a childish charade, we are not to know, for he continues to broadcast his happiness for all to hear.

KULIGIN. I am content. I am content, I am content!
MASHA. I am bored, I am bored, I am bored!

She is telling him plainly her opinion of her life with him; but at the same time she also carries the excruciating knowledge that there is no escape with her colonel, as the febrile joking suggests. Does Kuligin know that he has only to wait before Masha must come back to him?

Chekhov drops a new bombshell, one exploding with even more force. Andrey's losses at cards have till now reflected only his own character; now they will affect the fortunes of the whole family. To make the point strongly to the audience, Masha gets up from her sofa where she has spent most of the time while on stage, and as if suddenly shaking off her personal worries, announces,

And there's something I can't get out of my head . . . It's simply revolting. It sticks in my head like a nail; I must speak of it. I mean about Andrey . . . He has mortgaged this house in the bank and his wife has grabbed all the money, and you know the house does not belong to him alone, but to us four! He ought to know that, if he is a decent man.

Kuligin in his self-centred way ignores news which does not affect him directly, and leaves still declaring his happiness to the world with a little tune. In any case, the loss would make Masha entirely dependent on him. But Irina has heard, although only the audience sees the larger implications of the debt: she still thinks of the mortgage only as it affects Andrey. Indeed, she is more concerned by her brother's reputation than by his solvency. His career at the university has been forgotten, and he is content to be on the council in a position of subservience to the hated Protopopov – 'the whole town is laughing'. Without saying as much, she also expresses her disgust at Natasha's continuing affair with her influential lover. As for Andrey, he does not care any longer: when the fire broke out, he stayed in his room playing his violin.

The youngest of them is ready to break down, and as the scene approaches its peak of tension the sisters are at last alone, with nothing to restrain their feelings. When Olga comes in again, Irina collapses. Her voice rushes on until she is crying in Olga's arms almost in distraction, 'Where? Where has it all gone? Where is it?' The older sister is here the maternal figure, and like a child Irina moans with pathetic irrelevance that she cannot remember her Italian. We learn that she managed to change her dreary job at the telegraph office for one with the town council, but the new work is no less tedious than the old. She is now twenty-three and has grown 'thin and old and ugly'. We watch her in the paroxysms of despair. Gradually her strained tones die away in her tears, and Olga tries to comfort a quietly sobbing little girl, telling her what *she* would have done, and what we would have told her ourselves: 'Marry the baron!', ugly as he is. With extreme pathos Olga adds wistfully that she would have married without love – 'even . . . an old man'. Idealism can be carried too far: accept things as they are. This painful moment Chekhov does not relieve with comedy, and the first light of morning finds the world looking bleak indeed.

Chekhov supplies a visual symbol of their mutual dejection at this crucial moment. He has Natasha make one of her stiff, fleeting entrances, out of key with the rest of the scene, suggesting the presence of a world which is extraneous, but which may not be ignored. There are some coldly going about their business, creating havoc, causing misery, while the sensitive ones must merely look on and suffer. 'NATASHA *with a candle in her hand walks across the stage from door on right to door on left without speaking*',[1] and Masha's dry comment, 'She walks about as though it were she had set fire to the town', links the victims of the night with the dispossession of the sisters. The obliquity of Chekhov's symbolism does not disturb the naturalistic surface.

The tension breaks in Masha too. Now that she is alone with her sisters, her voice quivers as she announces with a touch of bravado that she has a confession to make: 'I can't be silent.' She is in love, in love with the Colonel. Her sisters look at her in shock. Stanislavsky's staging of this climactic moment made its central importance explicit:

Masha stands up quickly, she is excited, she has made her decision, she is nervously wrought up, she nervously stretches out her arms, she

---

[1] Stanislavsky expanded this by having Natasha angrily slam doors. This is not true to what Chekhov wanted when he wrote to him, 'You tell me that in Act III, when Natasha makes the rounds of the house at night, she extinguishes the lights and looks for evil-doers under the furniture. But it seems to me it would be preferable to have her walk across the stage in a straight line without looking at anything or anybody, à la Lady Macbeth, with a candle – that way the scene would be shorter and more blood-curdling' (2 January 1901, in Hellman, p. 280).

gets down on her knees, as does Olga, by the head of Irina's bed; she puts one arm around Irina, the other around Olga. She speaks in a low voice ('I love this man . . . I love Vershinin') as she draws their two heads closer to her own. The heads of the three sisters are close to one another . . . Masha looks up at the ceiling dreamily and with a glow on her face, recalls her whole romance . . .[1]

Chekhov wrote about the episode to Olga Knipper when she was playing Masha, and was most particular about her tone and attitude:

Masha's repentance in Act III isn't repentance at all, but only frank conversation. Take it nervously, but not desperately, don't scream, smile just occasionally, and the great thing is to do it so that the exhaustion of night may be felt. And that it may be felt that you are cleverer than your sisters, think yourself cleverer, anyway.[2]

Masha is nervous, but she must speak with a degree of self-composure, for she is the only sister who feels she has a straw to cling to: 'that's my fate'. Yet in this harsh environment she knows that her position is unreal. She admits that her affair with Vershinin is the kind of thing one reads about only in novels; it is too trite, too romantic, to be true. Then, is she wrong? Is she mad? She will be silent like the anonymous clerk of Nikolay Gogol's comic story *The Diary of a Madman*, who finds everyone about him insane except himself.

Masha's revelation troubles her sisters more than it does herself. Irina accepts Masha's caress in unbelieving silence,[3] and soon retires behind her bed-screen without another word. Her sister's positive action beside her own passivity has silenced her. As for Olga, she goes behind her screen instantly. She is stunned: 'Leave off. I don't hear anyway.' Herself ready to marry at any price, she cannot accept this flouting of society; she cannot accept adultery.

---

[1] Stroyeva, p. 52. However, this interpretation with its tendency towards a symbolic grouping implies the unity of the sisters over Masha's unconventional behaviour, and also seems falsely to anticipate and detract from the closing tableau of the play.

[2] Letter of 28 January 1901, in Garnett, p. 76.

[3] At the Barnes Theatre, London, in 1925, Komisarjevsky, probably following Stanislavsky, had Irina begin crying again here: 'Irina with her arms entwined about her sisters bursts into a storm of weeping. The grouping here is pyramidal, and it is as much the visual effect as the skill of the words which gives an effect of dolour such as may not be compassed by the précis-writer' (James Agate, *The Contemporary Theatre, 1926*, London, 1927, p. 57).

But we see that, in the face of Olga and Irina's tenuous dream of Moscow, Masha's Colonel, at any rate, is more substantial.

Masha's passing happiness is sharply set against Andrey's misery. We are to see the last and weakest member of the family in the scene's final image. During the fire, Andrey has been too wrapped up in his own anxieties even to move from his room: he is one who does not care, and upon his entrance, we find the change in him appalling. Old Ferapont has forgotten to address him as 'your honour', and the master is in a nasty temper. He is becoming touchy about his status, and some of Natasha's contempt for the lower classes has brushed off on her husband. We witness the evil creep on. Now he asks Olga for 'the key of the cupboard' (is this for access to money? to alcohol?), but she, still the mother, is reluctant to part with it, and the pauses speak for her. When, finally, she comes from behind her screen and gives it to him without a word, he flares up with a guilty conscience. He is spoiling for a fight in any case, and finding the three girls together alone, decides that this is the moment to challenge them in spite of their fatigue.

ANDREY. Let us have things out thoroughly, once for all. What have you against me? What is it?
OLGA. Leave off, Andryusha. Let us talk tomorrow (*nervously*). What an agonizing night!
ANDREY (*greatly confused*). Don't excite yourself. I ask you quite coolly, what have you against me? Tell me straight out.

The tension in Andrey is greater than in any of them, but Olga cannot face a quarrel, and behind her screen Irina is perhaps sobbing quietly to indicate her presence to the audience and her withdrawal to her brother. Masha wants none of him either, and hearing Vershinin's 'Tram-tam-tam!', echoes him with a 'Tra-ta-ta!' and escapes. Olga goes behind her screen without saying good-night to Masha, and the strained relationship between the two older sisters remains unrelieved.[1]

[1] According to Stanislavsky's production, Olga relents and kisses Masha at the door like a mother commiserating with a wayward child, and then goes again behind her screen (Stroyeva, p. 53). He conceived the idea that Masha's confession should unite the sisters, and Olga's kiss was to indicate that 'she really understands Masha, and realizes deep down that she would do the same thing in her place. Now she no longer criticizes her but pities her'. This, of course, is at variance with what Chekhov asked: Olga in her maternal role must be seen to be shocked.

Act III

Both Olga and Irina are motionless behind their screens[1] and strikingly silent; but Andrey will not go. He must speak. He is coherent, for he has marshalled all his arguments. Nevertheless, to the audience, listening with the ears of Olga and Irina, every one of them sounds specious. 'First, you have something against Natasha'; and with a bluster he asserts that he respects her as 'a splendid woman, conscientious, straightforward and honourable'. He waits upon the *'pause'* for a reply, which does not come. Second, why are they annoyed that he is not a professor? He is a county councillor, 'and I consider this service just as sacred and elevated as the service of learning'. Again he pauses; again no answer. He begins to falter when, third, he apologizes for mortgaging the house, but he argues that while they have an annuity, he has no independent source of income. Again, nothing from behind the screens. Each of his points concerns his honour: he respects his wife, he respects his job and he justifies his action over the mortgage. But he protests too much. The audience, like the sisters, recognizes the spinelessness of the excuses, and, because each touches an open wound without going to the source of the infection, the sisters are in pain. What Natasha has done to sap their vitality, the evaporation of the Moscow appointment and Andrey's escape into gambling, with the resulting loss of the house, reflect their own debility and are symptoms of a disease which has spread through the family.

The silence from behind the screens implies that the sky has fallen about their heads. Andrey stands helplessly before the inhuman barrier of the screens, trying to control his emotions. He does not move when Kuligin puts his head round the door asking for Masha and disappears again. Andrey paces the strip of stage, persisting with 'Natasha is an excellent, conscientious woman'. Still there is silence from the sisters as we watch how they isolate the brother on whom they had pinned their hopes. Finally,

[1] John Gielgud reported of Komisarjevsky's 1925 production that the girls retired with their candles behind 'a chintz-covered partition some four feet high stretched across the stage, dividing it in two', so that 'one saw, on the wall above, their huge shadows, as Irina sat up in bed crying and Olga came across the room and leaned over to comfort her' (*Early Stages*, London, 1953, pp. 106–7). James Agate saw this effect symbolically: 'The younger sister's flood of passion is not yet stilled, and as you listen to the last of its ebb you see the giant shadows of these two figures of grief thrown by the candle upon the upper wall and ceiling' (*The Contemporary Theatre, 1926*, London, 1927, p. 57).

he breaks down; the mask drops; he weeps. He cannot sustain the pretence a moment longer. 'Dear sisters, darling sisters, you must not believe what I say, you mustn't believe it . . .' He has gone, unable to listen to the horror of the truth from his own mouth. Kuligin, more agitated this time, calls again for his missing Masha, reminding us that there are more overwhelming problems than Andrey's, like the loss of one's wife to another man.

'*The stage is empty*'. We stare at the neglected muddle of the night, mirroring the confusion of the characters. More distantly now, the fire-alarm is heard for the last time: the distraught scene has been sandwiched between these urgent bells. The drunken Doctor is heard knocking from below, and, as the curtain does not fall, time hangs in suspense.

From her bed, Irina looks round her screen, and we see that she is no longer crying. In a new voice, subdued and a little frightened, she tells Olga that the brigade is being posted. 'Then we shall be alone . . .' For the first time Irina weighs the terrors of being marooned on this desert island. A short pause, and she calls to her sister again. She has made a decision of sorts: she 'respects'[1] the Baron – she is careful not to say 'loves' or even 'likes' – and she will marry him. Yet immediately her thoughts of him are flooded by the overwhelming obsession, and it is clear that the poor man runs a bad second in her desires. 'I will marry him, I consent, only let us go to Moscow! I entreat you, do let us go! There's nothing in the world better than Moscow! Let us go, Olya! Let us go!' The naïve Irina speaks for them all, as they dare not, in clinging to the dream. At the curtain we hear her voice echo that reiterated 'Moscow!' as if it were carried from the end of Act II on the flames of the fire. It has never sounded so forlorn as at the end of this, the most unrelieved scene that Chekhov wrote.

1 *Uvazhat* (to esteem, respect) does not necessarily include affection.

Act Four

In spite of another change of tone and tempo, the fourth act of *Three Sisters* maintains consistency of character among everyone in an unusually large cast, newly stresses the specific contradictions of thought and feeling in the action, and restates the problem the play has been proposing.

For the first time the scene is set outside the house, and the two worlds, within and without, are visible on stage. Significantly, only Natasha and her lover are in the house, but we are not so far from it that we are unaware of her presence. James Agate saw the setting as symbolic to a degree: 'The poetic and the commonplace are curiously mingled. The birch trees on one side of the house are for apostrophizing, on the other side hangs out the clothing of Natasha's babies.'[1] More importantly, the sisters are to end their play trapped at the house, while the wider world mockingly beckons them to come: '*a long avenue of fir trees*' leading to '*a view of the river*' and thence to a wood on the far side of it, take the eye out and away. In addition, there is a street beyond the garden, and from time to time men and women are seen passing upstage: '*five soldiers pass rapidly*'. Thus this outside world is vivid and active around the sisters. By constant movement and offstage hallooing, the bright midday bustle of departure animates the scene until the regiment has gone.

Four years have passed since Irina's springtime party. For all its animation, the scene is autumnal, and Stanislavsky had leaves falling throughout the act, probably to remind his Russian audience of the imminent onset of the harsh continental winter. It is another of Chekhov's going-away scenes, but this time it is to be done with a flourish all the more ironic for its gaiety. The champagne is on the table for the conventional toast of departure. The Doctor for the first time is seen to wear his army cap; he is sitting

[1] *The Contemporary Theatre, 1926* (London, 1927), p. 58. Agate was describing Komisarjevsky's production.

in an easy chair as usual, although he has given up even taking notes. The Schoolmaster, who is now the new second master, has shaved off his moustache in honour of his beloved superior, and is wearing a decoration on his chest: for the occasion he is in formal dress, matching the military. The officers are in full service dress, their brilliant colours making them look more like picture-book soldiers than we have seen before. In the sunlight, it is altogether a dazzling scene, contradicted only by the leaves of autumn.

Irina and the Baron, in his civilian clothes, are saying goodbye to a small group of lieutenants, while Fedotik is trying to take a parting snapshot with the camera we saw in Act 1. He manages only with some difficulty because everyone is far too excited to hold still for the photograph. There are tears, and exclamations, and the small talk of saying farewell, and troubling sentiments like those expressed to Tusenbach by his old companions in arms that they will not see him again.

RODDEY (*taking a long look at the garden*). Good-bye, trees! (*Shouts*) Halloo! (*a pause*) Good-bye, echo!
KULIGIN. I shouldn't wonder if you get married in Poland . . . Your Polish wife will clasp you in her arms and call you *kochany*!1 (*Laughs*)
FEDOTIK (*looking at his watch*). We have less than an hour.

The young men only partly feel the tensions between the past and the welcoming future, and Roddey's calling to his echo is a neat vocal effect to suggest the attraction of what is to come. Kuligin's apt sentiment about a Polish wife for Roddey at once intimates to them that he knows the language, and tells us the destination of the regiment (presumably as part of the policy of policing Russian Poland at this period); at the same time he indicates his own need and desire for an affectionate wife. But withal it is a happy speech, and Kuligin seems overjoyed to see them go. Even Fedotik's remark on the limited time left to them catches the excitement, while it also suggests the sadness of parting. Some are going, others are staying; some are happy and hopeful, others are miserable. Chekhov so casually seems to mix the tonal ingredients associated with departure. 'Peace and quiet will descend upon the town', with 'And dreadful boredom too'. All is mixed feelings and dramatic ambivalence. Roddey's hallooing dies away as he goes,

1 'beloved' (Polish).

his voice fading like a memory of the past, yet resounding like a call into the future.

Only Tchebutykin remains contentedly indifferent to the sensations both of going and of staying. Oh, he is going, but he has arranged to be retired in a year's time, and he thinks he will return and live his life 'quite differently'. As he puts one newspaper into his pocket and takes out another, we suspect that he will nevertheless continue as before. He sings a snatch of the tune which will be heard from him intermittently throughout the act: 'Tarara-boom-dee-ay!', an extension in song of his frighteningly unchanging attitude of 'It doesn't matter!' At the time of disaster, when the emotions of other people are stretched to breaking, the Doctor is anaesthetized, passively thinking only of his pension.

Andrey is another who has been reduced by experience to a deadening indifference to what is going on about him. It is enough for him to be seen pushing a pram across the back of the stage. The Professor has descended from his books and music to the minding of babies – one of them probably not his own – a progress of degradation and emasculation.

Suddenly amid the desultory teasing of Tchebutykin and Kuligin, Irina introduces a matter of urgent personal importance.

IRINA. Ivan Romanitch, darling, I am dreadfully uneasy. You were on the boulevard yesterday, tell me what was it that happened?
TCHEBUTYKIN. What happened? Nothing. Nothing much (*reads the newspaper*). It doesn't matter!
KULIGIN. The story is that Solyony and the baron met yesterday on the boulevard near the theatre . . .
TUSENBACH. Oh, stop it! Really . . . (*with a wave of his hand walks away into the house*).

The Baron has been curiously silent, and his stillness in a busy scene takes the spectator's attention. There has finally been a full-blown quarrel with the Captain. Usually so full of plans, Tusenbach is torn between his officer's code and his hopes for a life with Irina. His refusal to discuss the matter of the quarrel is a gesture of helplessness, in its own way a fatalistic acceptance of the blow that events can deal, parallel with the paralysis of the sisters.

The Doctor's disclaimer provides the ugliest insight into his frigid character that we see. It was within his power, indeed it was his duty, to put a stop to this duel, but he does not lift a

finger. Does he want Solyony and Tusenbach to destroy each
other if it means that he can preserve intact his fatherly relationship with Irina? However, her feelings are relieved, and a thin
joke from Kuligin helps to distract the troubled girl, at least temporarily. But when offstage the cry from the future comes again,
'Aa-oo! Halloo!', she shudders, and the audience knows there is
more to come. Solyony's malevolence towards Tusenbach from
the beginning of the play is Chekhov's way of pointing a pistol
at the Baron's head, and in obedience to his own rule of writing,
that 'If in the first act you hang a pistol on the wall, then in the
last act it must be shot off. Otherwise you do not hang it there'.[1]
Irina's intuition of something sinister about to take place matches
our own. Like the past, the future is mixed of hope and fear.

Irina's tone changes, and in a voice which is girlish with her
desires for the future, she announces that the Baron and she are
to be married tomorrow. They are going to live near the brick-
yard, and with her new diploma she will start teaching. Two
building industries! But Chekhov has taught us by now how to
interpret evidence that a character too readily furnishes: his whole
method of playwriting is an education in social observation.
Tusenbach has never worked before; Irina has already rejected
two jobs. As a schoolmistress, we see her in Olga's shoes, weary
and frustrated; and if she is not marrying for love, as a wife we
see in her the shadow of Masha also. So the family revolves, one
sister repeating another. Kuligin, who knows what hard work
both marriage and teaching are, is unimpressed either by her
prospective union or by her choice of a career.

Nevertheless, in this scene Kuligin is happier than we have seen
him before: he is almost beside himself with joy at the departure
of the regiment. He is constantly declaring his love for Masha,
cracking his jokes, wishing everyone well. He thinks of himself
as a lucky man – he has even been awarded 'the order of the Stanis-
lav of the second degree'!

Well, today the officers will be gone and everything will go on in the
old way. Whatever people may say, Masha is a true, good woman. I
love her dearly and am thankful for my lot!

His juxtaposition of the army's departure with his love for his

---

[1] Reported by A. Gurlyand and quoted in Simmons, p. 190.

wife confirms what we already suspect: the absence of Colonel Vershinin, he thinks, will send his Masha running back to him. His ironic judgment that she is 'a true, good woman', like Andrey's pronouncements on Natasha, puts him along with the others who feed on fantasies. No one is listening to his ramblings, and the doleful playing of 'The Maiden's Prayer' inside the house – it must be Natasha herself who is playing – seems to answer his excess of happiness. We may guess what Masha herself is thinking.

The song certainly speaks to Irina. She is thinking of her wedding and believes she will soon be saved from spinsterhood: 'Tomorrow evening I shall not be hearing that "Maiden's Prayer" '. And she adds that Protopopov, from whom we have not heard for some time, is in the drawing-room. The music is evidently to entertain him, and at last he has achieved regular admission into the house of his mistress. The liaison is almost regularized! 'He has come again to-day' – on this of all days. To top this, 'The Maiden's Prayer' is Natasha's attempt to cover his visit with a suitable decorum, and for these two the choice of the music is superbly ironic.

We learn from Irina, too, that Olga has become headmistress of her school, and able to live there. Irina has therefore been living alone in the house with Andrey and Natasha – and Protopopov. The last daughter to leave their father's house, Irina is now casting off all this embarrassment. But if Irina's marriage with the Baron rescues her from a home life she now loathes, this is yet another indication of a loveless union. Chekhov touches in the expository details which show how matters have progressed. Meanwhile, like spectres at the feast, Tchebutykin still hums his 'Tarara-boom-dee-ay!' and Andrey pushes his pram round the garden for a second time.

As for Masha, she has lost her colonel. She comes up beside the Doctor as he reads his paper, and sits down in silence looking the picture of woe. Unexpectedly, she urges a question on him: 'Did you love my mother?' Chekhov is picking up a forgotten thread, and at the same time showing how Masha is obsessed by the need to discover evidence of human love, of any kind, in any form, even illicit.

TCHEBUTYKIN. Very much.
MASHA. And did she love you?
TCHEBUTYKIN (*after a pause*). That I don't remember.

Even though the spotlight is on Masha's unhappy predicament, Chekhov cannot help but balance one experience with another and stress their parallelism. Unrequited love comes in old men as well as in young women. Tchebutykin has devoted a lifetime to a dead woman, and is here evading a painful enquiry, but his refusal or failure to recall the essence of the experience, their mutual response, is desolating indeed for the young woman; her thoughts leap naturally to the source of her problem, Kuligin. 'Is my man here? It's just like our cook Marfa used to say about her policeman: is my man here?' Her ability to jest at her misfortune, albeit sardonically, is well within the character Chekhov has built up. The remark embodies both her lack of respect for her husband and for herself: she grants herself as much romance as we allow cooks and policemen.

For a third time Andrey pushes his pram across the garden. He is like a chorus figure calculated to reduce every tragedy to the scale of dull normality. In the first version of the play Chekhov gave Masha the line, 'The person I'd like to give a jolly good hiding to is brother Andrey. The stuffed dummy!'[1] In the final version, he has no need to say this: 'Here is our Andrey' is enough. Masha's distaste for his baby-minding at this juncture, especially if it is Protopopov's baby he is minding, helps us to see him as her male counterpart, another slave to a loveless, humdrum marriage. But Andrey's thoughts are on the giant problem of getting Sophie to sleep: why do they not stop the noise in the house?

'*The sound of a harp and a violin being played far away in the street*' begins to grow upon us as the pace of the scene slows down. Coupled with the lifeless sounds of the piano from the house, the melancholy of distant strings reproduces the spirit of provincial monotony, of which the modest street noises of Act II were a part. Andrey comments, 'The town will be empty. It's as though one put an extinguisher over it (*a pause*).' The joyless strains winding across the countryside capture the *taedium vitae* of all three on stage.

There now begins a long sequence of terrifying relentlessness. The Doctor has been looking strangely at his pocket-watch. 'Soon', he has been heard to say. Now he looks at it again. At last he admits

[1] See Hingley, vol. III, p. 312.

that something is afoot, but his 'It was nothing' is tantalizingly non-committal. However, he has not been thinking of the time of the march. We are to learn that a duel is to be fought between Solyony and Tusenbach at half-past twelve, a precise half-hour before the troops move out. Chekhov is counting the minutes to the departure in this act, sustaining the tension we are to share with the sisters. Tchebutykin has not stirred from his armchair; his only interest is in the time of the event, suggesting that he is expected to officiate. Indeed, he seems to find the encounter amusing: 'The doctor enjoys being at a duel,' Chekhov wrote in his rough notes on the play.[1] With a laugh, he says he thinks it funny that Solyony imagines himself to be like Lermontov, but adds ominously, 'Joking apart, this is his third duel.' The implication is that Solyony is used to the sport, and that he has succeeded in surviving twice before. Masha immediately expresses our own anxiety for the little Baron, but Tchebutykin's indifference to the fate of others, both as a doctor and as one who professes affection for the Baron's fiancée, is sharp and definite. 'The Baron is a very good fellow, but one baron more or less in the world, what does it matter?' This line was specially inserted in the final version of the play, and it is Chekhov's intention here not only to complete his portrait of Tchebutykin, but also to increase our sense of personal urgency.

A new pulse is felt in the scene, the thrill of a gradually approaching crisis. If Tchebutykin has made no move to stop the duel, neither has Andrey, who merely comments on the immorality of duelling. Masha walks away in disgust: 'How they keep on talking, talking all day long.' And through her Chekhov sends an icy chill into the theatre as she remarks the signs of approaching winter: 'The birds are already flying south.' The birds suggest the mindless compulsions which determine their lives. As Masha sees these birds high and free in the sky, taking their own farewell, she thinks of her earthbound prison, and we of the infinite space and time which dwarfs us all.

Having started the tension, Chekhov refuses us relief and instead revives the surface torpor of an earlier mood. Alone with the Doctor, Andrey thinks of the family home soon to be empty of love. What about his wife? 'A wife is a wife.' The brutal

[1] See H. Popkin, *Anton Chekhov: The Three Sisters* (New York, 1965), p. 135.

answer sums up his resignation and his meaningless loyalty. The legal bond is the final justification of his apathy. All his ambitions have been smothered in a marriage to a little *bourgeois* wife. In a neat counterpoint with Kuligin's kindly view of his Masha, Andrey says,

She is a straightforward, upright woman, good-natured, perhaps, but for all that there is something in her which makes her no better than some petty, blind, hairy animal. Anyway, she's not a human being.

He knows that Natasha is *poshloy*, 'commonplace', 'trivial', but mind and heart have, as so often, proved irreconcilable, and his voice falls away in irresolution: 'I can't account for my loving her.' The Doctor's advice is simple: put your hat on, leave and never look back. Andrey has too much conscience, or is too much a coward, for that. He is silent as he stands pensively jogging his pram.

Captain Solyony arrives to fetch Tchebutykin to the duel, and the tempo is crisp once more. 'It's time! It's half-past twelve.' The Doctor is suddenly testy, but the Captain is in the highest spirits,[1] theatrically quoting a line or two from Lermontov's thickly romantic poem 'The Sail', which depicts the poet's soul at sea in a storm. Tchebutykin counters with the two lines from Krylov heard in Act I, but the comedy becomes sinister on the lips of a man about to preside at a killing, and the contradiction in tone injects the occasion with a touch of insanity. Solyony sprinkles more scent on his hands and remarks that he has just used up a whole bottle, but they still smell 'like a corpse'. Solyony's mysterious gesture of evil, only a joke at first, is renewed at the time of crisis.

[1] John Fernald finds the moment of Solyony's brief appearance charged with his own feeling, 'which, true to his character . . . he is quite incapable of expressing in words. Beneath their cover he suffers a frustrated romantic desire for Irina, a hunger for the respect of his brother officers (which has always been denied him) and a craving to be thought an intellectual by the people he meets.' Fernald would have him left behind by Tchebutykin for a moment: 'Left alone at this point of crisis, he can invest that pause with almost all that he has ever longed for and all that he has ever failed to achieve. When the dam of the reservoir "breaks", however, it must break into action. And the longer the pause, the greater the super-charge, the more compulsive the action . . . In the case of Solonyi, the action, since he is clearly obsessed by Irina, is a kiss blown at her window. But it can be a long time, as he stands there, before he need do anything at all.' And he reports that when Livanov played the part in Nemirovich-Danchenko's production at the M.A.T., 'his pause before this exit held the audience successfully for a minute and a half' (*Sense of Direction: The Director and his Actors*, London, 1968, pp. 98–9).

Act IV

The immediate object of our apprehension, the Baron, looking ridiculous in a new straw hat, enters nervously with Irina. He is anxious to go, but she is troubled, even more so when he speaks to her with a tremor in his voice he can hardly control. He kisses her hands and gazes into her eyes, oblivious of deaf old Ferapont waiting patiently upstage with papers for Andrey. He is deaf, but he can see, and by his disbelieving presence he turns to humour the sweetness of the scene. Tomorrow they will work, they will be rich and all their dreams will come true. 'There is only one thing, one thing: you don't love me!' The poignancy of Tusenbach's present situation is acute. Irina admits she does not love him, ironically unaware of her cruelty, when within the hour he might be killed. She cannot love, only dream about love: hers is a terrible affliction. As for the Baron, he is not afraid of dying, only of dying without love: a more sympathetic condition.

TUSENBACH. Say something to me . . . (*a pause*). Say something to me . . .
IRINA. What? What am I to say to you? What?
TUSENBACH. Anything.
IRINA. There, there! (*a pause*)[1]

Those pauses are heavy with numbness. She cannot bring herself to speak the word he wishes to hear.

Yet in another way Tusenbach is curiously happy. As he looks at the trees in the avenue, he says he feels as if he were seeing them for the first time. Recalling Vershinin's story in Act II of the prisoner watching the birds from his cell window with childlike eyes, we guess that the Baron is seeing the trees with the sharpened perceptions of a condemned man. These are the very trees which Natasha later says she will cut down. 'What beautiful trees, and, really, how beautiful life ought to be under them!' He is sensing death. But there is also a mystical optimism in his thinking: just as the dead tree 'waves in the wind with the others', he feels that even when he is dead he will still 'have part in life, one way or another'. The calls of his seconds, 'Halloo! Aa-oo!', exactly echo the calls of those who came to say goodbye.

His farewell, considering he 'will be back directly', strikes Irina as suspiciously emotional. Alarmed, she wishes to go with him.

---

1 Hingley renders this line, 'Oh, please don't talk like that' (vol. III, p. 132), but Garnett's version hits the insipidity of Irina's answer.

Perhaps she has known in her heart from the beginning of the act that he was going to be killed,[1] which makes her inability to speak a word of love the more shattering. But it would be impossible for her to go, and as Tusenbach hurries off through the trees he searches for an excuse to keep her at the house. Will she have them make him some coffee? Irina stands impassive, then turns back in silence and sits motionless on the swing upstage, deeply disturbed.[2]

The crisis is almost upon us, and it is indirectly reproduced, not in Irina, but in Andrey. He again appears with his pram, and Ferapont approaches him with the batch of papers. Since we saw Andrey last, his mind has been working over the problem of his marriage, and his thoughts have come to a head. His voice is raised, and Chekhov insisted that in Andrey's speech 'He must be just about ready to threaten the audience with his fists!'[3]

Why on the very threshold of life do we become dull, grey, uninteresting, lazy, indifferent, useless, unhappy? . . .

He is talking of himself, and his manner is restless like his lines, those of a caged animal. People 'only eat, drink, sleep, and then die'. It is the same from generation to generation: 'An overwhelmingly vulgar[4] influence weighs upon the children' – he uses the same word with which he described Natasha – and 'they become the same sort of pitiful, dead creatures, all exactly alike, as their fathers and mothers . . .' By this tirade Andrey seems to show that he knows that his wife is unfaithful and that as her husband he has been deceiving himself. One of the children to be

---

[1] Mary McCarthy's view upon seeing the New York production in 1943. See *Mary McCarthy's Theatre Chronicles* (New York, 1963), p. 59.

[2] Stanislavsky visualized the parting thus: 'The music comes closer [these are the wandering musicians who enter a moment later: J.L.S.] . . . Tusenbach caresses Irina, smoothes her hair, wraps her shawl more snugly around her, kisses every finger on her hand. Irina concentrates completely on Tusenbach. She never takes her eyes off him . . . He pats her on the head. She clings closely to him . . . Tusenbach says: "I feel so happy" [this line now associated with his love of Irina, not of life: J.L.S.]. He is much more spirited, livelier . . . Then, "Now I must go, it's time". He quickly kisses her hand, goes to the garden gate, and takes hold of the latch to open it. Irina rushes after him with an anxious look, grabs his arm and holds him back. Tusenbach forces himself to smile. Irina embraces him and lays her head on his shoulder. Tusenbach looks wistfully in the direction of the garden' (Stroyeva, pp. 53–4).

[3] Reported by V. V. Luzhsky in *Chekhov i teatr*, p. 353, and quoted in Hingley, vol. III, p. 316. See also Magarshack, p. 247.

[4] *Poshloy.* See p. 220, above.

crushed by vulgarity is in the pram he pushes, and he will never rid himself of his philosophy of despair.

In his anger he swings round on the deaf old man, but Ferapont's blank, uncomprehending expression calms his master down. There follows another characteristically Chekhovian sequence. Ferapont's obtuse response to Andrey's tortured heart-searching is to remark that rumour has it that there were two hundred degrees of frost in St Petersburg last winter. We cannot miss Chekhov's comic disruption of Andrey's heated mood, and with it his temper softens further. Andrey is still young, and to think about the future at all is hopeful. He half smiles at a fleeting vision of himself as a father with his children, working and living a life 'free from sloth, from kvass, from goose and cabbage, from sleeping after dinner, from mean, parasitic living . . .' This is the other side of the coin, in contrast with the picture of a family of dead creatures. But Chekhov is still pursuing his disruptive tactics, and has his Ferapont continue to ponder the disasters of last winter: 'Two thousand people were frozen to death. The people were terrified. It was either in Petersburg or Moscow, I don't remember.' *That* was something to worry about! – again the old man is used to deflate the nonsense of unreal visions.

Andrey's feelings change direction yet again.

ANDREY (*in a rush of tender feeling*). My dear sisters, my wonderful sisters! (*Through tears*) Masha, my sister!
NATASHA (*in the window*). Who is talking so loud out there? Is that you, Andryusha? You will wake baby Sophie.

Andrey has not spoken like this of his sisters before. We see in the two faces the tell-tale juxtaposition: on the one hand, the brother aware of the values of human affection, and in particular the worth of the long-suffering Masha, the mirror-image of himself; on the other, the wife with her brusque insensitive authority. Between them is the child for whom they are responsible and by whom they are bound. Ferapont is told to take the baby away, and Andrey is relieved of his pram. As a sober husband goes into the house reading the papers from the office, we hear the wife raising her voice within, demonstratively being the epitome of loving mothers in front of Bobik's 'auntie Olya' and the unseen guest Protopopov. For Andrey, the trap is closed.[1]

[1] At this point, Stanislavsky had a deep bass laugh, that of Protopopov, resound

At the critical moment, the melancholy sounds of the violin and the harp, now near at hand, swell up. A man and a girl, street musicians, come into the garden playing. The music brings Vershinin out of the house with Olga and Anfisa; Natasha does not appear. Irina joins them, and the sad little gathering stands in silence listening. For a moment there is a hiatus in which the nostalgic notes speak for them.

This use of a sound effect is a Chekhovian opportunity to introduce a dramatic effect of distancing for the whole theme, showing the concerns of the characters in a totally new light. The poverty of the street musicians which would drive them to this degrading form of livelihood appears in their hungry faces and tattered clothes; these are set against the comparative prosperity and the handsome dress we have seen exclusively till now. The contrast comes as a shock. The misfortune of the musicians is also part of the external world. How fundamental, we wonder, is the distress of the sisters? The intrusion is fleeting, like that of the beggar in Act II of *The Cherry Orchard*, but a tiny stroke sets in motion a whole train of thoughts. The old peasant Anfisa has known deprivation herself, and it is she who says, 'Poor things. People don't play if they have plenty to eat.'

Natasha has succeeded in evicting Anfisa after all. She has moved her things to the school with Olga, who has found the old woman a room rent-free'in her official flat. She mentions it with delight: 'I have a room to myself and a bedstead.' Her demands upon life in her last years are small, and she declares with complete sincerity that 'There is no one in the world happier than I!' If the sisters take no note of the implicit comparison with themselves, the audience does. Anfisa, like the street musicians, puts the sophisticated desires of the family into a glaring perspective.

from the house, and linked Natasha's world with the crisis on stage by having Bobik's ball bounce from the verandah into the garden, so that Anfisa had to retrieve it. At one time he even considered bringing Protopopov himself on stage in person: 'Make a try at having Protopopov himself pick [the ball] up; in this way he would appear before the public for a moment. It might turn out magnificently or dreadfully. It should be tried at one of the dress rehearsals.' He adds his impression of Protopopov: 'Just imagine: suddenly a fat man with a cigar between his teeth would unexpectedly leap from the balcony; he would run after the ball, bending over several times since he could not catch it at once. Then he disappears forever with the ball' (M. N. Stroyeva in Jackson, p. 130).

Act IV

The Colonel's thoughts are certainly elsewhere, dwelling both on his Masha and on his regiment. He glances at his watch – the gesture keeps the clock ticking – and asks where Masha is. He has been delayed by the Mayor's farewell luncheon, and now there are only a few minutes to say goodbye. He waits with growing impatience, while Irina and Anfisa go off calling for her, and Olga in embarrassment tries to substitute for her sister. Since Masha's confession on the night of the fire, a kind of acquiescence, a fatalism, has settled upon Olga.

OLGA. Nothing turns out as we would have it. I did not want to be a headmistress, and yet I am. It seems we are not to live in Moscow . . .
VERSHININ. Well . . . Thank you for everything . . . Forgive me if anything was amiss . . .

They are talking the same language. Olga's personal ambitions were not those of a provincial success, but those which would return her to the elegance of her life as a girl in Moscow. Her claims on the future were as unreal as Vershinin's when he talked of unborn generations, or as Masha's, in love with a married man. In the Colonel's stock phrase of farewell, 'Forgive me if anything was amiss', is a deeper resonance and an implicit acknowledgment of the self-deception of the past few years. However, after the maidenly shock she felt at first, Olga is now beyond reproving her sister for clutching at passing happiness.

Masha's secret love is all they have in common as Olga and Vershinin wait uncertainly in the garden for her to come. Vershinin tries to break the ice. He asks forgiveness for talking too much, but proceeds to make a speech in his customary way. His speeches delighted them all in the beginning, but now they sound more and more hollow. His tired voice offers only platitudes to the miserable Olga for consolation. 'Life is hard . . . yet we must admit that it goes on getting clearer and easier . . .[1] If, don't you know, industry were united with culture and culture with industry . . .' Olga has heard it all before, as we have. And even Vershinin's heart is not in what he says, for he keeps glancing at his watch. His voice reproduces 'the flatness of a gramophone record'.[2] There is no longer that old sonority in his tones.

[1] Hingley translates these platitudes pleasingly as 'Life isn't a bed of roses . . . Still . . . it does look as if we'll see a real break in the clouds before very long' (vol. III, p. 135).
[2] Desmond MacCarthy, *Drama* (London, 1940), p. 121.

Masha comes in breathlessly, and Olga is well relieved. She *'moves a little away to leave them free to say good-bye'*. The elder sister knows to withdraw, but her distressed presence provides that second audience on stage which keeps our eyes the drier. Masha faces her middle-aged lover for the last time, and in a slow, stumbling exchange his speech flows smoothly no longer.

VERSHININ. I have come to say good-bye . . .
MASHA (*looking into his face*). Good-bye . . . (*a prolonged kiss*).
OLGA. Come, come . . .

This is the crisis for Masha. Olga's plea is to be brave, and under the stress of time, words and kisses seem perfunctory and cruel. The parting is not prolonged. Vershinin gives the sobbing girl to her sister and in a moment he has gone.

Kuligin's prompt entrance suggests that he has been waiting for Vershinin's exit. He stands on the opposite side of the stage watching his wife crying in Olga's arms, for us as isolated a figure as Masha as he witnesses helplessly the distress of the two women in each other's arms. He is happy, but his is a sadly inverted happiness: his wife's tears are for another man. His attempt at consoling her is devastating. He will not blame her; rather, 'We'll begin the old life again.' But in his access of generosity, he has said the wrong thing. Kuligin would like, no doubt, to revert to the old teacher-student relationship of their early marriage, but after Masha's romantic escapade the prospect hurts her more than the loss of her lover. Chekhov has her articulate her agony of mind by having her speak the familiar phrases from Pushkin. They are now no more than a jumble of words and moans, but they are the fullest means within the convention of expressing her edge of hysteria: 'I am going mad.' Olga, the practical one when a maternal call is made upon her, tells Kuligin to fetch Masha some water, and he runs to the table upstage for it. Slowly the sobs die away.

One blow follows another. As Masha strains to keep her self-control by forcing herself to recall Pushkin, we hear *'the dim sound of a far-away shot'*. Those around Masha seem not to hear it, but the audience, prepared as it is, is simultaneously reminded of the problem of the youngest sister and the treacherous incident of Solyony's duel. Irina's entrance a moment later visually confirms the association properly to be made with the sound, although she, too, does not recognize it. The emotionality of Masha's broken 'By the sea-strand an oak-tree green . . .' thus embraces all three of them.

The sisters are together again for the first time since the fire of Act III, and more in harmony than at any time in the play. They sit closely together for a brief moment in silence under the autumn trees, Olga and Irina on either side of Masha, comforting her. The stage is at rest. The sisters come together in mutual compassion, the stage acquires a visual symbolism and the action grows to its final crisis.

Nevertheless, Chekhov is not the artist to allow the sentimentality of the scene to wash thoughtlessly through the theatre. Kuligin is still on stage, writhing in embarrassment and with a sense of guilt he cannot understand. In the pause, he searches for a way to ease the tension and cheer them up.

I took a false beard and moustache from a boy in the third form yesterday, just look . . . (*puts on the beard and moustache*). I look like the German teacher . . . (*laughs*). Don't I? Funny creatures, those boys.

He struts like a clown upon the stage, laughing to encourage his little audience to a response. The three women try to laugh, and even Masha admits that he looks like the German teacher, but Olga has to laugh for her as she dissolves in tears again at the effort. Some of those tears are shed, no doubt, at the prospect of having to live the rest of her life with a fool. Kuligin is somewhat disconcerted that his performance has produced more tears, and can only encourage his own flagging confidence: 'Awfully like . . .' If he has not cheered them up, neither has he eased the tension we still feel. No comic relief, this: the pain is there worse than before.

For the enemy herself is close at hand. Chekhov has left Natasha's entrance in this act until almost the end, so that the final sequence of the play shall overwhelmingly clinch the victory of the forces of Philistinism.

Unusually for Chekhov, Natasha's last appearance in the play is almost written for solo performance, once precise in tone and tempo, finally clarifying her relationship with each of the other characters, richly summing up her place in the pattern of the

play's meaning. Especially, it is conceived by its author as movement and style in what might be called 'the Natasha mode'. The
visual image is of her rapid circling of the stage, glancing at this
person, remarking on that object, constantly restless, her manner
completely at variance with the still centre of the three sisters,
who seem to huddle closer together in self-defence. Chekhov has
held such an entrance back until this crucial moment.

Natasha flashes in with a remark over her shoulder to the maid
in the house. She is, in this last glimpse of her, such a busy, self-
important creature: 'Now what was it? Oh yes . . .'[1] Her life has
become one long business of giving orders to others, arranging
their lives for them, running her empire. Her remark to the maid
is in effect designed to deploy her menfolk. Protopopov will
watch Sophie; Andrey will push Bobik. 'What a lot there is to do
with children . . .' Her eyes address the sky from the verandah,
but she is never seen to work herself.

She has paused momentarily at the foot of the steps into the
garden, her eye taking in Irina as she sits tensely on the bench.
Irina is leaving tomorrow, and a word in parting is called for: so,
Will she not stay on? But Natasha hastens to add, 'Just another
week.' The departure of Olga and Irina suits her book perfectly;
she has conceivably been working towards this from the beginning. As she sweeps on without waiting for an answer, she
comes abruptly face to face with Kuligin still wearing the comic
beard and moustache, and '*utters a shriek*' in her own inimitable
voice of refined alarm. Yet in a moment she has returned to Irina
and to the subject that is on her mind. She hovers momentarily
as she visibly calculates the new situation in the house, and her
transition from the past to the future as Chekhov writes it is
wonderful indeed: she regrets Irina's parting, but in the same
breath announces that Andrey shall have her room, where he
can 'saw away' on his violin to his heart's content, and baby
Sophie can therefore have his. Natasha's tentacles are to creep
through the whole house, and another man's child is finally to
usurp Andrey's own domain.

Oblivious to the pain her lack of tact is causing, she rehearses
again her performance as the loving and considerate mother as
she comes upon Ferapont with Sophie's pram. 'Adorable,

[1] Hingley's rendering (vol. III, p. 137) of her first word, '*Shto?*' ('What?', 'Well?').

delightful baby! Isn't she a child! Today she looked at me with such eyes and said "Mamma"!' No character in the play has concurred with Natasha's evaluation of her own children, and her tasteless charade with the babies is aggressive, as if challenging anyone to contest her authority. Thus she exerts her maternal superiority over all these childless women. As she pauses and looks round for a response, it is Kuligin who supplies it, partly out of his customary good-nature, and partly to appease the trouble-maker: 'A fine child, that's true.'

Chekhov naughtily arranges that Natasha shall also echo earlier sentiments on emptiness and loneliness variously expressed by Vershinin, Tusenbach, Tchebutykin, Andrey, Olga, Masha and Irina, especially by those who are to be left behind by the departing regiment. With a great sigh, Natasha now says, 'So tomorrow I shall be all alone here.' But the words are empty, the tone is a sing-song of superficiality and the too-vocal sigh is cut short by her racing mind. She has already swept on and is looking upstage to the path through the trees. The first thing she will do, she says, is to have the avenue of firs cut down. This would complete the dispossession by the loss of the natural beauty of the garden itself, an idea which Chekhov pursued in his last play, where the cutting down of the cherry orchard is enlarged to become a blow aimed at life itself. When Tusenbach looked at these trees as if he were seeing them for the last time, he was showing the spectator how to regard them in preparation for this moment. And when Natasha indicates that the next to be felled is the dead maple which the Baron felt in its windswept beauty to share life with the living, likening it to the way people in the future might see him after death, her stark words are terrifying, like an order to kill and desecrate the body. 'It looks so ugly in the evening.' By such a method of recurring imagery as this, the play has passed into the mode of poetic drama.

Natasha has circled the stage and returned at last to Irina, who sits in apprehension of her unexplained fears. 'My dear, that sash does not suit you at all . . . It's in bad taste. You want something light.' A neat riposte after four years! – and for the audience after more than two hours. She has all this time harboured the memory of the cut she received at Irina's party, and is finally in a position to insult Irina as Olga had insulted her. Irina's present distress makes her words especially vindictive. She has almost completed her general inspection of the property, and the people on it, but as she climbs the steps of the verandah, she sees a garden fork lying on a seat. The provincial wife is indignant. The last we hear of the shy Natasha is her voice raised against the maid as she marches into the house, the shrill tones dying away as she moves through the inner rooms.

The tyrant leaves a miserable silence behind her. Only Kuligin makes a comment: 'She is at it!' That is all that needs to be said. As Andrey warned, her pettiness, selfishness and opportunism will infect the next generation of Sophies and Bobiks. She epitomizes the creeping evil against which dignified ineffectuality and dreamy fatalism have no chance.

The 'facts' of the play are now nearly all given. Chekhov prepares his last disturbing impressions with music. In the quiet after Natasha's voice has ceased, the faintly strident sounds of the regimental band are heard afar off, brassily playing a march in quick time to move the files of men smartly away to the railway station. The jaunty sound continues to the curtain, slowly fading. Like Brecht's use of a victory march in counterpoint with the suffering of the ordinary people in *Mother Courage*, the music ironically accompanies the pathos of Chekhov's ending. Its confident rhythms suggest the movement of men and horses, and this in turn emphasizes the paralysis of the characters on the stage, inducing in the audience that bitter taste of dark comedy.

Slowly Masha and Olga come alive and prepare to go. Masha in resignation looks for her hat and coat to take up life again with Kuligin; Olga must face her duties as a headmistress. But Chekhov arrests the stage for a last time. Tchebutykin has come in: we have been waiting for him for what seems an interminable time. He whispers to Olga that the event has happened which we have been anticipating: Solyony has killed Tusenbach in the duel. The old Doctor's bleak apathy was never shown with such force as in his reaction to Olga's shock. 'Such a business . . . I am so worried and worn out, I don't want to say another word . . . (*With vexation*). But there, it doesn't matter!' The infectious fatalism learned from Andrey and Olga is already present in the young Irina, and is felt again when she does nothing other than cry quietly, murmuring to herself, 'I knew, I knew . . .' Chekhov wrote to I. A. Tikhomirov that in spite of what Irina says in this line, she knew nothing, for 'When a woman guesses, she says, "I knew it, I knew it".'[1] Does Irina feel that Tusenbach has allowed himself to die because she refused him her love?

This is the last blow, aimed at the youngest and most defenceless of the sisters, the one who has hoped for most. The crisis is complete. As Tchebutykin settles down again to his everlasting newspaper, he mutters, 'I am worn out . . . Let them cry . . .' and we hear again his snatch of the devil-may-care army song, 'Tarara-boom-dee-ay'. Olga and Masha cannot leave Irina alone in her newest affliction, and in trying to comfort her they come together almost formally. They cling to each other and their eyes stare as they listen to the lively notes of the military band. We absorb the music, too, through their distress.

In this curiously choric manner, an extension of the ending of *Uncle Vanya*,[2] Chekhov appears to break the naturalistic convention in order to underscore and energize the catastrophe by a formal tableau. The sisters have come together visually, just as their thinking coalesces; sharing each other's pain equally, they speak as one woman. As if the everyday action of the play has stopped, each sister speaks in turn, echoing one another's thoughts.

The words are simple in the extreme, and general without being abstract. Masha begins, and the note sounded is the familiar one of resignation.

Oh, listen to that band! They are going away from us; one has gone altogether, gone forever. We are left alone to begin our life over again . . . We've got to live . . . we've got to live . . .

The original manuscript included the direction to Masha to look up and see a flock of passing birds, as she did before. She spoke

[1] Letter of 14 January 1901, in Hellman, p. 281. John Fernald comments on Chekhov's stage direction for Irina ('*weeping quietly*') that 'no actress and no director can leave it at that . . . The power that Irina has generated and stored throughout the play must burst the flood gates: it breaks out in a cry of animal pain. If the power is as great as it can be, a mere discharge of sound is not enough to carry it: the force of emotion spills out into movement, and Irina sweeps *upstage* for twenty feet before coming to rest.' Fernald reports that the actress Stepanova played Irina like this in Nemirovich-Danchenko's production (*Sense of Direction: The Director and his Actors*, London, 1968, p. 100). This is uncomfortably 'stagey' for the mature Chekhov, and in any case turns on the nature of Irina's shock. For how much did she love Tusenbach?

[2] As Chekhov admits in his letter of 15 January 1901, to Stanislavsky (Hellman, p. 282). He thought the repetition 'a minor evil' in the play.

of the mystery of their instinctive flight and natural freedom.[1] The recurrent image of birds elsewhere in the play was probably in Chekhov's mind as he wrote the first version, but by omitting the lines, he made the dramatic decision to avoid poeticizing Masha's attitude unduly. There is a greater strength in the bald simplicity of her statement in the final version. The poignancy of 'We've got to live' does not need reinforcement if the ambivalence of the whole play is behind it. The spectator must be left free to criticize Masha's acceptance of God's mysterious, but exasperating, purpose. For are we to be uncritical of Masha? Does she make any attempt to understand Kuligin?

Irina, her head on Olga's breast, echoes Masha's pace and tone at a higher pitch. But she extends Masha's acceptance of life with more particularity and direction. 'A time will come when everyone will know what all this is for, why there is this misery; there will be no mysteries and, meanwhile, we have got to live . . . we have got to work, only to work!' In view of the news Irina has just received, her fortitude has the more power. The mystery of her strength to carry on is balanced against the trend of the scene, with its sense of defeat. Her words ring out ironically to complete the contradiction. For are we to be uncritical of Irina also? Lost in her dreams, she was prepared to offer her lover a stunted marriage like Masha's.

In her role as mother, Olga, standing between her sisters, speaks half to comfort them, half to comfort herself. 'The music is so gay, so confident, and one longs for life!' But her voice quavers. 'O my God! Time will pass, and we shall go away for ever, and we shall be forgotten, our faces will be forgotten, our voices, and how many there were of us.' They will be forgotten, just as the memory of their father has grown dim. This is desperate thinking. Olga searches for consolation, and decides, like Sonya in *Uncle Vanya*, that if there is purpose in existence, it must be hidden in the future. 'But our sufferings will pass into joy for those who live after us, happiness and peace will be established upon earth, and they will remember kindly and bless those who

[1] The omitted speech read, 'There are migrating birds up there, they fly past every spring and autumn, they've been doing it for thousands of years and they don't know why. But they fly on and they'll go on flying for ages and ages, for many thousand years, until in the end God reveals his mysteries to them' (translated by Ronald Hingley, vol. III, p. 311).

Three Sisters Act I

Three Sisters Act III

Three Sisters Act IV

have lived before.' The inconsistency in these oscillating sentiments is intentional. There is to be no invitation to the audience
to elect the way of either an easy optimism or an easy pessimism.
In a play which presents the fortunes of life in as realistic a way as
possible, we are given insight into the normal human quandary.
As the brass band '*grows more and more subdued*', the focus is on that
normality, and the very ambivalence of the situation constitutes
the energizing power of the scene. It is not Chekhov's purpose
to resolve the enigma of realities and aspirations.

If the ambiguity of the ending does not admit the nostalgia and
melancholy of so many Western productions of *Three Sisters*,
neither does it admit the treatment of the play as a manifesto, a
vision of a new order, with Vershinin as its prophet. N. A.
Gorchakov described the typical Soviet handling of this sequence,
from the M.A.T. production of 1940 directed by Nemirovich-
Danchenko:

The sisters take each other by the hand. Their faces are stern and
solemn. They speak little about what is in their hearts. Their eyes talk.
Their eyes sparkle, not with tears, but with a stubborn belief in the
future. And the three sisters begin to show that they are great and
strong . . . A magnificent type of Russian womanhood, with its suffering, self-renunciation, and moral strength.[1]

Michel Saint-Denis reported that, in keeping with this kind of
solemnity, this production was speeding up in tempo and simpli-
fied, shortening pauses and cutting Stanislavsky's noises.[2] This
sense of the play's purposefulness is also argued by E. J. Simmons,
Chekhov's American biographer:

As in the conclusion of *Uncle Vanya* . . . Chekhov distils from frustration and failure a renewed faith in life and its purpose. Though this
ending may be interpreted as another illusion of happiness, given the
natures and values of the three gallant sisters, one suspects that this
was not Chekhov's intention. As the band plays and the troops march
off, Masha declares that she and her sisters must start their life anew;
they must live. Irina agrees and adds that she will dedicate herself to
work in service to those who need her. Olga embraces them both in
affirmation.[3]

[1] Quoted in F. L. Lucas, *The Drama of Chekhov, Synge, Yeats, and Pirandello* (London, 1963), pp. 94–5.
[2] In *Theatre: The Rediscovery of Style* (New York, 1960), p. 53.
[3] Simmons, p. 523. This view is also represented by Stroyeva, pp. 55–6.

Saint-Denis also approves the optimistic emphasis as one realistic of our times:

The words of Vershinin in *The Three Sisters*, those of Trofimov and Lopahin in *The Cherry Orchard*, announcing happiness in the future, may still be exaggerated or even ironical, but they have now a much more positive value than twenty or thirty years ago. To me it is a matter of fact and not of interpretation; the characters who represent the 'new world' have grown in stature; they are neither prophets nor heroes, as the Russians represent them in their new productions, but they have, naturally, a much greater impact on a contemporary audience than before.[1]

This emphasis in performance follows the activist view of Chekhov's drama, that it affirms life and foretells the Revolution. The playgoer must judge for himself whether the sisters here represent a 'moral victory' over the bourgeois Philistinism of Natasha and her kind, a final liberation of the spirit from provincial slavery, or whether they appear powerless in the face of it. Chekhov does not deny the sisters their hope, certainly, but he resolutely refuses to allow a dream to come true. In any case, if it is hope for a better society, what could conceivably remedy the ills Chekhov is concerned with in this play?

However, the evidence for Chekhov's intentions is not yet complete. In the beginning, Chekhov had asked that the body of Tusenbach should be seen carried across the back of the stage.[2] From a practical point of view, Stanislavsky doubtless felt that this would damage the ritualistic quality of the stage composition at the end, especially since the sisters would have to react to it: 'The sisters have got to see the corpse. What are they to do?' In his letter of reply, Chekhov acknowledged that Stanislavsky was right: 'a thousand times right, it wouldn't do at all to show Tusenbach's body. I myself felt it when I wrote the play and spoke to you of it, if you will recall.'[3] And Stanislavsky found a number of other reasons to omit the Tusenbach incident. 'It would be necessary to insert a crowd scene, the noise of the

---

[1] Introduction to John Gielgud's version of *The Cherry Orchard* (London, 1963), p. x. Saint-Denis first remarked the less melancholy trend in English-speaking productions in *Theatre: The Rediscovery of Style* (New York, 1960), p. 53.

[2] The first version of the play had the stage direction, '*There is a noise at the back of the stage. A crowd can be seen watching as the body of the baron, who has been killed in the duel, is carried past*' (Hingley, vol. III, p. 311).

[3] 15 January 1901 (Hellman, p. 282).

people carrying Tusenbach's body; otherwise it would be a ballet.' Carrying the body would rock the scenery. The noise of feet 'would cause an irritating, dampening pause'. And he concludes, 'We shall miss our main quarry, which is to present the author's final and optimistic summing up, which compensates for the many sad parts of the play.' It would be a bore, a nuisance and 'terribly depressing'.[1] In any case an audience would have found it a sensational and sentimental distraction to see the dead body of the most likeable character in the play. In addition, the choric speech of the sisters has, at this stage, taken us beyond mere particularities to a more universal position. The fact remains that it was originally Chekhov's idea to complete the picture of disaster, but that for practical reasons the excision of the incident tipped the balance towards a less unequivocally tragic curtain. The last emphasis must not be on the death of the Baron, on fate playing one more unkind trick: rather, the events of the last act – the loss of Vershinin and Tusenbach, two embodiments of the sisters' hopes – are to seem part of the normal course. The question-begging choric speech is to convey and stress their own lack of self-knowledge.

Nor is the evidence of ambivalence finished. The sisters in their tableau remain still, but other people, with a careful disjunction of convention, continue to go about their business. As they enter, Kuligin and Andrey trace contrasting movement patterns, one quick, one slow: a contrast one with another, and both with the sisters. Kuligin happily brings Masha's hat and coat, the hat the same that she nursed in Act I but did not put on, almost symbolic of the old life to which she is returning. Andrey pushes his pram along the stage yet again, and the pram remains in the mind as his eternal cross. Tchebutykin reads his newspaper and carelessly sings his monotonous 'Tarara-boom-dee-ay!'[2] Chekhov intends the stage to be alive again as we hear Olga's last whisper – which is not a challenge to God, not a cynical rasp in the throat, but a humble *doubt*: 'If we only knew, if we only knew!' In the final chorus, the sisters complete their cycle and return to their

---

1 Stroyeva, p. 55.

2 Garnett does not translate the rest of the couplet, '*Sizhu na tumbe ya*', which is, literally, 'I'm sitting on a roadside stump' (i.e., drunk), and is variously rendered, 'I'm sitting on a tomb today', 'I'm sitting on a stump today', 'This is our washing day', 'Sit on a curb I may', 'I'm getting tight today', 'Let's have a tune today'.

sterile beginning, caught between the forces of indifference and the struggle in their minds to understand, between Tchebutykin's 'Nothing matters!' and Olga's 'If we only knew!' As the curtain falls, the stage is busy again with the triviality of everyday – in Chekhov's words, 'that grey dawdle'.

Are the attitudes of the sisters symbolic of a 'new order', a 'new society'? We have simply to ask whether Chekhov was so naive as to think that in any conceivable new society people would not, then as now, be insensitive or over-sensitive, turn cynical or destructive, fail to realize themselves or to exercise their gifts, suffer unrequited love or make bad marriages.

The spectator's final impression is therefore complex. The play is about the doubts of particular people; but in a larger way, it is also about the uncertain pressure of past and future time on the life of the present. In 1960 I wrote: 'This is a play about time, time that the sisters cannot restrain; their life is a dream that deludes them into inertia; they represent people searching for answers they will never hear because they are asking the wrong questions. Chekhov is too gentle to have them appear stupid, but at the end of the play time is still slipping through their fingers; even if Moscow has faded, they still hug their dream; do they not still ask the same questions as at the beginning? To define our final sensations by the final words of the sisters, simply because they speak, is to treat fictions as truths, characters as mouthpieces, and to disregard the contribution of the whole series of impressions. Is this a play of hope? Rather, of resignation and endurance.'[1] I see no reason to change this judgment. I would only add that Chekhov's advance in dramaturgy in *Three Sisters* enables his audience to re-experience, exquisitely, the double values that too many people adopt when confronted by time's categorical demands.

[1] *The Elements of Drama* (Cambridge, 1960), p. 207. Written to challenge the simplistic view (e.g. in Magarshack, ch. xxiii) that the play is a 'gay affirmation of life' and 'ends on a note of triumph'.

The Cherry Orchard

A Comedy in Four Acts

1904

The Cherry Orchard

ΩΩΩΩΩΩΩΩΩΩΩΩΩΩΩΩΩΩΩΩΩΩΩΩΩΩΩΩΩΩΩΩΩΩΩΩΩΩΩ

The Cherry Orchard, the supreme achievement of the naturalistic movement in the modern theatre, was Chekhov's last play. It was written and revised when its author was a dying man, his tuberculous condition forcing him to live in the milder air of Yalta on the Black Sea, six or seven hundred miles from rehearsals at the Moscow Art Theatre. Luckily, he had married Olga Knipper, one of the M.A.T.'s leading actresses, on 25 May 1901, and he and his wife corresponded freely about the details of the play, so that our first-hand knowledge of its author's intentions is very full.[1]

Chekhov told Nemirovich-Danchenko that he had spent three years preparing the play,[2] and it seems that he was already planning it during rehearsals for *Three Sisters* in 1901. Two years later he had only just begun to write, and the first draft was not finished until October 1903. This teasing and weighing of his material is characteristic of Chekhov at the end: he used this long period of gestation as Ibsen might have done, until, as he said, the play was completed in his head.[3] It is clear, for example, that at the beginning he intended to make his play more of a light comedy, and he described it as a 'vaudeville', a term synonymous with 'farce', although he may have been speaking idiosyncratically in order to emphasize his comic intentions to those who thought of him as a writer of tragedy.[4] At all events, the detail

---

[1] Chekhov saw some rehearsals in December 1903, and was present on the opening night.

[2] Letter of 2 November 1903 (Hellman, p. 317).

[3] Letter to Stanislavsky of 5 February 1903 (Hingley, vol. III, p. 318). Nemirovich-Danchenko asserted, 'Not a single play, not a single story, did he write so slowly as *The Cherry Orchard*' (Nemirovich-Danchenko, p. 214).

[4] See Nemirovich-Danchenko, pp. 214–15: 'If I write anything that resembles a play it will be a vaudeville piece.' Cf. his letter to Lilina (Stanislavsky's wife): 'Not a drama but a comedy emerged from me, in places even a farce' (Simmons, p. 604). The point is reiterated in a letter to Olga Knipper: 'The last act will be merry, and indeed the whole play will be merry and frivolous' (21 September 1903, in Garnett, p. 306).

of the working compelled him to modify his first ideas, and he finally called the play 'A Comedy in Four Acts'.

As with *Three Sisters*, Chekhov was again able to plan his play with the actors in mind, but this time the facility was more of a headache. Olga Knipper, then aged thirty-four, was first imagined in the part of Varya, then of Mme Ranevsky and then of Charlotta, since he wanted an actress with a sense of humour for the part; she finally played Mme Ranevsky.[1] The part of Charlotta, first conceived for Lilina or Olga Knipper, was finally played by Muratova. Lilina herself was thought of for Varya, who as a character accordingly became a more attractive young woman, then as Charlotta, but she finally played the young girl Anya. Stanislavsky was at first to play Lopahin, but he cast himself as Gaev, and Lopahin was in fact played by Leonidov. This juggling suggests that, far from gaining any easy verisimilitude for his characters by a close acquaintance with the players, in his last years Chekhov had grown as fussy about his characters as a mother about her babies.

The play was first performed in Moscow by the M.A.T. on 17 January 1904, on its author's forty-fourth birthday. It was published in June of that year, a few days before he died (1 July 1904).

In spite of the play's slow gestation, Chekhov's advances in craftsmanship in *The Cherry Orchard* suggest a complete confidence in what he was doing at the last. One might point to the progress of the setting of the play from act to act, moving from the house out to the estate itself (almost, indeed, to the town beyond) and back to the house again; and, within the house, from the most intimately evocative room, the nursery, to more public rooms, and back again to the nursery. Parallel with these visual changes, Chekhov makes a more thematic use of the weather and the seasons, passing from the chill of spring with its promise of warmth to the chill of autumn with its threat of winter. In this, the lyricism of *The Seagull* returns to Chekhov's dramatic writing. The growth of the year from May to October is precisely indicated, and the cycle of the cherry trees, from their blossoming to their fruiting and their destruction, matches the cycle of joy and grief, hope and despair, within the family. As in *Three Sisters*,

[1] She was still playing this role for the three hundredth anniversary performance of the play in 1943, when she was seventy-three.

time and change, and their effects wrought on a representative group of people, are the subject of the play. But in feeling for this, Chekhov knows that the realism of the chosen convention can dangerously narrow his meaning until it seems too particular and finally irrelevant. He thus works hard to ensure that his play projects a universal image, giving his audience some sense that this microcosm of the cherry orchard family stands, by breadth of allusion and a seemingly inexhaustible patterning of characters, for a wider orchard beyond.

The cherry orchard is a particular place and yet it is more. It represents an inextricable tangle of sentiments, which together comprise a way of life and an attitude to life. By the persistent feelings shown towards it, at one extreme by old Firs, the house-serf for whom the family is his whole existence, and at another by Trofimov, the intellectual for whom it is the image of repression and slavery; by Lopahin, the businessman and spokesman for hard economic facts, the one who thinks of it primarily as a means to wiser investment, and by Mme Ranevsky, who sees in it her childhood happiness and her former innocence, who sees it as the embodiment of her best values – by these and many other contradictions, an audience finds that the orchard grows from a painted backcloth to an ambiguous, living, poetic symbol of human life, *any* human life, in a state of change.

Inseparable from these patterns are those into which the cherry orchard characters are woven by their brilliant selection. Chekhov claimed that his cast for the play was small, but in performance they seem curiously to proliferate. Offstage characters increase the complexity, like the lover in Paris, the Countess in Yaroslavl, Pishtchik's daughter Dashenka, Lyubov's drowned son Grisha. But the true reason for this sense of proliferation is because the same dozen players, each supplied with a character of three-dimensional individuality in Chekhov's impressive way, are encouraged to group and re-group themselves in our minds. He had always been meticulous in delineating the social background to his situation. Now he plans the play's context as a living environment. What is 'a cross-section of society'? It may be a division by birth and class, by wealth, by age, by sex, by aspirations and moral values. Chekhov divides the people of the cherry orchard in a variety of ways, so that the orchard and its sale take on a different meaning for each group.

By birth and class, we see the members of the land-owning upper middle class, Mme Ranevsky, Gaev, Anya and, accordingly, the foster-daughter Varya, slipping from their security: we are made to feel what it is like to be uprooted. Lopahin, Epihodov, Yasha and Dunyasha, the servants and former peasants, are straining, comically it may be, to achieve a new social status. For some, Charlotta, Trofimov and Pishtchik for much of the play, their future security is in doubt. Forty years after the Emancipation,[1] each character is still making a personal adjustment to the social upheaval according to age, sex or rank, and according to his lights. As a group, the cherry orchard people demonstrate the transition between the old and the new, bringing life to Chekhov's idea of an evolving social structure. The passing of time is thus represented *socially*. The three classes on the stage, owners, dependents and the new independents like Lopahin, are a social microcosm at a given point in time, so that any shift in the pattern of dependence forces an audience to acknowledge the reality of social time.

From economic considerations, the one-time wealthy land-owners, Mme Ranevsky, Gaev and Pishtchik, are in great distress. The responsible ones, Lopahin, Charlotta and Varya, are intimately concerned: to those who must battle the real world, money matters. However, the new generation, Trofimov and Anya, are largely indifferent, and the servants are unaffected. But money is the least of it.

By age, those of middle years who live in and for the past, like Mme Ranevsky and Gaev, the sale of the orchard is a blow striking at their very souls. For Anya, Trofimov, Dunyasha and Yasha, the young who, naturally, live for the future, the event is an opportunity for enterprise of one kind or another, self-interested or altruistic as the case may be. For those who are neither young nor old, for Varya, Lopahin and Charlotta, those concerned with the pressing problems of the present, the auction is an urgent call for decisions and practical measures. Firs, aged eighty-seven, is beyond time. *The Cherry Orchard* is thus, in part, a 'generations' play, marking the conflict between the old and the young, the substance of a thousand dramatic themes. To watch

[1] The Act of Emancipation of 1861, indirectly one of the better results of the Crimean War, freed some fifteen million serfs, although for many years they continued paying for the land they were allotted.

the interactions of the four age-groups is to watch the cycle of life itself. Time will be alive on the stage, and the characters will seem human milestones.

By sex, the departure from the orchard means an assessment of marital needs and opportunities, and the spinsters, Charlotta, Varya and Dunyasha, are troubled in varying degrees. But Pishtchik, Lopahin and Yasha, because of other pressures, fail to respond. While Anya and Trofimov claim idealistically to be 'above love', at least for the time being, Mme Ranevsky is thrown back on her other resource, her Paris lover; as instinct or impulse brought her back to the orchard, so one or other drives her back to Paris. Only Firs has arrived at that time of life when nothing, neither status, money, past nor future, can affect him any more. With exquisite irony, it is he whose neglect by the family in the last act passes the final comment on them all.

This is not the best place to indicate the echoes and parallels and parodies built into this restless group of people: these are better observed as the action of the play proceeds. Mme Ranevsky finds her counterpart in the feckless optimist Pishtchik, the neighbouring landowner. Epihodov the clerk counters Pishtchik's trust in fate with an equally pessimistic fatalism. While Epihodov declares that he has resigned himself to his position, Yasha, who aspires to higher things than the life of a servant, is treading on necks as he climbs. When Gaev finds Yasha, a servant, playing his own aristocratic game of billiards, the valet's impertinence measures his master's own precarious status. Gaev, sucking his caramels, will, in spite of his disclaimers, never do a day's useful work, and Chekhov sets this weakness against the practical energies of Lopahin. And Lopahin against Trofimov. And Trofimov against Mme Ranevsky. *La ronde* continues ceaselessly.

Patterns of characters, then, make patterns of dramatic emphasis, and this 'plotless' play is one with *too many* plots, however fragmentary, to permit analysis finally to untangle all its threads. In *Three Sisters*, Chekhov traced the passing of the months and years from scene to scene, and we watched the visible transformation of the people of the play. In *The Cherry Orchard*, time past, present and future are at the last all one, the play's last act an integrated moment of revelation. We know the orchard must go, just as surely as the curtain must fall, and in Act IV Chekhov counts out the minutes, as in the first three acts he counted out the days to the sale. As the minutes pass, we scrutinize the whole family. Every exchange, between Lopahin and Trofimov on their futures, between Mme Ranevsky and Pishtchik on the vagaries of fate, between Varya and Lopahin in their abortive proposal scene, refocuses the image of the play. When Varya seems to strike Lopahin with a stick, the notions both of differences in class and of sexual need are by one gesture violently yoked together, simultaneously reintroduced to contradict one another. When Trofimov refuses Lopahin's generous offer of a loan, the student's youth and idealism are in pathetic contrast with Lopahin's maturity and common sense. When Mme Ranevsky gives away her purse to the peasants at her door (her name 'Lyuba' means 'love'), we see in the gesture her failure to be realistic about her financial circumstances as well as her paternalistic affection for all the orchard stood for in the past. One incident comprehends and generates the next, endlessly, and the last act is a masterpiece of compact concentration.

'The entire play is so simple, so wholly real, but to such a point purified of everything superfluous and enveloped in such a lyrical quality, that it seems to me to be a symbolic poem.'[1] So wrote Nemirovich-Danchenko, early recognizing the gratifying contradiction that a play can be naturalistic and poetic at the same time. *The Cherry Orchard* has the poetic strength of simplicity. The interweaving in the play, the relationships between one generation and another, between master and servant, between the love-lorn and the less concerned, with the ebb and flow of such relationships, are the source of *poetic* energy in the play. But the subtle shifts across the social fabric are also the source of the play's *comic* energy, compelling its audience to remain both alert and amused as it watches. In *The Cherry Orchard*, Chekhov consummated his life's work with a *poetic comedy* of exquisite balance.

The Cherry Orchard was conceived as a comedy, but its author had difficulty in persuading Stanislavsky and his company that it was not full of tearful people. 'Where are they? Varya's the only one, and that's because Varya is a cry-baby by nature, and her tears shouldn't distress the audience.'[2] He wanted his Moscow audience to laugh at tears. 'There isn't a cemetery in Act Two,' he expostu-

---

[1] Nemirovich-Danchenko, p. 218.
[2] Letter to Nemirovich-Danchenko of 23 October 1903 (Hingley, vol. III, p. 326).

lated. It is evident from his letters to Olga after the first production that he felt Stanislavsky and Nemirovich-Danchenko had created a *drame*, as indeed they advertised it.

Why is it that on the posters and in the newspaper advertisements my play is so persistently called a drama? Nemirovich and Stanislavsky see in my play something absolutely different from what I have written, and I am ready to bet anything that neither of them has once read my play through attentively. Forgive me, but I assure you it is so.[1]

In spite of Stanislavsky's ecstatic praise of the play, he had misunderstood it. E. P. Karpov reported the same reactions from Chekhov after a provincial performance of the play at Yalta.

Is this really my *Cherry Orchard*? Are these my types? With the exception of two or three roles, none of this is mine. I describe life. It is a dull, philistine life. But it is not a tedious, whimpering life. First they turn me into a weeper and then into a simply boring writer. However, I've written several volumes of merry tales.[2]

In the role of Gaev, Stanislavsky had 'dragged things out most painfully' in Act IV.[3] The whole thing was played flamboyantly. What is the truth behind this difference between conception and realization? Farce, which prohibits compassion for human weakness, and tragedy, which demands it, are close kin. The truth is that *The Cherry Orchard* is a play which treads the tightrope between them, and results in the ultimate form of that special dramatic balance we know as Chekhovian comedy.

An audience, of course, will find there what it will, depending upon how it approaches the theatre experience. If, like recent Soviet audiences, it wants rousing polemics from Trofimov, it can hear them. If, like many Western audiences, it wishes to weep for Mme Ranevsky and her fate, it can be partly accommodated. It is possible to see Lyubov and Gaev as shallow people who deserve to lose their orchard, or as victims of social and economic forces beyond their control. It is possible to find Anya and Trofimov far-sighted enough to want to leave the dying orchard, or ignorant of what they are forsaking. But if production allows either the heroics of prophecy or the melodrama of dispossession, then all of Chekhov's care for balance is set at

---

[1] Letter to Olga Knipper of 10 April 1904 (Garnett, p. 380).
[2] Simmons, p. 624.
[3] Letter to Olga Knipper of 29 March 1904 (Hingley, vol. III, p. 330).

nought and the fabric of his play torn apart. Chekhov himself must have known that he was taking this risk, and it is for us to ask why.

In *The Cherry Orchard*, Chekhov struck his final blow at nineteenth-century theatrics. There is no shot fired, either on or off the stage. In Act II, Charlotta has a rifle and Epihodov a pistol, but these weapons are now handled by comedians purely for the joke, and they are not mentioned again. Even the amorous pairing of characters common to the earlier plays has been turned entirely into comedy: the 'love scenes' between Varya and Lopahin are illuminatingly still-born; between Anya and Trofimov they remain pathetically ludicrous; and between Yasha and Dunyasha they border on farce. The play is 'about' the purchase of a great imperial estate by a former peasant who at one time worked on it, but Chekhov makes nothing political of this; rather, it is emphasized that the man who buys it had no intention of doing so, and Chekhov takes immense pains to subvert any easy alignment of the spectator either with the old or the new owner. If the 'action' concerns the sale of the orchard, its fate is sealed from the start, and Chekhov denies his audience the satisfaction of a sensational crisis. In its place the play that Chekhov wrote allows only an intelligent, objective curiosity about how the sale of the estate will affect the individual lives of those who live there. Chekhov takes no stand on the issues themselves; there is no triumph, no villainy, no message, no lesson, no argument. But 'there is not five minutes space, anywhere in the dialogue, which would not, like a drop beneath a microscope, be found swarming with life',[1] and, in the theatre, to this life we are forced to attend.

Chekhov's anti-theatricalism was more obvious in *Uncle Vanya*, where it appeared as an almost sensational anti-sensationalism. The technique in *The Cherry Orchard* is more subtle, more submerged and pervasive, and a stage examination of this pervasiveness may go some way towards resolving the controversy about the genre of the play. In *The Cherry Orchard*, every detail fits, not just by a progressive illumination of a character's roots or the ramifications of a social situation as in any good naturalistic play, but by its contribution to an embracing structure of comi-tragic

[1] Desmond MacCarthy, *Drama* (London, 1940), p. 87.

ambivalence. 'Undercutting' as a method of objective communication in the theatre has become a style and a mode on *The Cherry Orchard* stage. Chekhov knows that by reversing a current of feeling, muting a climax, toppling a character's dignity, contradicting one statement by another, juxtaposing one impression with its opposite, he is training his audience to see the truth of the total situation. To be compassionate and yet cool at the same time is to take a big step nearer this truth, and Chekhov's final, hard discipline is to prove that the truth is relative by trying it dialectically on his audience's feelings. In this Chekhov is again the scientist and the doctor, and the result is perfect comedy – Chekhovian comedy.

At the same time his unrelenting methods of undercutting lend the play a vitality which penetrates and activates its audience's perceptions. This nourishment is at the source of all good theatre, and has nothing to do with the final direction his story takes. His procedures on the stage result in a lively extension of our involvement with the play. In the last act, when with outrageous baby noises Charlotta mimics the bitter-sweet dreams of Anya and her mother on the sofa in the chilling nursery, Chekhov is both setting the play back on its course of comic objectivity and demanding of his audience a newly creative frame of mind. In the control of an audience's response, this is pruning for stronger growth.

Ambivalence is the source of all that is truly participatory in comedy. By promoting in his thousand and one details at once our sympathy with his characters and our alienation from them, Chekhov has refashioned for a proscenium arch drama the time-honoured ironies of the traditional aside. For ambivalence as it flourishes in *The Cherry Orchard* reveals its author's sense of the playhouse as well as his sense of the play. Compensating us for the loss of an earlier participatory theatre, he must draw us into the world of the characters at one moment, into the illusory world through the arch, and at the next push us back into our seats, more critical than before. The tone of his play therefore constantly edges on satire, without being distinctively satirical. He divides us against ourselves and splits our attention in order to arouse us.

A split theatre is a dialectical theatre. The director Michel Saint-Denis has tried for many years to sound the true note of

Chekhovian comedy, and he thinks of it as one which strikes the perfect dialectical balance. For him, it is Mme Ranevsky herself who exemplifies this balance, a balance between her fear of the ill-fated situation she is in and the irresponsible, if charming, behaviour with which she tries to avoid it. We must neither condemn nor condone. He argued that the English tradition of Chekhovian production militated against the complete success of his work on the play when he presented it at the Aldwych, London, in 1961.

The 'connoisseurs' have fallen in love with the scenery, with the dear creatures, representing the threatened past; they mock Trofimov and have little sympathy for Lopahin; they were bound to resent the degradation of romantic values purposely displayed in my recent production. The contradictions of the Press contributed to the liveliness of the public's reactions; some complained they were not moved enough while others regretted not being given more opportunities to laugh. It is my belief and my hope that our interpretation has brought many people, particularly among the young, to a new understanding of this many-sided masterpiece.[1]

It is this balance on the stage, producing an exactly irritating result in the auditorium, which can be tested only in performance.

Chekhov's achievement in naturalism, therefore, was to do more than create the conditions for our belief in the happiness and misery on the stage. They had to be conditions which he could also control by calling up sympathy at one moment, and dispelling it at the next. The human personality is many-faced, just as Mme Ranevsky may be sad and yet smile, be stupid yet generous, or as Lopahin may be a tough businessman and yet a clumsy lover, a peasant's son always calling himself a pig and yet a man with a gentle nature who loves the poppies he must destroy. Social and human 'doubleness' touches every line of dialogue in the play, and 'Chekhovian' is the endearment that describes as much our response as Chekhov's characteristically quizzical way of looking at life. Just as the best tragedy engages the intelligence, so the best comedy, in spite of Henri Bergson, engages the emotions.

[1] Introduction to *Anton Chekhov: The Cherry Orchard*, a version by John Gielgud (London, 1963), p. xi.

The Cherry Orchard Act I

The Cherry Orchard Act II

a. The Cherry Orchard Act III

b. The Cherry Orchard Act IV

Act One

The Cherry Orchard compels a sense of Chekhovian time from the
rise of the curtain. Both chronological and immeasurable time are
evoked almost continuously by the characters' multiple awareness
of the moment. The audience watches the clock and the calendar,
and feels the boredom or the suspense of the present; but we also
capture the nostalgia of the infinite past and try to chase thoughts
that fly off into the impenetrable future. Where in *Three Sisters*
the audience witnessed the passage of time, in *The Cherry Orchard*,
it lives in the sensation of time passing. The play begins this process by presenting its first contrast in class and age.

The stage is in half-light. Dawn is breaking, but the sun is not
yet up; in any case, the shutters on the windows are closed,
allowing only the palest streaks of light to filter across the room.
With the half-light, the house seems half deserted: in due course
it will be peopled, and at that time the audience will seem to
people it too. At the beginning, we *are* the empty house waiting
to be inhabited. At the end, the stage will look like this again,
and again we shall seem to be the house that has been abandoned.

The position of the doors will give us an architectural sense of
the rest of the building, but now the light from the tall shutters
takes our attention to the great windows behind them. Eventually
we shall get increasing glimpses of the white blossom on the
cherry trees through these windows,[1] for it is May and the trees
are in brilliant flower. The same windows will pull us beyond the
immediate illusion of the stage set, beyond the family to the world

[1] Stanislavsky wrote in a letter of 2 November 1903: 'I think I have just found the
set for the first act. It is a very difficult set. The windows must be close enough to
the front of the stage so that the cherry orchard will be seen from the entire auditorium; there are three doors; one would wish to show a bit of Anya's room,
bright and virginal. The room is a passageway, but one must be made to feel that
here (in the nursery) it is cosy, warm, and light; the room has fallen into disuse,
there is a slight sense of vacancy about it' (*Stanislavski's Legacy*, ed. and trans. E. R.
Hapgood, New York, 1958, pp. 124–5).

outside. But Chekhov adds that characteristic touch, an implicit direction for every actor who enters to communicate the chill that is in the air: the orchard is cold with the light frost of early morning. Here is a first hint at the uneasiness which will haunt the joy of the homecoming.

The merchant Lopahin, shivering a little from sleep, slowly follows Dunyasha's candle into the room. By the light of this candle we see the room and its grandeur more clearly. It used to be the nursery, and we judge this from the ancient nursery furniture and the old-fashioned toys still in the room. It is a stroke of genius by Chekhov to begin and end the play in this room, for in the nursery each member of the family, even the youngest, will have some vivid, personal memory. The oldest too will remember their childhood days, and all the mothers and children whose invisible presence this nursery conjures up will in the end be invoked at its destruction. Here Lyubov will see herself as a child, and here we shall *see* Lyubov as a child when we watch her own daughter Anya. Here an old bookcase can be an omniscient presence, since it has witnessed so many generations of small children. And only in this room can the death by drowning of a little boy of seven several years before remain green in the memory. A nursery is a symbol of all innocent, created life.

Lopahin, dressed in his white waistcoat and tan shoes,[1] very much the dapper businessman, is from the start the play's conscious time-keeper: 'The train's in, thank God. What time is it?' He and Dunyasha the maidservant have been waiting through the night. He came to meet the family at the station, but dozed off with a book, an awkward error of behaviour we shall find characteristic of him. For a man of mature years accustomed to rising at five and working hard all day, two o'clock in the morning is not the happiest time, and now with a yawn and a stretch of the limbs he lolls listlessly in a chair. Dunyasha, on the other hand, with the appropriate vitality of her youth, is all expectancy. The differences of attitude in these two are immediately illustrative of the humour of the situation: when the one contradicts the other, the audience receives as comedy the visual mixture of the excitement and lethargy of waiting. In this double mood, we the audience receive the family on their arrival too, and recreate the

[1] Chekhov's letter to Nemirovich-Danchenko of 2 November 1903 (Hellman, p. 317).

happiness and the tensions of the reception. Yet the comic tone insists that we view the exuberance on the stage coolly: we are to see exactly how matters stand.

First we learn that Dunyasha had forgotten to wake Lopahin, who, as a result, is tetchy. In her excuse, 'I thought you had gone', we observe no special respect for her superior. And his annoyance is aggravated by the lateness of the train: 'two hours, at least'. Tardiness is typical of the people the train is bringing home, and no one is likely to be more irritated by it than Lopahin. The exposition of time, in its most literal sense, has begun.

Conventional exposition of the past, such as we find in Act I of Ibsen's *The Wild Duck*, in which one footman tells another what he must already know in order that the spectator should know too,[1] is not Chekhov's way here. It seems natural, as the man and the girl wait, listening for the sound of the carriages at the door, for the elder to reminisce to the younger about the past, for Lyubov has been away for five years. Chekhov manages his expository beginning unobtrusively through Lopahin's yawns. His sleepy rambling seems at random, and marks a complete break with the purposive dialogue of the contemporary French and Russian theatre. Yet while we learn much about the lady who is soon to arrive, we learn more about the man who is musing.

Lopahin remembers the great lady of the estate only with affection. Hers is not the stereotyped image of an indifferent aristocracy, and before we get a glimpse of her person, we are to feel the generous warmth of her gentle patronage: 'She's a splendid woman. A good-natured, kind-hearted woman.' But Chekhov is interested in more than the impression she makes on others, and is probing for a sense of time longer than five years.

Lopahin's memory slips back easily to the time when he was a peasant boy of fifteen. Indeed, it is hard for him to forget. In those days, the drunken shopkeeper, his father, used to hit him as a peasant might be expected to. In this, Chekhov is drawing upon his own memory: he himself was the son of a small shopkeeper and the grandson of a serf who had bought his freedom, and he too became the owner of an estate when he bought Melikhovo.

[1] Cf. Sheridan, *The Critic*; *or A Tragedy Rehearsed* (1779), Act II, scene ii:
DANGLE. Mr Puff, as he *knows* all this, why does Sir Walter go on telling him?
PUFF. But the audience are not supposed to know anything of the matter, are they?

The spectator makes an estimate of how far the peasant boy from the village has come as he watches Lopahin lounging in an easy chair in his fashionable clothes. Yet as we listen to him, we do not hear him as a 'loud, noisy man', but as 'soft' and gentle.[1] And we see how different is the life of Dunyasha, not much older now than he was then. In the flickering light, Lopahin is reliving those lost days. Lyubov, the mistress, was 'a slim young girl' who had comforted him in 'this very room'. Thus is the nursery given meaning for Lopahin too. The room pulls them all together and Lopahin can understand something of the lives of both master and servant.

'Don't cry, little peasant.' He remembers Lyubov only for her kindness, but he is also reminded of his birth. He will remember it again, painfully, when he comes to buy the estate in Act III, and when he is urged to marry Lyubov's foster-daughter Varya in Act IV. On that day in the nursery long ago, Lyubov had said to comfort his tears, albeit as a light colloquialism, 'It will be well in time for your wedding day.' Chekhov's weighty *'pause'* at this point, as well as serving to recall his peasant origins and emphasizing his hard-earned wealth, lets us know also that marriage is on Lopahin's mind from the start of the play. The context of this pause quietly makes the connection between his class and his marriage. This is the beginning of the 'love story' of Lopahin and Varya, and if every subtle reference to it is recognized throughout the play, an audience will have no difficulty in understanding its fruitless outcome in Act IV.

Lopahin falls silent. In the distance a dog barks, and the new morning outside the hushed room is felt to be alive with creatures stirring. However, Dunyasha has not been listening to Lopahin's dull reminiscences of a bygone age. She is on pins with an excitement of her own: 'The dogs have been awake all night, they feel that the mistress is coming.' She is speaking of her own sensations, and Lopahin notices it.

A peasant is the best, at any rate the harshest, judge of another peasant. 'What's the matter with you, Dunyasha?' Her hands are shaking; she thinks she is going to faint! But Lopahin's response to this display from one of his own kind is to tell her that she is spoilt. She is 'dressed like a lady' with her hair 'done up'. She is certainly not to be another version of forlorn Varya, who as an

[1] As Chekhov insisted in a letter to Olga Knipper of 30 October 1903 (Garnett, p. 335).

unmarried girl will have her hair fastened in a plait behind her back. The Moscow audience, accustomed to seeing only the heroine of a melodrama with her hair dressed like Dunyasha's, might well feel that Chekhov was parodying the work of his contemporaries, even if only by flighty little Dunyasha's aping her mistress.[1] We may also recognize in her, too, the innocent stirrings of social change, for Lopahin is there to remind us of them: 'One must know one's place.' There speaks at once the conservative peasant who has a conscience about buying the orchard, and the *nouveau riche* who is capable of being the new master.[2]

The gentle satire of their exchange gives place to the broader comedy of Epihodov the clerk. Three 'peasants' are now seen comparatively. Epihodov's part was written for a natural comedian, and was to be played by Luzhsky or Moskvin; this is clear evidence that Chekhov intended to keep his play buoyant. But even the farce of this role admits its opposite quality, pathos, since no character on so realistic a stage may be wholly a clown, even though Epihodov, poor man, is 'madly in love' with a flirt like Dunyasha.

His laughable appearance immediately uplifts the play. He is over-dressed for the great 'occasion' he takes this to be. He is wearing new boots and they squeak at every move. His voice is as affected as his preposterous style of speech, a bundle of malapropisms and stilted turns of phrase. He brings a bunch of flowers from the gardener (the whole estate is alert to the return of the mistress), and he promptly drops them. Gathering them up, he awkwardly thrusts the bedraggled bunch at Dunyasha like a bouquet, and the girl responds with a flutter, her pretences towards being a lady suitably encouraged. The whole episode shifts the scene into a new key, and the comedy of the *amours* of Epihodov and Dunyasha is accentuated when Lopahin packs her off to get some kvass and puts a stop to the nonsense.

Epihodov stands there squeaking faintly, as Lopahin begins to nod again in his chair. Why does the fellow not go? Epihodov

[1] Until Ostrovsky's theatre reforms of 1853 'silk and French hairdressing were obligatory for the heroine' (see P. Hartnoll, *The Oxford Companion to the Theatre*, London, 1951, p. 688). But stage traditions die hard.
[2] Chekhov made the point that Dunyasha and Epihodov should stand in Lopahin's presence; to match this deference, Lopahin 'behaves like a squire and calls the servants "thou", while they call him "you"' (letter to Stanislavsky of 10 November 1903, in Hingley, vol. III, p. 329).

wants to see Dunyasha, of course. So he begins an elaborate discourse on – the weather. (Even here Chekhov manages to insinuate a hint of the frost on the cherry trees outside the windows.) Then he talks about the 'climate'. Perhaps an absence of response from Lopahin dozing in the chair, perhaps a squeak from a shifting foot, makes Epihodov change the subject to his boots. Whatever the topic, everything is spoken in the same earnest tone. Again the comedy is emphasized by the complete indifference of the auditor on the stage: 'Don't bother me.'

Flattened, Epihodov nevertheless seems to take a pleasure in the rebuff. 'Every day some misfortune befalls me.' And he smiles fleetingly, painfully cracking his face before it resumes its mask. As Dunyasha comes in with the kvass, the little clerk goes, stepping back and knocking over a chair. With a note of triumph in his voice, as if proof that the fates are against him has been conclusively demonstrated, he cries, 'There!' Epihodov serves to introduce in miniature the glancing theme of unrequited love, one of the less happy results of change. Yet, a very polite clown is Epihodov, designed by Chekhov to contrast with Yasha's gross new ways with Dunyasha later in the act.

For Dunyasha, Epihodov is one more excuse to indulge her pathetic dreams of grandeur, but she would no more think of marrying as lowly a millstone as Epihodov than Yasha would now think of marrying a peasant girl. Into the unheeding ears of the yawning Lopahin she pours the endless stream of her excited reactions to Epihodov's recent proposal of marriage. He is a strange man, but he does, after all, love her to distraction, which must count in his favour!

To all this and much more Lopahin offers only weary grunts of fatigue, and thus by forcing a 'soliloquy' upon Dunyasha, Chekhov leads us to a fair estimate of her pretensions. Were it not for the comedy, this is a slow, even subdued, beginning to the play, preparing the stage for the burst of activity to come. For Lopahin is sufficiently awake to catch the sound of carriages in the distance, and in a moment the submerged excitement rushes to the surface. 'Will she know me?' from the man. 'I shall drop this very minute!' from the girl. Without protocol, the two of them scurry off to greet the family on their return, and the stage stands empty.

With confidence in his power to build upon the interest he has started in the audience, Chekhov leaves us alone with his bare, half-lit stage. During the pause, noises off, faint at first, strain our ears, and we are pressed to reconstruct in imagination what is happening outside the room by the careful selection of gathering sounds. Lopahin's and Dunyasha's quick exit prompts a new pace in the action against the slower tempo of the opening. Now the old servant Firs, for all his great age, hurries across the stage with the help of a stick. He is no sooner seen than he is gone, and his momentary appearance heightens expectancy. The noise swells, individual voices are raised. All at once the door flies open, the sound bursts upon us, everyone talking at once, and a small crowd of strangers in travelling clothes pours on to the stage, with Lopahin, Dunyasha and other servants bringing up the rear. The audience is overwhelmed by the excitement of the arrival.

Anya must run in first with all the vitality of her youth, for she is hardly more than a young girl. Michel Saint-Denis reports how Stanislavsky handled this moment when he saw the M.A.T. at the Théâtre des Champs Elysées in 1922.

Anya . . . who has been brought up in that nursery, jumps on to a sofa and, crouching on it, is caught up by a fit of that high-pitched laughter which is induced by a combination of tiredness and emotion. And on that piece of wordless acting the audience of two thousand five hundred people burst into applause.[1]

On her heels comes the lady of the house, Lyubov Andreyevna, Mme Ranevsky,[2] of whom Lopahin has just been speaking. She is leading a procession through the house, and talking at the top of her voice. Her gaiety betrays signs of exhaustion, and she dabs at her eyes as she looks joyfully about the nursery with wide eyes as if it were a fairy palace. She comes to a stop in the centre of the room, and others flow in behind her: Charlotta the tall, thin governess trailing a small lapdog on a lead behind her;[3] Varya,

---

[1] *Theatre: the Rediscovery of Style* (New York, 1960), p. 41. In his letter to Nemirovich-Danchenko of 2 November 1903, Chekhov wrote, 'Anya can be played by any actress you'd like, even an utter unknown, if only she is young and looks like a young girl, and talks in a young, resonant voice' (Hellman, p. 316).

[2] Chekhov wrote to Olga Knipper in a letter of 14 October 1903, that Lyubov 'is dressed with great taste, but not gorgeously. Clever, very good-natured, absent-minded; friendly and gracious to everyone, always a smile on her face' (Garnett, p. 322).

[3] 'Charlotta speaks with a good accent, not broken Russian, except that once in a while she gives a soft sound to a consonant at the end of a word rather than the

the adopted daughter, in a black coat like a peasant's *babushka,* and with a scarf tied round her head also in peasant style.[1] Lyubov's brother Gaev is there, together with a fat neighbouring land-owner, Semyonov-Pishtchik,[2] both talking at once.

The audience of course cannot at first distinguish one character from another in this way. Chekhov has refused to introduce his many characters in a conventionally theatrical way, one by one, or by pairs. Instead, he fills his stage with a crowd, a 'family', as if to warn us that his play is about people rather than persons, a group rather than individuals. Nor can we distinguish much of what is being said: all express the incoherence of exuberance by expressing the coherence of the whole group in its general excite-ment. Chekhov's requirement of ensemble acting begins early in *The Cherry Orchard.*

Against Lyubov's pleasure at seeing the old nursery again, it is given to Varya to make an undercutting comment on the cold weather. Varya had evidently been left in charge, and she claims to have kept Lyubov's rooms 'just the same as ever'. We shall increasingly hear this kind of sentiment as the play progresses, but we shall hear it ironically, for the real situation will constantly belie the endeavour to conserve the past. However, Lyubov is too overcome to hear anything. With a laugh in her voice, she recalls her childhood – 'I used to sleep here when I was little' – and we see a vision of her as a younger Anya, and beyond that vision generations of happy cherry orchard children. Lyubov is kissing everyone: Varya, who is 'just the same as ever, like a nun'; Dunyasha, who she recognizes from the little girl she was.[3] Again Chekhov commences a gently deflationary process, for Gaev is pronouncing judgment officiously on the lateness of the train, and Charlotta is telling Pishtchik that her dog eats nuts, the crea-

hard sound that is proper, and she mixes masculine and feminine adjectives' (Chekhov to Nemirovich-Danchenko on 2 November 1903, in Hellman, p. 317).
[1] 'Varya's part is more on the serious side ... Varya does not resemble Sonya or Natasha; she is a figure in a black dress, a little nun-like creature, somewhat simple-minded, plaintive and so forth and so on ... Varya wears a black dress and wide belt' (*ibid.* pp. 316–17).
[2] 'Pishtchik is an old Russian fellow broken down with gout, old age and satiety, plump, dressed in a long Russian coat ... and boots without heels' (*ibid.* p. 317).
[3] In Tyrone Guthrie's production for the Minnesota Theatre Company (1963), Jessica Tandy as Lyubov hesitated a moment before speaking Dunyasha's name, and in this moment the audience delighted to see her trying to recognize the child of five years before.

Act I

ture bred in his mistress's image as a circus performer, it seems. The first words heard from Pishtchik, 'Fancy that!', fly from his mouth wide open in astonishment, the phrase and the facial contortion his own recurring mannerism. Chit-chat and nonsense bubble on the surface, and lightly ridicule the heartfelt emotions of the homecoming.

The spectator is allowed this merest glimpse of the family before they sweep on in their tour of the house. They have paused in flight before us for a confused, ill-composed snapshot.

Only the young girls, Anya and Dunyasha, are left. They share the natural friendship of young people of the same age, and Dunyasha is soon telling Anya the whole story of Epihodov's proposal of marriage. In a serious voice she prepares to announce that the clerk proposed to her just after Easter. But she forgets that in matters of the heart a hint of jealousy always exists between teenage girls. Add to this that Anya is exhausted after a long journey from Paris, and Chekhov's next line smothers Dunyasha's earth-shaking news with an anticlimactic 'What now?' Pressing the comedy home, Chekhov has Anya catch sight of herself in the mirror on the wall, and instantaneously a matter of greater substance is on Anya's mind: 'I've lost all my hairpins.' Dunyasha's moment has passed. 'Each lives in his or her bubble of egotism', was Desmond MacCarthy's view of the characters in *The Cherry Orchard*.[1] Without making Dunyasha a caricature of a pert maidservant or the silly *soubrette* of nineteenth-century farce, Chekhov neatly touches off the comedy of her overcharged heart.

Dunyasha's voice runs on, but Anya is already looking through the door to her own room. A glance and immediately she echoes her mother's delight at renewing her acquaintance with her possessions. In the morning she will run out into the orchard itself – 'I'm home!' Again we see in her the image of her mother as a girl.

In a new, confidential tone, Dunyasha announces that a certain Petya Trofimov is here, 'asleep in the bathhouse . . . afraid of being in their way'. Anya looks up. Dunyasha was holding back this news, and now uses it as a sure way of claiming Anya's attention. So we learn of the girl's interest in him, and gain a first insight into the curious and complex reticence of this young man

[1] *Drama* (London, 1940), p. 89.

who seems fearful of his place in the household, but who cannot stay away. Chekhov continues delicately to probe the individual problems of the young people of the family. He is meticulously surveying the general mixture of their several concerns before he drops his bombshell among them.

Varya has taken off her coat and we see at her waist the keys which signify her special authority in the house. The only responsible one, Varya hides her worries behind tears of joy, so that we are unable to tell whether she is happy or unhappy. She sends Dunyasha on her way to make coffee for Madame, and the maid-servant hastens to obey with more alacrity than she showed when Lopahin sent her for kvass. Varya waits for her to go: she and Anya have been anticipating this moment of intimacy. Alone at last, the two sisters embrace in silence.

Against the continuing sounds of shrill laughs and exclamations through the house, we listen to the confidences Varya and Anya share. Charlotta had to chaperone Anya on the journey to Paris; they had set out in Holy Week, in the cold (Chekhov yet again reminds us of the season). The intimate tone of the girls indicates a close friendship we did not observe between Anya and Dunyasha. Anya is seventeen, Varya twenty-four, ages sufficiently near to justify this familiarity, yet sufficiently apart to persuade us that Varya feels more responsible than the younger sister. Although Chekhov repeatedly refers to Varya in his letters to Olga Knipper as 'a foolish girl', 'a good-natured fool' and 'rather stupid',[1] she is at that realistic age when she senses the needs of the moment in a way which is denied to Anya. In the unit of action that follows, Chekhov convincingly establishes the precise relationship between the girls, and at the same time exposes in some depth what is worrying the family.

Anya's narrative of her visit to Paris has in summary form all the richness of suggestion of Chekhov's short stories, in which the total experience is often suggested by fleeting personal impressions. The sordidness of Lyubov's Paris is as vivid as Anya's mixture of embarrassment and fear.

We got to Paris at last, it was cold there – snow. I speak French shockingly. Mamma lives on the fifth floor, I went up to her and there were

[1] See the letters of 11 February, 22 February and 14 October 1903, in Garnett, pp. 275, 280 and 323.

a lot of French people, ladies, an old priest with a book. The place smelt of tobacco and so comfortless . . .

And she suddenly felt sorry for her mother, clasped her and could not let her go. We may be tempted by Anya's plaintive performance, but with her tremulous account of Lyubov's tears, and with Varya blubbering herself, we can afford to remain objective.

There is reason enough to follow. How much sympathy does Lyubov deserve? She must selfishly have left Anya for her Paris lover when the child was only twelve. In any case, her Parisian escapade was foolishly indulgent and expensive. Just as she will forfeit the orchard, as a last desperate measure she sold her villa and 'had nothing left, nothing'. On the journey back she ordered 'the most expensive things' at the restaurants, and tipped the waiters extravagantly. Even Charlotta and Yasha the manservant had the same food that they had. The theme of the insolvency of the estate[1] makes its incisive entrance in this exchange, although it is the symptom and not the cause of the family's difficulties. In case the point is missed, Anya seems vaguely to change the subject, only to return us to the same question.

ANYA. Well, tell me – have you paid the arrears on the mortgage?
VARYA. How could we get the money?
ANYA. Oh, dear! Oh, dear!
VARYA. In August the place will be sold.
ANYA. My goodness!

Anya's surprise at Varya's admissions expressed the wide-eyed vacuity of a young girl who has never had to handle money herself. And from the moment that 'August' is mentioned, the clock begins to tick insidiously: there are only three or four months in hand.

The pieces of the puzzle fit smoothly together. Laughter is still heard in the other rooms, but beneath the general mood of happy reunion is heard the irksome rumbling of bad news. Into the jubilant present intrude the ominous mistakes of the past.

There is no time, however, to linger on such thoughts, for hard on the heels of one worry comes another. Lopahin peeps round

---

[1] In the crisis that followed the Emancipation in the second half of the nineteenth century, the landed gentry in Russia were generally threatened by economic pressures they had not known before, as the industrial growth of an emergent Russia drew upon the peasant labour force which had previously populated the great estates.

the door at Varya as if to speak a word of greeting and affection perhaps, thinks better of it and '*moos like a cow*'. He then disappears again as quickly. Inarticulate in his personal relationships, this is both Lopahin's way of teasing the girl he is expected to marry and his way of making love to her. But Varya is in no mood for a joke. She shakes a fist at him, clearly as distressed as she is angry. We laugh, but behind the comedy lurks the story of her personal tragedy. More signs of Varya the 'cry-baby'[1] appear. And Anya's question as she tries to comfort her sister, 'Varya, has he made you an offer? . . .' firmly introduces the new theme.

At her age, how can Anya understand the complexity of Varya's and Lopahin's relationship? Varya's love problem is of a different order from Dunyasha's, and Anya's 'What are you waiting for?' betrays a youthful ignorance of the forces dividing these mature lovers. Adopted into the household at an early age[2] to be brought up as one of the family and earn her keep as housekeeper, Varya is in the spinster's abject position of dependence upon Lopahin's decision. She also suffers in her own way from shyness: she is 'nun-like', as Lyubov remarks, and it is not surprising that Lopahin seems to take no notice of her beyond teasing her. For he too has his inhibitions. He regards her as one of Mme Ranevsky's family and a well-bred girl, and his own peasant background, to which he constantly refers, prevents him from asking for her hand. Varya's mortification is the more acute because 'everyone's talking of our being married' – how upsetting, and how provoking!

The girls, each in her individual way and each afflicted by her individual burden, reflect the prevailing mood of the orchard family. Such apparently disjointed dialogue as this reads strangely until its function is felt in the theatre.

VARYA. . . . Everyone's talking of our being married, everyone's congratulating me, and all the while there's really nothing in it; it's all like a dream. (*In another tone*) You have a new brooch like a bee.

ANYA (*mournfully*). Mamma brought it. (*Goes into her own room and in a light-hearted childish tone*) And you know, in Paris I went up in a balloon!

VARYA. My darling's home again! My pretty is home again!

1 Hingley's translation in the letter of 2 November 1903 to Nemirovich-Danchenko (vol. III, p. 328).
2 The suggestion has been made that Varya is the illegitimate daughter of Lyubov's late husband, but there is no hint of this in the text, and if it were true, Chekhov could not have avoided supplying one in Lyubov's remarks about her.

Act I

The switchback of their emotions, happy and unhappy, romantic and realistic, troubled by the past and simultaneously overjoyed by the excitement of the moment, is here epitomized in the changes of voice and gesture. Anya most obviously, as a young girl, vacillates between joy at coming home and anxiety over her mother. Chekhov's characters experience opposite sensations without recognizing the contradiction which the audience sees immediately. So the girls chatter on, and their dreams come and go. If only they could marry Anya to a wealthy man – that would solve their problems! Then Varya would wander from convent to convent – she would be a nun who would see the world! All this is only the airy talk of a girl who feels herself growing old without a husband. As the morning bird-chorus is heard in the orchard, the bright sunlight of the new day streaks across the floor, and Anya and Varya have drifted into Anya's room.

Broad comedy is used again to dispel the note of despair, and Chekhov seeks a rapid change of focus to the servants' comic world of dream and reality. Yasha has enjoyed his taste of Parisian life in Lyubov's service,[1] and he tries hard to look flashy and fashionable: his hair is parted in the centre and plastered down with oil. Now he minces across the stage towards a blushing Dunyasha who has come in to pour the coffee. 'May one come in here, pray?' is his pretentious manner of address. His performance might be a parody of Lyubov's French lover – 'H'm! . . . And who are you?' – for Yasha shares with Dunyasha ideas above their station. If he lights a cigar, he does it ostentatiously, with half an eye for the impression he is making on the girls. He and Dunyasha are well matched: she responds like the caricature of a lady. After looking round to make sure he is not seen, a gesture which reveals the conflict between his origins and his unwillingness to acknowledge them, Yasha gives her an over-dramatic kiss, behaving to the servant-girl much as he imagines the master would have done. With appropriate refinement, she gives a polite scream, drops a saucer and wipes at a tear. Brief and mocking, the tiny scene offers a quick perspective on the social life of civilized Paris, the same that has so obsessed Lyubov and troubled Varya and Anya. And

[1] It is belittling to Lyubov, and too visually distracting from the main business, to imply more than this, that perhaps Yasha is on terms of undue familiarity with his mistress. He may take liberties in the social sense, provided that this makes him seem forward without demeaning her.

Yasha's short way with women is in sharp contrast with the emotional contortions of Epihodov and Lopahin.

Chekhov continues his oblique exposition. Anya wanders in and suggests that her mother should be warned that Petya Trofimov is in the house. The mystery of Trofimov grows clearer: he was the tutor of Anya's little brother before the boy was drowned, and no doubt the sight of him will recall a horrible memory. More than this, the death of Lyubov's husband had occurred just before the drowning, and the two tragic blows had together been the cause of Lyubov's flight to Paris. These details compel us to adjust our earlier judgment of the lady, and we find it easier to justify the love which it is evident everyone in the family feels towards her. In this way also, we are being prepared for Lyubov's next entrance.

Further to prepare us, Chekhov allows a closer view of old Firs, the family servant formally dressed in footman's tail-coat, white waistcoat and white gloves. He is the visible embodiment of how life went on in this house in the past, during the halcyon days of the cherry orchard. He fusses at the coffee-pot and snaps at Dunyasha for neglecting to bring the cream. 'Ech! you good-for-nothing!' – the phrase and the growl have over the years become a reflex. He will have everything as it should be, that is, as it was in a bygone age. And he too weeps for joy at Madame's return: 'Now I can die.'

The elderly group of Lyubov and her brother Gaev comes in talking animatedly, again urging upon us an awareness of the meaning of the nursery: 'We used to sleep together in this very room.' Pishtchik and Lopahin[1] follow behind them. Gaev makes an energetic arm motion, perhaps with a cane if he carries one, as if he held a billiards cue in his hand. This mannerism, usually accompanied with a billiards call,[2] we shall see several times in varying contexts. It is Chekhov's way of communicating Gaev's particular state of mind at different stages of the play, while at the same time conveying that he is at a loss for words. An imaginary billiards cue is an appropriate upper-class emblem for Gaev:

[1] Chekhov omits Lopahin's entrance in his text.
[2] In a letter to Olga Knipper of 14 October 1903, Chekhov declared that he put down the billiards terms 'at random' and asked the actor Vishnevsky to listen for appropriate words spoken by men when playing the game (Garnett, pp. 322–3).

billiards and caramels appear to sustain his life. They are also intended to reduce him to ridicule in our eyes: can such a man save the orchard? Gaev's thoughts, like Lyubov's, are suffused with the past, and he announces that he is fifty-one, 'strange as it seems'. But the pathos in his voice is dispelled by a desultory exchange that is as much Pinteresque as Chekhovian.

LOPAHIN. Yes, time flies.
GAEV. What do you say?
LOPAHIN. Time, I say, flies.

Lopahin is probably thinking of the hour, Gaev of the year, the audience of generations. And 'How like you are to your mother!' is the line Gaev addresses to Anya which again identifies the young girl with the older woman.

Anya at last goes to bed. General weariness affects everyone on the stage. Varya hints to Lopahin and Pishtchik that they should leave. But Lyubov, with the perpetual enchantment of her smile, sits splendidly before her circle of admirers, arranges her attractive Parisian dress and declares that she will drink Firs's coffee before she retires. 'Thanks, dear old man', she says to Firs as she kisses him; 'I'm so glad to find you still alive'. Chekhov kills the sentiment immediately with Firs's reply: 'The day before yesterday.' He was too deaf to catch her remark.

Lassitude descends more heavily on the company. It is three o'clock. Lopahin announces that he has to leave for Harkov at five. The particularity reveals the mind of a businessman. And it is clear that he too is conscious of the difference between his hosts and himself. Gaev had once called him a peasant out for what he could get. So? His father was a serf. But he has forgotten that. He loves Lyubov as though she were 'kin'. Yet the word does not sound right on his lips, and the warmth of his gesture with his arms looks incongruous.

Lyubov cannot sit still. With new life, she jumps up, kisses the bookcase and touches the nursery table as if she were stroking the family cat.

GAEV. Nurse died while you were away.
LYUBOV (*sits down and drinks coffee*). Yes, the Kingdom of Heaven be hers! You wrote to me of her death.

The momentary exuberance has passed. The house and its furniture may be the same; her sitting down again emphasizes the fleeting notion that other things at least have changed. Time past, with its best memories and also its regrets, is singularly alive in the nursery: the old nurse belonged there too. But Lyubov's customary smile quickly returns and her mask covers what she may be feeling. For the moment, a restful content pervades the room, and the homecomers bask in their warmest thoughts. It is into this calm that Lopahin offers to bring his 'good news'. His confidence is wholly ironic, for what he is about to propose juxtaposes a prescription for both the preservation and the destruction of what is dear to them. Walking the room while the others sit, glancing at his watch as usual, he speaks to them in a voice strong with pride in his idea.

The orchard must be sold on 22 August, the day now absolutely precise. However, if they lease the land for summer cottages (*dachas*), they will have an annual income of 25,000 roubles.

The reaction of Lyubov and Gaev to this pronouncement is one of incredulous silence. For them, Lopahin's plan to 'cut up' the estate would destroy the orchard as much as the sale of it. Gaev is abrupt: 'That's all rot, if you'll excuse me.' Lyubov is more polite: 'I don't quite understand you.' Lopahin's 'very pleasant and cheering' news has fallen on their ears like lead. His intention was only to help, but he has spoken out of turn, not fully realizing the intensely personal meaning of the orchard to the family, a meaning, however, that the audience has itself begun to fathom. Lopahin is not quite blind to the effect of his words: he is not a brash man, for he loves the poppies he must cut down, presumably as he loves the cherry trees that must be felled. And he shifts his position in relation to Lyubov, softening his tone as he speaks, changing the form of his address from 'if *you* say the word' to 'if *we* don't decide on something'. But Lopahin is a realist who can reject sentiment if he must, and this Lyubov and Gaev cannot do. Their obstinacy increases the sense of death in the nursery.

Lopahin continues to make his calculations. Of course the house will have to go, and the orchard be *cut down*. The words are repeated. Lyubov's response is wonderfully irrelevant. 'Cut down? My dear fellow, forgive me, but you don't know what you're talking about. If there is one thing interesting – remarkable indeed – in the whole province, it's just our cherry orchard.' To this Gaev adds that the orchard is even mentioned in the Encyclopaedia, a comically particular extension of the musty past. And Lyubov grows increasingly silent after this: her mood of joy behind her bland smile has changed. This the audience can understand. In spite of the fact that Lopahin points out that no one wants to buy the cherries, and that the whole place will be sold anyway on 'the 22nd of August' – again the particular date is heard, and again on this line he glances at his watch – the audience can appreciate well enough the refusal to entertain even the thought of the proposal. The orchard has more than material value. It may not represent a geographical landmark, or even a piece of history, but it has the qualities of a living thing: it stands for a way of life.

At the mention of cherries, Firs feels that he has something to say on the matter. Gaev tells him to be silent, but Firs's rather selective deafness protects him from criticism. In a ludicrous interpolation, he speaks of the way the cherries were dried or preserved for a good profit 'in old days'. If Gaev brushes this aside, Lyubov actually asks about the recipe as if she might yet consider using it; it is evident that not even she in her time had bothered to think the cherries worth growing. Anyway, the recipe is forgotten; at the end of the play, Firs himself will be equally forgotten. And Pishtchik has already changed a subject which he can see is disturbing his friends, asking Lyubov whether she ate frogs when she was in Paris. Pishtchik has a cherry orchard problem too, for he also has a mortgage whose interest he must meet; but he and his 'dear lady' will sink or swim together. Thus are Lopahin's well-meaning efforts belittled, and from this episode the spectator has the strongest sense that the irresponsible attitude of the family is one which nothing can alter. Lopahin tries a second time to raise the matter of the sale, but Gaev's peremptory 'What rot!' finally silences him.

Two telegrams have been kept for Lyubov in the old bookcase that stands in the nursery. The piece is not often used, and Varya opens it *'with a loud crack'*. We glance towards the noise, and Varya hands the telegrams to Lyubov. Throughout the play she will receive such telegrams. They tell us what little it is necessary to know of the unseen lover in Paris. It seems that he has fallen ill and is beseeching her to return. By having us watch what Lyubov does with each telegram, Chekhov can intimate with all economy of means the current state of her feeling towards the man. Here, with a somewhat ostentatious flourish, she tears them up without reading them. 'I have done with Paris.' Paris was an escape from the orchard, just as now the orchard is an escape from Paris. Nevertheless, the telegrams have momentarily made her dwell on her other life, and she has left the problem of the solvency of the orchard far behind. By means of the telegrams, fluttering in pieces at her feet, the audience has a dual vision of her two great personal disasters past and future, her guilty experience in Paris and the loss of the cherry orchard.

Meanwhile, Gaev has begun a speech to the bookcase, and Pishtchik listens in amazement. The speech is self-consciously emotional, almost a parody of a hundred after-dinner flights of bombast: 'Dear, honoured, bookcase! . . .'[1] In this unexpected outburst we recognize Gaev's affection for his home and have again a sense of its history. Yet, strangely, in the actual words of the speech, we hear a comic extension of his feeling about the orchard itself: 'Though it's an inanimate object, still it is a *book case*.' If Gaev cannot embrace an inanimate object like the orchard, he can caress the bookcase, and he does so, talking vaguely of virtue and justice, faith in a better future, ideals of good and social conscience. There follows an excruciating '*pause*' in which no one knows what to say.

LOPAHIN. Yes . . .
LYUBOV. You are just the same as ever, Leonid.
GAEV (*a little embarrassed*). Cannon off the right into the pocket!

Lopahin has had his rebuff, and perhaps he expected nothing better. Meanwhile, Lyubov's remark guides us to smile at Gaev's emotion, and Chekhov with a neat inconsequence smothers the rising sentiment.

Now Pishtchik is used rapidly to lighten the atmosphere and complete the switch of attention with some finality. When Yasha reminds Madame to take her medicine, Pishtchik empties the whole bottle of pills into his hand and swallows them. The incident has no dramatic meaning except to demonstrate Pisht-chik's high spirits and hence everybody's delight that Lyubov is

[1] The point of the parody was well made when on the opening night at which Chekhov was present, one of the speeches in his honour began, 'Dear, honoured Anton Pavlovich . . .', and Stanislavsky, playing Gaev, caught Chekhov's eye, as much as to say, 'The joke was a good one!' Hingley gives a full account of the story in vol. III, pp. 331–2.

home again. Pishtchik, we are to learn, claims in jest to be descended from the horse which Caligula made a member of the Senate: Lyubov calls him a glutton, and everyone laughs. Firs caps the sequence by telling them that at Easter Pishtchik came and ate 'a gallon and a half of cucumbers'. Again there is general laughter, and when the old man does not find the matter funny, the laughter is redoubled. The problems of the play seem to be disintegrating in farce. For, next, Lopahin tries to kiss the hand of Charlotta, the gawky German governess, who in a little performance of mock modesty says, 'If I let you kiss my hand, you'll be wanting to kiss my elbow, and then my shoulder.' 'I've no luck today!' cries Lopahin, and the scene dissolves in yet more empty laughter. But the audience off the stage cannot laugh at this fragmented series of jokes with the same freedom as those on it.

The apparently disruptive laughter has not diminished our consciousness of the imminent sale of the orchard. In spite of the horseplay, we may not forget the real issues. Has the family forgotten them? Lopahin's departure at this point, a gay one as he goes round the circle kissing and shaking hands with them all, is carefully used to remind us of the prickly moments of the previous scene. For we observe that he reserves for Varya a somewhat awkward hand-shake, and manages to remind Lyubov of his plan. Thus, when Lopahin goes, Gaev is still angry with him for his preposterous proposal for the orchard's future, and Varya for his indifference to hers: 'Well, do go, for goodness sake.' As the family speaks to her of his suitability as a husband, the themes of money and marriage are interwoven.

Here a wildly comic vignette from Pishtchik seems to summarize Chekhov's highly indirect and economical method of exposition.

He is, one must acknowledge, a most worthy man. And my Dashenka . . . says too that . . . she says . . . various things (*snores, but at once wakes up*). But all the same, honoured lady, could you oblige me . . . with a loan of 240 roubles . . . to pay the interest on my mortgage tomorrow?

Pishtchik seems to live in a private world of unreality and wonder, like a great child. He has an implicit trust in the judgment of others, and defers to them whenever possible. We never meet his daughter Dashenka, and do not need to. But we can well imagine that she has her hands full, not only with keeping their own estate solvent, but with her father too. For Pishtchik is always trying to borrow money, and, as we surmise from Varya's anxious 'No, no!', with a miserable eye on Lyubov, he seems in this family to get it. He is a man who is everlastingly hopeful that something will turn up, and, surprisingly, it seems to. Like that other innocent, Gaev (out of the corner of our eye we watch Firs fussing over him like an old hen, muttering, 'What am I to do with you?'), Pishtchik is ridiculously fatalistic. He is the comic counterpart of all the insolvent landowners of *fin de siècle* Russia, and a maddening mirror image of the cherry orchard family itself, representing a distorted version of their position. He dreams, he drops asleep, and wakes to remember the ever-present need for money.

Pishtchik's snore also advises that the pace is slowing again. Anya has gone to bed, Lyubov is ready for it, and Chekhov again reminds us of the time. The bustling stage is at last still. Quietly, Varya and Gaev open the shutters and the sunlight floods in. It is the magic moment of early morning in the orchard. 'What exquisite trees!' . . . 'The orchard is all white': from Varya's and Gaev's ecstasy the picture of the scene beyond the stage charms the spectator more than any painted set.

Lyubov looks through the window for us and extends our vision with her own: 'Oh, my childhood, my innocence!' The guilt behind the inflection of the word 'innocence' mixes with her childlike laughter as she thinks of her happy years as a girl. 'In those days the orchard was just the same, nothing has changed.' We know the sentiment to be false, but we relish her pleasure and warm to her laugh, which we hear as an echo of Anya's on her first entrance into the nursery: 'All, all white!' Doubtless for this scene Lyubov could herself be dressed in white, for Chekhov wrote to Stanislavsky that he had an image of whiteness in his head from the conception of the play, as if Lyubov's view of the past were one of absolute purity.[1] The orchard is young again, like the season, like Lyubov. They have renewed their life for the homecoming. But, just as Gaev's voice as he addressed the

[1] Letter of 5 February 1903: 'Cherry trees can be seen in bloom through the windows, the whole orchard a mass of white. And ladies in white dresses' (Hingley, vol. III, p. 318).

bookcase was a little shrill, so also is Lyubov's as she apostrophizes her orchard. For she has married unwisely, taken a lover and lost her son as if it were a punishment. And with an abrupt change of mood, she passes from joy to sorrow: 'If I could forget the past!' To Lyubov the orchard now recalls both an innocent and a guilty past. Subtly Chekhov has injected the visionary moment with a sense of the real conflicting with the romantic past. Even more disturbingly, he begins also to tinge it with the reality of the present, and has Gaev call the sale to mind. But Lyubov shrugs off such cruel realities with 'See, our mother walking . . . all in white, down the avenue!' And once more we see in the white figure of Lyubov a mother who had a mother like herself, and we see in her a symbol of the generations which delighted in the sunlit orchard as they stretch backwards in the imagination. But we also know that the woman in white in the orchard is dead. The woman is Lyubov herself, the image of all the dead mothers clothed in white innocence, an innocence which is also a shroud. Lyubov for an enchanted moment is herself the orchard in its contradictions.[1]

Chekhov must bring her, and us, down to earth with a bump, and he does so by ordaining at this juncture the entrance of Trofimov. Petya, in his shabby student's uniform, peering into the room through steel-rimmed spectacles, his wisp of a beard making him look merely unshaven, is here the reality of the immediate past. His voice at a new low pitch of emotion stops Lyubov in her transport, and his presence abruptly changes the pace and the mood. He kisses her hand as she stands transfixed in silence, seemingly bewildered by his nervous figure. He announces himself: 'Petya Trofimov, who was your Grisha's tutor . . . Can I have changed so much?' As if recognition comes suddenly, Lyubov quickly embraces him and in a moment the whole party is in tears. As they look at him, they do not see Trofimov, but the drowned boy Grisha. We hear Varya's pious voice whimpering as she mops her eyes, 'It is God's will.' With Varya as their spokesman, the assembled company feels the touch of fate.

[1] Chekhov in his letters always referred to Mme Ranevsky as an old woman: 'a woman along in years' (to Vera Komissarzhevskaya, 27 January 1903, in Friedland, p. 157); 'the old mother' (to Olga Knipper, 11 February 1903, in Garnett, p. 275); 'an elderly lady' (to Olga Knipper, 11 April 1903, in Garnett, p. 300); 'the old lady' (to Olga Knipper, 15 April 1903, in Garnett, p. 301).

Grisha was part of Lyubov's past also, a part she wanted to forget.

Only like a mother speaking to her own son could Lyubov say what she now says through her tears to Trofimov: 'Why have you grown so ugly? Why do you look so old?' Her words are spoken with affection, and Trofimov turns them with a wry-faced joke. He is losing his hair and now wearing spectacles; and he is still a student.[1] She speaks casually as she moves slowly to the door, almost as an after-thought. She is going to bed: this last encounter is too much. Trofimov too is a reminder of time passing, and the whole incident of Lyubov's reunion with her son's tutor is a configuration of their close relationship unbroken by the years.

Pishtchik again serves to undercut the tensions of the moment, and the pace accelerates.

PISHTCHIK. 240 roubles . . . to pay the interest on my mortgage.
LYUBOV. My dear man, I have no money.
PISHTCHIK. I'll pay it back, my dear . . . a trifling sum.
LYUBOV. Oh, well, Leonid will give it you . . . You give him the money, Leonid.
GAEV. Me give it him! Let him wait till he gets it!

The sentimentality is quite submerged in the comedy of the two penniless landowners. Yet behind Gaev's indignant outburst lies the sobering thought that the lady remains frighteningly ignorant of her own pressing needs. She is richly endowed with the gift of ignoring what is unpleasant. Only the audience recalls the ugly theme of bankruptcy.

Gaev, Varya and Yasha remain, and a little of Yasha's story is hinted. Gaev tells him he smells like the henhouse. More is indicated than Gaev's dislike of Lyubov's servant: his constant criticism never allows Yasha's somewhat sinister vulgarity to be anything but comic. For his true function in the play, as will be seen, is to extend the notion of social change by showing it at work at the lowest level of society. When Varya tells Yasha that his mother has been waiting to see him since yesterday, 'Oh,

---

[1] Chekhov explains part of Trofimov's story as a student revolutionary in a letter to Olga Knipper of 19 October 1903: 'Trofimov has been in exile over and over again, he is continually being sent down from the University, and how is one to express these facts?' (Garnett, p. 325).

bother her!' is his insolent response. After his Parisian experience
he does not want to be reminded of his peasant origins.

The next few minutes are all Gaev's, and they fall like a sorry
anticlimax after Lopahin's exit. Is Leonid Andreyevitch, the
gentleman of the estate, indifferent to its future? Against Varya's
typically pious contribution, a tearful appeal to God, her uncle
offers only the silliest of solutions, those which are least likely to
come about. They could hope for a legacy. Anya might marry a
wealthy man. They could apply to their rich aunt in Yaroslavl,
the Countess. Gaev's second thoughts, that the Countess does
not like them, is a sad admission which immediately betrays the
comic unreality of his thinking.[1] His woebegone tone conveys
his feeling of being a poor relation. Why did Lyubov marry a
lawyer and not a nobleman? And what of her immoral ways?
Anya's entrance, sleepless from her room, puts a stop to this line
of thought, and Gaev again exerts himself to find an answer to
comfort the girls. He reports, but none too confidently, that there
is a possibility of borrowing some money. Or Lyubov can always
appeal to Lopahin. Anya can visit her great-aunt in Yaroslavl.
Between them, they are bound to succeed. Gaev will not let it
come to an auction: 'I swear on my honour, I swear by anything
you like.' And as if to seal the bargain with himself, he pops a
caramel into his mouth. He has managed to comfort Anya at least,
and his niece comforts him with flattery in return: 'How good
you are, uncle, and how clever!' But we are hardly convinced by
his assessment of the situation, and that simplest of gestures with
the caramel destroys all confidence in him. Spoken with the mouth
full and a lick of the fingers, 'Upon my soul I swear it' does not
sound too brave. The next moment, Firs comes to put him to
bed like a small boy, and off he goes, elatedly making a mimic
shot with his imaginary billiards cue, one shot that cannot miss.

Varya and Anya sit alone sleepily, the last of the crowd, in the
bright rays of the sun. Varya, the worried housekeeper, begins
faintly to talk of her problems, the immediate and practical
problems of running the house on a shoestring. The quick
picture she touches in of all the old servants and tramps still
living on the estate reminds the Moscow audience of the chaotic

[1] The comic method of showing Gaev's 'optimistic fantasies . . . at odds with his
sense of realism' is analyzed in detail by John Fernald in *Sense of Direction: The
Director and his Actors* (London, 1968), pp. 110–16.

conditions in rural Russia, and of the breaking up of the old patriarchal order. The problems of the cherry orchard, indeed, are very real.

Anya has fallen asleep in Varya's arms, and Varya's voice drops away as she leads the exhausted girl back to her room. Pace is now at a minimum. Trofimov, crossing the stage, stops as he catches a glimpse of Anya as she goes, and we hear him murmur, 'My sunshine! My spring!' In spite of the sense of disaster lingering in the room, we are left with the strangely optimistic feeling that it is spring, that there is a new day and that a new generation promises that life will go on. From far away a shepherd's pipe is heard playing, and with it Chekhov brings down his first act curtain. As it slowly falls, the sweet sound in the stillness, coupled with Trofimov's ecstatic tone, beckons us beyond the house to a world that is less transient. It also beckons us into the open country of Act II.

Act Two

Chekhov found his second act the most difficult to write; he feared that it was 'boring and monotonous, like a spider-web'.[1] Always experimenting, he was here trying to create a static, lyrical scene, one with no development of the action in any accepted sense. He planned the scene to catch time in flight, to halt the narrative element and review the situation, as if the play were designed musically. Before the crisis of the third act, his second movement was to provide a quiet revelation to the audience.[2] Also, for a sense of comic equilibrium, and in contrast with the uncertain optimism with which the first act ends, Chekhov opens this next movement with an amusing study of the private lives of all the servants except Firs. Charlotta, Dunyasha, Yasha and Epihodov are four melancholy Jaques playing on different strings. Individually, each thinks only of his own needs and desires; together, four comedians accentuate the comedy of one another. The first five minutes of Act II constitute the overture *buffo* before the principals enter.

For a wider perspective, Chekhov has also moved the play outside the house, even beyond the orchard itself. It is the open country on a hot summer evening in June at about sunset: the scene has the appearance of the twilight of a way of life. Stanislavsky, as always, was keen to indulge his passion for noises off, here with the sound of corncrakes and frogs. Chekhov, as always, tried to restrain him. 'Haymaking usually takes place from about the twentieth to the twenty-fifth of June, during which time it seems the corncrake and the frogs are over their summer music and are silent. Only the oriole can be heard.'[3] He was wielding his knowledge of farming at Melikhovo over the ignoramus from

---

[1] Quoted by S. D. Balukhaty (Jackson, p. 145).
[2] Not to give the *characters* a fresh sense of their doomed position, as Francis Fergusson suggests in *The Idea of a Theater* (New York, 1953), pp. 185–6.
[3] Letter of 23 November 1903, in Hellman, p. 319.

the city, for, as a dramatist, he wanted a peaceful scene. The heat, with the time of day, was to encourage that lassitude in which his characters might seem to muse upon their deepest thoughts. Chekhov at first wanted a river in the scene – the one in which Lyubov's son had drowned – but thought this less 'peaceful' than its absence. But he did call for 'a real green field, and a path, and a horizon wider than is usual on the stage'.[1] The space surrounding his characters was to make them seem smaller than in Act I, to dwarf them, for their struggles were not to be permitted to loom too large. We shall see, too, that Chekhov also had it in mind to blast the idyllic scene with his own brand of subversive comedy.

The details of the setting are indicated with great care, for they are to inform the conflicts within the action. The visual statement is designed to be specifically ambivalent. On one hand is *'an old shrine,*[2] *long abandoned and fallen out of the perpendicular; near it a well, large stones that have apparently once been tombstones'*. The image of the setting is one of dissolution, but Chekhov insisted that it should not seem funereal. 'There is no cemetery – there had once been one, but two or three gravestones leaning in disorder are all that remain.'[3] He wanted only a few bizarre suggestions of the dead past as a background for the old bench upon which some of the characters sit.[4] Linking this scene to the orchard is a road leading to Gaev's house, its direction outlined by a line of dark poplar trees. I believe a glimpse of cherry trees is also necessary to orient the scene for the audience.

The same road going the other way leads the eye to *'a row of telegraph poles'*, and *'far, far away on the horizon there is faintly outlined a great town'*. Chekhov's ideas here were brilliant. In the last decades of the nineteenth century, industrial expansion in Russia was rapid, and the development of textiles, steel and coal encouraged an extensive growth in railways. The telegraph poles are to state this simply, although Stanislavsky also wished to

[1] Letter to Nemirovich-Danchenko of 22 August 1903, in Friedland, p. 158.
[2] *Chasovenka* implies a small chapel protecting a Greek Orthodox icon.
[3] In the same admonitory letter to Stanislavsky. Also remarked in a letter to Nemirovich-Danchenko of 23 October 1903 (Hingley, vol. III, p. 327).
[4] In place of the 'old garden seat' which Chekhov asked for, Stanislavsky substituted hay: 'To the left in the foreground, a mown field and a small mound of hay, on which the scene is played by the group out walking. This is for the actors, it will help them get into the spirit of their parts' (in a letter of 19 November 1903, in *Stanislavski's Legacy*, ed. and trans. E. R. Hapgood, New York, 1958, p. 126).

include a passing train. This would have destroyed the quiet atmosphere that Chekhov wanted. 'If you can get the train into the action without noise, without so much as a single sound – go ahead', was the author's polite rebuttal, knowing that this condition was impossible to fulfil.[1] On the same day he wrote to Olga Knipper, 'Stanislavsky wants to have a train pass in Act II, but I think he must be restrained from that.'[2] The outcome was a more direct impression: telegraph poles, staccato against the horizon, are to be set against the graceful poplar trees, marks of both man and nature, telling at once of the future of the Russian countryside and of its past, with the people of the cherry orchard caught between them in the precarious present. Perspective scene-painting sets the cherry orchard into historical perspective too.

The bench is occupied by the lovers Yasha and Dunyasha; they wish to be alone, but, tiresomely, two other people are with them and will not leave. One is Epihodov, playing his guitar and playing gooseberry, hovering uncertainly near them on the other side of the stage. He stands apart, separated in space and mood from his beloved Dunyasha as she flirts with another man. She has already made a choice, it seems. Epihodov may be trying to improve himself with books, but Yasha is the one who has 'prospects', and intuitively she knows it. Even on this trivial level, the audience feels the pressures of social change. The other unwanted intruder is Charlotta, who sits on the bench at the other end from the lovers, an awkward third. At the rise of the curtain, everyone is *'plunged in thought'*. Thus the scene opens without animation of any kind, and, except for Epihodov's soulful strumming, in bleak silence. The heat bears down. The pace is slack.

We have had intimations of Charlotta's self-conscious clowning

[1] Letter to Stanislavsky of 23 November 1903, again, in Hellman, p. 319.
[2] Garnett, p. 348. Stanislavsky had written, 'Let's hope the scenery will be successful. The little chapel, the ravine, the neglected cemetery in the middle of an oasis of trees in the open steppes. The left side and the centre will not have any wings. You will see only the far horizon. This will be produced by a single semicircular backdrop with attachments to deepen the perspective. In the distance you see the flash of a stream and the manor house on a slight rise, telegraph poles, and a railroad bridge. Do let us have a train go by with a puff of smoke in one of the pauses. That might turn out very well. Before sundown there will be a brief glimpse of the town, and toward the end of the act, a fog: it will be particularly thick above the ditch downstage. The frogs and corncrakes will strike up at the very end of the act' (letter of 19 November 1903, in *Stanislavski's Legacy*, ed. and trans. E. R. Hapgood, New York, 1958, pp. 125–6).

from her brief appearance in Act I with her nut-eating pet dog. She now takes on three-dimensional life. Chekhov thought of her at the last as 'the best part', perhaps because, for all her buffoonery, she is the most sane and sceptical character in the play.[1] Wearing a man's peaked cap, she sits angularly on the bench adjusting the buckle of a shot-gun. Here is a distinctly masculine image, that of the new woman, the independent spirit. However, this role is unwelcome to her, for when she breaks the silence with her clipped accent, she seems to speak like a child.

She is lonely and unloved, and we learn about her restless childhood. Her parents were performers, and when she was a small girl she 'used to dance the *salto-mortale* and all sorts of things'. After their death she was educated by a German lady and became a governess: the incongruity between the upbringing and the profession she was presumably compelled to adopt is visible in the odd figure she presents. That is all she knows of the past; for her, the rest is pathos. She thinks of herself as a girl, but she does not know how old she is, or who she is. As she sits there, to the embarrassment of her younger companions, she throws out the statement, 'One wants to talk and has no one to talk to . . . I have nobody.' Heart-rending? It might have been, had she not at this very moment glanced at the lovers on the bench and taken a cucumber[2] deftly from her pocket and crunched it between her teeth. The remainder of her melancholy refrain is punctuated, therefore, by munching. Again, a simple but ludicrous gesture makes ambiguous all earlier impressions of her. Everyone continues to ignore her, and she continues to eat the cucumber as if she were laughing at her own ill-luck. 'Who I am, I don't know', she says, but she has chosen her own sardonic identity, that of a clown.

Undercutting what is already a 'throw-away' line about Charlotta's empty existence, Epihodov has begun to sing a popular ballad to his guitar, appropriately a serenade on the need for love. Is this not a love scene? But no one is listening to Epihodov's cry of distress either. Now he suddenly stops singing, as if to call for attention.

---

[1] Letter to Olga Knipper of 29 September 1903 (Garnett, p. 311).
[2] An earlier version of the text associates Charlotta with a gherkin, not a cucumber (see Hingley, vol. III, p. 324). Chekhov doubtless realized that a sizable cucumber would better project the comic effect he sought.

Act II

EPIHODOV. How agreeable it is to play on the mandoline!
DUNYASHA. That's a guitar, not a mandoline.
EPIHODOV. To a man mad with love, it's a mandoline.

To mark her indifference to him, Dunyasha examines herself in a hand-mirror and dabs at her nose with a powder-puff, just as Madame might have done, only in private. She is more concerned with her immediate object, that of ensnaring Yasha, and she is used by Chekhov to take the wind out of Epihodov's sails. The little clerk, however, tries again: 'were her heart but aglow with love's mutual flame'. This time Chekhov has Yasha join in, and two voices in chorus comically spoil the homage Epihodov wishes to pay to his Dunyasha. He is effectively squashed.

Each of the four characters has the most serious of pretensions in the scene; as elsewhere in Chekhov, each wishes to play the tragic hero; each is incapable of striking the right note. Now it is Dunyasha who tries to steal the limelight, and in the coy tone of a lady in her salon, she turns to Yasha and says, 'What happiness, though, to visit foreign lands.' Yasha, like a man of the world, yawns and lights a cigar: 'Ah, yes! I rather agree with you there.' The cigar is his Parisian affectation (in Act I, Anya found her mother's apartment smelling of tobacco). In his turn, Epihodov tries to regain the initiative, and with his high-flown, half-assimilated phrases, begins a long and garbled account of the Byronic precariousness of his life. 'I always carry a revolver,' he declares, and for Dunyasha's benefit he produces it with a clumsy flourish.

Epihodov's romantic gesture with the pistol produces no kind of response from the girl. Only Charlotta, the realist in the group, speaks: 'I've had enough, and now I'm going' – a reaction worth worse than nothing to the lovesick Epihodov. With mock fear, Charlotta adds as she passes him, 'All the women must be wild about you. Br-r-r!' She moves off slowly, perhaps in the faint hope that someone will call her back. No one does, and Epihodov is left to drone on in his melancholy voice, overstating melodramatically the disasters that seem to stalk his life: a spider on his chest that morning, a cockroach in his kvass. He pauses. No response. He tries again, this time with a bright new conversational opening: 'Have you read Buckle?' Again, nothing. Finally, he speaks more directly to Dunyasha: 'I should be desirous to speak with you alone.'

However, Dunyasha will not be cornered, and knowing how far away the house is, she sends him for her cape. 'Bring me my mantle,' she says, and, as if a reason is needed, she adds affectedly to Yasha, 'It's rather damp here.' She is still aping Madame, and Epihodov at last seems to recognize that he has been rejected in favour of Yasha, the social climber: 'Now I know what I must do with my revolver.' But the audience need not fear for his safety, since Chekhov has him go off strumming his guitar, and the other two take absolutely no notice of his threat. He seems, in any case, happiest in his role of abject suitor, and no doubt he would not know what to do with a flirt like Dunyasha if she accepted him.

With Yasha and Dunyasha alone at last, the girl can practise her carefully planned arts of sophisticated seduction upon her Parisian beau.

God grant he doesn't shoot himself! (*A pause for Yasha to be suitably impressed by her having a lover willing to sacrifice his life for her. No answer.*) I'm so nervous, I'm always in a flutter. (*She bats her eyelids, and makes the slightest of movements along the seat towards Yasha for protection.*) I was a little girl when I was taken into our lady's house, and now I have quite grown out of peasant ways (*Please do not think of me as a girl with the manners of a peasant*), and my hands are white, as white as a lady's. (*She waves them before his eyes for proof, and perhaps just touches his cheek.*) I'm such a delicate, sensitive creature, I'm afraid of everything (*her voice here exquisitely coy*). And if you deceive me, Yasha, I don't know what will become of my nerves. (*There! That is proof enough: only real ladies are permitted to have nerves.*)

In this humorous monologue, Chekhov reveals his gift of caricature, and realizes his Dunyasha completely, suggesting every intonation and gesture. By stressing such pretensions even at the bottom of the social scale, Chekhov touches the nerve of delicate satirical comedy.

It is even suggested that Yasha and Dunyasha have already enjoyed an illicit relationship this summer. But, unluckily for the girl, Yasha does not treat her with the respect she desires. On the outrageous line, 'You're a peach!', he kisses her most inelegantly. In his new role as a gentleman, Yasha thinks he knows how to treat a servant-girl. Of course, she 'must never forget herself'; he does not like 'flighty' behaviour in a woman. Evidently Dunyasha is satisfied with this, for she asserts that she is 'passionately in love' with him, adding the lame reason, 'You are a man of culture'. With which sentiment he can only agree, affecting another yawn. Yasha's cynical yawns throughout the play typify his notion of superiority.

Unluckily again for Dunyasha, her lover hears Lyubov and the family coming up the path. He pushes himself away from the girl's impulsive embrace and announces that they must not be seen together. This is hardly another of his gestures towards gentility; it is more fear for the mistress's esteem and his own false dignity should Dunyasha be found with him alone. So he saves face and returns to his cigar as Dunyasha trips off like a lady, attempting a refined little cough: 'The cigar has made my head ache . . .' At least she knows that it is impolite for a gentleman to smoke a cigar in a lady's presence. Thus, with her prim reprimand, this parody of gentility ends a mocking prelude to the entry of the master and mistress.

That so much time is given to such seemingly unimportant characters and their petty affairs may surprise us in view of the necessary economy of dialogue in naturalistic drama. But in *The Cherry Orchard* the servants are not to be thought of as constituting a 'subplot'. In as closely integrated a play as this, the concept is untenable. Apart from the social shifts which Yasha and Dunyasha represent, their scene contributes centrally to the rhythm and feeling, and therefore to the experienced meaning, of the whole. In the world of the cherry orchard there is no narrow focus. Yasha and Dunyasha tell us of the forces at work in the family as well as Lyubov and Gaev. Even more important, this light-weight opening exactly sets the serio-comic tone for the rest of the act.

Dunyasha's silly gentility, communicated to the audience by powder-puff and cigar smoke, represents the general transition within all their social attitudes, and the sense of change so far developed in the play is now pointed sharply by Lopahin. With all three elegantly dressed for an evening walk, Lopahin follows Lyubov and Gaev in, talking boldly to his friends. The significant words ring out after the subdued nature of the previous episode. 'You must make up your mind once for all – there's no time to lose.' Time presses. Action is wanted. As Lyubov and Gaev seat themselves comfortably on the vacant bench, two patterns of speech and movement indicate the conflict on the stage. While his listeners sit relaxed in some comfort after their walk, the merchant marches up and down uncomfortably in his smart brown boots and urges a decision: 'Yes or no?' Lyubov's reply immediately turns the issue aside and recalls the mood of the prelude, incidentally contrasting for us her honest reaction to Yasha's cigar with Dunyasha's affected one: 'Who is smoking such horrible cigars here?' But in her evasion, Lyubov is the lady still. Gaev, all 'softness and elegance'[1] in his summer straw hat, is equally evasive, but for the audience his reply is more ironically informative: the railway is so convenient, for they were able to go into town for lunch. The real meaning of the advance of mechanized life is measured against Gaev's innocent assessment of its advantages. Is to have lunch in town all that a railway is good for?

Lopahin is temporarily defeated, and sits despondently upon a tombstone. The heat of the evening forbids further argument. Sprawling on the bench with a yawn, Gaev announces that he would like to play billiards. Looking in her purse, his sister muses upon the way money slips through her fingers. She is not unconscious of the trouble Varya is having in order to stretch the house-keeping allowance while her mother squanders roubles in a restaurant. In any case, it was 'a wretched place with its music and the tablecloth smelling of soap'. To reinforce the point, Chekhov has her drop the purse so that all the money is scattered on the grass. It is, appropriately, Yasha who picks up the coins. So the conversation drifts on. At lunch, Gaev had drunk too much and, as usual, had talked too much. How ridiculous for him to talk to waiters about the Decadents![2] Again appropriately, it is Yasha who laughs.

Lopahin returns to the attack in more specific terms: 'Deriganov, the millionaire, means to buy your estate.' Like the naming of the day of the auction itself in Act I, the naming of the enemy makes the threat of losing the orchard more personal and more real. Gaev retaliates defensively with a suggestion that is not much of an advance upon his expectations in Act I, that their Yaroslavl aunt has promised them some money. Neither he nor

[1] Letter to Olga Knipper of 23 September 1903 (Garnett, p. 307).
[2] A derogatory term for the early *symbolistes* of the 'art for art's sake' movement in late nineteenth-century European art and literature. Whether Gaev approves of the Decadents we cannot be sure; the irony is that he talks of them at all. Although as a realist Chekhov laughed at Konstantin in *The Seagull*, he was not unimpressed by what the movement was attempting, and in *The Cherry Orchard* itself he assimilates its techniques in his own gentle, anti-didactic symbolism.

Lyubov speaks with much confidence, however, and Lopahin again introduces the idea of building summer cottages. This time he is charged with vulgarity, and, exasperated, he gets up to leave. Yet Lyubov is terrified of losing the security which she intuitively recognizes Lopahin to represent. He is the only one among them who can cope with the forces of the external world. As he hesitates before his exit, Lyubov's sudden moment of terror is dismissed by her lame compliment, 'With you here it's more cheerful, anyway', and as if peace were restored, Gaev resorts to his habitual comforter, a caramel. 'They say I've eaten up my property in caramels.' Hopelessly unrealistic though Gaev is, nevertheless this touch of self-criticism is attractive, and thus is the ambivalence sustained.

Not until this second act does Chekhov allow a complete exposition of Mme Ranevsky's story. In this his method is reminiscent of Ibsen's retrospective exposition, whereby details of the past are reserved until the time when the audience's familiarity with the persons of the play makes the information felt more personally, and the delay in retailing information about the past itself acts as a stimulus to the vitality of the present action. In the hiatus of Lopahin's silence, Lyubov remembers her 'sins'. Her husband died of champagne. She had the misfortune to love another man. Grisha drowned, and she ran away. She nursed her lover for three years in her villa in Mentone. He robbed and deserted her in Paris. As the orchard will be, the villa was sold to pay the debts incurred by her way of life. But the memory of this lover, it is clear, cannot be easily erased, and at this juncture, Chekhov has her produce another telegram, this time from her own pocket. She has already read this one and has been keeping it on her person. For as long as she carries it, Paris comes that much nearer. Only now does she tear it up, but slowly and uncertainly. The story of the Paris lover moves in parallel with that of the sale of the estate.

The group is silent as the audience listens to the careful tearing of the paper. And this sound merges with the nostalgic strains of music carried faintly across the fields. Ready for the crucial scene of the ball in Act III, Chekhov here plants information about 'our famous Jewish orchestra', oddly, and thinly, composed of 'four violins, a flute and a double bass'; it is 'still in existence', suggesting that it is somewhat old-fashioned in the music it plays.

From Lyubov, 'We ought to send for them one evening, and give a dance.' With characteristic subtlety, Chekhov leads us towards the party scene and simultaneously belittles all the lady's remorse for her sins. And to cap this, he has her turn on Lopahin with, 'How grey your lives are!', as if to justify her frivolity. The reproach, of course, is more appropriate to herself.

Lopahin accepts the criticism. He is still no more than the peasant he was when he was beaten with a stick by a drunken father. As in Act I, he likens himself to a pig,[1] emphatically denigrating himself. We are to remember his story of the stick and his image of himself as a pig when he enters in Act III to announce the result of the auction. But why does he not marry Varya?

LYUBOV. You ought to get married, my dear fellow.
LOPAHIN. Yes . . . that's true.
LYUBOV. You should marry our Varya, she's a good girl.
LOPAHIN. Yes.
LYUBOV. She's a good-natured girl.[2] She's busy all day long, and what's more, she loves you. And you have liked her for ever so long.
LOPAHIN. Well? I'm not against it . . . She's a good girl (*pause*).

Lopahin's desire to marry Varya is hardly overwhelming: that repeated phrase, 'a good girl', is altogether too lack-lustre. And Lopahin's pause, placed precisely, must also deny Varya hope for a successful outcome.

Gaev kills the topic by breaking into speech with the news that he has been offered a job in a bank. As he lounges in his elegant summer suit with an empty smile playing across his face, the idea of this feckless man's handling other people's money must strike us as preposterous. Even Lyubov recognizes how unthinkable it is. But Chekhov confirms the impression theatrically when at this moment he has old Firs come in with Gaev's overcoat and start to fuss over him like an old hen: 'You can't go on like this.' Gaev the financier cuts a sorry figure.

The presence of Firs and the comedy of his deafness maintains the wry level of the playing. But Chekhov has brought him into this rural scene for a reason other than the mockery of his master.

[1] *Svinya*, a word having the more severe connotations of 'swine' or 'hog'.
[2] Weak translation; Hingley translates, 'She's a nice simple creature.' *Prostich* implies 'from simple, ordinary people', but not necessarily of peasant stock, which tells us a little more of Varya's history. A man of Lopahin's class could marry her.

Act II

Unobtrusively, Firs's entrance re-introduces in high historical relief the sensation of time past and present change.

FIRS. I've had a long life. They were arranging my wedding before your papa was born . . . (*laughs*). I was the head footman before the emancipation came. I wouldn't consent to be set free then; I stayed on with the old master . . . (*a pause*). I remember what rejoicings they made and didn't know themselves what they were rejoicing over.
LOPAHIN. Those were fine old times. There was flogging anyway.

Lyubov winces. Lopahin's sarcasm hurts the cherry orchard family, but the audience smiles as the old man's vanity is deflated. Yet Firs is still thinking like a serf although the Emancipation was as long ago as forty years, and we recognize this affectionately. Narrow as his view of events is, we also see a truth in his automatic criticism of the change, for change must destroy in order to create.[1] However, Lopahin is of peasant origins too, but as a self-made man he sees both sides of the truth. His memories as a child are only of brutality: a punch in the face, a bleeding nose, a beating with a stick, public flogging. He reiterates his dry comments on the past throughout the play. Between Firs and Lopahin is a span of history and an age of experience. The immediate sale of the cherry orchard is placed precisely at the centre.

The sun is going down. The family group enlarges to include the younger members, Trofimov and Anya, with Varya trailing behind them as chaperone. Lyubov gently pulls the girls down to the seat beside her and embraces them both. An idyllic scene seems about to follow.

However, Lyubov's sense of unease on this hot evening, the particular frustration Lopahin feels about her inaction over the auction and his niggling displeasure at being reminded of his obligation to Varya, have already cut into the blissful atmosphere. Automatically, Lopahin vents some of his spleen on Trofimov,

---

[1] The audience of 1904 was well acquainted with the problems which followed the Emancipation. While the economic and technological revolution was under way, Westernization threw the peasant masses into new insecurity, and the sufferings of the people remained the greatest problem of the period up to the Revolution of 1917. Not only were the peasants burdened by taxes and payments for their land, the price of their freedom, but the famine of 1891–2 decimated those who were trying to live on holdings which barely supported them at the best of times. Even those who escaped to the towns became the victims of uncontrolled industrial growth. A new slavery succeeded the old.

for he is the one man whom he cannot understand. A practical man, one for whom time is money, Lopahin is temperamentally the antithesis of this eternal student who grows old, does no work and stays poor. 'He'll soon be fifty, and he's still a student.' It is spoken half in joke, but it is enough to rile Trofimov.

In some heat, Trofimov offers his own judgment of the merchant and snaps at him in his own pseudo-academic terms: 'Just as in the economy of nature a wild beast is of use, who devours everything that comes in his way, so you too have your use.' Trofimov's pedantic language and posture strike the listeners on the stage and in the auditorium as funny, and the sting of his criticism is soothed. But although Trofimov too is half joking, within his joke the barb of truth remains. Lopahin is no wild beast: throughout the play he repeatedly reveals an impassioned love for the land he grew up in. But hidden in the comedy is also the formal subject of Chekhov's whole play, 'the economy of nature', and Lopahin, his money and his instincts are indeed an integral part of that economy.

The ladies encourage Trofimov to continue talking, and fully within character the student is thus drawn into his major speech in the play. As we know from his letters, Chekhov shared with Trofimov many of his views on the passivity of the intelligentsia,[1] but he is careful to ensure that the audience remains objective about what Trofimov is saying, and there is no hint that he is his author's mouthpiece. It is entirely natural that a student should be the one to make a didactic and polemical speech, and, the more eager Petya is, it is natural that what he is saying in his squeaky voice should be continuously deflated by the amusement on the faces of his older listeners, and by their winks and glances. Only Anya, of Trofimov's own generation, and rather infatuated with him in any case, listens in wonder and says nothing. The general mockery is confirmed when Trofimov is rewarded by remarks like Lyubov's kindly, but uncomprehending, 'How clever you are, Petya!' and Lopahin's sarcastic 'Fearfully clever!' Above all, the spectator may not forget that the comments on

[1] In Chekhov's first version of this speech, Trofimov's lines which described the condition of the working-class and its degradation were censored, together with those which declared that the upper classes were parasites (see Hingley, vol. III, p. 321). Garnett's translation is of the speech which Chekhov substituted for performance.

human pride come from a self-regarding youth who has himself achieved nothing. 'One must give up glorification of self. One should work, and nothing else' sounds hollow from a person who knows only how to sponge on others. We allow Lopahin his stricture from a man who has worked all his life without the benefit of an education like Trofimov's.

It is true that, below all the ridicule, Trofimov in his clumsy way is articulating the human issues that lie in the situation, and at this midway point in the play no audience can be unaware of them. It is the family's pride, blind, unthinking, even 'mystical' as Trofimov says, that has made them bankrupt and the orchard sterile. Nevertheless, while this notion lingers in our minds, substantiated by our own cumulative sense of the family's false dignity after two acts of the play, Trofimov's own pride is also suspect. 'Humanity progresses, perfecting its powers. Everything that is beyond its ken now will one day become familiar and comprehensible, only we must work, we must with all our powers aid the seeker after truth.' As Trofimov, the 'moth-eaten gentle-man' who has twice been sent down from the university, blinks breathlessly behind his steel spectacles, the audience has hardly listened to his clichés, and it can understand when the stage audience grows bored. Even though the boredom we see warns us to listen more intently, only a deliberate misreading of the text can make Trofimov's speech into one of prophecy. Maxim Gorky early recognized the fallacy of taking this abstract idealism at face value,[1] but Soviet directors continue to inflate this and other speeches of Trofimov to heroic proportions.[2] His indict-ment of Russian intellectuals[3] who 'air their theories' while they

[1] *The Note-books of Anton Tchekhov together with Reminiscences of Tchekhov by Maxim Gorky*, trans. S. S. Koteliansky and L. Woolf (Richmond, 1921), p. 24.

[2] See the discussion of this issue in H. Popkin, *Anton Chekhov: The Three Sisters* (New York, 1965), p. 10: 'Western criticism tends to find Chekhov more impersonal and to regard the optimistic elegies as speeches in character, not orations in behalf of the dramatist. The difference in interpretation is readily apparent in production. Trofimov is rather impressive and almost heroic in the Slovenian National Theater of Ljubljana and in the Moscow Art Theater, but his weaknesses are more evident when Jean Louis Barrault undertakes the role at the Théâtre de France.'
The audiences of 1904 would have recognized Trofimov's thinking as that of one of the 'intellectuals' himself. It was the kind of thinking that followed the assas-sination of Czar Alexander II in 1881 and the repressive measures which resulted. The period just before the 1905 Revolution was one of great, if vague, hope. See M. Slonim, *From Chekhov to the Revolution: Russian Literature 1900–1917* (New York, 1962), p. 71.

'do practically nothing' and ignore the squalor about them is ostensibly a straight-from-the-shoulder attack on the Muscovite audiences of the time; but since the description of the intelligentsia exactly fits Trofimov himself, Chekhov has, as usual, managed to undermine the argument for comedy. As he does with Irina and the Baron in *Three Sisters*, Chekhov makes a point of putting the cry for work into the mouths of characters who are never seen to do a stroke.

Nevertheless, in the quiet of the evening, as Trofimov finally comes to a stop, his voice of pained appeal has touched a spring in Lopahin. The merchant, still rather in irritation, but now more reflectively, begins to remind the company that he at least works. 'You know, I get up at five o'clock in the morning, and I work from morning to night . . .' It is not lack of work, Chekhov implies, but lack of vision that limits them. For Lopahin too, in spite of his business activities, has had his vision. 'Oh! Lord, thou hast given us immense forests, boundless plains, the widest horizons, and living here we ourselves ought really to be giants.' These words, coming from so efficient and circumspect a worker, sound a more genuine note than Trofimov's. The practical man can also love his Russia, and there is more poetry in Lopahin's soul than in the impractical student's. Yet Lopahin is not any the less a victim of material pressures, certainly no giant to command his environment.

The scene, the most static among Chekhov's major plays, has passed into one of ironic discussion drama. But, more than this, an elusive lyricism is also present, one not inappropriate to this resting place in the action. The family's thinking has reached stalemate, and Epihodov passes across the back of the stage strumming his mournful tune on his guitar. It seems to sum up the common mood.

LYUBOV (*dreamily*). There goes Epihodov.
ANYA (*dreamily*). There goes Epihodov.

Their tones echo each other and the guitar. Every touch is designed to make the scene's lyricism more fragile. Gaev begins softly to make a speech to nature, to its beauty and to its indifference to life and death. Nature – 'thou dost unite within thee life and death! Thou dost give life and dost destroy!' The heart of Chekhov's truth lies there too, but Gaev's quavering voice reduces the impact of his meaning and feeling, as the girls make clear.

VARYA (*in a tone of supplication*). Uncle!

ANYA. Uncle, you are at it again!

The omnipotent divinity of nature has been made a jest by its human creation, and Chekhov laughs at his own most profound thoughts. Gaev dries up like the lonely old comic actor Svetlovidov in Chekhov's *A Swan Song*: 'a squeezed lemon, a miserable nonentity, a rusty old nail'.[1]

Thus the mood is lyrical but still light, and '*all sit plunged in thought*' exactly as others did at the beginning of the act. The effect is cyclical. The audience strains in the silence, and hears only Firs's husky muttering as he stands awkwardly against the skyline upstage. Suspended, we may wonder in what direction Chekhov will take us next. He takes an extraordinary risk, and comes up with the unexpected. '*Suddenly there is a sound in the distance, as it were from the sky – the sound of a breaking harp-string, mournfully dying away.*' For purposes of practical theatre, Chekhov is planting, familiarizing us with, the sound that is to be used to greater effect at the end of the last act, so that it will not then disrupt the experience of the whole by its strangeness, but tie this moment with that. In the present silence, the merest pluck of a 'cello string would electrify the tense audience. Here, the sharp, piercing, uncertain noise lingering on the air miraculously captures the mixed mood of wonder and regret, and fixes the tableau like an unexpected snapshot. The characters on stage are as startled as we, and by trying severally to explain the sound they speak for us; this too will save the need for explanation in Act IV. But, with each isolated in his own world, each is incapable of seeing the whole; only the audience is invited to do that. Lopahin explains it scientifically, as might be expected: a cable in the mines must have broken. Gaev offers the improbable suggestion of a heron; Trofimov counters this knowingly with an owl, symbolic of foreboding. Anya is seen silently to sob a little. With a shudder, Lyubov expresses merely her feelings of uneasiness. Her 'What's that?' makes the unreal effect more real within the dramatic framework: she expresses our feelings too, for that incomprehensible, seemingly supernatural, sound effect strangely binds the

[1] Trans. Hingley, vol. I, p. 45.

family and the scene with the audience. As music might, it introduces an aural symbol of time; it traps in our heads time past
and time passing. Yet it also signifies the break with the past.
To do all this, it must, like the artifice of the theatre itself, seem to
stop time.

After a new pause, Firs conveys some such notion in words
when he takes his turn to comment. With a curious clarity in his
voice, he is heard to say that similar effects were experienced when
the serfs were freed. Comic as he is, this ancient man speaks with
some truth, and his words recall the disorder, dispossession and
famine that followed the Emancipation. With almost primitive
superstition, Firs implies that, in his view, the omen is bad. But
the past is irretrievable. Thus the single sound of the breaking
string is encouraged to grow in the imagination long after the
stage effect has died away.

In addition, it redoubles its meaning by being juxtaposed with
a visual incident which is equally unexpected. The unnatural
sound will finally signify the threat of things to come. The company is preparing to leave as a passer-by, a shocking figure looking
like a tramp and rather drunk, stumbles into their midst. When
the tension is at its highest, Chekhov disturbs everybody with
an uncalled-for entrance. What can the 'Wayfarer' represent?
Perhaps one of Firs's unhappy dispossessed peasants. Yet his
polite speech and forage cap may make him one of the landless
gentry. It is, either way, the image of real, ugly poverty that now
faces them, and from his tone he might be Gaev himself in the
future. He asks the way, then wildly utters a line or two of
rhetorical poetry, 'My brother, my suffering brother! . . .' In his
drunkenness he seems to be speaking for all mankind, but, we
comfort ourselves, only as drunks sometimes do. Suddenly he
turns and lurches at Varya and asks for money. The notion of
borrowing returns yet again. Varya shrieks, and Lyubov in a
panic hurriedly fumbles in her purse. 'Here, take this . . . I've no
silver. No matter – here's gold for you.' Lyubov is able to make
her vice a virtue, but underlying her reckless generosity is the
whole story of her hidden guilt towards the poor, and in particular the serfs at one time under her care.[1] And after the intruder has gone, Varya between her sobs fills in the hard facts of

[1] Valency writes of the need of the cultivated classes to make self-sacrificing gestures
like Lyubov's: 'At no time in the course of the century were the economically

life in the family: 'The servants have nothing to eat, and you gave him gold!' Against the background of his own idyllic scene, Chekhov probes the diseased parts, examines the past and foretells the future. In this way the spectator is made to feel the present chaos of values.

Laughter helps a release of feeling, and the pace picks up. In the deepening twilight, the gathering again prepares to return to the house, and the sense of doom lifts somewhat. Lyubov jokingly congratulates Varya on having found a husband, whereupon the girl again dissolves in tears: but we are by now ready to smile at her outbursts. Partly to disguise his own embarrassment, partly to cheer her up, Lopahin makes another joke of her nun-like propensities by addressing her as Ophelia, comically mispronouncing the name and misquoting Shakespeare.[1] Against the general laughter, we may reflect that their love can be only as tragically fruitless as that of Hamlet and Ophelia. So this bizarre assortment of people ambles off into the night. However, just as they have gone, we hear Lopahin's same clear, warning voice, the same heard upon his entrance. 'Let me remind you, ladies and gentlemen: on the 22nd of August the cherry orchard will be sold. Think about that! Think about it!' A fine example of a strongly pointed exit speech in the old tradition of sensational theatre – if it were not for the fact that there is no one either on or off the stage who is listening to it. It therefore has the properties of a throw-away line, in which Lopahin's tone of urgency is mixed with both disgust and jocularity. He is afraid to say the wrong thing, having been rebuffed on this point twice before. Now he too, bringing up the rear of the party as it picks its way back to the house in the dark, has gone. But we in the audience recognize the renewed insistence on the actuality of the sale, marked again by an authentic date. It must be soon now.

Trofimov and Anya are alone at last in the twilight. There is no sign of any response to Lopahin's threat from the young people,

privileged wholly free from guilt-feeling with respect to the labouring classes which sustained them' (Valency, p. 20).

[1] Magarshack argues that Lopahin shows his contempt for what he thinks is Varya's refusal to marry beneath her, by vulgarizing 'Ophelia' as 'Okhmelia' and misquoting Hamlet's line as 'Okhmelia, O nymph, remember me in your prayers!' (Magarshack, pp. 278–9).

only an irrelevant laugh from Anya, pleased that the intruder has frightened the others away. Like a child's, her tears have rapidly given way to joy. Varya and Lyubov hope for a rich marriage for Anya, but in her consternation Varya has forgotten her duties as chaperone.[1] Anya, only wanting to be left alone with Trofimov, is delighted.

In these circumstances, with a wooded setting, a romantic moon rising, a balmy evening, a convenient bench, and a young man and woman, the audience expects a love scene in the old tradition, and Trofimov himself talks of love. But Chekhov has his anti-romantic surprises in store. The young couple may embody hope for the future, but this is not the pair upon whom to place much trust, either to rebuild upon the ruins of the orchard or to make love. Just as Lopahin evaded an emotional commitment to Varya, Trofimov moves uneasily away from Anya as she seats herself expectantly upon the bench. Instead of speaking words of endearment, he begins to address an imaginary throng of people as from a platform, speaking over the girl's head, and announcing confidently that they are 'above love'. Trofimov is posturing, partly out of his disgust at Lyubov's affair in Paris, partly from his own youthful inadequacy. He falls back upon the style of speech he knows best, and his tone is the very opposite of what Anya anticipates. 'Forward! We go forward irresistibly towards the bright star that shines yonder in the distance. Forward! Do not lag behind, friends!' He speaks like a soldier, and his voice reaches Anya as if she were an army of militant idealists all of whom look exactly like Trofimov himself. However, her momentary disappointment is replaced by her unquestioning admiration of him, and she responds appropriately by clapping her hands and crying, 'How well you speak!' We observe that, ironically, she emphasizes the manner and not the matter of his speech, and that her one pair of hands mocks the thunderous applause his way of speaking seems to expect.

Anya is always animated like a child,[2] always on her toes

---

[1] In an earlier variant (see Hingley, vol. III, p. 323), Chekhov made it clear that Varya did not think it right for Anya to be left alone with a young man. When Trofimov later teases Varya, it is, according to Gorky, out of boredom, but her conservative attitude of protectiveness towards Anya would provide a better motivation for the bantering of an advanced thinker like Trofimov, and his contempt for Varya here would support this view.

[2] 'Anya is first and foremost a child, light-hearted all through, knowing nothing of

running and bouncing, spontaneous with her bright smiles, and she makes her gesture of clapping hands unaffectedly. But try as she may to please this clever young man, she herself is not above love. After a deliciously ironic pause, she prompts her supralover with the pathetic coquetry of 'It is divine here today.' Trofimov in a dead voice answers as if he had heard an irrelevant question from the back of the gallery: 'Yes, it's glorious weather.' If Anya's 'divine' expressed her feelings, Trofimov's 'glorious' means less than it says. Again leading him on, she asks him how it is that he has made her less fond of the orchard. Doubtless she is naively trying to please and catch her man; she means to flatter him. She is telling him plainly enough that it is he who has all her love, and that she will follow him wherever he goes. Yet, through this troubling remark, Chekhov does indeed intend us to know that a girl of seventeen, with the shallow roots of her extreme youth, must inevitably be fickle in her loyalty to the orchard.

Unluckily for Anya, her prompting encourages him to take up his prophetic theme again. He does so with the most entranced, and the most abstract, speech in the play: 'All Russia is our garden.'[1] From the lips of this odd-looking young man, this eternal student with a wispy beard, are heard the words that are part history, part politics, and yet part vision, part poetry. It is a set-piece, spoken in the dusk in rapt tones, a patriotic speech such as the audiences of the time of Nicholas II would have expected at this place in an Ibsenite problem play.[2]

Think only, Anya, your grandfather, and great-grandfather, and all your ancestors were slave-owners – the owners of living souls – and from every cherry in the orchard, from every leaf, from every trunk there are human creatures looking at you. Cannot you hear their voices?

life, and not once crying except in Act II, and then she only has tears in her eyes' (Chekhov in a letter to Olga Knipper, 21 October 1903, in Garnett, p. 327):

[1] The Russian word *sad* is of course the same as that in the title of the play, 'orchard', and should be translated so.

[2] Several critics take the play to be socio-political, interpreting this speech as socialist-realism. Simmons is characteristic of these: 'In these words . . . lies the real symbolism of the loss of the cherry orchard – Chekhov's favorite theme of the destruction of beauty by those who are blind to it. Trofimov expresses another favorite theme of Chekhov, that of hard work as a solution for the ills of Russia. Even the merchant Lopakhin . . . is a lover of beauty. But Lopakhin, whom Chekhov regarded as the central character, also destroys beauty if it gets in the way of his accumulation of wealth' (Simmons, p. 616).

For Trofimov, every tree in the orchard is a symbol of the bad social order of the past. We are to remember these words when the axe is heard in the last act. It is not one particular estate that is being swept away, but a chapter in human history.

Nevertheless, Chekhov, more as a Bernard Shaw would have done, is using this strikingly contentious speech to question the very attitude which prompts it. He is playing his sensitive audience carefully. Trofimov, the representative of the new generation, comes to his point. If they are 'to begin to live in the present', they must make a clean break with the past. This is the truth of the matter in the eyes of a young man for whom the orchard is not part of his own flesh. Sitting in our Olympian seats in the theatre, it is for us to weigh these feelings with Lyubov's. When she awoke to the orchard each morning, happiness awoke with her. For her, the orchard stood for peace and love. Now it is as if we are to choose between her values and Trofimov's, or, by comic extension, between those of the superannuated Firs and those of the precocious Yasha. Of course, neither is 'right', and we perceive that this is not a play of moral choices. The spontaneity of Anya's response to Trofimov's polemics might have warned us. Nor can we miss the error of Trofimov's conclusion: breaking with the past does not expiate it; rather, it only destroys some of the living tissue of the present.

In naive ecstasy Anya gives Trofimov her word that she will 'leave' the house. Throw the keys in the well! the young man enjoins. Be free, free as the wind! Happiness is coming, Anya! The moment is idyllic, charming, ridiculous. And to match it, Chekhov tries an unusual effect to conclude his scene, employing a gamut of aural and visual effects suitable to the realism of the picture-frame stage. As Trofimov runs off pulling Anya upstage towards the river, Epihodov is again heard playing his comically soulful guitar. At the same time, the moon is rising, as Anya's line reminds us, bathing the poplar trees in silver light. While the curtain falls inch by inch, Varya's plaintive voice is heard calling, 'A-anya! A-a-anya!', first nearer then farther. A generally lyrical scene ends with an excess of lyricism in preparation for what is yet to come, and a succession of evocative devices gathers great cumulative strength. The effect is not one of diffusion, because our eyes and ears are entirely on Anya, whose name we hear and whose figure we see all in silvery white running away from the orchard, as if she were the lost girl of the folk tales.[1] Anya escapes into the future, leaving the wistful image of her innocence lingering in the theatre. And from Act I we recall her mother Lyubov and Lyubov's mother, women all in white in a white orchard, as they fled into the past.

[1] W. B. Yeats used this ghostly effect in *The Land of Heart's Desire* (1894), in which a fairy child tempts Mary Bruin away from her home in a setting of singing and dancing figures; and it is also to be found in J. M. Barrie's *Mary Rose* (1920), in which the heroine is drawn away to fairyland by 'a celestial music' that calls her name.

Act Three

The elusive, wistful end of Act II, mistily set in a scene of natural beauty, touched with intimations of a dreamy future, charmed by the innocence of two young people, soft and delicate in tone at the end – all this is sharply dispelled for Chekhov's climactic third act. The new action is noisy, jarring and shot through with ironies of thought and feeling. From the start we feel the contrast as the curtain rises on an animated, brilliantly lit and quickly crowded scene. We are back in the house, in the middle of a party, yet at the same time thrust again among the worrying realities of the present. It is the most ceremonial scene Chekhov could devise, using nearly the whole assembly of players and even bringing on stage a few representatives of the rest of the community. It is the scene of Madame's promised ball, and Chekhov has arranged it to coincide with the day of the auction, the sale of the very place which houses the festivities. In 1906, Meyerhold expressed the scene's ambivalence exactly:

The author conceives the act thus: the leitmotif of the act is Ranevskaya's presentiment of impending disaster (the sale of the cherry orchard). All around her, people somehow live vacantly. Here are the complacent people, moving to the monotonous rattle of a Jewish orchestra, and, in a nightmarish whirl, circling in some dull contemporary dance in which there is no enthusiasm, no excitement, no grace, not even lust. These smug individuals are unaware that the ground they dance on is slipping from under their feet. Only Ranevskaya foresees Misfortune, and waits for it restlessly, and for a moment stops the moving circle – this nightmarish dance of puppets in a farce.[1]

To make the ironies work, Chekhov borrows from the first act of *Three Sisters* the idea of a double stage made up of two acting areas, which extend the proscenium-arch stage by creating

[1] Vsevolod Meyerhold, 'Naturalistic Theater and Theater of Mood', trans. J. C. Vining, from *Teatr. Kniga o novom teatre. Sbornik statej* (St Petersburg, 1908), quoted in Jackson, p. 64.

a frame-within-a-frame. The difference here is that the real audience will be conscious of a stage audience looking through the upstage frame, so that the main acting area within the downstage frame will seem to be the truly inner world. The action we shall see most clearly will represent the life within a life. Like the platform of the Elizabethan theatre, the 'forestage' will be the area where a character can voice his more intimate thoughts at closer proximity to the audience, moving over a focal space in a scene which can nevertheless remain in a state of constant flux. The nearer setting shows the drawing-room of the palatial house, but upstage there is a wide arch through which a more brightly lit ballroom draws us into the party. In the drawing-room itself we shall be loaded with the anxieties of the present, while the action in the more formal ballroom beyond represents a parody of the gay past, the fading sights and sounds of innumerable parties on the estate from generation to generation. The sounds pull us into the past, where, indeed, from time to time we escape with members of the family.

At the rise of the curtain, a dance is in full swing in the ballroom and the forestage itself is empty. In Act I we saw only the nursery; now we sense the true scale of the house. We see the brilliance of the chandeliers and the fine furnishings. Chekhov referred to the grandeur of the room's style in a letter to Stanislavsky: 'The furniture is ancient, stylish, solid; ruin and debt have not affected the surroundings.'[1] But as we catch glimpses of the figures dancing past the archway and listen to their shouts and laughter, we also hear how thin and squeaky is the music of the Jewish band with its four fiddles, a flute and a double bass, the band to which Gaev referred. Hardly an appropriate ensemble for the dance in progress, a *grand rond*, a stately processional dance which calls for a full orchestra. Above all the noise we recognize Pishtchik's booming voice as he calls the steps in a breathless and laboured French: 'Promenade à une paire!' It seems that in the absence of Gaev as master of the house, Pishtchik has appointed himself master of ceremonies. He is very excited and quite delighted with his own performance, yet in himself he constitutes the most subversive critic of the solemnity of the dance.

Meyerhold recognized the importance of the dancing to the

[1] 5 November 1903 (Friedland, p. 161).

rhythm of the action, and he wrote an appreciative letter to the author.

> Your play is abstract, like a Tchaikovsky symphony. The stage director must above all feel it with his ear. In the third act, against the background of the stupid 'stomping' – this 'stomping' must be heard – Horror enters unnoticed by anyone.
> 'The cherry orchard is sold.' They dance. 'Sold.' They dance. And so to the end. When one reads the play, the third act makes the same kind of impression as the ringing in the sick man's ears in your story *Typhus*. Some kind of itch. Gaiety in which sounds of death are heard. In this act there is something Maeterlinck-like, frightful.

But he hastened to criticize the treatment of the scene by the M.A.T.

> In the Moscow Art Theatre one did not get such an impression from the third act. The background was not concentrated enough and at the same time not remote enough. In the forefront: the story with the billiard cue and the tricks. Separately. All this did not form a chain of 'stomping'. And in the meantime all the 'dancing' people are unconcerned and do not sense the harm. The tempo of this act was too slow in the Art Theatre. They wanted to convey boredom. That's a mistake. One must picture unconcern. There's a difference. Unconcern is more active. Then the tragedy of the act becomes more concentrated.[1]

As the ironies of the scene begin to be felt, suddenly the grand chain swoops through the arch and bounces with high steps round the stage and out again, the shouts and laughter swelling to a crescendo and then falling away. We see the whole company, as it were, at once, our eye scanning the general incongruity of the grotesque scene. Each couple is carefully arranged to make an ironic point. In the lead, as the antithesis of elegance, are the two clowns of the show, Pishtchik and Charlotta. The big man[2] in top-boots, his red face glistening with sweat, seems to rock the floor, and the stiff-backed governess in a black dress and checked trousers, 'the typical puppet theatre costume',[3] half mocks her ridiculous partner with her gawky strides and bland, expressionless face. With a student's gracelessness, and looking as moth-eaten as ever, Trofimov inappropriately leads Lyubov:

---

[1] Letter of 8 May 1904, trans. N. Beeson, and quoted in *The Tulane Drama Review* 25, vol. 9, no. 1 (New Orleans, Fall, 1964), pp. 24–5.
[2] See p. 256, n. 2, above.
[3] According to Meyerhold's report of the M.A.T. production (Jackson, p. 64).

a man who is above love is likely to be above dancing too. Anya, with whom we might have expected to see Trofimov, is unsentimentally paired with a complete stranger in a shabby uniform, as is Varya. The girls are not allowed to dance with their lovers, although at any rate their partners are in uniform. The reason is clear later, when Firs remarks, 'In old days we used to have generals, barons and admirals dancing at our balls, and now we send for the post-office clerk and the station master and even they're not overanxious to come.' The Post-Office Clerk and the Station Master constitute a cruelly subversive detail which points directly to the collapse of the old order. Varya is wiping away tears as usual: she is crying for no immediately apparent reason. She is the same Varya, her tears finally destroying the sympathy which might belong to a melancholy heroine.[1] Dunyasha, dressed like a lady, looks more at home than her mistress. When Pishtchik finally cries, 'Les cavaliers à genoux!', we get a glimpse of him as he struggles to the floor on his knee before an impassive Charlotta. A motley company of *cavaliers* indeed! The parody of a majestic ball is amazingly detailed.

The music stops and the noise dies down. After the boisterous movement, there is a complete change of pace. Firs, a mute testimony to the standards of the past, shuffles his way slowly across the drawing-room floor. As might have been appropriate fifty years before, he is wearing a formal tail-coat, having changed from his former livery to mark the special occasion. Faded as he is, he is too good for the scene before our eyes, and the bottle on the tray of glasses he carries is one of soda-water, no longer of champagne.

Coming downstage towards us into the drawing-room, the leader of the *grand rond* reappears with Trofimov. Pishtchik is obviously grateful to have relinquished his duties. He mops his brow and the back of his neck, and speaks in short, breathless sentences. 'I am a full-blooded man;[2] I have already had two strokes. Dancing's hard work for me . . .' If he is all wind, so is his party conversation, full of homespun proverbs and empty tags.

---

[1] 'Varya's a cry-baby by nature, and her tears shouldn't depress the audience': Chekhov in a letter to Nemirovich-Danchenko, 23 October 1903 (Hingley, vol. III, p. 326).

[2] Hingley's translation is more accurate: 'I've got high blood pressure.'

He sinks exhausted into a chair and turns to the topic always on his mind, his debts. In this, Chekhov has him speak in lieu of Mme Ranevsky to recall the real and pressing issues underlying the scene. But like Varya's blubbing, Pishtchik's reiteration of his worries undercuts the pathos of his situation. In any case, still speaking of money, he drops off to sleep with a snore and promptly grunts himself awake again. With his only listener a destitute young visionary who despises wealth, Pishtchik's performance is in no danger of a melodramatic emphasis.

Although because of the party the whole house is more superficially lively than it was during the homecoming of Act I (the music soon strikes up again, the sound of people playing billiards is heard from the adjoining room, short bursts of laughter come from the ballroom), the personal problems are more acute than before. The party has been flung at a wholly inappropriate time, as much a thoughtless as a defiant gesture by Lyubov. Varya, released by her Station Master, has escaped from the dance, looking for sanctuary. Trofimov insensitively joins in the family joke with a teasing sarcasm, 'Madame Lopahin!' Convinced that the 'nun-like' Varya does not want him to be alone with Anya, he taunts her with her own shortcomings in the matter of an amorous relationship.[1] She retreats, too upset to prolong an argument with Trofimov: 'Here we have hired musicians and nothing to pay them!'

With all the trivial conversation, the subject has quickly returned to money, and it is Trofimov's turn to make his contribution. Always the critic of the past, he tells Pishtchik that with all the time he has wasted in his search for money, he 'might in the end have turned the world upside down'. But Pishtchik is not listening. Instead, he plucks a name out of the air, as is his habit, and announces impressively that Nietzsche suggests forging banknotes. Trofimov pricks up his ears: philosophy is his prerogative. 'Why, have you read Nietzsche?' No, as we might have expected, it was his daughter Dashenka who reported this extraordinary advice. A short sequence, this, of delightful human comedy, playing off naivety against illiteracy, and gently pursuing illogicality to an absurd extreme, one in which both men look foolish. In the only way it could have done, the incident

---

[1] See the discussion of the motivation for this teasing on p. 290, n. 1, above.

collapses completely into farce. Pishtchik feels in his coat for his borrowed mortgage money, and it has gone. A cry, tears, a frantic search through his pockets. Then he finds some banknotes in a tattered lining. Laughter. Thus is this unhappy man's anguish over his finances viewed through Chekhovian eyes.

We have been reminded of money, of material things, but about the major issue we are to remain in suspense until the end of the act: has the orchard been sold ? Chekhov now increases the tension, for we are to understand that this is the important day, 22 August. Lyubov comes in with Charlotta, and in spite of the worries of the moment, Madame still wears her gracious smile and poses beautifully as she sits. Defensively, perhaps, she is humming the Lezginka, a popular Russian dance tune. But while her singing recalls the pleasant times of parties long ago, she also reveals that she cannot take her mind off the auction: 'Why is Leonid so long?' Gaev's absence is thus accounted for: he is presumably at the sale. Still thinking of their financial crisis, Lyubov graciously asks Dunyasha to offer the 'orchestra' some tea, but even as she speaks, she shows that she is aware of the incongruity of celebrating the day of disaster with a party. 'Well, never mind!' The vapid remark suggests her despair. In a quick sequence of four or five apparently unrelated thoughts, Lyubov's stream of consciousness characterizes the contradictions within the woman and of the time. Downstage and close to us, she sits apart as the music plays gaily, a public figure in the private world of her anxiety. Others circle past her and about her, while her still figure embodies the inescapable issues of the moment.

For a few seconds while the audience concentrates on Lyubov, the pace has slowed, but the solemnity of her situation has triggered Chekhov's levity. Charlotta in her buffoon's costume hands Pishtchik a pack of cards with a flourish, and his childlike excitement at the prospect of a party-game runs through the assembly. With noise and laughter, everyone gathers inside the arch of the **drawing-room** to watch Charlotta at her tricks. Farce is again to counterpoint the suspense, and if it were not for Lyubov's prominent exclusion from the group, our thoughts would be distracted from the auction.[1]

---

[1] Meyerhold criticized Stanislavsky for confusing the point with excessive detail: 'The director of the Art Theater showed how the harmony of this act can be destroyed. Out of the [episode with the] tricks he made a whole scene with all kinds

'Ein, zwei, drei!' Charlotta's German accent makes her more of a magician than she is, and she invites 'my dear Mr Pishtchik' to look in his coat pocket, the one from which he had a moment before lost his precious roubles. There he finds the very card he had thought of. 'Fancy that now!' His utter amazement at these fateful cards is indistinguishable from his amazement in Act IV when valuable clay is discovered on his land. For Pishtchik's is a world of chaos and disorder, in which good and bad luck is dealt out arbitrarily like a card from a pack. His attitude to fortune farcically reflects that of all his generation in the play.

The younger generation, represented by Trofimov, stands sceptically by. This self-declared young realist is also above magic, and Charlotta senses the presence of an enemy. She turns on him for her next victim and asks him to name the top card. Ominously he names the card of death, the queen of spades. 'It is!' cries Charlotta, and she promptly turns back to Pishtchik and asks another card of him. In perpetual astonishment, and half in love with this fascinating lady, he coyly names the ace of hearts. She produces the right one again, claps her hands and the cards are gone. A round of applause and laughter from all the onlookers.

Now it is ventriloquism. Charlotta strikes an attitude and speaks to a mysterious stranger beneath the floor: 'You are my perfect ideal', and she is charmed to hear the voice reply, 'And I greatly admire you too, madam'. This is the Governess again wryly expressing her lonely spinsterhood.[1] As if used to seeing travelling fairground people and their performances, the Station Master makes it clear to everyone that he is familiar with the trick: 'The lady ventriloquist – bravo!' 'Fancy that now!' explodes again from the open-mouthed Pishtchik; 'I'm simply in love with you'. This Charlotta shrugs off with, 'Guter Mensch, aber schlechter Musikant', which might be loosely interpreted as 'You're a good fellow, but as a lover you're a poor performer'. Trofimov laughs (he shows that he knows German too), but these words fit him as well as Pishtchik.

of bits and pieces. It is long-drawn-out and complicated. The audience is forced to concentrate on it and loses track of the leitmotif of the act. And when it is over, the background melody is remembered, but the leitmotif has been muffled and has disappeared' (Jackson, p. 65).

[1] In an earlier version of the play, Charlotta also played a trick in Act I. In this she contrived a knock on the door, and this, she said, was made by the gentleman to whom she was engaged. See Hingley, vol. III, p. 323.

Charlotta has already started her third trick. How long can Chekhov sustain this diversion? But the last one is *la pièce de résistance*, and, oblique as they are, the tricks are each time more pointed. She picks up a rug from a chair and offers to *auction* it, no less. 'Doesn't anyone want to buy it?' No response. 'Ein, zwei, drei!' and the rug is swept aside disclosing Anya standing there holding back her laughter. Was it Anya who was up for sale? She laughs, bobs a quick curtsy and runs to her mother, thus bringing the silent Lyubov back into the stage composition. Again Charlotta raises the rug, and in an exquisite visual effect this time we see behind it Varya with a sad face, brushing away a tear. Doubtless as children the two girls had played this game in the nursery with their governess and their mother countless times, and countless times Lyubov had applauded them with a 'Bravo! Bravo!' The wistful past is vividly recalled, and the sudden contrast between the innocent Anya and the worried Varya is unmistakable. Charlotta coquettishly throws the rug at Pishtchik, who chases her off gasping out his eternal 'Fancy that now!' Lyubov's smile remains fixed, but her voice is flat as she remembers the auction that will bargain with the lives of herself and her children. 'And still Leonid doesn't come.'

The joke is over. We learn from Varya that the wealthy aunt in Yaroslavl sent some money, but not enough even to pay the interest. The object of the scene is now made plain: 'My fate is being sealed today, my fate . . .' And associated with the future of the orchard as usual is the future of Varya. Trofimov's teasing 'Madame Lopahin' promptly turns Lyubov's thoughts to the marriage of her foster-daughter. They all agree that Lopahin is 'a good man'; what is she waiting for? Varya has heard this so often, as we have, and her businesslike tongue in exasperation goes straight to the point: 'I can't make him an offer myself.' And, almost to herself, she argues that he is too busy making money to pay any attention to her. This may be partly true, but we have heard enough from Lopahin to know that his reluctance is more complicated than Varya allows. Unlike Trofimov, Lopahin is conservative to a fault in his personal relationships, as his constant reminder of his origins conveys: he has erected an impenetrable social barrier around Varya. It is one thing for Lopahin to tell Lyubov what to do with her property, another to tell her daughter what to do with her life. The audience is never to feel that marriage is the simple solution to Varya's problem. As for the girl herself, she would rather go into a convent. Or so she says.

Trofimov's sarcastic 'What bliss!' breaks the tension, and Yasha's momentary appearance to announce that the ill-fated Epihodov has broken a billiards cue completes the deflation. Yet all this is a distraction from the sale of the orchard, to which important business Lyubov now returns more anxiously than before. 'Why is it Leonid's not here?'

By turning to Trofimov for sympathy, Lyubov turns to the wrong person. He stands there in silence as if passing judgment on the older generation; youth confronts age.

TROFIMOV. What does it matter whether the estate is sold today or not? That's all done with long ago. There's no turning back, the path is overgrown. Don't worry yourself, my dear Lyubov Andrey-evna. You mustn't deceive yourself; for once in your life you must face the truth!

LYUBOV. What truth? You see where the truth lies, but I seem to have lost my sight, I see nothing. You settle every great problem so boldly, but tell me, my dear boy, isn't it because you're young – because you haven't yet understood one of your problems through suffering?

If Trofimov's brusque words make us feel like joining him in criticizing this silly, distressed woman, Chekhov is prompt to remind us that we must judge her on her own terms, measuring the depth of her feelings, those sacred to her. Who can know another's pain? She was born in this house, is part of it, like her mother before her, like her own dead child. And Lyubov kisses Trofimov as if he were her drowned Grisha, trying to lessen her isolation of spirit by physical touch.

Trofimov's answer is a perfunctory, 'You know I feel for you with all my heart.' That is not the way to say it, as Lyubov remarks, but she has already realized, as we have, that the young man cannot begin to understand. So Lyubov wisely turns to a matter more immediately his own. She would like him to marry Anya, but he must complete his degree. 'You do nothing – you're simply tossed by fate from place to place.' There is a gentle sarcasm behind what she says: is this not the Trofimov who would have her face the truth? And she adds with an affectionate laugh words that truly cut him down to size: 'You must do something with your beard to make it grow somehow.'

In fumbling for a handkerchief, Lyubov has pulled out a telegram from her pocket and it drops to the floor. She gets one every day, she says, and we have had one in every scene to mark the progress of her relationship with her Paris lover. The last she tore up; this one she has been keeping safely about her. In the last act there will be no telegram; instead, she will be off to Paris. Here she is still making up her mind, as if making a serious choice between Paris and the orchard.[1]

Why hide it or be silent? I love him, that's clear! I love him! I love him! He's a millstone about my neck, I'm going to the bottom with him, but I love that stone and can't live without it.

The cherry orchard is another affectionate millstone she cannot live without, equally personal, equally beyond her judgment; her speech about the French lover could as well be about the orchard itself. She presses Trofimov's hand and asks for his approval. But he is not the one to step aside when moral verdicts are invited, and he blurts out, 'For God's sake forgive my frankness: why, he robbed you!' To Lyubov, this is like the stroke of the axe on the trees in Act IV. She shrinks from what she does not want to hear, and she does not want to hear this, any more than she wanted to hear the facts about the orchard from Lopahin. She covers her ears in horror. The tension of the day, the irritating music from the ballroom, Trofimov's cold, puritanical tone, all contribute to rouse her temper. She has just complained that it is 'so noisy', and it may be assumed that the band is playing more loudly during the quarrel. Suddenly she sees the man before her as a callow, pretentious youth with but half a beard and even less experience of life. The fight is on, each antagonist arguing from a limited moral position, one of loneliness and the other of ignorance.

Within minutes of Charlotta's jolly party performance, the mood has completely changed. Lyubov challenges Trofimov in

[1] Olga Knipper portrayed a strong element of seriousness in Mme Ranevsky, and Hugh Walpole recalled an interview with her on this point: 'I remember very vividly her explaining Tchehov's intention – that Mme Ranevsky was not wholly feckless, that her speech about her return to her lover in Paris showed this, and that the cherry orchard was sacrificed for many reasons' (in James Agate, *First Nights*, London, 1934, pp. 215–16).

terms she knows will hurt: he is still a schoolboy and should be more of a man; he should fall in love and be less of a prig. 'At your age not to have a mistress!' Trofimov is horrified, just as Lyubov was a moment before, although an audience which witnessed his inadequate performance as Anya's lover in the moonlight of Act II must be delighted. Distraught, he rushes blindly into the ballroom clutching his head and running full tilt into the astonished dancers. He is immediately back again. 'All is over between us!', and as blindly as before he rushes out into the hall, Lyubov trying to shout an apology after him.

Trofimov's footsteps are heard running down the stairs; there is the sound of a crash mixed with a scream from the girls, then a short silence followed by a great burst of laughter. Anya runs in to say that Petya has fallen downstairs. Thus making exact use of his noises off, Chekhov punctures the tragic exit for comedy. Trofimov is not allowed to play the romantic: the hard reality of a staircase gets in the way. Even Lyubov's anger is softened, it seems, by the accident: 'What a queer fellow that Petya is!', she says with a smile. With her smile and ours, Chekhov reduces the melodrama of their fiercely antithetical dispositions, and within a minute she will be dancing with him again.

The party goes on. In the ballroom the Station Master with an impressive bass voice[1] begins to recite a party-piece from A. K. Tolstoy's 'The Magdalene'. There is a glancing irony at Lyubov's way of life in this choice, but the opening lines otherwise catch the party spirit: 'A bustling crowd with happy laughter . . .'[2] After a few lines in this vein the band strikes up a lively waltz, and the music smothers his voice. Lyubov takes Trofimov's arm and dances him from the drawing-room into the ballroom, followed by Anya dancing with Varya like two skittish children. Tempers are cool, all are reconciled, and the stage is left to the two manservants, Yasha and Firs. As they and we look upstage towards the dancing, Firs mutters about days gone by, and Yasha yawns his characteristic reply: 'It's time you were done with.' But Firs is really talking to himself, and Yasha does not look at the old man. There is no love lost between them. As they stand there,

[1] Chekhov in a letter to Nemirovich-Danchenko of 2 November 1903 (Hellman, p. 317).
[2] In Hingley's translation (vol. III, p. 335).

Act III

the one in his old-fashioned livery and the other in the smartest
style from Paris, they contribute to the picture of fifty years of
cherry orchard life.

This episode constitutes a short breathing space before Lyubov
and Trofimov dance back. Chekhov again increases the tension.
Lyubov sits apart as before, and just as Firs is serving her with
some refreshment,[1] Anya runs in with urgent news.

ANYA (*excitedly*). There's a man in the kitchen has been saying that the
cherry orchard's been sold today.
LYUBOV. Sold to whom?
ANYA. He didn't say to whom. He's gone away.

Anya's animation is in sharp counterpoint with the rigidity of
the stunned Lyubov. This is what she has been waiting to hear,
and it is also a fresh reminder to the audience of the momentous
event that has been taking place at the same time as the party.
Some people dance while others tremble. Yet it is news that tells
us nothing, merely making the muscles tense with frustration.
And Lyubov's question incidentally reflects her outlook: sold –
not for how much, but to whom? People, not money, are
important to her. She knows that the purchaser could not have
been Gaev, and she could not have entertained the idea of
Lopahin. Anya's flat answer is cruelly casual, and, dancing off
prettily with Trofimov, she leaves her mother transfixed in an
agony of mind.

Chekhov now uses Firs to tease Lyubov and the audience
further with a neat irrelevance. Reporting that Gaev has not yet
returned, he adds, 'He has his light overcoat on, *demi-saison*, he'll
catch cold for sure.' In some exasperation, Lyubov asks Yasha to
find out who bought the orchard; but Yasha does not move:

[1] Michel Saint-Denis saw the M.A.T.'s production of the play at the Théâtre des
Champs Élysées, Paris, in 1922, and reported how Olga Knipper played Mme
Ranevsky at this moment: she 'takes a cup of tea from the old servant while she is
engaged in talking to someone else. Her hand shakes, she's burnt by the tea, drops
the cup which falls on the ground and breaks. Fresh burst of applause. Why?
Because the reality of this action was so complete, so untheatrically managed as
to be striking even from a distance. It was enough to create enthusiasm. I had the
opportunity of asking Stanislavsky how he has achieved such balanced and convincing reality. He replied, "Oh, it's very stupid. She couldn't get it. We rehearsed
for seven months but she still couldn't get it; so one day I told the stage-manager
to put boiling water in the cup. And he did" ' (*Theatre: the Rediscovery of Style*,
New York, 1960, p. 42).

'He went away long ago . . . (*laughs*).' Lyubov must sit helplessly between these two, both her servants useless to her.

She notices Firs's wizened figure as he stands upstage behind her like death itself and instinctively she remembers her matri-archal role. Where will the old man go when the orchard is sold? At his age, there is no future and the question does not matter: 'Where you bid me, there I'll go.' Yasha is quick to step in and divert his mistress's attention from his apparent rival. Let her take Yasha with her to Paris! Here it is uncivilized, immoral and boring. 'The people have no morals' is sufficiently ironic, in the light of his treatment of Dunyasha, to betray his other criticisms as impertinence. If Firs is indifferent to the sale of the orchard, in Yasha speaks the man with a quick eye on the main chance.

The dance in the next room is at its height, and Lyubov in a daze is swept into it almost against her will. Pishtchik puffs and prances in to ask her for a waltz, and as he whirls her away he raises again with unwitting but painful irony the matter of the interest on his mortgage: 'Only 180 roubles.' The higher his spirits, the more they hurt. But she is already lost in the crowd of merry-makers, and in searching among them, we get only a glimpse of Charlotta in top hat and checked trousers clowning to shouts of general approval. The party flows on . . . interminably, it seems.

Again Chekhov, with a sly irreverence, chooses to interpolate the comedy of the servants, and now he uses Dunyasha. At the party, she is conscious only of her own affairs, oblivious of the suspense of the sale; she makes a perfect foil for her mistress. Perhaps to escape the attentions of Epihodov or to follow Yasha, the little maidservant has stepped from the ballroom to powder her nose. She sees her quarry, and promptly assumes her role as *une femme fatale*. She directs her words at Firs, but articulates them with care so that Yasha shall hear everything. She has been so much in demand! It is all too much for a lady like herself . . . 'My young lady tells me to dance. There are plenty of gentlemen, and too few ladies, but dancing makes me giddy and makes my heart beat.' After this mock modesty, she throws Yasha a glance to see whether he is listening. 'Firs, the post-office clerk said something to me just now that quite took my breath away.' Firs, of course, is the last person to be impressed by her pretensions. 'He said I was like a flower.' Firs and Yasha supply the visual contrast of

pure comedy as both deny her her satisfaction: Yasha strolls out
with his customary yawn, and Firs responds only with his customary reprimand: 'Your head's being turned.' Luckily, Epihodov is by to save her face, although it is small comfort to her
to be pestered by a suitor she does not want.

Epihodov has been hailing Dunyasha from the ballroom, for
he has been pursuing the girl all evening. He was not invited to
the party, and, according to Varya, he was certainly not invited to
play with the master's billiards and break the cues. (Varya has to
watch every detail to keep the house in order!) Now he complains
with his usual sigh that Dunyasha does not want to see him.
Again we hear a mocking echo of the major mood from a minor
comic character. Epihodov is now in 'a state of mind', not unlike
the vaudeville character Gregory Smirnov in Chekhov's one-act
farce *The Bear*.

But of course, if one looks at it from that point of view, if I may so
express myself, you have, excuse my plain speaking, reduced me to a
complete state of mind. I know my destiny. Every day some misfortune
befalls me and I have long ago grown accustomed to it, so that I look
upon my fate with a smile.

But Dunyasha is in a dream, it seems, playing with her fan like
the lady she aspires to be.

Varya is apparently destined to break up the love affairs of others,
and the level of humour is quickly changed when, more in key
with the tension of the act, she sees Epihodov from the ballroom
and chases him off. 'You do nothing but wander from place to
place and don't do your work. We keep you as a counting-house
clerk, but what use you are I can't say.' Thus Varya's house-
keeping concerns dispel dreams of romance, and in the contradiction curiously epitomize the all-or-nothing prospect of her
own fate. Overwrought because of the sale like Lyubov, she
attacks Epihodov's billiards playing as if she resents the social
change that encourages this liberty. Epihodov tries to counter
her anger by assuming the dignity of one with whom the whole
world is at odds, and taking a step in retreat, he retaliates with
words: 'I beg you to express yourself with delicacy.' At this,
Varya loses her temper completely. This nun-like girl snatches
the walking-stick that Firs has left by the door and aims a blow
at the unrequited lover. Dropping all pretence of dignity, Epihodov dodges out. A moment of farce, but also an incident which

suddenly heightens tension at the approaching crisis of the play. For Varya almost hits Lopahin instead.

Lopahin has arrived back from town at last, slightly drunk. In taking Epihodov's place at the door just as Varya raises her stick, he must feel that all her anger against the peasants is turned on him alone. The irony is that Lopahin is the man whom Varya hopes will be her husband. There is a shocked silence, since a moment before even the music had been subdued in cunning preparation for his entrance. Now the man and the woman look at each other in ludicrous surprise. Varya's bad temper is made to seem silly, and Lopahin's triumphant entrance is spoiled. The distance between them widens perceptibly and their exchange is acid.

LOPAHIN. Very much obliged to you!
VARYA (*angrily and ironically*). I beg your pardon!
LOPAHIN. Not at all! I humbly thank you for your kind reception!
VARYA. No need of thanks for it. (*Moves away, then looks round and asks softly*) I haven't hurt you?
LOPAHIN. Oh, no! Not at all! There's an immense bump coming up, though![1]

An ingenious sequence, which compounds a host of suppressed and contradictory feelings. Arguably, Chekhov has been building towards this moment from the beginning of the play. By the gesture with the stick, Lopahin, who has suggested to the audience again and again that he associates his peasant origins with the beating he received as a child, is suddenly reminded of his childhood: he is again the recalcitrant peasant boy and Varya is his superior. The illuminating shock of the incident, with the extended pause which follows it, gives us an immediate under-standing of his submerged feelings, and after he ducks the blow so ignobly, the false dignity of the tipsy man and the mock gentility of his words belie his embarrassed sense that he is still an underling.

It is important, too, that it is Varya who shall appear to be

---

[1] Lopahin is joking. The stick does not hit him, for we are not to feel too sorry for him. In an earlier version of the play, Varya did strike Lopahin (see Hingley, vol. III, p. 325), but by just missing him, in the same way that Vanya just misses the Professor in Act III of *Uncle Vanya*, the incident is relieved of its more serious implications and turned into a joke.

delivering the blow, which not only expresses their contentious relationship, but also enacts their social differences. For a moment, Varya becomes the landowner's daughter beating the serf, but ironically so, since it is this very serf who, as the new owner, is about to threaten her security. Yet to describe the effects of the gesture in this way is to stress its symbolism too strongly, for the incident is inconsequential, fleeting and essentially comic in quality. Nevertheless, in being denied his moment of glory from the start, Lopahin is made to seem an intruder, and not an owner.

The episode also performs an important function theatrically. Lopahin's entrance with the news about the sale of the orchard might have been sensational, but it has been brilliantly modulated into comedy. Varya's gesture is the first of a series of master-strokes designed to suppress an emotional response to the climax of the play's action, for Chekhov is playing upon his Russian audience with great care. He is not only anxious to avoid theatrics which by overstatement at a crucial time might throw a wrong emphasis on his subject, which is not that of the sale itself, not that of serf-become-master: these matters are merely symptomatic. He also wishes to subvert any automatic reaction from his middle-class audience, who would find a triumphant Lopahin a brute and his victims overwhelmingly pathetic. This is not a drama of stereotypes, either in plot or in character.

'Lopahin has come!' The cry goes up and the pace is quick as the company hurries to greet the traveller, still grinning ruefully and touching the pretended bump on his head. Raised voices are heard from the ballroom and the dancers gather under the arch, an increasingly mute chorus of public opinion. Pishtchik, not Varya, comes to embrace Lopahin, although without thought of the reason why: 'There's a whiff of cognac about you!' Thus Lopahin's performance to the end of the act is belittled by seeming to be that of an inebriated man. Lyubov follows Pishtchik, but she asks for her brother, not for Lopahin: it has still not entered her head that anyone but Gaev might have taken part in the auction. She speaks to him as if he were a peasant: 'Was there a sale? Speak!' Lopahin evades the question, *'afraid'*, as the stage direction indicates, *'of betraying his joy'*. The auction was over by four, but they missed the train. Lyubov's agitation at this point, of course, is ours too.

At last Gaev himself appears. Laden with parcels and wiping

away tears, he too makes a sorry entrance, and his sister hastens over to him. He is a changed man, drained of his resources. The watching group closes in a pace or two. 'Well, Leonid? What news?' But Gaev's overwrought feelings are also used to prolong the suspense: he is too exhausted to speak. Mechanically he gives his parcels to Firs, the only person he has left to turn to, and without saying a word to his sister, explains that they contain anchovies and herrings. His childish preoccupation with eating is evident still, but at this moment anchovies and herrings are an outrageously irrelevant detail. In the pause, Gaev hears the insufferable Yasha playing billiards, playing *his* game! On top of all the disagreeable experiences of the day, he cannot face Yasha's smirk and promptly stops his crying and goes off with the faithful Firs to change, ignoring his frantic sister. He cannot even enunciate his customary 'Cannon off the red!' That the valet has displaced him in the billiards room hurts more than that the peasant has bought his home.

Lyubov has only Lopahin left to tell the tale, and everyone now turns expectantly to him.

PISHTCHIK. How about the sale? Tell us, do!
LYUBOV. Is the cherry orchard sold?
LOPAHIN. It is sold.
LYUBOV. Who has bought it?
LOPAHIN. I have bought it. (*A pause*).

The stichomythic echoes of these clipped lines fall on all ears with a harsh finality. Someone motions the music to stop. All in an instant, after the long delay, the fact is out. Lopahin, hoping to make a grand announcement, is left with the bare admission. As everyone turns to look at her, Lyubov, whose rising emotion Chekhov has been carefully graduating throughout the act, is the focus of attention during the pause. She almost collapses. The strain upon her is over, but she knew the orchard had to go, so Chekhov's stage direction that she is '*crushed*' points to her astonishment that it is Lopahin who has bought it. This is confirmed by the nature of her questions preceding the revelation – who? who? – and confirmed again when Varya throws her household keys to the floor. We do not hear Lyubov's voice again in this act, but her unspeaking grief is implicit. One of Chekhov's contemporaries might have been expected to have her mouth a voluble, accusatory speech, to secure an easy moral condemnation from the audience. Instead, Varya's heavy bunch of keys flies crashing to the floor.[1] Thus she throws her whole life at his feet, and her irate departure severs their relationship. Here at the climax of the play, the reversal of the existing order is complete.

Chekhov wishes his audience to see this clearly, but in human terms, for his subject is *change*. He is concerned that we should not feel that Lopahin is a designing scoundrel, an upstart and a villain. In a letter to Stanislavsky, Chekhov wrote,

Lopahin, of course, is only a merchant, but he is a decent person in every sense, should conduct himself with complete decorum, like a cultivated man, without pettiness or trickery, and it did seem to me that you would be brilliant in this part, which is central for the play. (If you decide to play Gaev, let Vishnevski play Lopahin. He won't make an artistic Lopahin but still he won't be a petty one. Lujski would be a cold-blooded foreigner in this part and Leonidov would play it like a little kulak. You mustn't lose sight of the fact that Varya, an earnest, devout young girl, is in love with Lopahin; she wouldn't love a little kulak.)[2]

Lopahin was not planning in secret to buy the orchard. As he stands looking at the bunch of keys, he too seems astonished that the chance to do so came his way. At the time of the play, Russians were well aware of the ferment which was to bring about the revolution of 1905. Thus for the Moscow audience of 1904, Chekhov handles with great delicacy a provocative and explosive situation, one which does not avoid showing the upsetting of the social establishment.

Chekhov wishes us to see a realistically balanced Lopahin, and when he composes his actor's major speech, he makes it frank and even charming in its naivety. Lopahin is tense like Lyubov and Varya, but for his big moment he wants an appreciative audience. However, the onlookers have instinctively moved away upon hearing the news that he was the one who bought the orchard, and he has to call them back. Nevertheless, they remain a silent and critical group framed in the archway. The new owner is astonished that everyone is not pleased that a friend has secured

[1] If Varya fumbles at her waist for an instant as she tries to unhook the bunch of keys, the melodrama of the gesture is nicely undercut.
[2] 30 October 1903, in Hellman, p. 315.

the estate, and he is hurt that no one seems to understand his position.

His words tumble drunkenly over one another, and his story grows with his excitement. He does not shout;[1] rather, he tells the tale joyfully. He is not speaking to hurt Lyubov, whom he loves too dearly, but to convince himself of the reality of the day's events.[2] With laughter in his voice, he explains how he outbid the dreaded Deriganov. 'Now the cherry orchard's mine! Mine!', and he repeats and repeats his own name as if he cannot believe it. He laughs, and, still the ungainly peasant, he stamps his feet: 'Tell me that I'm drunk, that I'm out of my mind, that it's all a dream.' Again he appeals for general approval. 'Don't laugh at me!', he cries, but no one is laughing. And, quite overcome by the enormity of his achievement, he seems to address the cherry orchard itself.

If my father and my grandfather could rise from their graves and see all that has happened! How their Yermolay, ignorant, beaten Yermolay, who used to run about barefoot in winter, how that very Yermolay has bought the finest estate in the world! I have bought the estate where my father and grandfather were slaves, where they weren't even admitted into the kitchen.

Pacing up and down, arms flapping, feeling his feet in his own house, he comes upon Varya's keys. With a smile he picks them up and looks at them as if receiving her censure, like the blow with the stick a moment ago. He sees in these keys both his new position and Varya's rebuke. But the irony of the situation has made him smile: always the optimist, he quickly rejects the notion that she was condemning his action, and explains, 'She threw away the keys; she means to show she's not the housewife now.' After the momentary hesitation, his spirits rise again, and he jingles the keys. Hearing the orchestra tuning up – in spite of his triumph, the party is continuing as before – with a kind of bravado he calls for it to strike up. He is too realistic a man to dwell long on the past.

[1] At rehearsal, Chekhov told the actor Leonidov, 'Listen, Lopahin doesn't shout. He's a rich man, and rich men never shout' (from *Chekhov i teatr*, ed. E. D. Surkov, Moscow, 1961, quoted in Hingley, vol. III, p. 330).
[2] Rather in the manner of Chekhov's own letter to his brother Alexander upon the purchase of the estate at Melikhovo in 1892. In this he signs himself 'Landowner A. Chekhov' with the same mixture of jocularity and pride we find in Lopahin (Simmons, p. 266).

Act III

Come, all of you, and look how Yermolay Lopahin will take the axe to the cherry orchard, how the trees will fall to the ground! We will build houses on it and our grandsons and great-grandsons will see a new life springing up there. Music! Play up!

This is too much. In his enthusiasm Lopahin has forgotten Lyubov, and at the mention of her loss, coupled with the release of her tension at the end of her long wait for the news, she crumples crying in her chair. At the same time gay sounds swell up from the musicians in the ballroom.

The mixture of music and tears characterizes the end of the scene. As at the end of *Three Sisters*, the music grates on the ear, and the contradiction completes the pattern of ambivalence started at the beginning of the act. Lopahin tries to comfort Lyubov in tones that betray both his pleasure and his concern; he wants the orchard and yet he does not want to see her suffer: 'My poor friend! Dear lady, there's no turning back now.' Thus Chekhov identifies the crisis as one of time and change. There shall be victors and victims, and Lyubov's miserable figure represents a silent criticism of events.

Pishtchik with unexpected understanding steps forward to lead Lopahin away from Lyubov and out of the room. In the confusion of his conflicting feelings, Lopahin seems willing to be guided by anybody who offers a suggestion, even Pishtchik. But even now he tries to make a grand exit. He strides towards the door uncertainly, calling again for the band: 'Here comes the new master, the owner of the cherry orchard!' A fine exit line, but, typically, Chekhov does not allow the champion to depart so simply. Lopahin's triumphant announcement marks his glory and his blunder. He '*accidentally tips over a little table, almost upsetting the candelabra*'. Chekhov is showing us how poorly he assumes his new role: it is the fool Epihodov's function to knock over tables. This is the actor of farce who trips over the rug as he takes his leave. The audience laughs and Lopahin's pretensions are reduced to absurdity. However, he is still the man we know, for his first instinct, that of the peasant, is to pick up the table. Halfway down, he remembers that it is now his own table to knock over as he pleases, and his last words, thrown over his shoulder as he goes, are, 'I can pay for everything!'

Lyubov is finally alone, forlornly trying to collect her thoughts. The music is quieter, but still playing. Anya comes in with

Trofimov, and she goes on her knees to comfort her mother, while Trofimov stands centrally upstage within the arch watching the two of them. His position makes him the ambiguous overseer of the scene, silently reinforcing Anya's false confidence in the future. Chekhov allows the action a flush of emotionality, but the audience cannot avoid perceiving it as inopportune optimism: 'We will make a new garden, more splendid than this one . . .' Anya merely parrots Trofimov, and in the circumstances of Lopahin's triumph, her words come across as sheer sentimentality. The bland expression of approval on Trofimov's boyish face is hardly a reassuring comment on the future. Meanwhile, Lyubov, hunched in grief, is thinking only of the past.

In the fine dramatic writing of this episode, Chekhov weaves the attitudes of all his main characters, Lyubov and Gaev, Varya and Lopahin, and Anya and Trofimov, as each responds to the fearful event of the sale. Its meaning is the sum of all the possible ways of regarding it.

Act Four

After an instant of shock, the audience should recognize the first act set.[1] The scene has returned to the simplicity of the nursery of Act I, and the cherry trees should be seen again, but this time almost bare of leaves. It is October, not May; the summer has passed, and the Russian winter is threatening. But above all, the earlier simplicity of the room has changed to a new starkness, for the curtains are down and the pictures have gone, leaving only discoloured shadows on the walls. Furniture and baggage are piled in the corners of the stage, and only the sofa is there to sit on, covered in a dust sheet. '*There is a sense of desolation*', reads the stage direction. The stage tells its own story: the family is on the point of departure, and the orchard has passed into its final phase.

'The last act will be merry', Chekhov wrote to Olga Knipper,[2] but it will be the surface gaiety of desperation. This act can be only anticlimactic after the tension of the party scene, but in Chekhov's design, the return to the setting of the first act, the cyclical balancing of departure with arrival, and of autumn with spring, must make this a scene of echoes. Structurally, the last movement of the play is going to rehearse the details of the past nervous months and summarize their implications. As the last phase in a cyclical experience, Act IV will complete a temporal image of life turning upon itself, repeating without repetition and changing without change. Back in the nursery, all the cumulative feelings of the family's loss will be represented in their attitudes. Francis Fergusson found this last act the 'epiphany' of the play: 'We see the action, now completed, in a new and ironic light.'[3]

---

[1] In the first production, the M.A.T. used the same set for Acts III and IV. This did not help the actors' cues for feeling sentimental towards the nursery, or Chekhov's attempt in the play to catch the circular rhythm of life.

[2] Letter of 21 September 1903 (Garnett, p. 306).

[3] *The Idea of a Theater* (New York, 1953), pp. 176–7.

The action begins with silence on stage and noises off. The house is alive with activity, and only Lopahin and Yasha in the deserted nursery seem alone. Listening with us to the cries of farewell from the peasants at the door and to Gaev's husky 'Thank you!'s stand the two men of the new order. The servant does not care, but the master of the cherry orchard is pitifully lonely as he surveys what he feels now to be his own handiwork, the breaking up of a home. His eye falls on Yasha standing beside a tray full of glasses, and he senses that the occasion is too momentous for the traditional champagne he has provided; everybody is too overwhelmed even to acknowledge the gesture. He suffers a new exclusion. Only Yasha speaks, and that a word of haughty criticism of the villagers, for he is returning to his beloved Paris.

Lopahin does not respond to Yasha, but flaps his arms momentarily in a mixture of impatience and embarrassment. He is sober enough now after his hysterical outburst in the party, and the audience should see him as Chekhov himself did:

[Lopahin] flails his arms when he is in motion, takes long strides, is lost in thought when he moves about and walks in a straight line. He doesn't cut his hair short, and so he frequently tosses his head back; in reflection he strokes his beard back and forth, i.e., from his neck to his lips.[1]

We are not to judge this man; rather, we share his embarrassment. We can understand exactly how he has come to find himself in this unlovely situation. Nevertheless, his unease is ironic, since he is caught in a flood of sentiment of his own that he can recognize, but cannot rationally indulge.

Chekhov emphasizes Lopahin's confusion with the same stage device seen in the first act, a device in naturalistic drama that only he has used. Lyubov and Gaev hurry in from the hall, cross the full width of the stage and go out through the far door. The lady is overwrought, hastening to escape the burden of affection showered upon her by her people; her brother is questioning that typically impulsive action of hers: 'You gave them your purse, Lyuba. That won't do – that won't do!' The audience has only the most fleeting impression of the scene outside, and is hardly free to digest it for watching Lopahin. The two have gone before

---

[1] Letter to Nemirovich-Danchenko of 2 November 1903 (Hellman, p. 317).

he can stop them. They did not give him or his champagne so much as a glance. He calls after them, half chases them: 'You will take a glass at parting?' Lyubov's rejection of him is a measure of her distraction, for she would not otherwise have hurt his feelings. He is left gesticulating through an empty door.

Lopahin takes his long strides back into the room, nervously stroking his beard, fingering his watch. The stream of his thoughts outlines the many facets of the man: he would not have bought the champagne had he known that nobody would want any – his words indicate partly his pride, partly his thrift; well, he will not drink any either – perhaps once again he has made a social gaffe among these incomprehensible people; Yasha can have some – at least the opened bottle will not be entirely wasted, especially at eight roubles; but how cold it is! – unexpectedly sensitive, he feels the chill of winter, and of despair, in the deserted room, a remark that is sharply illuminating because so incongruous with the surface level of his thinking; nevertheless, it is good building weather – his mind is also working over the immediate problems of his new business undertaking; he even wishes that everyone might go and be done with it, especially since he is, it seems, responsible for their catching the train – 'The train goes in forty-seven minutes; so you ought to start for the station in twenty minutes.' The sequence concludes. Through Lopahin his time-keeper, Chekhov is going to count these precious last minutes on the nerves of his audience, and count them exactly. We are not to wonder when the end will come, only how it will be endured.

Yasha is not the most sympathetic listener Lopahin could have had. Upon the invitation, he takes the first glass of champagne without hesitation and with his assumed Parisian *savoir faire* promptly declares that it is 'not the real thing'. He nevertheless does not put down the glass, but continues to work his way through the bottle during the scene, swaying more and more uncertainly at his post upstage. That marks the height of his response to the situation, and his presence on the stage in what follows is like a distorting smear on the canvas. Lopahin is left to fall back upon reassuring matters of business to lessen the pain of feelings he cannot control.

Trofimov enters with another reminder of the pressure of time. In his own newly officious way, as if it were his plan that they should go, he too feels responsible for the success of the family's journey: 'I think it must be time to start.' The audience hears the echo, but also hears Trofimov's dubious addition, 'I think'. And immediately his assiduous attitude is undermined by his undignified searching among the bags and bundles. Not only has he misplaced his galoshes, but he must call Anya to his assistance. A humble detail makes Chekhov's point.

Chekhov has arranged this last confrontation between the ineffectual student and the practical man of business, not to set up an irresolvable debate between youth and experience, idealism and pragmatism, but, surprisingly, to show us how alike in sympathies these two really are.

On this terrible day, Lopahin is pleased to have even his arch-critic to talk to; indeed, Trofimov is the only one in the family who will pay him the least attention. Lopahin explains that he is off to Harkov on the same train with them all, intending to go on with his work there, but his remark is an implicit criticism of the eternal student. 'I can't get on without work. I don't know what to do with my hands, they flap about so queerly, as if they didn't belong to me.' The comic mannerism is Lopahin's nervous counterpart to Trofimov's petty problem with his galoshes; Lopahin flaps as Trofimov hunts. The relationship between these two has never been so strained, but the image of them both together is an acknowledgment that they share human failings equally. In irritation, Trofimov returns Lopahin's humility with his familiar tone of sarcasm: 'Well, we're just going away, and you will take up your profitable labours again.' But Lopahin in a winning gesture of friendship ignores that exclusive 'we', turns the other cheek and awkwardly offers the student a glass of champagne. Trofimov is incongruously on his hands and knees at a trunk when the offer is made, and with youthful abruptness it is refused. Audience sympathy for the older man is the stronger at this moment, and it is Trofimov who is first to be judged.

Yet Lopahin can be spiteful in return, and he falls back on the usual joke. If Trofimov is off to Moscow, no doubt the professors are waiting for him. With this, the quarrel is on. Trofimov spits out an annoyed, 'That's not your business', and as if nonchalantly resumes the search for his galoshes. Suddenly he stops and faces his critic, seeming to have decided to grasp the nettle. Their differences in wealth and status are strikingly obvious, and only from a position of moral superiority can Trofimov give Lopahin a piece of his mind. With blustering seriousness he makes two amusingly incongruous points: for a start, Lopahin should stop waving his arms about; but just as stupid is his whole idea of cottages for small-holders. Everything about Lopahin, it seems, irritates the young man, both his person and his thinking. As we listen to this, it is Trofimov who is mentally waving his arms about, whereas Lopahin, for all his social *gaucherie*, at least has a head on his shoulders.

Unexpectedly, Trofimov softens – an afterthought by Chekhov, who added the next lines in his final version[1] – and seems to see his rival for the first time as a man like himself. Perhaps he suspects that his criticism of Lopahin's person has hurt far more than his aspersions about his business methods. He indicates that Lopahin's lack of the social graces means nothing to him, and remarks a quality in the merchant which the audience itself may gather from Lopahin's affection for Lyubov and the family, as well as from his love of Russia's forests and even the poppies in his own fields. 'You have fine delicate fingers like an artist, you've a fine delicate soul.' If Lopahin's antagonist could sense this much, says Chekhov, we must all agree; with typical generosity, the author is insisting that his audience get the true measure of his most complicated character. It was a neat stroke to choose Trofimov to speak like this, and only Trofimov in the play could have praised Lopahin's soul to such effect. Sensitivity has nothing whatsoever to do with wealth or education or social class. Chekhov's respect for human worth – so important for an understanding of Lopahin's failure to propose marriage to Varya, and so important for an estimate of what is finally of value to those who inhabit the world of the cherry orchard – is summed up in the Chekhovian concept of *nezhnij* ('delicate', 'tender'), with its connotations of love and affection.[2]

If Chekhov had ended their quarrel on this note, the episode would have seemed glib. While he believed that there is hope for progress in the unity of culture and industry[3] and above all in tolerance between social classes, nevertheless, as a good dramatist, he must let the audience deduce this for themselves. Thus his play

---

[1] See Hingley, vol. III, p. 325.
[2] With typically subversive humour, Chekhov also has Dunyasha use this word to describe her feelings to Yasha.
[3] As emerges particularly through the notions of Tusenbach in *Three Sisters*.

maintains its tenor of comedic insight when he allows the quarrel to flare up again. Not only is this realistic in maintaining consistency in characterization, but it also revives the spectators' interpretative energy. This is how Chekhov manages the transition:

LOPAHIN (*embraces him*). Good-bye, my dear fellow. Thanks for everything. Let me give you money for the journey, if you need it.
TROFIMOV. What for? I don't need it.
LOPAHIN. Why, you haven't got a halfpenny.
TROFIMOV. Yes, I have, thank you. I got some money for a translation. Here it is in my pocket, (*anxiously*) but where can my galoshes be?

Lopahin knows the value of money, and guesses the immediate problem for Trofimov in Moscow; but his generosity touches Trofimov on his raw spot, his personal dignity. Lopahin has made another gaffe. Trofimov snaps his answers in further criticism of what he thinks is Lopahin's vulgarity. No doubt poor Petya is telling a half-truth about his translation: he will hunt through his pockets in a pathetic pantomime, until he avoids Lopahin's amused eye by returning to the subject of his lost galoshes. The evasion suitably belittles his pride.

Chekhov has, not Anya, but Varya, find Trofimov's silly galoshes. She flings them at him from Anya's room, narrowly missing him, and the young man is as startled as we. But Varya's nerves are at breaking point, and we are sharply reminded that the tension between the two men on stage is duplicated among the others offstage. Varya is less angry with her idle tormentor Trofimov, but more with her ineffectual suitor Lopahin. However, it is the student who chances to catch the full brunt of her temper. 'Why are you so cross, Varya? h'm! . . . but those aren't my galoshes.' In this way the tension is released by a trivial detail.

Lopahin is unable to understand Trofimov's obstinacy. He has made a profit of forty thousand roubles on three thousand acres of poppies.[1] 'And when my poppies were in flower, wasn't it a picture!' – in the midst of business, his simple pleasure in natural beauty must charm us. He can afford the money: 'I'm a peasant, I put it to you straight.' And he drags out his wallet.

As the two men face each other centre-stage, Chekhov uses the

[1] Poppies were grown for their oil, which was then used for making fuel, food, medicine, soap and other products.

tiny crisis of their comic dispute to make exact his meaning.
Lopahin's father was a peasant, Trofimov's a chemist. What has
birth to do with it? Lopahin is thinking only that Trofimov
finds him his inferior, and is unable to forget their social differences, especially since he has had to pay for his freedom to rise
above his station. For Trofimov, on the other hand, it is freedom
to be independent of money that he values most.

TROFIMOV. I can get on without you. I can pass by you. I am strong
and proud. Humanity is advancing towards the highest truth, the
highest happiness, which is possible on earth, and I am in the front
ranks.
LOPAHIN. Will you get there?
TROFIMOV. I shall get there (*a pause*). I shall get there, or I shall show
others the way to get there.

With a large gesture, Trofimov has swept himself into the posture
his grand cliché suggests, that of a leader of men. However,
neither the merchant nor the idealist is right. Trofimov is again
making a speech to an imaginary army of militants as he did when
he was with Anya, only this time there is a heckler who deflates
him with the simple question, 'Will you get there?' In the pause,
Trofimov's bubble is pricked, and all youthful revolutionaries are
seen as slightly ludicrous. Meanwhile the vision of a glorious
future remains carefully obscured.

The comic debate between the merchant and the intellectual
makes a preliminary statement of contradictory extremes before
the rich spectrum of attitudes closes the play. By himself, neither
Lopahin nor Trofimov is so unequivocal a character as to speak
the whole truth, but somewhere between the pragmatism of the
one and the idealism of the other the audience is given a glimpse
of the need for human compromise. When in a moment Chekhov
adds to this some of Anya's unaffected buoyancy and a good deal
of Lyubov's warmth, he begins to furnish a sustaining image for
the future.

A very real axe is heard on a tree far away, and all philosophical
discussion ends. The axe on the tree is like the ticking of the clock
which counts the minutes to the end of the orchard. While it
reminds Lopahin of the imminent arrival of the train, it impels
Lyubov, who wishes to hold back the clock for as long as possible, to ask that the destruction should not begin until she has

gone. There is no sense in quarrelling, says Lopahin to Trofimov: 'We turn up our noses at one another, but life is passing all the while.' By this indisputable conclusion, he speaks for the axe on the tree, which, with the insistent regularity of its sound, is the unmistakable reality of the present.

It is Chekhov's practice in this play to grant a situation comic perspective whenever it seems overcharged, and for this purpose he regularly calls upon the servants. In any case, he has yet to complete the sad story of Dunyasha and her silly affairs of the heart, and he already has the bumptious Yasha upstage quaffing glass after glass of champagne. The stage is ready for lighter stuff, and Chekhov quickens the pace by a series of four 'entrances', if this is the appropriate term for what is merely coming and going. In fact, Anya appears at the doorway, Varya speaks from the next room, Epihodov passes through from the hall where he has been roping a box, and Dunyasha simply slips in with some bags.

If Chekhov allowed him to be, Yasha would be some sort of villainous accomplice of melodrama, the smart servant aping his superiors, seducing young girls like Dunyasha, cheating his mistress, devoid of sympathy with the aged, and taking advantage of the misfortunes of others. Summarized like this, he would seem to be all that his author despised in human *poshlost* ('banality', 'triteness'). Certainly he would demonstrate the worst of all possible worlds, even hinting at what might become of other young people like Trofimov and Anya when time and change overtook their innocence. But this is to describe a character of another theatre, and Yasha is kept from the centre of the stage and never allowed to be more than the merest shadow of Lopahin, whose sensitivity and generosity of spirit more than outweighs Yasha's vices. He remains comic in his sinister shadow work, too uppish to be taken into serious account. His cigar-smoking made its social point and was used simply as a joke to set off Dunyasha's affected gentility. Now in drinking the master's champagne, he presents only the ridiculous figure of a lackey who has made himself drunk. If soon he may seem to break Dunyasha's heart, that organ was only as fragile as it suited her to make it.

The single aspect of Yasha's worldly attitude which will hurt an audience beyond laughter is his callous disregard of the older generation, in particular of his peasant mother and his foil, the

faithful old Firs. 'Has Firs been taken to hospital?' asks Anya, a
question which is repeated by Varya in a more urgent tone a little
later. 'I told them this morning' is the assurance that Yasha gives
as he returns to his champagne. 'Tell him his mother's come to
say good-bye to him', Varya calls again. But 'They put me out of
all patience' is Yasha's irritable response as he shrugs off any
unwelcome reminder of his former days. And he pours another
glass. His cruelty sufficiently suggests that human values suffer in
the name of progress.

Yasha's malignity provides only a fleeting image, if a bitter
one. Fleeting, because Chekhov keeps a clear eye on the comedy.
Epihodov has crushed a hat-box, and the spectator is persuaded
to a response of broad laughter, set in motion here and sustained
through the next episode. Dunyasha has been waiting her opportunity to capture her young man on his own, and now she
employs the tactics she thinks appropriate for a maiden deceived.
Their scene together smacks of the novelette: the girl weeps and
throws her arms about the proud neck, but the man for his part
has no intention of marrying a peasant girl. The tone is frivolous,
not tragic.

Yasha, moreover, handles the embarrassing situation he finds
himself in while still toasting himself in champagne with his free
hand. Dunyasha's mixture of mincing tones and histrionics makes
no difference to him. 'Tomorrow we shall get into the express
train and roll away in a flash.' Dunyasha tries all the blandishments she knows, but she finally realizes that she has lost. Powder-
ing her nose, she pleads in a plaintive voice, 'I'm a tender creature,
Yasha.'[1] The gesture and the voice are in delicious contradiction,
and we need not worry too much about her broken heart, for it
will mend with lightning rapidity. And as before, Dunyasha's
tryst is broken up by the sound of people coming. The encounter
is brief, yet Chekhov has touched in the complete history of the
lovers. Dunyasha will recover, for Epihodov, or perhaps the
Post-Office Clerk who praised her at the party, will be within call.
Yasha will find his own kind in Paris, away from all this 'ignorance'. When Gaev comes in and spots the upstart with his plastered hair, his comment is a total judgment: 'What a smell of
herrings!'

[1] See p. 319, n. 2, above.

The family returns with another reminder of the clock from Gaev and Lyubov: 'We ought to be off. There's not much time now . . . In ten minutes we must get into the carriage.' Ten minutes. We catch at our breath as the life of the cherry orchard drains away like water in sand. Chekhov gives his stage people those ten painful minutes and has us share them.

Again is heard the evocation of place: 'Farewell, dear house, dear old home of our fathers!' Lyubov's words are chosen to bring the house alive again in terms of the generations who lived there.[1] 'How much those walls have seen!' Lyubov addresses the room she stands in, the nursery, and then obliquely addresses us. The actress will move around those walls until the audience too can feel their reality as we anticipate their destruction. Chekhov uses every pathetic device, every sentimental word and gesture, while at the same time inserting that edge of critical ambivalence and ironic comedy we have come to expect.

Against Lyubov's affecting embrace of her daughter, we hear the lady's insistent demand for reassurance.

LYUBOV. Are you glad? Very glad?
ANYA. Very glad! A new life is beginning, mamma.

It is Lyubov who is plagued by doubt and regret. In the thrilled tone of Anya's reply, the answer of a young and unfledged creature, we hear how untried is the 'new life'. The irony is redoubled by Gaev's brightly echoing, 'Yes, really, everything is all right now.' He confirms the ambiguities of the mood, for he too is reassuring himself. But he also makes his little speech to comfort those he loves, earnestly asserting the belief that now they all feel 'calm and even cheerful', as if saying makes it so. To cap this, the one man who has no sense of money informs us that, of all things, he got the job at the bank: 'I am a financier!' At any rate, Lyubov has money in her pocket, the money the rich aunt in Yaroslavl sent them to save the estate.

Lyubov sits on the white sheet covering the sofa. Elegantly dressed to the last,[2] she wears a magnificent outfit for travelling. Anya embraces her like a small child, curled in her mother's

---

[1] *Stariy djedushka* (literally 'dear old man') is a term of affection which would be used of a *person*, such as an uncle or grandfather.
[2] Chekhov made a point of telling Olga Knipper, playing Mme Ranevsky, that it was necessary 'to know how to dress' (letter of 25 October 1903, in Garnett, p. 331).

arms. The girl dreams of studying and passing her examinations at school. Mother and daughter will read books together 'in the autumn evenings'. The voices are sweet and soporific, the mood dreamy and sentimental.

ANYA. Mamma, come soon.
LYUBOV. I shall come, my precious treasure.

An idyllic vision of mother and child. But with her golden fancies and the bright eyes of youth, the girl might be comforting the older woman herself. The spectator is expected to feel a lump in the throat.

This is just the moment when Chekhov, having put us to sleep, slaps us awake. Charlotta had come in with Anya, and has been watching the pretty scene with a jaundiced eye from the sidelines. As Anya's tones grow dulcet, the Governess starts to hum a tune, her accompaniment an ironic echo of Anya's voice. Gaev directs the audience's attention to Charlotta's presence, but misinterprets her mood entirely: 'Charlotta's happy; she's singing!' She is far from being happy. As a practical woman perforce, a woman as aware of present realities as Lopahin is, she senses disaster. Unexpectedly, she picks up one of the bundles left in the room and nurses it in her arms like a baby. 'Bye, bye, my baby', she croons, and with her ventriloquist's gift she mimics the 'Ooah! ooah!' of a howling infant. 'Poor little thing!', she concludes, and throws the bundle down with a squawk, 'Ooah!' The performance is ridiculous, and we laugh easily. But the point is well taken. Charlotta has wickedly parodied the archetypal image of mother and child, belittling any automatic sentiment, shockingly juxtaposing pathos and comedy. Come down to earth, she is saying, and she is saying it to both the mother nursing her daughter on the stage and to us in the auditorium. 'You must please find me a situation, I can't go on like this.' Even as we remember from Act II that she hardly knew her own mother, that she has had to fend for herself for many years, our laughter is turned to wormwood. This is *il sentimento del contrario*[1] of Pirandello and other twentieth-century absurdists, the contradiction of feeling that shatters an audience's equanimity. It was always Chekhov's injunction to his correspondents who wanted to know how to

---

[1] Luigi Pirandello, *L'Umorismo*, 2nd ed. (Firenze, 1920), p. 179.

write a story that an author should write about misery and misfortune only when in a rational state of mind: 'Yes, you must be
cold.'[1]

Chekhov accelerates the pace and raises the spirits once more; to
do this he has been holding Semyonov-Pishtchik in reserve.
Scant of breath, sweating like a horse, Pishtchik explodes into
the room and comes to rest centre-stage. 'The freak of nature!' is
Lopahin's affectionate aside to Lyubov. Perhaps the old warrior
has come to borrow money for the last time, even at the eleventh
hour. Gaev's scuttling escape from the room suggests that he at
least thinks so. Chekhov has reintroduced Pishtchik not only to
retrieve the play for comedy, but also to complete a calculated
part of the play's pattern of meaning.

The fat man calls for a glass of water, greets Lyubov, greets
Lopahin. He fumbles in his pocket with one hand, swallows water
from the glass with the other, gives the tiresome glass to Lopahin,
takes it back, thrusts instead a bundle of banknotes into Lopahin's
hands. At the very last moment, he has come to repay some of his
debt. '400 roubles. That leaves me owing 840.' Everyone on
stage is dumbfounded. Mopping his brow, gulping the water, he
tells his story little by little. A miracle has happened, one as
wonderful as a card-trick by Charlotta. Modern technology has
arrived for Pishtchik: 'Some Englishmen came along and found
in my land some sort of white clay.' For a man who finds everything equally astonishing, this piece of good luck might almost
have been expected.

It is a fact that foreign capital was being invested in Russia in
the 1890s, but Pishtchik does not ask the reason why. He merely
expresses his joy and amazement that someone, something turned
up. It is his perpetual belief in the beneficence of other people that
irradiates all about him. With this irrepressible confidence goes his
naive faith in the obscure wisdom of 'philosophy'. If it is not

[1] Thus two letters to Lydia Avilova: 'When you portray miserable wretches and
unlucky people and want to stir the reader to compassion, try to be cooler – to give
their sorrow a background, as it were, against which it can stand out in sharper
relief. The way it is, the characters weep and you sigh. Yes, you must be cold' (19
March 1892, in Hellman, p. 163). 'You may weep and moan over your stories,
you may suffer together with your heroes, but I consider one must do this so that
the reader does not notice it. The more objective, the stronger will be the effect'
(27 April 1892, in Friedland, pp. 97–8).

Nietzsche proposing a solution to financial difficulties by the forging of banknotes, it is another 'great philosopher' (Schopenhauer?) who advocates suicide as a way to end human anxiety: just jump off a roof, and that will solve the problem. Pishtchik passes on this momentous notion in deadly earnest. 'Fancy that, now! Water, please!' Perhaps even this jolly fellow, the life and soul of every party, has had thoughts of taking his own life. His farcical counterpart is Epihodov, but for him threats of suicide were never more than a joke. His serious counterpart is Lyubov, but for her there has been no white clay. Here are three fatalists of whom only one has been rewarded by a benign providence. The other two are no less subject to chance, and by leaving us with such a thought, Chekhov touches on the tragic potential of his play.

Lopahin is interested at once in the business prospects the discovery of white clay holds out. 'What Englishmen?', he asks. But Pishtchik is too excited to say more. He cannot stay. He has to see Znoikovo. And Kardamanovo. All his creditors. He has drunk his second glass of water and almost gone. Lyubov calls after him, and her tone arrests him in the doorway. They are just leaving for town and she is going abroad!

Pishtchik stops and slowly looks about him. In his confusion he has not noticed the bareness of the room, the heaps of luggage, the hats and coats. The pace is checked and his voice falters as he recognizes at last what has happened to his old friends: for them the magic Englishmen did not come, and his money is too late.

Never mind . . . be happy. God will succour you . . . no matter . . . everything in this world must have an end (*kisses* LYUBOV ANDREY-EVNA'*s hand*). If the rumour reaches you that my end has come, think of this . . . old horse, and say: 'There was once such a man in the world . . . Semyonov-Pishtchik . . . the Kingdom of Heaven be his!' . . . most extraordinary weather . . . yes.

This is a speech exquisitely calculated to evoke in the spectator the characteristic mixture of painful concern and wry humour. We have never seen Pishtchik so sober before. The negative aspects of his optimistic fatalism are suddenly brought home to him. The predetermined sale of the orchard is in parallel with the irrational chance by which Pishtchik's own orchard is saved.

Pishtchik is used to show the droll side of the victims of time.

At one moment blustering about his hard luck, at the next bewildered by unexpected good fortune, he is the clown who is
shown to be pathetically human. He '*goes out in violent agitation*', but
with the masterly detail of his comedy, Chekhov hurries him back
for a second time to say, 'Dashenka wishes to be remembered to
you.' In this last glimpse of him, the empty-head is consistently
true to himself when, in spite of the inappropriate circumstances,
he still parrots the message from that wonderful daughter of his.
As Henri Bergson explained of comic characterization, there is
usually 'something mechanical encrusted on the living'.[1]

Each exit brings us one step nearer the end of the orchard.
Everyone is ready to go. Lyubov looks at her watch: there are
five minutes remaining, but she still has two people on her mind.
One is Firs. Anya's reiteration, 'Firs has been taken to the hospital', plants the doubt in the spectator's mind that Yasha in
despite did not in fact see that this was done, but it at once re-
assures Lyubov. The other problem is Varya. With a voice un-
mistakably directed at the embarrassed Lopahin, she tries to
capture his pity for this plaintive creature who has no work to do,
who has grown 'thin and pale' and is always crying. Lyubov is
astute in trying to accomplish a mother's last duty towards a
daughter: Lopahin is just the man to want an industrious wife,
and who at the same time might be expected to respond to a
demand on his protective sympathies. When it comes to her
feminine wiles, Lyubov can be as practical as the next woman.
To crown her argument, she tells him that Varya loves him, a
certain appeal to his male vanity. There is still time for a proposal
of marriage, as Lopahin agrees – indeed, a whole five minutes!
Thus the private torments of years are to be resolved by a
frighteningly hasty bargain: 'A single moment's all that's
necessary.'

Lopahin seems as weary of countering the assumptions of the
family as Varya is herself. 'Let's settle it straight off': here the
man of decision speaks; it makes no sense to procrastinate. But
another voice immediately shows his inner doubt: 'Without you
I feel I shan't make her an offer.' And with mounting alarm he
watches the mother hustle away Anya and Charlotta, and then
Yasha and herself, until they have all deserted him. Chekhov is

[1] *Le Rire*, trans. C. Brereton and F. Rothwell (Paris, 1900).

careful first, however, to set the tone for comedy by having Lopahin see for the first time what has been happening to his champagne: a smothered hiccough from Yasha as he goes tells all.

Lopahin is alone again in the bare nursery. Lacking Lyubov's grace, he strides awkwardly back and forth a few paces in his customary way, and comes to a halt at the window farthest from the door through which Varya will come. Chekhov is careful to give his actor business by which to convey his embarrassment: Lopahin glances at his watch and grunts a 'Yes' to himself. The audience is held by this pause in the action until Lopahin's discomfort is almost its own. Chekhov gives us a few moments to see the cherry orchard situation as it is newly reflected in the prickly relationship between the two people who are about to come together. The abortive 'proposal' scene which follows revives the central notion of the play that human lives are tender, fragile things which may be bruised or broken by the relentless advance of tomorrow. Time plays the joker in this scene and strengthens the undercurrent of comic tension. The pressure of time, signified by the waiting carriage, by the approaching train, and now by Lopahin's glance at his watch, allows him only so much breathing space. In counterpoint with this restriction is Lopahin's wish to hold back the clock, and the nervous flapping of his arms indicates the shuttlecock of his mind. Perhaps he feels too settled in his ways to marry, or keep pace with the times. Rapid social change, which demands the violent disruption of age-old class barriers, takes no account of feelings. Five minutes is all the time granted to arrange a marriage between a girl brought up in a well-to-do family and the son of a peasant. It is true that their economic positions are somewhat reversed, but it hurt when Lopahin bought the orchard, and now at the back of his mind is the knowledge that marriage with Varya would be a second breach in the social structure, another blow of the axe on the cherry trees. Both the mother and the foster-daughter want this marriage, but in his heart Lopahin knows that it is impossible.[1] Chekhov's character is not the one to say defiantly, 'I'm

---

[1] Valency makes the suggestion that the real reason why Lopahin will not marry Varya is that Lyubov is the secret love of his life and his ideal of womanhood (Valency, p. 273). Chekhov does not, it seems to me, plant enough evidence in the play for this.

master now!' when it comes to forcing Varya to sell herself to the only bidder. Lopahin can buy an orchard, not a human being; he has no respect for slavery.

It follows that the scene between Lopahin and Varya must be played with a sensitive awareness of its pace and variations. Against the haste of Lyubov's exit, we must feel that the clock has stopped while the hands race round. Lopahin's torment is apparent as he hears '*smothered laughter and whispering*' behind the door. The whole family seems to be eavesdropping, waiting for his decision. '*At last*' Varya enters, or, rather, seems to be pushed in by Lyubov and the girls and all the women in the world. She quickly surveys the scene of her encounter and the empty stretches of the room, and sights Lopahin with his back to her on the far side. Her instinct, too, is to run. She turns away and buries herself in a pile of bundles on her side of the stage, pretending to look for something: 'It's strange, I can't find it anywhere.' But we know that Varya is not the one to mislay anything, and we watch her pantomime with amusement.

There follows a series of false starts by Lopahin. 'Where are you going now, Varvara Mihailovna?' He has hardly turned, their eyes have not met, but it is a bright opening gambit that might have led to some such question as, 'Why not join me?' Every rising tone will raise Varya's romantic expectations, and every falling away will defeat them. 'I?' she answers, as if the room were filled with other people. 'To the Ragulins. I have arranged to go to them to look after the house – as a housekeeper.' So Varya's life as a spinster is measured out for her. The Ragulins live at Yashnovo, seventy miles away, in another world; it will be exile, and this will be the extent of the global travelling that Varya so desired. Her voice mixes her hope and her terror.

'So this is the end of life in this house.' After the pause, Lopahin starts again, as if to say, 'Why not begin your life again with me?' But he has said the wrong thing, conjuring up, as he does, a bleak vision of a derelict building and a dead orchard. Varya is already suppressing tears, and partly out of maidenly modesty, but mostly in the anguish of her frustration and nostalgia, burrows again into the luggage.

'And I'm just off to Harkov.' Encouragingly, Lopahin tries yet again. But as he thinks about his work, he seems to forget why Varya and he are here, and instead tells her of his plan to leave

Epihodov in charge. Varya's 'Really!' is dull with her hopelessness. The same nostalgia grips them both, and with a brilliant
stroke of perception, Chekhov has Lopahin call up the past instead of the future. 'This time last year we had snow already, if
you remember; but now it's so fine and sunny. Though it's cold,
to be sure – three degrees of frost.' The last remark, spoken to
the amorous expectations of Varya, is wildly funny; but it has a
dying fall. From Act I, the audience recalls the frost warmed by
the sun; now it is the sun which is chilled by the frost of the
coming winter. Chekhov has slyly invoked the weather to characterize the emotional chill in the room and in the hearts of Lopahin
and Varya. Symbolism is introduced without disturbing the surface of naturalism, for Lopahin's estimate of the temperature has
the accuracy of a man born on the land. But poor Varya can
only explode with a tearfully exasperated 'Our thermometer's
broken!'

Chekhov has stretched our feelings and taunted us with the
bitter humour of his situation as far as he may. As though they
were the automata of a farce, Lopahin and Varya have not yet
looked each other in the eye.[1] Suddenly the tension is broken by
the sound of a voice offstage, probably Epihodov's, calling Lopahin from beyond this prison of male obligations and female
sensibilities. In a moment, *'as though he had long been expecting this
summons'*, Lopahin has gone and Varya is left to collapse on her
knees into the bundle she has been perfunctorily turning over.
She is at last free to cry without restraint.

The precious moment, so carelessly snatched, so foolishly
thrown away, has passed. Human inadequacy has aided time the
thief in robbing Lyubov of her tidy satisfaction. As with the sale
of the orchard, so with Lopahin's proposal, we expect the result
when it comes, and thus pay a different kind of attention to its
causes. The multitude of small details which go to make up a
human relationship grows momentous. The amusing proprieties
in the man and the fragments of gentility in the girl illuminate
the whole pattern of cherry orchard behaviour. Neither can
adjust, nor can be expected to adjust, to the demands of change.
They both see themselves subjectively, and they are both buffeted

---

[1] In his production at the Aldwych Theatre, London, in 1961, Michel Saint-Denis
had Lopahin and Varya in a close embrace at this point. This grouping is surely
too emotive not to deny the humour implicit in the scene.

by forces they cannot recognize, much less control. Against these forces, their social decorums are laughably out of place.

As if she has been waiting outside the door, Lyubov immediately enters, but *'cautiously'*. 'Well?' is all she says. At a glance she sees Varya on the floor in tears and recognizes the fact she knew and feared in her heart all along. 'We must be going.'

For the last phase in this protracted departure, Chekhov characteristically fills the stage in order to empty it. At the same time he supplies an ironic reflection of the traditional Russian family assembly before leaving. Not only the family, all dressed in travelling clothes, flows into the room, but, to gather the luggage, servants and coachmen too; by this procedure, the audience is soon to have a renewed physical sense of the empty house. As in Act I, the crowded stage bustles with life, although this time with the urgency of departure. The nursery temporarily loses its identity to show a moving panorama of all the cherry orchard people like an animated curtain-call. Yet they are not heard as a simple chorus, for their varied attitudes and fragments of individual feeling are to be both blended and distinguished in a total image of farewell, mixed of hope and loss.

There is profound regret in Lyubov's toneless 'Now we can start on our travels', for she is not thinking of the excitement of the journey. But this mood is immediately contradicted by Anya's uplifting voice expressing her joy at the thought of new prospects: 'On our travels!' The cross-currents of feeling which have run through the whole play here begin to rush together. In voices and familiar phrases, gestures and movements, we hear and see the past and the future at odds with each other. And reducing all the incongruities to the level of humorous comedy, Gaev overtops everyone with the beginnings of an expected speech, 'My friends – my dear, my precious friends! Leaving this house for ever, can I be silent? . . .' As is his habit, he has slipped from sentiment to rhetoric, until the girls, as is theirs, implore him to stop.

All is animation on the stage, Trofimov officiously gathering the travellers together, Lopahin calling for his coat from his new man Epihodov, servants with luggage winding their way through small clusters of people. Only Lyubov is quiet, sitting upstage centre at the window, looking out at the orchard for the last time, as if unable to move from the spot. She catches our attention by her stillness.

LYUBOV. I'll stay just one minute. It seems as though I have never seen before what the walls, what the ceilings in this house were like, and now I look at them with greediness, with such tender love.
GAEV. I remember when I was six years old sitting in that window on Trinity Day watching my father going to church.

She is caught in the web of her memories, and in a pose we saw once before at the beginning of the play. With Gaev, Chekhov uses Lyubov to support the concentrated weight of emotion he has built up from the outset. Again the vision of generations past is prompted by that gentle reference to Gaev's father. Finally, Lyubov shakes herself from her trance to ask whether the luggage has gone; Lopahin and our eyes confirm that it has, for the room itself looks a degree more bleak.

Simultaneously with such effects of pathos, Chekhov continues to tease his audience with disturbing strokes of humour, and Epihodov, the most outright buffoon in the play, is used to create the next shift of feeling. A frog in his throat surprises us with an unexpected sign of the warmth of his emotions. Even a fool can be affected by an irrevocable departure. Whether or not he was play-acting, we have never thought of Epihodov as a person deserving anything but laughter; now like Lopahin, we are startled into a moment of characteristic uncertainty, and Yasha's derision is no longer laughable either.

Attention returns quickly to Lyubov, who is thinking only about the lost orchard: no one will be left there when they have gone. 'Not till the spring', Lopahin responds brightly, trying to allay the fear and despair he hears in her voice; at the same time he indicates that he still has his mind on practical matters. However, he has again said the wrong thing, and Lyubov recoils. For her, spring suggests the orchard in bloom, a return to the happy time of the homecoming, a flight back to innocence and childhood.

Lopahin knows as soon as he has opened his mouth that he has spoken out of turn, and he is reminded that he must assume some of the responsibility for this melancholy occasion. Chekhov stressed his sense of guilt before, when Lopahin made his entrance in the third act to announce his purchase of the estate and found Varya brandishing a stick at him, as if he deserved a beating like a peasant. Now Chekhov echoes that little crisis in another spirit. He has Varya suddenly pull an umbrella from a bundle; it flies up and just misses Lopahin again. There is a suspended moment when the lively stage is stock-still as everyone sees Varya's unintended threat and Lopahin's hasty stoop as he instinctively shields himself with his arm. He has dispossessed the family and jilted Varya: the blow would be well deserved, and Varya's gesture reviews his contribution to the general disaster. But again Chekhov renounces melodrama. The incident is over in a flash, and the whole company laughs as Lopahin '*makes a gesture as though alarmed*'. With his hands before his face in mockery, he performs a little pantomime which relaxes the tension between Lyubov, Varya and himself. All are friends once more.

The stage at once becomes animated again, as though someone had thrown a switch. Trofimov pompously calls for the party to get into the carriages. Varya finds his galoshes at the very last moment, her action simultaneously clearing up a last detail and deflating Trofimov's assumption of dignity. Still giving orders, he incongruously finds himself struggling upon one leg, trying to put the galoshes on. 'And what dirty old things they are!' is the appropriate thought from Varya the housekeeper; yet there is also a warm note of reconciliation in her voice. As for Gaev, the poor man is in a whirl of emotion, unable to contain himself, but trying to collect his thoughts and stem his tears: 'The train – the station! Double baulk, ah!' Lopahin is busy counting heads, locking a door here, ushering servants out there. And we watch the family go one by one in a broken, sorry little procession.

Naturally, the youngest leave first, anticipating an unbounded future, uncomplicated by regrets about the past. With Trofimov wearing his dirty old galoshes, adjusting his steel spectacles, he and Anya hail a new world, their voices ringing with joy.

ANYA. Good-bye, home! Good-bye to the old life!
TROFIMOV. Welcome to the new life!

Varya follows, but with a contrasting reluctance, uncertain of the future, only too aware of the vagaries of the present reality. Yasha presses impatiently behind her, and Charlotta crosses the width of the stage leading the pet dog we saw on her arrival; as always, she displays her gawky version of cool dignity by a stiff back and an enigmatic smile. Lopahin brings up the rear with a gay, thoughtless cry, 'Come, friends, till we meet!' Thus Lyubov and Gaev are alone in the nursery at last, alone with their cherry orchard, if only for a few fleeting seconds.

The brother and sister, the older ones, have avoided breaking down until they are alone, two lost creatures clasping each other in the middle of a large, bare stage, sobbing quietly on each other's shoulder. The whole drama has been gathering towards this fragment of time, and now in their isolation they seem to embody the cherry orchard itself. Gaev, for once, is beyond speech, and it is Lyubov who addresses the orchard, speaking through tears of her life, her youth and her happiness. Yet at the same time her words cannot be heard without invoking that unspoken, bitter-sweet comment of those who cannot afford this self-indulgence, especially Lopahin, Varya and Charlotta.

We hear the unspoken criticism, too, of those who look with confidence to the future, and the impatient, excited voices of Anya and Trofimov outside break into the reverie. Anya with her ringing tones is heard calling 'Mamma!', the word suited to the lyrical effect of a reverberating call intended here; this is followed by Trofimov in an echoing effect of 'hallooing through empty rooms'.[1] They pull us from the deserted nursery into their other world beyond, where they are ready to plant another cherry orchard. The spectator, nevertheless, must remain behind in the nursery, feeling its emptiness. The sobbing on stage is in counter-point with the fading cries offstage, and we listen transfixed to the sounds of the past and the future, unable to escape the prison of time that Chekhov has built. Suddenly Lyubov says, 'We are coming', and the stage is empty.

Like the house itself, the audience is deserted. The curtain should fall, but it does not. The stage returns to the twilight of the play's beginning. We strain to see, and the filter of light through the barred shutters leaves only shadowy outlines of the room we knew before. Chekhov, the master of meaningful sound effects, is, at the end of his career as a playwright, about to exploit the most daring sequence of noises the naturalistic theatre has known. The noises off have the effect of a limitless, timeless pause, painfully long, but by their sequence controlling the tempo

---

[1] Thus described by John Gielgud, who played Trofimov for J. B. Fagan in 1925 at the Oxford Playhouse (*Early Stages*, London, 1939, p. 88).

of our thinking. Chekhov will have us digest his meaning before we stir from our seats.

As the cries die away, we hear the sound of bolts shot home, of doors being locked. It is as if the audience itself were being locked in the theatre. We hear the jingle of harness as the carriages pull away, and for an unusually long time[1] their clinking is left to fade slowly until imperceptible to our ears. Then '*There is silence*', and we are prisoners again. In the stillness the sound of an axe is heard monotonously striking a tree, a chastening thud, thud, thud, its repetition a sign of an irremediable destruction that is cruel and yet just. Nevertheless, the impersonal stroke on the tree, important though it is in the lives of these people, is insignificant in the span of time.

Still the curtain does not fall. The audience has been *prepared* for listening, and now it hears even the sound of old slippers shuffling towards the door. In the half-light old Firs in his jacket and white waistcoat enters, crosses, tries a door-handle unsuccessfully and then moves slowly down to the sofa covered by its dust-sheet. Although Chekhov earlier provided strong hints that the family might forget Firs in the confusion of departure, we too have forgotten him until now; Lyubov's and Gaev's own emotions have distracted us. In this final, overwhelming irony of the play, we see this ancient man, who seems to symbolize the history of the cherry orchard in his person, certainly its most permanent feature, abandoned like the house, like ourselves. 'They have forgotten me . . . Never mind . . .' He is impassive in the face of his situation. At eighty-seven, he has no future beyond these walls, and the world outside has no meaning for him. He is not quite indifferent to the passage of time which so disturbed all the others, for he feels some sense of loss when he says, 'Life has slipped by as though I hadn't lived.' He is, however, never indifferent to personal relationships. These matter to him. At the last, he is still thinking of Gaev who has probably gone off in his summer coat. A final prick of comedy is felt in his irritation as he mutters under his breath, 'These young people . . .' Time and his great age have reduced the whole family equally to the level of children who do not know what they are doing. In this concluding notion, time has become of no account. His last words,

[1] Even a full sixty seconds is supportable, as the director John Izon established in a production at the Gate Theatre, Dublin.

and Chekhov's last speech as a playwright, are, 'Ech! I'm good for nothing.'[1]

As Firs falls back feebly on the sofa, still the curtain does not fall. That enigmatic sound of the breaking string, louder, it seems, this time, off tone, dying slowly away, resounds through the theatre.[2] The accumulated mixture of all the thousand and one ambivalent details of the play is in that sound. But it adds a strange element of cosmic mystery. It suggests time in its most inscrutable mood; it is the passing of one order of life, with what seems its irreparable loss; but it is also the mark of change, ushering in the new order, both hopeful and frightening because it is unimaginable. To interpret that sound is to interpret the play.

In the renewed silence which follows the dying sound, we hear again, both near and far away, the sound of the axe on the trees. So the audience is returned at the last to the immediate and particular plight of the cherry orchard, and yet finds itself contemplating the passing of all cherry orchards. And only then may the curtain fall, and the audience be released.

---

[1] *Nedotyopa* is rendered variously as 'duffer' (Magarshack), 'nincompoop' (Hingley), 'useless lumber' (Valency), etc.

[2] In one performance, the sound coincided with a last lifeless arm movement by Firs, so that he seemed to have been shot by an arrow from some supernatural bow. Firs, of course, is not seen to die; he sleeps. In any case, Epihodov has been left behind by Lopahin and would no doubt find him.

Postscript

Critics still talk about a 'definitive' production, using the term not as a pejorative but as high praise. These commentaries are not an attempt to finalize some such imaginary entity as an ideal production. Like all great theatre, Chekhov will remain alive and self-renewing with each performance. In his case, this quality is notably linked with his objectivity as a dramatist.

For all his demand for accuracy in his abundance of detail, and his expectation that every detail should fit into an exact pattern, Chekhov's great plays can never suffer from petrified production. While he called for the most carefully planned ensemble work, at the same time he satisfied most adequately the drive of creative improvision dear to all good actors. Because his many details grow organically together, they challenge the stage every time to engender new life. We may go to the theatre hoping to see the definitive production of a Chekhov play, but this can never be. We shall always see something new in Chekhov, just as we do in Shakespeare.

Lillian Hellman explained the disagreements between Chekhov and his director very simply.

Stanislavski was a man of intelligence and great ability, and one can wonder why he did not present the plays as Chekhov wished them to be presented. The answer is simple: Stanislavski's interpretation had made the plays popular. What Stanislavski put upon the stage was what the public wanted, or at least what the *avant-garde* section of the public wanted.[1]

In 1940, Nemirovich-Danchenko revived *Three Sisters*, but not his earlier production. He sought a new tone which eschewed cliché 'Chekhovianism', as he called it: 'Dismal whinings, protracted rhythms, elegiac intonations.'[2] In 1961, Michel Saint-

---

[1] Hellman, Introduction, pp. xxiv–xxv.
[2] G. Tovstonogov, 'Chekhov's *Three Sisters* at the Gorky Theatre', *The Drama Review*, vol. 13, no. 2 (New York, Winter 1968), p. 147.

Denis accounted for his dry, 'farcical' *Cherry Orchard* in much the same way, believing that he was suiting the play to a new post-war, absurdist audience.[1] We should be pleased that a body of drama exists that can seem to change with the times.

It is true that Chekhov's emphasis on detail of tone, gesture, mood and rhythm satisfies the special need of the naturalistic theatre of illusion to have the spectator identify and recognize the world of the stage as real and convincing; but this is not all there is to a play, which lives on and off the stage. The indispensable party to a play is the audience, and the play is created in their minds or nowhere. Chekhov's kind of detail also forces, as Stanislavsky discovered, a subtextual approach to production, but this in turn forces them to share in the activity of interpretation: they are urged to 'participate'. Therefore the play must change as all the parties to the play change. This is especially true of Chekhovian comedy.

Chekhovian comedy appears as a series of checks and balances. The playwright must first draw the spectator, sitting remotely like a *voyeur*, through the proscenium arch to engage him intimately with the lives of the characters, especially if they represent a dull normality of existence. The more remote the stage, the more solid the invisible curtain of darkness, the more the actors play to each other and not to the spectator, then the more effective must the subtext be to hold his attention. All considered, the proscenium arch theatre affords the most unnatural conventions in which to produce a naturalistic play. Yet only after the playwright has demolished the barrier of the picture-frame can he begin the work of 'distancing' necessary for the comic response. The intricacy of the subtext must meet all these demands, those of the subject, the conditions of performance and the kind of comedy. Chekhov's new techniques, like his experiments with the empty stage, his use of sounds to enlarge the area of our perception or to illuminate the condition of a character, his injection of farcical business into an emotional scene, and many others, are designed to make his subtext especially compelling. The subtextual controls applied by the writer must be both strong and elastic, and to say this is to pass a value judgment on the quality of the drama.

[1] See the Introduction to *Anton Chekhov: The Cherry Orchard*, version by John Gielgud (London, 1963), p. xi.

In particular, there is a special link between Chekhov's insistent deflationary methods and the degree of involvement and revelation they occasion. The undercutting process of his stage is an undercutting process in the auditorium. If it is impossible to deny that Chekhov is an impersonal, non-didactic dramatist, one completely committed to a kind of dramatic 'negative capability', a poetic suspension of self and an acceptance of objective reality, it is also impossible to deny that he educates his audience towards a similar capability, and that this is a tremendous source of *energy* in his plays.

This is to argue that what makes Chekhov a great and objective dramatist is at bottom his *stage* technique. The many famous statements he made about objectivity in the writer were all about the craft and not the themes of writing, albeit of prose fiction:

To chemists there is nothing unclean in this world. A man of letters should be as objective as a chemist; he has to renounce ordinary subjectivity and realize that manure piles play a very respectable role in a landscape and that evil passions are as inherent in life as good ones.[1]

The artist should not be a judge of his characters or of what they say, but only an objective observer.[2]

You are right to require a conscious attitude from the artist toward his work, but you mix up two ideas: *the solution of the problem and a correct presentation of the problem*. Only the latter is obligatory for the artist.[3]

You scold me for objectivity, calling it indifference to good and evil, lack of ideals and so on. When I portray horse thieves, you would want me to say that stealing horses is an evil. But certainly this has always been obvious without my saying so. Let the jury pass judgment on them, it is my business solely to show them as they are.[4]

Yet each of these exhortations and explanations is most aptly applied to the modern theatre. In the last letter quoted, Chekhov goes on to say something that could explain also why his dramatic technique will ensure that his plays stay alive in the theatre of the future.

[1] Letter to Maria Kiseleva of 14 January 1887 (Hellman, p. 20).
[2] To Alexei Suvorin, 30 May 1888 (Hellman, p. 54).
[3] To the same, 27 October 1888 (Hellman, p. 57).
[4] To the same, 1 April 1890 (Hellman, p. 98).

Postscript

When I write I count upon my reader fully, assuming that he himself will add the subjective elements that are lacking in the telling.[1]

As the audience changes, so their image of the plays will change, and this is as it should be. To every man his own subtext. Chekhov's search in the theatre was for the perfect economy of means, not to ossify his meaning, but to ensure that the spectators' contribution would give his meaning new life. In *The Cherry Orchard*, he achieved this object supremely well.

Like metaphor and imagery in a poem, Chekhov's fugitive subtextual details, contradicting one another to have us perceive the ambiguities of life, will satisfy us only to the extent of our willingness to discover them. At the same time, they will also leave us feeling dissatisfied with our own effort at interpretation, as all great poetry does.

[1] *Ibid*. p. 99.